QuickCASH

Quick CASH

THE STORY OF THE LOAN SHARK

Robert Mayer

NORTHERN

ILLINOIS

UNIVERSITY

PRESS

© 2010 by Northern Illinois University Press

Published by the Northern Illinois University Press, DeKalb, Illinois 60115

Manufactured in the United States using postconsumer-recycled, acid-free paper.

Design by Julia Fauci

Library of Congress Cataloging-in-Publication Data

Mayer, Robert, 1960–

Quick cash : the story of the loan shark / Robert Mayer.

   p.   cm.

Includes bibliographical references and index.

ISBN 978-0-87580-430-9 (clothbound : alk. paper)

1. Usury. 2. Loans. I. Title.

HB551.M39 2010

332.8'3—dc22

2010014718

Contents

Acknowledgments

Like the tree from the seed, this book began as a paragraph in a paper I presented at an academic conference a decade ago. In the paragraph I used the payday loan as an example to illustrate the nature of an exploitative transaction. That paragraph later grew into a paper, and that first paper spawned several more on the problem of payday lending. Eventually I thought it necessary to write an entire book on the subject, in part because my curiosity had not been slaked but also because it surprised me that nobody else had written a volume on what has become a fifty-billion-dollar-a-year business. The loan sharks had returned in large numbers by the start of the twenty-first century, but nobody had yet told the story of their resurgence and transformation. The book I thought should be written about today's check lenders would connect the present to the past and try to glean some lessons from previous efforts to contend with the payday creditors of yesteryear. We cannot know what to do now until we learn what has been done before. We will probably make fewer mistakes ourselves if we try to profit from the mistakes of those who came before us.

The seed with which I began was only able to grow into a tree because others helped to nourish this project along the way. I am grateful to the reference librarians at Loyola University Chicago, Northwestern University, the University of Chicago, and the Chicago Historical Museum for their help in hunting down the forgotten documents upon which the early chapters in this study are based. I am also grateful to the clerks and the presiding judges in the bankruptcy courts in the Northern District of Illinois and the Eastern District of Wisconsin for giving me access to the filings of countless debtors, whose disclosure forms are like a window into the sweatshops of the payday lenders.

I benefited from conversations about payday lending with representatives of the Consumer Federation of America, the Woodstock Institute, the Monsignor John Egan Campaign for Payday Loan Reform, the Community Financial Services Association, the Illinois Small Loan Association, Check Into Cash, the Illinois Department of Financial and Professional Regulation, the Wisconsin Department of Financial Institutions, the *Chicago Tribune*, the *Las Vegas City Life*, and the Legal Aid Society of Milwaukee. I received useful feedback from conference participants at the Midwest Political Science Association, the American Council on Consumer Interests, and the Illinois Asset Building Group. I am especially grateful to a talented group of undergraduates at Loyola University Chicago who discussed early drafts of some of the following chapters in a freshman seminar I taught several years ago on the return of the loan sharks. I received invaluable help from Lendol Calder, Claudio Katz, Christopher Peterson, and Nicole Pileggi, each of whom read the entire manuscript and offered many good suggestions. I also wish to thank Sara Hoerdeman and the staff at Northern Illinois University Press for shepherding the manuscript along the path toward publication.

Some people nourish the germinating ideas that grow into books by locating documents, or answering questions, or telling anecdotes, or pointing out mistakes. But some people who nourish a project do so without any intention of being helpful. They might actually try to distract you from the work because they think what you are doing is rather silly. I want to thank my daughters, Emma and Sally, who nourished this work by distracting me from it whenever possible. I dedicate this book to them.

The Evolution of the Shark

The loan shark is a predatory invader in a field of social

and economic necessity. —Robert Kelso, St. Louis

Community Fund, 1941[1]

In the popular imagination today the "loan shark" is a mobster. He belongs to a crime syndicate and beats up or kills people who won't pay the "vig" on their high-interest debts. His victims are gamblers or small businessmen in need of cash, and these borrowers offer their bodies as collateral for the money they receive. This loan shark is not a figure with whom most people have any personal experience now, but he is familiar to us from movies like *Mean Streets, Barbershop*, and *Get Shorty*, or television shows like *The Sopranos*. Tough and sometimes colorful, the loan shark is an exotic creature from an underworld that has shrunk in size and seems far removed from the place where ordinary people live and work.

Such loan sharks did and still do exist, but these violent predators are actually a later incarnation of a species of creditor that first emerged in the United States sometime after the middle of the nineteenth century. The original loan sharks were not mobsters, and they did not specialize in breaking the arms of debtors who could not pay. Rather, the class of lenders who first bore the epithet "shark" lurked about offices and factories and did much of their work on payday. They advanced small sums for short periods of time and at high rates of interest to working people who lived from pay packet to pay packet. These entrepreneurs liked to call themselves "salary brokers" or "salary lenders," but in everyday conversation they were referred to as "sharks." Their loans were usurious, with interest rates that were always triple-digit, yet these cash advances were not secured with the body of the debtor. Instead, the original loan sharks bound their customers with legal instruments that were recognized by the courts. Although loan-sharking from the start was always a kind of extortion racket, in its early days that racket was dignified by official-looking documents to which the borrowers affixed their signatures, mortgaging their future wages and, effectively, their jobs for the sake of a loan until payday.

The first loan sharks were widely hated figures at the turn of the twentieth century because they ensnared so many working people in the bondage of debt. At the height of the business, before reform efforts restricted its scope, the salary lenders were said to be advancing cash to every third or fourth wage-earner in the larger metropolitan centers. These debtors were being charged 10% or 20% a month for their loans, and various tricks were worked to inflate that high rate still further. With a heavy burden of interest, loans that were intended to be short-term often had to be rolled over again and again, or the customer might borrow from one shark to pay another in an expanding cycle of debt. The loans might go on for years, with payments extracted through aggressive collection methods from people afraid of losing their jobs. The relationship smacked of debt peonage because the shark would not let go but collected tribute in installments that were due every payday.

In the beginning, then, it was not the recourse to violence that qualified lenders as loan sharks. They did not have to draw blood to be likened to a predator. What was thought to be shark-like about their transactions was not the method of collection employed if the loan went into default but rather the initial structure of these extensions of credit. As one observer put it, "The essence of loan shark deals is small amounts for short terms, with an effort to keep the principal out all the time to secure repeated renewals of the interest charge." Loans that could not be paid back, loans that were interest-only: that was the defining trait of loan-shark credit. "Loan shark evils," this same author noted, "appear where the method of lending requires the entire indebtedness of the wage-earner to mature at one time. Inability to pay anything but the interest on the loan almost inevitably results from this method of lending money."[2] The short repayment schedule was the feature of the transaction that gave it its bite. Too much was demanded too soon from people too poor to borrow at a lower rate of interest. While the loan shark always charged an exorbitant price, another commentator noted, "he does more than this. He loans for too short a period of time, making the payments too high, and encouraging renewals or refinancing." The payments were structured in this way because "the real aim of loan sharks is to keep their customers eternally in debt so that interest (for the sharks) becomes almost an annuity."[3] In a loan-shark scheme, it was said, "the loan itself is so designed as to handicap repayment." Hence, "a chief test of a desirable system is the existence of [an] opportunity for the borrower to become free of debt."[4] You were not a shark, in other words, if the loans you made were paid off on schedule. According to another observer, "This insistence upon planned, orderly liquidation of the loan is one of the hallmarks of the honest lender. The unlicensed loan shark, on the other hand, seldom wants his principal so long as he gets his interest."[5]

That is what loan-sharking was in the beginning—not a violent method of debt collection but a way of lending small sums that trapped cash-strapped debtors. The pit from which these borrowers could not escape was the short-term, single-payment loan, an expensive credit product that requires debtors to return the principal in one lump sum. If customers could not scrape together the cash needed to retire this unamortized debt, they were required to renew the contract for an additional, hefty fee. The victims were bled dry in interest-only installments that never reduced the principal. Lending in this predatory way qualified you as a loan shark a hundred years ago, even if you never laid a finger on your debtors.

Progressive reformers waged a vigorous campaign against this model of lending after the turn of the twentieth century. At first they groped for a solution, but eventually the progressives hit upon the idea of starving the sharks by fostering lower-priced alternatives to the salary loan. Within a few decades they thought they had exterminated the loan sharks in most places outside the South. Victory was declared and the reformers moved on to new causes. But then, at the end of the twentieth century, the loan sharks reappeared in America's cities. They were not noticed at first, but their numbers proliferated rapidly during the 1990s. By the turn of a new century there were more than 12,000 outlets spread across the country, hawking short-term, high-interest cash advances, and this number would double again during the next decade. According to industry estimates, 19 million people—that's one in twelve adults—made use of this credit product during 2008. The vendors logged more than 150 million transactions during that year, advancing cash against the security of a postdated check. They lent $50 billion in subprime (or high-interest) credit and collected more than $8 billion in fees.[6] These new lenders called their credit product the "payday loan."

If we employ the epithet in its original sense, today's payday lenders are the loan sharks of the twenty-first century. The product they vend now bears a striking resemblance to the salary loans that proliferated in this country after the Civil War. Like those "ten-minute loans" of yesteryear, the payday advance is an expensive and unamortized extension of credit that is timed to mature on payday and is pitched to credit-constrained consumers. Then, as now, the annual interest rate is always triple-digit. Then, as now, a large number of customers roll these loans over again and again or pay off one with the proceeds of another. Then, as now, many who patronize these lenders seem trapped by their debts. Their ostensibly two-week loans may stretch on for months or even years. Where it is legal, sizable numbers of customers will borrow from several or many lenders simultaneously. They will pyramid their loans in a kind of reverse Ponzi scheme, feeding many sharks instead of one.

What has happened before is happening again. The loan sharks have returned. They are swarming once more in population centers across the country. The aim of this book is to explain why this return has occurred and to think through what, if anything, ought to be done about the resurgence of high-interest lending in the United States at the start of the twenty-first century. To answer these questions, in this book I tell the story of the trade in small sums, from its origins around the Civil War and through a series of evolutions down to the present day. I recount the history of loan-sharking and the efforts to fight it, but I tell that history always with an eye to the present and to the policy choice we now face. Some today would like to prohibit payday lending while others would like to unshackle it; others favor the middle course of regulated toleration. Before we can decide what to do, however, we need to know why payday lending exists, where and why it thrives, what its consequences are, and what the results of regulation have been thus far. The current debate about payday lending lacks historical depth. The history of loan-sharking has been forgotten. Advocates and opponents both would profit if their fight was placed within the context of an enduring struggle over subprime credit—a struggle that has unfolded over the last century and a half. In this book I offer the first comprehensive history of payday lending in the United States.

One thing revealed in this history is that the loan shark is not a single species. Different breeds have flourished, often alongside one another. We are now living through the third wave of loan-sharking in the United States, and perhaps its most striking feature is the breakthrough to legality that today's payday lenders have achieved in most states across the Union. Loan sharks now are licensed. They operate in a white market and have become corporate. Some are conglomerates. Despite that fact, it is surprising how little we know about the newest payday lenders. The first of their kind evolved during the 1980s but thus far no book has been written about this new industry. Little scholarly research has been published.[7] One task of the present work is to synthesize what is known about the current trade and the customers who patronize it. Before we can judge the payday lenders, we must know what they do and how their customers fare. We must try to understand the dynamics of supply and demand that made possible the rapid proliferation of this new species of subprime creditor.

In the political arena and in the newspapers, the policy fight over payday lending is often depicted in contrasts of black and white. The lines are starkly drawn, and opponents disparage the motives of those with whom they contend. But an analysis of payday lending in the various forms it has assumed over the course of time reveals the complexity of the problem. If the lenders often seem guilty of taking unfair advantage of their customers, for example, it is also the case that the customers often seem guilty of foolishness, profligacy, and self-deception. While gaining at the expense of such people may be wrong, the payday lenders frequently offer a better deal than the alternatives and may seem to their customers like the lesser evil. These creditors do not create the context within which their customers must choose, a context shaped by more powerful institutions that are also frequently engaged in taking unfair advantage of working people. The loan sharks are bit actors in the larger drama of modern society, and for some of the people these lenders serve they are benefactors, not villains. They lend cash in a hurry and without asking a lot of questions. They lend when others won't. They perform a service that the do-gooders despise. In my analysis I seek to render these shades of gray and the moral complexity that seems inherent in the trade in small sums. While the shark may be a brutal predator, we should not forget that it has a part to play within the larger ecosystem. It fits into the whole, and the sudden disappearance of this predator might be extremely disruptive to the sensitive balance of species that has evolved over the course of time. It is even possible that its prey might be worse off if the shark did not exist.

The question that drives this analysis is the question of prohibition. Would society be better off if high-rate lending was illegal? Should we try to exterminate the loan sharks or, instead, make our peace with them? When I began this study I was skeptical about the idea of prohibition.[8] Standard economic theory teaches us that the consequences of prohibition ought to be worse than the consequences of deregulation. Suppression of a trade can have unintended effects that render the least advantaged groups even worse off than they were before. The history of America's Prohibition, enacted by the Eighteenth Amendment, seems to confirm this theory and is an object lesson that cannot be ignored. Banning the manufacture and sale of alcoholic beverages had disastrous black-market effects that seem immediately relevant to the case of high-rate lending. If we ban payday lending, it is natural to think, we will call back into existence the mob sharks of yesteryear that seem to have died off in the present age. Throughout this study I have tried to keep an open mind about subprime credit and its utility and to be as skeptical about what the progressives say as we should be about the self-serving claims of the payday lenders. In writing the final chapter, however, I had to make up my mind about what is to be done about payday lending, basing my decision on the evidence assembled in the previous sections. In the end, and to my surprise, I have convinced myself that prohibition of high-rate lending would have better consequences than either free trade in this product or the defective schemes of regulation that have been tried out by the states over the last decade. Payday lending ought to be suppressed, preferably in combination with new policies that foster better alternatives for cash-strapped wage-earners. But in explaining how I reach that conclusion, I also try to show that our choice is only between lesser evils and that every policy in this domain will impose significant costs and confront us with dilemmas. Each option has perverse consequences. No matter what we do, there will be dirt. The best we can do is try to minimize it. Based on the evidence I have mustered, prohibition now seems like the least messy option. It will not do away with loan sharks, for that is a hardy breed. But prohibition in the twenty-first century stands the best chance of minimizing deprivation, which ought to be the aim of policy in the "field of social and economic necessity" (as Robert Kelso puts it) with which we are concerned.

America is a large and complicated country, but I want this book to be accessible and clear. Each state has its own regulations about consumer lending, and it can be confusing to try to keep fifty different stories straight. The history of loan-sharking over the past century will have more coherence if it is located in a particular place, one that is both representative and colorful. The place I have chosen is Chicago. Loan-sharking has always been disproportionately an urban phenomenon, so it makes sense to focus on the cities. And, among American cities, Chicago stands out because it was the birthplace of one of the small loan products whose history we will trace. Over the past century Chicago's neighborhoods have nourished each of the three waves of loan-sharking that will be examined in this study. Chicago was reputed to be the capital city of salary lending around the turn of the twentieth century, but it was also the scene of a vigorous and well-documented fight by progressive reformers lasting nearly twenty years. In the middle decades of the last century, Chicago was, of course, a thriving center of organized crime, and its gangs made a lot of money in the underworld business of advancing cash. Those gangs eventually went into decline, but late in the twentieth century the loan sharks reemerged in Chicago, in hundreds of storefront offices that push the payday-loan product. At first Illinois was an unregulated state, but over the last decade politicians and reformers have groped toward a regulatory formula that could tame the sharks and end their abuses. The project is still a work in progress, but the story of its twists and turns can serve as a case study in the complexities of consumer protection. Whenever new rules are enacted, the Illinois payday lenders adapt and recraft their product so that it still takes a bite. They exemplify the tenaciousness that has always been a characteristic of this breed of lender.

The setting for my story, then, is Chicago. Developments elsewhere will not be ignored, but I think we are likely to learn more about the business and its regulation through a rich case study of one shark habitat. It also helps that I happen to make my living in this habitat, where there is a trove of source material at hand through which one may sift for clues about a predator that tends to shun the light.

In the first chapter of this study I describe the origin of the species and identify the forces of supply and demand that gave birth to the loan sharks in their first incarnation, as salary lenders. We will see who borrowed from the loan sharks and why, and how these customers were enticed into the scores of dimly lit offices clustered in the Loop or around the Stockyards. Once inside the door, we follow the transaction from initial application through every step to the methods of debt collection. That journey will reveal to us the techniques of the sharks and how they managed to make so many of their customers miserable early in the twentieth century.

The response to this misery and the fight against the loan sharks is the topic of the second chapter. It took some time for salary lending to come to the attention of elite strata in Chicago, but when it did, the business provoked numerous reform schemes. Judges, journalists, lawyers, politicians, and captains of industry each had their own ideas about how to tame or kill the loan sharks, and victory was proclaimed again and again by these different groups. But the loan sharks proved resilient, and the first campaign against them lasted nearly twenty years. It culminated in the passage of the Uniform Small Loan Law, which legalized one breed of shark but proscribed another. The outlaw breed refused to die, however. When salary lending became illegal, it invented salary buying and other variations of the product. The original loan sharks continued to cling tenaciously to a trade that remained lucrative despite the new risks, because working people without collateral still needed cash right away.

In the third chapter we examine the darkest phase in the evolution of loan-sharking, when the market became black. The Uniform Small Loan Law turned high-rate lending into a criminal enterprise, and the crime syndicates that had grown strong during Prohibition were available to step into the place of the old loan sharks who found it increasingly difficult to do business in public. This new form of loan-sharking was the kind we associate with the word even today. The transactions were more furtive, unencumbered by contracts or wage assignments, and a different type of security was pledged by the debtor. In case of default it was understood that the lender would resort to violence to extract payment, although this did not occur in every case. Indeed, alongside syndicate loan-sharking there existed in this black market other, less violent networks of lending that spread through workplaces and neighborhoods to provide cash until payday. Newspaper reports would sometimes expose these networks to the light, but most of the attention in this period was devoted to the mob lending and its outrages. A series of highly visible campaigns were directed against the Mafia loan sharks, and by the 1970s it seemed they had been hunted down and driven to the verge of extinction. A few might remain to feed on the gamblers and businessmen who could not secure a loan, but their ranks had been drastically thinned, and they no longer seemed to be the plague of payday.

But then the loan sharks returned. That is the topic of the fourth chapter, in which we trace the rise of the modern form of payday lending. The origins of that industry lie in the 1980s, in the confluence of new forces of supply and demand. In this chapter I identify those forces and then chart the rapid growth of this industry over the next two decades. The impact of this product on customers is described, together with the business practices of the lenders. Payday lending in its modern form represents a rather brilliant innovation. It is a product of the credit revolution that began at the end of the 1970s and that remade the infrastructure of liquidity. Depository institutions were undergoing large changes at this time, and the practices to which they were driven by the forces of competition opened a feeding ground for a new generation of loan sharks. Banks and payday lenders became bound to each other, as we shall see, in a relationship of competitive symbiosis.

In the fifth chapter I explain why and where the payday lenders were able to achieve what the original loan sharks could not—legal protection for high-interest loans. At the turn of the twentieth century, 20% a month was a scandal; today the average payday loan is twice as expensive as that, but in most states—including Illinois—these high rates are legal. An explanation will be offered for this transformation and also for the unevenness of its progress. A number of states clustered in the Northeast have retained their traditional usury statutes, which render payday-lending transactions illegal. That approach is favored by many consumer protection advocates elsewhere, but their demand for prohibition has failed in most states thus far. We shall treat the regulatory battles in Illinois over the last decade as a case study in the modern effort to domesticate loan-sharking. The policy arena will be viewed as a market in which the forces of supply and demand operate. The motives and strategies of the contending parties will be laid bare. As we shall see, those forces that have demanded reform in Illinois have been continually outflanked by the lenders and their lawyers. The payday creditors have proved themselves adept at recrafting their product in such a way that it can always slip through the loopholes that remain in every regulatory formula. In states like Illinois, the equilibrium point in the market for credit regulation seems to have converged on a regulatory net that is extensive and expensive but also shoddy in its construction and full of holes.

The sixth chapter is evaluative. In it I make the case for prohibition. That case is based on the consequences, with priority given to the least advantaged group. Where payday lending is permitted, the fraction of customers that gain from having access to this expensive credit tend to be better off and to use the product lightly. Those who roll over loans repeatedly or remain indebted for long periods of time produce the bulk of the revenue for the payday lenders and clearly seem trapped by their debts. These customers form a sizable group wherever payday lending is legal, and they count as the least advantaged population. However, if prohibition is enforced, we must take account of black-market effects. One of my tasks in this chapter is to estimate those effects based on the fragmentary evidence available to us. I show that the black market in payday credit has evolved over time and is not as big a threat as is sometimes imagined. The idea that prohibition of payday lending will revive the mob loan sharks is not compelling, in part because the involvement of organized crime in this trade during the middle decades of the twentieth century was largely a historical accident. The circumstances that called into existence that violent breed of lender have disappeared. Black-market lending in the twenty-first century is taking a different and less dangerous form, and shrewd policy initiatives could limit this threat. The optimal policy now would pair prohibition with incentives for the depository lenders to fill the vacuum in subprime credit that will appear when the payday lenders are put out of business.

The unfolding credit crisis today presents policy makers with the opportunity to reshape the supply of subprime credit in ways that would be beneficial to its consumers. That crisis is the background against which this study has been written. The rapid swelling of subprime lending during the era of financial deregulation helped to inflate the credit bubble that has now burst so disastrously. Whether policy makers will act creatively to reconfigure the ecosystem of our credit markets in such a way as to drive off or to starve the loan sharks remains to be seen. But the analysis of this study suggests that, unless policy makers fix the banks and other depository institutions, we can expect some breed or other of the loan shark to survive into the future. After all, this is an ancient predator. It probably cannot be exterminated once and for all, but public policy can certainly encourage or discourage its propagation. It has done so, often unwittingly, for the last 150 years. The aim of this study is to explain how.

The Origin of the Species

Perhaps the man most to be despised is he who, under the guise of offering

help in a difficulty, takes advantage of that difficulty to his own gain.

—Guy Blake, Legal Aid Society of Chicago, 1911[1]

The idea that lenders might bite is as old as the biblical injunction against usury. One of the Hebrew words in the Old Testament that is translated as "interest" is *neshek*, which literally means "to bite." From the late medieval period forward it was common in discussions of usury to draw a distinction between interest that does or does not "bite." But the image of a "loan shark" is a more recent innovation. The phrase is an Americanism and seems to have come into usage near the end of the nineteenth century. Linguistically, the "loan shark" is a descendant of the "land shark" and the "money shark." The connection between the shark and sharp money dealing seems to have arisen in port towns early in the nineteenth century. A "land shark" was originally a boardinghouse landlord or unscrupulous trader who preyed upon sailors returning from a long voyage. He would charge exorbitant prices for his services and often befuddle his victims with grog and bawdy entertainments. Within a few days the hapless stranger would have been fleeced of all his money by "John Shark."[2]

As the nineteenth century wore on, a new breed of "land shark" was discovered inland, hunting among the class of small farmers. Speculators and predatory lenders earned that epithet by charging homesteaders usurious rates for a loan or refusing to sell until the price of land had been bid up. This midwestern land shark was such a hated figure in the Farm Belt because "he victimized those who should have been protected, made huge profits upon his business, and put upon the homemaker a burden heavier than he should have been allowed to bear."[3]

Near the end of the century some of the rural "land sharks" who were lenders also became known as "loan sharks." The first reference to this predator in the *Chicago Tribune* came in an 1888 article on the plight of Minnesota farmers: "Loan sharks lent them money and charged exorbitant interest." But the phrase quickly became identified with an urban genus of lenders, not those who took homestead deeds as a security but, rather, chattel mortgages or wage assignments. By the 1890s the "loan shark" was known to hunt in the big cities among wage-earners, lending small sums at high rates of interest to people who lacked collateral. The phrase became closely associated with this industry, especially after the turn of the century, but sometimes these lenders were also known as "loan spiders" or other creatures of prey. The *Tribune* once referred to them as "the South Clark Street condors."[4]

The loan sharks of the early twentieth century were divided into two breeds, depending on the type of security they took. Chattel-mortgage lenders advanced money on the security of a debtor's furniture, which remained in the owner's possession but could be seized in case of default if the lender filed a claim in court. Salary lenders, by contrast, secured their cash advances with a wage assignment, which could be filed directly with the debtor's employer and did not require a court order to become effective. These salary lenders were the predecessors of today's payday lenders, the focus of this study, and we will therefore seek out this particular variety of loan shark in its Chicago habitat. We will learn something about the other variety, too, but the chattel-mortgage lending business evolved in a different direction with the enactment of the Uniform Small Loan Law. It became the personal finance industry, which makes installment loans that are larger in size and less costly than the payday-loan product. Government regulation, as we shall see, tamed and transformed one breed of the loan shark but drove the other further underground. Late in the twentieth century, a new set of businesses figured out how to make salary lending a legal enterprise in many states. In this chapter we examine salary lending in its first incarnation, when it was synonymous with loan-sharking.

Loan-sharking evolved within the market—in particular, the market for cash advances. The demand for cash called forth new products; supply met demand. In this chapter I will tell the story of the origin of loan-sharking, beginning with demand and then turning to supply. I will describe who the salary borrowers were and why they came to swim with the sharks. I will then describe the salary-lending breed of sharks and how they hunted in Chicago. The Second City is an excellent place to study this breed; it was often described as "the center of the loan shark business of the world." As one reformer, Earle Eubank, explained, "Chicago has long been known by all the money lenders as the safest and most liberal city in the United States in which to operate. For that reason, the loan companies are probably more numerous there than in any other city."[5]

The Demand for Quick Cash

Lending money is an old business, but payday lending is comparatively new. Its precondition is a critical mass of urban wage-earners, one of the consequences of industrialization. These wage-earners possessed two traits that made loan-sharking possible as a distinctive type of credit transaction: regular paydays and decent incomes. Without the latter, prospective borrowers would lack a surplus out of which to fund debt repayment. Loan-sharking isn't feasible in a population that ekes out a bare subsistence. It also isn't feasible if the debtors lack a steady income stream. Only people with recurring paydays can get payday loans. The phenomenon of payday is a product of the industrial revolution and its routinization of wage labor. Factory-hands and office workers became employees—people whose services were engaged on a more or less continuous basis and who were paid not at the end of the harvest but every week or month. As David Caplovitz observes, "the bureaucratization of the world of work is a structural prerequisite for the credit society."[6] Loan sharks were present at the birth of our credit society, and they were spawned in the income stream of a swelling mass of wage workers who lived from payday to payday.

However, without some means to secure or collateralize the debt, lending to this new class of wage-earners would have remained prohibitively risky. As Clarence Wassam pointed out in his 1908 study of the salary lending business, "The very fact that it is necessary for an individual to borrow to meet living expenses is evidence that it will be difficult for him to meet his obligations."[7] The office clerk or skilled worker might now be consuming above the level of subsistence, but if such individuals needed to borrow to sustain their standard of living this indicated that the surplus had not been saved, or that savings out of this surplus were insufficient for emergency expenditures. A lender of even small sums would be taking a big chance of losing the principal or not turning a profit unless some means of enforceable security could guarantee the loan.

But those legal instruments already existed; in fact, they predated the rise of the new wage-earning class and constituted an unintended extension of credit to ordinary people on a massive scale by the legal system. The two instruments that made the loan-sharking industry possible in the nineteenth century were the chattel mortgage and the wage assignment, which gave people property rights they could alienate in exchange for cash. The one device allowed consumers to mortgage the furniture they had purchased with their increased incomes without having to put it into hock; the other device allowed employees to mortgage their future earnings as a security for debt. The innovation of the loan shark was to recognize that these older mortgage instruments could be exploited in the new context of bureaucratized patterns of work and remuneration engendered by the process of economic development.

The main purpose of the new lending products was—in the terminology of the economists—to smooth household consumption over time. As Rolf Nugent explained, "Urban wage-earners needed not only capital financing for their households, but also some means of refinancing these credits and of meeting maladjustments between income and expenses that occurred only too frequently in spite of the best-made plans."[8] Some of these maladjustments resulted from external "shocks" to the household budget—either to income or to expenses, or in the worst-case scenario, to both simultaneously.

Loss of employment represents the sharpest shock to household income, but lenders were unlikely to advance money to people who were unemployed, especially those who lacked other tangible assets. In the salary-lending business, your job is your credit, hence people without jobs rarely get loans. But disruption of a household's income stream can take milder or more temporary forms, and these less intense shocks created a large demand for small, short-term loans in Chicago.

The business cycle was volatile in the late nineteenth century. Many wage-earners experienced temporary layoffs or reductions in hours of employment. These disruptions created a demand for short-term credit. But the most visible form of these milder shocks afflicted public employees.

Though the *Chicago Tribune* in 1900 railed that "the men in the public employ get larger salaries on average than those in private concerns for the same grade of work," the payroll of these civil servants was frequently held hostage to the vagaries of local government. Sometimes tax receipts would fall short; other times the budget would be delayed because of wrangling between the legislative and executive branches. A November 1896 article in the *Tribune* reported that employees in the Cook County Recorder's Office had not been paid since August due to mismanagement of funds. "Loan sharks, it is also said, have nearly pauperized the force by loans at usurious rates of interest and brought about a condition of complete demoralization."[9] Such disruptions of the government payroll would recur every few years, followed by reports that the loan sharks were hunting in these waters. At one time or another, and often more than once, articles would report that teachers, firemen, sheriff's deputies, police officers, election officials, sanitary district workers, and so forth had gone to the loan sharks in large numbers while they waited to be paid.

When the city or county could not pay its employees, it issued scrip instead. These vouchers could not be cashed at a bank, but loan sharks would buy them at a discount of 15–30% and redeem the paper later.[10] Employees who wanted the full amount they were owed would have to go into debt to the loan sharks, paying them interest until enough could be saved from future paychecks to retire the principal. The local governments did not compensate employees for the hardship they caused by failing to pay them in a timely fashion. Instead, the city and the county adopted a policy of suspending or firing civil servants against whom a wage assignment was filed.

The local governments, however, were not the only culprits. From time to time the *Tribune* ran stories about disruption in pay for the soldiers stationed at Fort Sheridan, north of the city. The troops would pawn what few possessions they had to the saloonkeepers and then turn to the loan sharks, who were drawn to the base by the scent of desperation. One private reported that "the loan sharks are bombarding us with letters, and many of them have come out here and offered terms that some of the men found impossible to refuse."[11]

Even if income was not disrupted, a sudden increase in household expenses could create the demand for short-term credit that fed the loan sharks. The need to pay for medical treatment drove many wage-earners into the small-loan market. Some observers claimed this was the single most important source of the demand for loan-shark money. Dozens of articles on loan-sharking in the *Tribune* are filled with sad stories of householders turning to the salary lenders to pay medical bills for a sick child, wife, or mother. A man might earn $20 a week, but it could cost $100 to deliver a baby. Wage-earners didn't have health insurance or a welfare state to fall back on. A household's plight was even more dire if the breadwinner became ill; then income fell as expenditures rose. A death in the family also figures often in the stories told about why people turned to the loan sharks. Parents might go into debt to pay for the funeral of a child. In general, as one reporter observed, "Vital statistics are closely allied to borrowing statistics. Births, deaths, sickness, and even marriages cause thousands of men to get into debt for the first time in their lives."[12]

Housing was yet another source of extraordinary expenses. Renting an apartment might require a security deposit or an extra month's payment. There was also the cost of the move.[13] If the household lacked savings, it might have to mortgage future income to pay for pressing needs today.

These shocks to income and expenses account for part of the demand for short-term credit. But the truth is that maladjustment between income and expenditure did not always result from hard luck or external forces. Many observers recognized that bad planning or extravagance drove people into the clutches of the loan sharks. A large number of employees were paid only once a month at this time, and some had difficulty budgeting carefully. Teachers were under contract only ten months a year and had to rely on the loan sharks if they didn't save enough to carry them through the summer. But one school principal speculated that the real reason so many teachers borrowed from the loan sharks was because "their style of living must be luxurious and vain." She thought these spendthrifts set a bad example for their students and ought to be fired.[14]

Others agreed that the demand for "easy loans" arose in part from irresponsible behavior. The head of the Chicago Relief and Aid Society insisted that "many of the victims themselves are to blame. They live beyond their means and run into debt through improvidence and ignorance." An article in the Sunday *Tribune* magazine concurred: "Doubtless of all the causes which force men into the pawnshops or to borrow money, gambling and drinking are the most in evidence." This was also the view of a police commander, who declared that "the racetrack has been the chief cause of the loan shark trouble." He believed that "there is no reason for a man earning $1000 a year to be without money. He earns enough to have a home."[15]

Sometimes victims of the loan sharks would admit they were to blame for going into debt. One bank clerk embezzled a large sum from his employer in order to pay off the loan sharks. In his confession he did not tell a hard luck story: "My daily expenses were not large, but I would go out for a good time once or twice a week, and sometimes I'd spend $15, $20, or $25."[16] Salary lending made it feasible to live for the day by mortgaging one's future income, but accumulating debt at this pace on a bank clerk's salary would quickly plunge one into dire straits.

Gambling one's wages at cards or the racetrack fueled the demand for cash advances, but so did more respectable forms of gambling. One article in the spring of 1901 reported that office workers all over town had been caught up in a frenzy of speculation at the commodities exchange. "Thousands of clerks have become so absorbed in the craze that they have bargained their wages for weeks ahead to loan 'sharks' and are playing chance with the yet unearned salaries." In an interview one clerk at the Board of Trade laughed off the hefty interest rate charged by the salary lenders: "Ten per cent a month? Why, sure; the fellows are tied up every way. But just wait until things pay out. We'll all go into the money-loaning business ourselves."[17]

Opinions varied about whether need or extravagance was the more important cause in creating the demand for small loans. Wassam reported the view of a New York City loan shark, who guessed that three-quarters of his customers were family men with legitimate needs, but the other quarter were simply profligate. No matter what the proportions were, the *Tribune* editorial board thought it was folly and short-sightedness, at bottom, that led wage-earners to the loan sharks. "If he finds himself in need of money during the early part of the month he had better live on bread and water, if necessary, until the next payday rather than secure an advance of his next month's salary."[18] People who were thinking clearly ought to be able to see that a loan at ten or twenty percent a month would not smooth household consumption over the long run but reduce it.

To people without urgent needs or wants that conclusion is indeed obvious; they were not the source of the demand for quick cash. The demand came instead from people who discounted the future steeply because their present fear of loss—or desire for gain—was so intense. These consumers experienced a sharp disjunction between short- and long-term interest that the new lending products were designed to exploit. As we shall see, these loans were structured in such a way that, at any given moment, the lesser evil for many customers was to keep paying even though the debt was rather obviously a losing proposition over the long run.

The sort of people who patronized the salary lenders needed a steady job and an income above the level of subsistence, but if they had savings or assets to fall back on, they were unlikely to borrow at such steep prices. In 1900 the average savings depositor in Illinois had $310 in the bank, but less than 5% of the population owned one of these savings accounts. The wage-earners who went to the loan sharks were "unbanked"; they did not have an account and, without collateral, were ineligible for bank loans. In any case, banks did not execute notes for less than $100, in part because strict adherence to the usury statute made small loans unprofitable.[19] And most banks would be reluctant to get into a business that required lenders to employ such harsh collection methods—methods that were likely to earn firms an unsavory reputation.

The effective demand for cash advances, then, arose neither from the top nor from the bottom of the income scale but from those somewhere in between. The working and middle classes were the waters in which the sharks hunted. The professions from which large numbers of wage-earners were said to have become entangled with the loan sharks included streetcar employees, railway clerks and mechanics, stockyard workers, telegraph operators, government clerks of every sort, police officers, sheriff's deputies, firemen, and teachers. There were conflicting estimates about which of these occupations were most in thrall to the small-loan companies. One article in September 1907 claimed that "street car employees and mechanics are the most inveterate borrowers," but another insisted that this group shared the prize with railroad men and telegraph operators.[20] Within these various professions a sizable fraction was said to be in debt to the loan sharks at any given time. Mayor Carter Harrison claimed that half of Chicago's three-thousand-man police force in 1900 had assigned its wages to the "ten-percenters." A few years later the Cook County Controller complained that half the firemen in the city had claims filed against them at the payroll office, and he thought the rate was nearly the same for other classes of government workers.[21] Such large numbers in these prominent occupations helped to fuel the sense of crisis that motivated numerous reform efforts in the early decades of the twentieth century.

In his study of salary lending in New York City, Wassam gained access to the files of one loan shark firm and was able to build up a profile of the typical debtor: a man in his twenties or thirties, usually married, and earning between $51 and $75 a month, which placed him in the second (or lower-middle) quartile of the income distribution. But the incomes of some of the occupations listed above, like police officer, were better than average, and this meant that the demand for quick credit stretched into solidly middle-income groups. In his account of the small-loan market Clarence Hodson estimated that one-quarter of the urban population in the United States borrowed from loan sharks. Arthur Ham, the man who spearheaded the fight for the Uniform Small Loan Law, thought the number was more like one in five, but in the largest cities one-third of wage-earners might have been in debt to the illegal lenders.[22]

As is to be expected, most of the salary borrowers were men. In fact, the salary loan was the better product for husbands who wanted to conceal their debts. Chattel mortgages usually required couples to sign together; in any case, the loan couldn't be kept secret because the lender's agent would call at home to appraise the furniture that served as collateral. Salary loans, by contrast, were backed by a wage assignment rather than by household possessions; they had the reputation of being sought by "drunkards, gamblers and men with no permanent residences, whereas the chattel mortgage is almost invariably given to a family man whose wife joins him in it." Still, not every salary borrower was shiftless or dissolute, and plenty of female wage-earners mortgaged their future income too. Teachers were a case in point. And shrewd loan sharks recognized that the female market had not been fully exploited. One prominent broker created a new product just for housewives. They would be permitted to borrow against their "allowance" if they could find two cosigners to join them in the loan.[23]

In addition to being mostly male, the loan-shark clientele in Chicago was also overwhelmingly white. At the turn of the century African Americans accounted for only about 2% of Chicago's population.[24] The incomes they earned would have prohibited most from borrowing from the loan sharks. In the South there was extensive loan-sharking among the black population (often the $6-for-$5 racket), but in Chicago, salary lending at this time was a white market. This may help to explain why so many establishment voices were alarmed by the phenomenon and joined together to reform this business. The clientele of today's payday-lending business, by contrast, is disproportionately nonwhite and female, and it isn't as visible within the division of labor as the loan-shark victims of old.

One last factor that may have intensified the demand for small loans at the end of the nineteenth century would not have been so obvious to observers at that time. This was a period of growing income inequality as wage-earners near the top of the distribution moved more quickly ahead of those further below. Based on the fragmentary evidence available to us, we now know that "the stretching in the nominal pay structure between 1896 and 1914 reflects the last great surge in American urban equality"—until the late twentieth century.[25] Over the last generation, income inequality in the United States has grown at a pace that roughly matches the surge a century ago, and scholarly studies of the trends in recent decades have shown that this elongation of the income distribution has fueled the demand for credit. Growing income inequality is accompanied by a rising household debt burden as those behind in the race borrow against future income in order to sustain a socially acceptable level of consumption.[26] If the association we observe today is a general pattern, then the demand for new forms of credit that we witness at the end of the nineteenth century was driven in part by the widening gap in compensation between more and less skilled labor. The less favored groups had to consume more than their current incomes in order to try to keep up with the fortunate minority that was pulling ahead and setting the pace of consumption. It is a striking coincidence that salary lending in its loan-shark and payday-loan guises emerged or reemerged precisely in periods of accelerating income inequality. These products are symptomatic of the stresses wage-earners in the bottom half of the distribution experience when they fail to keep pace with the cohort ahead of them.

The Spawning of the Sharks

A progenitor of the loan shark was the dealer in scrip—promissory notes issued by large employers in lieu of wage payments. Local governments distributed scrip whenever the tax receipts fell short, but private employers might also substitute certificates for cash payment when they couldn't make the payroll. In February 1856, for example, the Chicago, Alton and St. Louis Railroad Company issued scrip to its employees, many of whom promptly sold the notes at a discount of as much as 30%.[27] The dealers in this scrip—who were sometimes called "shavers"—didn't lend the workers money or tie them up in debt. For this reason we can't classify them as loan sharks. When the shavers purchased scrip they were actually lending money to the employers, not the employees. But it was the employees who paid the interest on this debt when they accepted less in cash than the face value of the certificates. The transaction amounted to a pay cut for the workers, who suffered because their employers had run short of cash. While the practice wasn't quite loan-sharking, it was a related form of exploitation. In this case the employer's scrip served as the instrument of security for the cash advance.

But there were other kinds of note shavers operating around the middle of the nineteenth century, and one of these discovered the utility of the wage assignment as a form of collateral. It is impossible to say when and where the trade commenced, but large concentrations of government employees seem to have been the original feeding ground of the first salary sharks. One of these early entrepreneurs was alleged to have been William H. English, a man who came within two thousand votes of being elected vice president of the United States on the ticket of the Democratic Party in 1880. Back in the 1840s, English was a clerk in the U.S. Treasury Department, and it was rumored that the young lawyer "was accustomed to shave the per diem and salary of his fellow-clerks, and to take assignments of pay." His charge was said to be as much as 10% a month. These "ten-per-centers" multiplied in and around the government bureaus in the nation's capital, where modest pay combined with job security to lure the money sharks. In the 1880s it was reported that "offices for [the] prosecution [of this trade] are numerous in the vicinity of the departments, and many private bankers, lawyers and real estate agents have a considerable run of this custom." One of the biggest operations in the city was said to have been organized by a former congressman from Virginia.[28]

Another early and notorious den of "salary harpies" was the Custom House in New York City. According to the *New York Herald*, "A class of curs known as 'salary brokers' have long been a most obnoxious pest and disgrace. These creatures have been for years in the habit of making advances of money to clerks in the different bureaus, and the clerks generally give them a due bill for the amount, presentable on the next payday." One of these salary brokers, Edward Winship, began in the Custom House and then set up shop on Wall Street. He lent money at 10% a month to government clerks and paid the investors who supplied him with capital one-third of that rate, but his business was a Ponzi scheme and it eventually collapsed. In the course of describing Winship's technique for "shaving the pay accounts," the reporter noted that "the business is a relic of the war, as the salary broker was then a parasite of the army, who, when the exchequer was depleted, relieved the necessities of the officers at exorbitant rates, and in most cases divided with the Paymasters, who secured them against loss."[29] According to this genealogy, salary lending began during the Civil War without the security of the wage assignment and continued afterward when profligate soldiers were rewarded with government jobs. Whether this sequence is accurate or not, it is certainly the case that what would come to be called loan-sharking in later years thrived first among government employees, both uniformed and civilian.

In Chicago a different type of note shaving was invented. This one relied on the chattel mortgage as its instrument of security. Some old-timers connected with the business recollected that mortgages on furniture were being made already back in the 1850s, but Robinson and Nugent in their fine study of consumptive lending could find evidence for such transactions dating back only to 1869. They combed the classified ads in the *Chicago Tribune* and found the first published offers of chattel mortgages in that year. Similar ads appeared in other big-city newspapers a few years later.[30] Such transactions were no doubt occurring some years before the ads began to appear, but it seems likely that this line of lending first emerged around the end of the Civil War. It is thought to have been the sideline of men with cash to lend—for instance, payroll clerks, pawnbrokers, and storage dealers—who first recognized the demand. As the market grew, some began to specialize in these loans and set up independent credit stores.

In Chicago the first consumptive loans were chattel mortgages. The debtor pledged household goods or jewelry but retained possession unless the loan went into default. Salary lending, or lending on a wage assignment, emerged later as a sideline of the chattel-mortgage business. Robinson and Nugent found evidence for the existence of such loans in cities on the East Coast dating from the early 1880s.[31] But the product was not advertised in the newspapers under the name "salary loan" until the 1890s, when the phrase "loan shark" was also coming into currency. There were no news articles in Chicago or New York about "salary lending" until the first decade of the twentieth century, which suggests that the product remained invisible to elite consciousness in the early period of its growth.

One civic group that we might expect to have paid attention to the product sooner than others—the Bureau of Justice, later renamed the Legal Aid Society of Chicago—made no reference to salary lending in its annual reports before 1899. In its first publication a decade earlier, the Bureau of Justice did mention "the chattel mortgage question," which it said "presents a great problem and demands our best thought." Its lawyers handled 45 of these cases in its first year of operation, and that number grew steadily over the next decade. In its report for 1892, the director declared that "the phrase 'chattel mortgage' is the modern synonym of the rack, wheel, and thumb-screw of an earlier age. It suggests usury, extortion and every form of financial trickery." Several years later we are told that "there are in this City hordes of human sharks," but it would be a few years more before the reports described wage assignment transactions. The bulletin for 1901 observed that "of all the instruments of persecution in the hands of the loan sharks this one is the most formidable." Within a couple of years the Legal Aid Society would be handling more wage-assignment than chattel-mortgage cases.[32]

The annual report for 1900 observed that the market for salary loans in Chicago was expanding quite a bit in the latter half of the 1890s: "We find that the greatest injustice is being done the small wage-earner today by the 'sharks' who loan money on unearned wages and take assignment of the borrowers' future wages as security for same. Until very recently these loans were made only to men earning $20 or more per week. In such cases we have felt it was not the province of this institution to intervene." But now the loan sharks were said to be lending to wage-earners who made $10 a week or less—people at or below the poverty line and thus eligible for legal-aid representation. This piece of evidence suggests that the product had been in existence for some time but that the market was deepening and drawing in new strata of workers around the turn of the century.[33]

The loan shark businesses operated under names that obscured the nature of the products they sold: "People's Loan and Trust," "Equity Finance," "Chicago Security and Credit," and so forth. Some even called themselves "banks" because there was no law in Illinois at that time regulating the usage of the term. These businesses were rarely incorporated, in part because their transactions violated the state's usury statute but also because they often changed names. "Chicago Loan and Trust," for example, became "People's Loan and Trust" and then the "Chicago Loan Association."[34] As Earle Eubank observed, the industry had "a mushroom-like character" that makes it difficult to chart its growth and size.[35] A single nondescript office might have operated under several different names simultaneously.

Ownership of the businesses also tended to be concealed because of their illegal nature. The true owner would purchase a proxy's power of attorney and claim this person was the main investor. As federal judge Kenesaw Mountain Landis observed, this was "just a device to break the thread between the borrower and the loan company" in case the former tried to file suit. One successful loan shark in Chicago paid an elderly dressmaker a small fee to front for him; it took weeks for Judge Landis to track her down. Another lender placed a chain of stores in the maiden name of his 80-year-old mother, who lived in Reedsburg, Wisconsin.[36]

Despite its illegal status at the turn of the century, the small loan industry was in fact a pioneer in the chain-store phenomenon. The man who was dubbed "King of the Loan Sharks of Chicago," Frank Jay Mackey, owned dozens of branches across the country, including several different firms in Chicago. He started his first chattel-mortgage business in Minnesota in 1878, made money, and then expanded across the Midwest.[37] He transferred the headquarters of his chain to Chicago in 1894. Mackey was not apologetic about how he made his fortune. He insisted that the business had improved the quality of life for people of modest means. When pressed by a reporter, he retorted: "Say, don't you know this business is a blessing to the poor. When we started in Minneapolis years ago the town was honey-combed with second-hand shops and we cleaned them all out. Chicago does not have half of the second-hand shops it had before collateral loan concerns started business."[38] His point was that chattel mortgages made it possible for people who didn't own real estate to raise cash without having to sell their possessions or put them into hock. Even if the loans were costly, they made it possible for debtors to maintain their standard of living.

The first phase in the history of loan-sharking was drawing to a close in 1916. By then, Mackey was said to own nearly seventy loan shops. The name his holding company would take a decade later was Household Finance Corporation, better known today as HFC.

Mackey's rival for the loan-sharking crown was Daniel H. Tolman. Though his chain was based in New York City, Tolman was said to have gotten his start in Chicago in the 1890s. He set up shop with $10,000 and, fifteen years later, had about as many branches across the country as Mackey. His son managed the ones in Chicago. Those operations were reported to have more than $100,000 on the books in 1912, in loans that began as $10 or $20 cash advances.[39]

Rapid growth was possible in this industry despite the risks associated with making usurious loans. C. Frank Taylor began loan-sharking in Chicago in 1910 with a tiny investment and was said to be worth $40,000 two years later. He boasted that his income from this loan fund exceeded $15,000 during the previous year.[40] In response to the demand for small loans, investment poured into this market. All of the businesses were privately held until HFC went public in 1928. In 1907 the Legal Aid Society of Chicago counted 125 small loan firms in the city. It also estimated that several hundred more individuals lent money at usurious rates as a sideline to other businesses. In the same year the *Tribune* pegged the total loan fund at more than $25 million for all loan-shark businesses combined. Roughly 200,000 Chicagoans, or one in five adults, were said to be in the clutches of the "loan octopus."[41]

A few years later Irwin Ellis, who frequently wrote about loan-sharking for the *Tribune*'s Sunday *Worker's Magazine*, reported that there were 161 loan companies currently in operation, plus another 100 part-time loan sharks. This was probably the highpoint of the loan-shark industry in Chicago, for the *Tribune* would launch its public campaign against the quick-cash businesses a few months later and shame some of them out of the market. Still, after years of bad publicity and a more hostile regulatory climate, a painstaking investigation by the Department of Public Welfare in 1916 identified 139 active offices, as well as an equal number that operated covertly or as part of other businesses. Half of the active offices dealt exclusively in salary loans. The report estimated that there were 150,000 live accounts for the industry as a whole. The total loan fund was approximately $11 million a year.[42]

The size of the small-loan industry in Chicago was comparable to that in other cities. The Russell Sage Foundation said that the average in the pre-reform era was one loan shark per five thousand inhabitants in cities with a population of at least twenty-five thousand. New York City had roughly three hundred lenders, Boston a hundred, Syracuse twenty-four, and Portland, Maine a dozen.[43]

There was a predictable number of loan-shark firms in most cities after the market matured because there was a limit to the number of customers any one office could serve. As is true in the payday-loan business today, convenience was an important factor in attracting a clientele for "five-minute loans." Borrowers favored locations close to work or home; they were unlikely to travel across town for a small loan. Wassam found that the typical salary lending office in New York serviced between 800 and 1,000 accounts. Once an outlet reached that size, it made more sense to open another branch in a new location rather than sink more capital into an office that had reached its saturation point. This is one reason why the chain-store model proliferated in the industry. Another reason was the economies of scale that could be realized by coordinating background checks, debt collection, and so forth.[44]

The size limit of offices ensured that there was always room for new entrants in the small-loan business. The start-up costs were not great, especially for a salary-loan operation. According to Robinson and Nugent:

> During the late nineties when the profits that could be made in the small loan business, especially in the salary loan business, began to be noised about, loan offices sprang up in the cities overnight like mushrooms. There are tales of chain salary lenders sending managers into new territory with $1000 of capital and expecting them to rent an office, buy furniture, pay salaries, and conduct a paying business without more capital. If this be true, these lenders must certainly have charged as much as the traffic would bear.[45]

To be sure, the risks in this line of business were great too. Many loans were likely to go bad, it was expensive to harass or track down deadbeats, and it was always possible that the government would crack down on a business that violated the usury statute. Savvy management was needed, but the lure of quick riches constantly enticed new capital into this market. The competition could be intense, but there was also collusion between lenders, as we shall see. Despite the large number of outlets, the competition was not perfect. The illegal and unsavory nature of the industry scared off reputable capital and increased prices for consumers. These businesses operated in a gray market, not unlike the sweatshop garment factories of that period. But instead of sweating their employees, the loan sharks sweated their customers.

The largest number of loan-shark outlets in Chicago was located in the Loop, where the clientele of clerks and government employees flocked to work. Dozens of firms were clustered in the office buildings around the intersection of Dearborn and Madison streets; sometimes there were more than ten different loan sharks in a single building. Another favorite location for the quick-cash businesses was transportation hubs in the city—near train stations, streetcar barns, and so forth. A large number could be found around the slaughterhouses on the city's South Side. A *Tribune* reporter uncovered "a nest of sharks at the Halsted street entrance to the stockyards," which targeted employees of the packinghouses.[46]

In the space of a decade or two around the turn of the century the Windy City had become infested with loan sharks. A ready supply of desperation and profligacy attracted a class of entrepreneurs willing to take risks for the chance to turn their capital over rapidly. The grayness of the usury market combined with a cash-strapped clientele forced these businesses to be inventive and sharp. In order to survive they developed a particular style of hunting and ways to coordinate their attacks. Though the species favored murky waters, the cries of its victims attracted much attention and motivated a number of observers to study its behavior. For that reason we may know more about how the loan sharks operated at this time than we know about many other businesses in Chicago.

How the Shark Bites

The first loan sharks were often likened to Shylock, but the new salary lenders did not bear much resemblance to Shakespeare's villain. Shylock loaned large sums for commercial purposes to members of the elite. He would not have bothered with small cash advances to clerks, especially if these loans were not backed by collateral. In turn, the typical salary lender was not motivated by vengeance to drive a hard bargain; he was just doing business in a tough market with a clientele that could be, or had to be, dunned. A pound of flesh would not have interested him. Above all, it is worth noting that the typical Chicago loan shark was not a Jew. The files of the *Tribune*'s Anti–Loan Shark Bureau "revealed an absence of Jews, both from the ranks of borrowers and lenders in chattel mortgage and salary loan transactions."[47] The loan shark in Chicago was usually a WASP; many of his victims were too.

Before the sharks could bite they had to lure customers into the office. Convenient locations made that easier, but more had to be done to ensure a steady volume of business. Many lenders advertised in the classified pages, until the *Tribune* and other papers eventually refused to take their money. One could find several dozen loan-shark ads every day in the *Tribune* before 1912; Eubank claimed the record was fifty-six.[48] Often the ads indicated the clientele of the business:

CLERKS, SALARIED MEN, MANAGERS AND EMPLOYEES can borrow money of us on plain note. Stevens & Dunlap, 1107 Chamber of Commerce.

LOANS TO HONORABLE EMPLOYEES—No security required: nothing but your plain notes; the fact that you hold a good position with a first-class firm is sufficient guaranty to us; we make no inquiries of your employer. Drexel & Co., 145 LaSalle St., Suite 409.

LOANS TO LADIES AND GENTLEMEN. Wholesale and retail clerks, firemen, school teachers, mail carriers, railway, and all salaried people with steady positions on their own names; no mortgage, no inquiries made of your employers or friends; everything private; low rates, easy payments. Call or address "The Manager." R. 16. 86 Washington.[49]

The loan sharks also advertised in professional publications. One board of education official complained about classifieds like the following that appeared in the teachers' papers after a salary cut was mandated:

PERSONAL—OF INTEREST TO TEACHERS. Private party will make loans to teachers at low rates.[50]

The sharks had a keen nose for detecting groups who were feeling the pinch and in need of extra cash right away.

Streetcars in the city were also plastered with ads, and many lenders passed out cards or handbills on the street.[51] A favorite marketing technique was to send targeted letters through the mail. Some city directories identified occupations as well as home addresses, and lenders could also buy the list of a business's employees for a penny a name from a firm on Halsted Street. The solicitations flattered the recipient and offered a "line of credit" on easy terms or advised a wage-earner to consolidate debts: "If your income is small we will arrange your payments in amounts so small that it will be no trouble for you to meet them. Pay a little each month. With this simple plan you have the use of a large sum just when it is of the most good to you, and pay it back afterwards in small installments that you will hardly miss. If you can use $10 to $300 to your advantage, call and get it."[52] Other letters sounded philanthropic, as if the lender specialized in saving people from other sharks. The *Tribune* claimed that thousands of these letters were sent each day, especially when business was slow, and certain classes of wage-earners would have received a steady stream of these offers in their mailboxes.[53]

These broadcast methods of advertisement, however, were scattershot. A thousand letters mailed would only bring in a handful of clients. The loan sharks therefore employed more direct methods of appeal. Many firms paid a commission to designated individuals in large offices or factories to steer business to them. A payroll clerk or foreman was likely to know which employees needed money and could also vouch for applicants or exert pressure on debtors to keep making their payments. Eubank reports that "in some of the buildings where loan offices are located, the elevator men act as solicitors, distributing cards to the elevator passengers." A few "touts" worked freelance in the city's social clubs, pointing their marks to a particular loan office in exchange for a 5% commission. Many salary lenders also offered discounts to current customers who referred a friend to the firm. A fee of $1 might be paid for the lead, but often the commission was withheld until both borrowers had retired their debts.[54]

The insider connections with the loan sharks sometimes resulted in scandal. There were persistent rumors that men in various government offices steered employees to the sharks. A representative of the Chicago Federation of Labor claimed that "a man going to work in city hall is handed a card by his superior officer, with the remark that 'you may need this'. It is an invitation to borrow money, the loan shark probably being located right in the city hall." In March 1906 an assistant city paymaster was found guilty of colluding with the lenders. The previous year a sheriff's deputy was investigated for steering men with pay vouchers to the "official" loan agent of the department.[55]

The biggest scandal of all involved loan-shark pals of the police chief trading on his name. Members of the Police Trial Board were also alleged to be working on behalf of the loan firms and coercing payments from patrol officers. And then it was revealed that a member of the Civil Service Commission was himself a loan shark and had arranged to sell copies of the lieutenants exam on the installment plan to sixteen sergeants. This scandal was matched some years later by the revelation that a director of the Legal Aid Society of Chicago was a loan-shark associate and had tried to collect on notes that were paid in full several years earlier. Scandals like these fed the rumors that the loan men paid protection money to city hall and got the politicians to tie up the payroll, so that employees would have to go to the sharks for emergency cash.[56]

Once inside the office door the customer was likely to be greeted by a woman. One in seven Chicago loan-shark firms in 1916 was thought to be owned by a woman, and often most of the employees were female too. Tolman hired women exclusively. There were many good business reasons for this preference. It was thought that "Women can be trusted where men cannot, they can be secured more cheaply, they give an appearance of harmlessness to the lending establishment, and an outraged borrower is not so anxious to kick the manager out of a window if she is a woman."[57] One reporter described the kinds of women who worked in these establishments:

> In one place it is a black-eyed girl with a slim figure, a pretty face, and considerable style. In another it is a woman of 30, intelligently attractive and

graciously at ease. In another appears a refined and sweet faced matronly person with white hair. In a fourth a girl with a severely parted coiffure of a ruddy color has the combination of the uncompromising and the artistic which suggests a musical college rather than a money lender's office.[58]

But not all of the women employed in these offices seemed so charming and harmless. Another reporter told a story of a female clerk who came around from behind the counter one day and punched a lawyer who was trying to settle a debt for his client.[59]

New customers, however, were treated much better. After the request for a loan was made, the individual completed an application form listing address, occupation and employer, salary, other debts, collateral, and references. No money was offered at this time, but the client was instructed to return in a day or two after the firm had conducted an investigation. The form was then passed to a "reporter" who made surreptitious inquiries at the office, in the neighborhood, and with merchants. Although the newspaper ads emphasized the "strict confidence" of the transaction, in fact the grocer or payroll clerk likely knew what such snooping meant and could be alerted to the applicant's financial embarrassment.[60]

A second vetting of the applicant occurred simultaneously. Several times a day "runners" stopped by many of the loan offices in the Loop and collected the names of new applicants. They returned to a suite in the Hartford building at the intersection of Madison and Dearborn that housed the Chicago Merchants' Credit Association. This was a clearinghouse that had been established by the principal loan sharks in the city back in 1895, in the early days of the business. In 1912 it was alleged to have more than sixty member firms that paid an initiation fee plus $5 a month for its services. A sort of primitive credit bureau, the clearinghouse verified whether an applicant owed money elsewhere, had skipped out on a loan with a member firm, or was employed by a blacklisted company that made trouble about wage assignments. The consortium was also said to collude in discouraging price shopping by quoting inflated rates to applicants who inquired at a second or third office. Each member firm was assigned a number by the clearinghouse, and the firms and the clearinghouse communicated among themselves in code to avoid revealing evidence of the conspiracy. One reporter described the clearinghouse as "a secret organization which in passwords, cryptic signs, and mystic numbers rivals the Ku Klux Klan in its palmy days."[61]

Some lenders preferred a more direct method of assessing applicants. Would-be borrowers might be quizzed in the office about their beliefs and lifestyle: "One man will not loan to married women who believe in race suicide [birth control], another tests their knowledge of the Bible, and with subtle skill discovers how keenly alive is their sense of right and wrong." Such methods of screening and investigation were necessary because some applicants had skipped out on other loans or were trying to scam the lender. They might be impersonating a stranger or planning to leave town without repaying the debt. Some accepted the money but then turned around and filed bankruptcy, hoping to have the debt discharged in court.[62]

Most investigations were completed within twenty-four hours. If the result was positive, the applicant was presented with a series of documents to sign. These included one or more promissory notes listing principal and interest, a power of attorney, and a wage assignment. Some lenders added a "statement of present indebtedness" to the stack of papers to be endorsed; it could be used to threaten delinquents with fraud for failing to disclose the extent of their financial difficulties when they borrowed. Some of these forms might be left blank and filled in later if the loan went into default. Frequently the papers were stacked one on top of the other with only the signature lines visible. Clients were discouraged from reading the forms and sometimes the offices were made purposely dim so that it would be hard to decipher the fine print. When an acquaintance of Irwin Ellis insisted on reading the documents first, "he was informed that if he meant to be so particular he was not desired as a customer." After signing the forms, the debtor was not provided with copies or a receipt for the transaction. The lender did not want to provide a paper trail that might lead into court.[63]

The crucial document in this pile of papers was the wage assignment. It secured the debt against the wage-earner's future income. In case of default, the loan shark could file the wage assignment at the borrower's place of employment. This lien on the wages prevented employees from collecting their pay until the loan shark signed a release. The lender did not have to go to court to make the claim effective, and wage assignments were given priority over any garnishment decrees. The instrument was more powerful than the chattel mortgage because the salary shark could "tie up wages without any legal proceedings." In bankruptcy court it was treated as a secured debt that could not be discharged until the borrower switched employers.[64]

The loan sharks did not invent the wage assignment; it was a creation of the common law. Such contracts first made their appearance in the 1830s in New England factory towns. Because many of the textile workers were strangers in the community and might therefore skip out on a bill, grocers would require them to assign their future wages in exchange for store credit. On payday the merchant was entitled to collect the wages that had been earned over the previous month or quarter, take the amount needed to settle the bill, and then turn the balance remaining to the assignor. By drawing the employer into the transaction between creditor and customer, the wage assignment "added to the obligation of a possibly irresponsible wage-earner the obligation of a responsible employer."[65] These novel contracts soon found their way into court and were judged to be valid instruments as long as the assignment was not indefinite and applied only to the wage-earner's current employer. Once the employment contract was terminated, so was any existing wage assignment, for otherwise the device would render the debtor an indentured servant.

It was not realized at the time what a massive extension of credit had been effected by the courts when they granted recognition to the wage assignment. Over the next few decades the instrument was employed only by merchants, but after the Civil War the small-loan companies discovered the device as a means of security when the debtor could not provide a chattel mortgage on household property. Now many more people would be eligible to borrow because the courts permitted them to mortgage their future income stream rather than an existing and tangible possession. The invention of the wage assignment was an unintended credit revolution.

For some, that revolution was emancipatory because it made it possible for them to maintain their consumption level during a period when money was tight. But this credit revolution plunged others into bondage, because the loan shark could hold their pay packet—and even their job—hostage. Although the loan secured by a wage assignment was usurious and therefore illegal, employers felt obliged to honor the instrument in order to avoid the possibility that the loan shark (a notoriously litigious breed) might file a lawsuit.[66] Hence, until a release was signed, employees could not draw their pay. This was bad enough, but worse still was the very real possibility that the employer would fire the debtor when a wage assignment was submitted to the payroll office. This was a common practice at the turn of the century, and the loan shark was in fact counting on that outcome as a means to coerce the borrower into making payments. The wage assignment was like a gun pointed at the employee's head and it transformed debt collection into an exercise in extortion.

Sometimes in the literature this policy of discharge is treated as an irrational prejudice of employers. But there were good reasons why businesses adopted this admittedly harsh rule. So many wage assignments were being filed that it slowed the process of preparing the payroll and required employers to hire extra staff to handle the flood of paper. Often the loan sharks filed wage assignments blindly as a means to trace "skips" who had disappeared from a different place of employment. They were trying to discover if their debtor now worked at this establishment, but the tactic only increased the paperwork to be handled by the payroll staff.[67] Yet if the employer decided to ignore the assignments, the loan sharks would file suit in a distant jurisdiction and subpoena the top executives to appear with all of the company's books. As one manager in a large firm explained, "In self-defense we have been compelled to weed out such of our employees as were in the habit of patronizing the loan sharks, and we now have a notice posted threatening to discharge any man who does business with them. It is only by this radical action we can protect the company officials from annoyance and serious loss of time."[68] The Cook County controller, for example, was virtually hunted by loan-shark operatives. A police officer had to be stationed outside his office door because so many tried to hand him wage assignments in person. Some snuck them into packages being delivered by merchants. Others waited on his doorstep at home and bothered his wife. The harassment became so bad he started to avoid the office, which was under surveillance from across the street by loan sharks equipped with binoculars.[69]

The fundamental grievance of employers against the wage assignment was that the instrument turned their payroll offices into a debt collection agency for the loan sharks.[70] They did not want that obligation, and so, many organizations adopted the policy of discharge to discourage employees from assigning their wages. This policy, however, did not reduce the employees' need for quick cash; it merely gave the loan shark a more effective tool with which to extract payment from people terrified of losing their jobs.

But the terrors of the wage assignment were unrecognized by most applicants when they signed the papers in the loan office. They needed money right away, and they also tended to assume they could make all of their payments on time and quickly clear the debt. Salary loans were often repaid on the installment plan, unlike today's payday loans, which require a lump-sum payment. But because many payday-advance customers now renew their loans again and again, the two products are actually quite similar.

In practice both often amount to interest-only cash advances in which the principal does not shrink but actually grows. The number of installments for a salary loan varied depending on the size of the loan, the borrower's income, and the frequency of pay. The payments on a typical $20 loan might be spread over twelve weeks.

The standard interest charge for a salary loan in Chicago ranged between 10% and 20% per month. This translates into an annual percentage rate of 120–240%. The rates were higher for this product than for chattel-mortgage loans, in part because the latter tended to be larger in size and longer in duration but also because the default rate was higher for debts secured by a wage assignment. The salary-loan interest rate had to be higher because those who paid were also paying for those who didn't. One loan shark claimed that "two in every five borrowers will not repay and he must gouge enough out of the other three to cover losses and make a profit."[71]

Because the maximum permissible interest rate in Illinois at this time was 7% a year, every single salary loan was illegal. But tricks were devised to conceal the true charge, such as requiring the borrower to purchase a life insurance policy with the loan or disguising the transaction as a stock sale. Some passed the interest charges off as fees: for example, to cash a check made out by the lender to the debtor and that had to be redeemed right there in the office at a 25% discount. Judge Landis quizzed a loan shark on the stand about a transaction in which the borrower received $10 but had to repay $12. The lender boasted, "I never collect any interest." Landis asked, "What was the extra $2 for?" "O, that's just a fee I charge for making the loan." The judge replied, "Well, usurious interest is usurious interest whether you call it a fee or not."[72]

Tolman's firms had a different way of concealing the true interest rate. They only made loans in odd amounts, for example $18 or $22.50. This made it more difficult for applicants to do the math in their heads and calculate how costly the loan actually was. Other lenders tried to get around the usury statute by assigning the notes to a dummy business that could claim to be an "innocent purchaser" of the debt.[73] The loan sharks and their lawyers were an endlessly inventive group. So are today's payday lenders.

A few sample transactions will give the reader a sense of how expensive these loans were. A client borrowed $25 on a six-month note at a rate of 18% per month. Payments of $2.25 were due each week, and after half a year the customer would have paid $27 in interest for the privilege of borrowing $25. However, like many debtors, this one fell behind on the payments and had to refinance the loan for additional fees. The principal grew, and so did the weekly payments, which were now $3.55.[74] Another example: a customer borrowed $25 and repaid the loan in twenty weekly installments of $1.90. The interest rate was 132% a year or 11% a month.[75] This transaction was unusually cheap.

Some loans were larger in size. A telegraph operator in a large firm borrowed $100 for one month at 20% interest. When he could not repay the loan after thirty days, the debt was rolled over for a fee of $20 every month. After a year he had paid $240 in interest but without reducing the principal at all. The loan was effectively an interest-only product. One loan shark put it this way: "The $20 is payable every month so long as the note is in force. We never press our patrons. They take their own time about repaying the principal."[76]

This sort of non-amortized transaction was all too common; it was called the "Extension Plan."[77] One man with a weekly salary of $20 borrowed $75 to finance medical treatment for his wife. He paid $9.75 each month for seven months and thought he was getting near the end of the loan: "He went to the loan company and asked how much remained due. He was surprised to learn that the firm claimed the original $75. He showed receipts for his payments and then was told that these payments represented merely interest and that the principal remained due."[78] Stories like this recur with monotonous regularity in the pages of the *Tribune*. The "easy payments" that were touted in the classified ads did not make clear that they covered only the interest, not the principal. After paying for quite a while the debtor was dismayed to discover that the loan shark would not accept partial installments on the principal but wanted a lump sum and would keep demanding interest until the borrower could scrape together the entire amount. As Irving Michelman noted, "often no planned retirement of the principal was provided for and the borrower could be counted upon to renew his loan over and over for a fee."[79]

In theory these small loans were supposed to be short-term, but in practice many of them were open-ended revolving accounts. In his survey Wassam found that 40% of the loans continued for at least twenty-four months. Some borrowers kept paying for a decade or more. One illiterate woman, it was reported in the *Chicago Tribune*, made payments for fifteen years until her son learned about the loan shark's threats; she had paid twenty times the principal in interest charges.[80]

Examples like this illustrate the gap between short- and long-term interest, which the salary-loan product was intended to exploit. At any given moment, the lesser evil seemed to be to make the payment, but on a cumulative basis the loan was obviously a bad bargain. It made no sense to pay $500 for a $25 loan, as the illiterate woman did, but each week she was terrified about what would happen if she defaulted.

If the debtor missed one installment, the lender was entitled to demand payment in full immediately. But, since this was impossible, the borrower would be forced to negotiate a new loan with the late fees and penalties added to the outstanding balance. Sometimes the initial lender would make out a new loan, but often those in default were directed to a different firm that might be secretly owned by the same shark or cooperating with him. This was called the "chain system," and it made the loan grow rather than shrink away. To cite but one example, a clerk borrowed $30 and was to repay $39 in three monthly installments. After two months the loan went into default, so a new note was executed for $58.50. After a few more months this one was replaced by a note for $81, and so it went for another two years. In that time the debtor never had use of more than $36 but he had paid $275 in interest and still owed another $85 in principal when the *Tribune*'s Anti–Loan Shark Bureau intervened. It was cases like this that led Judge Landis to exclaim, "We hear talk of 10 percent a month. There is no longer any such rate in operation here. A fellow caught doing business on that basis would be regarded as a piker."[81]

This is the way the sharks fed off their victims. Eventually many of the debts had to be written off, but the losses didn't really matter because by that point the lender had collected several times the principal in interest charges. Still, the sharks held fast to their victims for as long as possible and expended considerable resources to continue extorting payments. This is one of the reasons why the loans were so expensive—the sharks had to spend more than banks on debt collection services because the burden of salary loans could be so onerous. To make money a firm had to harass its delinquent customers, but organized harassment was an expensive business. One loan broker admitted that he was "no angel" but insisted "no man can be and stay in the business, with the number of deadbeats there are trying to do you."[82]

As soon as a borrower missed a payment, the harassment would begin. One could expect a phone call or a visit from an agent of the firm. This might be followed by "dun letters in glaring red envelopes, with the name of the loan company displayed in large type." These contained threats to file the wage assignment with the borrower's employer or to bring suit in court.

The phone calls would multiply until the harassed debtor disconnected the service. Then a "bawler-out" might show up at work. This was a female collection agent hired to make a scene and shame the delinquent into resuming payments. She would berate the poor fellow in a loud voice: "You call yourself an honest man and won't pay your legal debts?"[83]

If the lender filed suit in court, the debtor was at a severe disadvantage. The shark had the power of attorney and could confess judgment against the borrower. This was especially advantageous where there was a chattel mortgage, for now the lender could send a wagon to repossess the client's furniture. These suits were brought in the justice of the peace courts, which were notorious for their willingness to collude with the loan sharks. The "justice shops" operated on a fee system that encouraged litigiousness and legal harassment. Some even advertised themselves as a collection agency for lenders and could dispatch a rough-looking constable to demand payment. The ones favored by the loan sharks were located in distant suburbs, hard to reach, and thus requiring the defendant to lose a day's worth of pay in order to attend the proceedings. These courts were the scandal of the county until supplanted by a new municipal court system in 1906.[84] The establishment Merchants Club railed against these judicial rackets:

> Our justice courts, many of them at least, have come to be stench in the nostrils of the self-respecting citizens of this place. Instead of being a piece of legal machinery for administering justice, they have grown to be vicious, pernicious, courts of persecution. Men are sued in the most remote justice courts in the county at unseasonable hours and then if they do not appear, the case is continued from time to time. The fee system has come to be a method through which the weak and the unfortunate are persecuted by the unprincipled strong.[85]

Victory was proclaimed when the professionalized city courts came into operation, but even then the problem did not disappear. An article in 1910 reported that a justice shop in Oak Park had usurped the authority of the municipal court and was processing wage-garnishment suits on behalf of the sharks.[86]

In the face of this campaign of harassment, some debtors would switch jobs without telling their lender, or change residence, or even leave town. To hunt these "skips" the loan sharks employed "tracers" or "spotters." They were paid on commission and knew all the tricks about how to find those who wanted to be lost. They might wait outside a factory at shift change and scan the faces of those filing in or out. They might call under a false name with a phony offer to lure the skip out into the open or bribe a clerk at the utility company to disclose addresses. One of the worst tricks was to contact the debtor's wife at home during the day and tell her that her husband had been injured in a terrible accident. Caught off guard, she might divulge his place of employment. Then the loan shark could fill in one of the blank wage assignments that had been signed and file it at the debtor's new job.[87]

Even if the skips moved far away, the loan sharks could hunt them down. One of Tolman's female employees made the rounds of all the cities where he had offices so that information could be shared on the skips.[88] One of the efficiencies of the chain-store model was that it facilitated the hunt for debtors who had fled. There were stories of men chased from city to city. Each time they found a job, a wage assignment would soon be filed. The new employer would then discharge them, and this would go on until the debt was finally settled.

These "exquisite thumbscrew methods," as one attorney called them, made the salary-loan business an extortion racket. The debtor was placed *in terrorem* through a campaign of threats and harassment. Unlike the next generation of loan sharks, the small-loan brokers did not usually resort to physical threats, but even these methods were not unheard of at the turn of the century. Some loan sharks employed "rough house men"—"husky men of the strong arm type, whose success depends upon the borrowers learning from experience that to refuse payment is to invite a quarrel which results in a physical assault."[89] One woman who refused to make her payment was given a black eye by the collector. Another man was beaten by a hired thug when he took a loan shark to court. A florist who was behind on his payments had his shopwindows defaced overnight. The warning read "Dead beat—why don't you pay your bills." A skip who was traced to California received a letter advising him that "if he didn't voluntarily come back, he would be brought back if it had to be in a pine box."[90]

But physical threats and beatings were the exception, not the rule. The first loan sharks were not mobsters or connected to gangs and crime families. They viewed themselves as businessmen with a clientele that often had to be badgered into making payments, but in this trade it could be difficult to separate the entrepreneurs from the con men. In fact, the whole enterprise was a con because it violated the usury statute. But the loan sharks concealed the usury behind legal instruments meant to persuade "the borrower that the loan represented a legal obligation." As Arthur Ham explained, "the main value of a mortgage to the lender is often the moral effect it can be made to produce upon the borrower." The documents seemed legitimate, so the debtor felt compelled to keep paying. When one fraud failed, another might be tried. One loan shark was contacted by the Legal Aid Society about a client who wanted out of a debt. An agent of the shark then phoned the client: "This is the Chicago Legal Aid Society. Hurry over and settle up with the loan shark or he will get your job." The ruse worked. Another lender posed as a representative of a Chicago relief agency and persuaded grieving relatives to sign receipts for their inheritance—which in fact turned out to be loan contracts.[91] In many cases a client's experience with a loan shark consisted of one fraud after another, beginning with the advertisement and the contract and running through a series of shady collection practices. This wasn't a line of business in which capitalists with compunctions could hope to prosper.

Sometimes one fraudster would try to take advantage of another in schemes reminiscent of "The Sting." For a few years in the 1890s, a group of loan "hijackers" operated in Chicago. They would secure an exasperated debtor's new power of attorney and use it to demand surrender of the loan notes from the original shark. Then the pirate shark would turn around and begin squeezing the debtor anew, and anything collected was pure profit because no principal had been advanced. This scam worked for a couple of years until the more established firms refused to deliver papers to the pirates.[92]

These were the methods of the sharks. They operated in a gray market that was technically illegal but to which there were attached no criminal penalties in the state of Illinois. In this line of business (lending to people of modest means who were short of cash), sharp practices may well have been necessary to survive, and the grayness of the market only sharpened the shark's teeth. It was sometimes said that there were good and decent sharks alongside the predators, but the latter variety overshadowed the former in the public consciousness. The moneylenders were constant objects of opprobrium in the local papers and also the butt of many jokes:

> Victim—"I've paid this debt twice over, and you know it. Why can't you let up on me now, for heaven's sake!"
> Loan Shark—"Because I'm not in the business for heaven's sake."[93]

The Urban Peon

Like other entrepreneurs, the loan sharks were in the business mainly for the money. But they also claimed to be performing a valuable service, and some of their customers shared that view. After the *Tribune* launched its campaign against the loan sharks in 1912, several readers complained about this war on the "poor man's bank." One exasperated borrower wrote, "There you are putting up a fight on the only class of loaners I can get it from." If the critics didn't like how the loan sharks did business, he challenged them to set up a lending shop for people like him and charge lower rates.[94] The salary lender extended credit to the workingman when nobody else would. Why wasn't that an honorable service?

It could be, the critics replied, but not when the lenders were making windfall profits. Hard evidence about profit rates in the loan-shark business is scarce, for obvious reasons. The industry was illegal, the firms were privately owned, and they did not have to file an annual report with any regulatory agency. Still, it was widely agreed that the salary-loan businesses realized a higher rate of return on average than the chattel-mortgage houses. This was due in part to the fact that, "of these two forms of loan, by far the more oppressive in the obligations it imposes and in the effects it produces is the salary loan."[95] The wage assignment was the superior instrument of extortion, and the higher rate of interest this product could command permitted the low-overhead salary-loan businesses to turn over their capital more quickly in the course of a year.

Everything about the loan-shark industry would lead us to expect an unusually high rate of return for those firms that were able to survive. In the first place, the risks were greater and had to be compensated with a premium. Frank Mackey made this point in his typically brash manner: "High rates of interest? Yes, as high as 20 per cent or more, and what of it? Is it anybody's business but mine? I am not ashamed of it. Of course I charge high rates of interest, but no more than I should, considering the risks I have to take." Those risks arose both from the nature of the clientele, which was hard up, and the illegality of the transaction. Mackey acknowledged the latter point and turned it into a justification for high rates: "The borrower has all the protection of the state and we have nothing."[96] Only a fool would risk capital in a shady market without the expectation of making a handsome profit.

But aggressive returns were also likely because the lenders colluded in various ways, as we have seen. The *Tribune* made this point categorically: "Cases brought to light establish beyond question that loan shark concerns work for their mutual advantage. When a victim has borrowed from one several times he is cited to another to make further loans for the purpose of reimbursing the first." The competition in this market was imperfect, and it was reduced still further by its grayness and the unwillingness of reputable entrepreneurs to enter the field. To compensate for the opprobrium loan sharks had to endure an additional premium would have to be paid by their customers. As circuit court judge Edward F. Dunne observed, "No respectable man would engage in the business. The calling of a highwayman is decent in comparison."[97] The only reward that would make it worthwhile to put up with abuse like this was living well and getting rich.

The successful sharks did grow fat in these hunting grounds. Mackey admitted that his average profit rate was 18% a year. In 1909 the Legal Aid Society was able to audit the books of six firms, both chattel-mortgage and salary lending, and it found that net income ranged from 7% to 35% per year. Wassam reported a profit rate of 29% for a typical New York City salary lender, and he cited examples of men earning an annual income of more than $30,000 from an investment of $10,000 in this business.[98] Plenty of the survivors in this rough-and-tumble market could tell authentic rags-to-riches stories. Tolman and Mackey both became multi-millionaires through the fine art of sweating borrowers.

The combination of super-profits and borrower misery provoked the numerous reform efforts that would be undertaken after the turn of the century and which culminated in the adoption of the Uniform Small Loan Law in many states—the topic of the next chapter in this study. If there were satisfied customers of the loan sharks, their voices were drowned out by the countless stories of men and women who had been mauled by the sharks. The industry obviously had a serious public relations problem. The articles about high rates, obscene profits, and captive borrowers were bad enough, but many other articles recounted the extremes to which debtors were allegedly driven by their financial desperation. A kindly postman in Hyde Park blamed the sharks when he was caught robbing the mails. A clerk in debt said the "hounding of the loan sharks" led him to mug a diamond broker. A bank employee caught passing bad checks claimed "the loan sharks have put me where I am"; "it was loan sharks and drink that did it." A bookkeeper arrested for forgery explained that "the money all went to the loan sharks. They kept threatening to garnish my wages, and I knew if that happened I would lose my job and be able to do nothing for the children." The unshakable grip of the lenders was a recurrent mitigating circumstance to which the accused appealed.[99]

But the damage ascribed to the loan sharks was greater still. "Loss of positions innumerable, separations of hundreds of families, wrecked homes, and suicides can be traced to their machinations," thundered the Bureau of Justice. In 1904 it received 291 complaints from wives about nonsupport or misconduct by husbands tangled in debts. "Mackey Agents Drove Woman Insane," blared another *Tribune* headline. But the saddest story of all concerned an elevator operator who lost several jobs in succession when his loan shark kept filing wage assignments. In despair he drank a bottle of carbolic acid, a favorite method of suicide in those days.[100]

In the eyes of many observers after the turn of the century, the loan-shark credit revolution had degenerated into a reign of terror. Wage-earners in large numbers and from respectable occupations were being harassed, impoverished, and demoralized by the quick-cash products. Instead of rising up, these wage-earners were falling down, and that fall was made all the more bitter by the fact that it was not the result of a single blow. One could recover from a temporary misfortune, but the problem with the loan sharks was that they would not loosen their grip. They held fast, collecting their interest payments week by week, and making it impossible for debtors to recover from their financial embarrassment and move forward once again. The lure of "easy payments" ensnared all too many in "the bondage of financial slavery." For them the credit revolution of the late nineteenth century had introduced a new condition of "economic peonage" or indentured servitude. That was the most damning charge in the indictment of the critics.[101] The right to mortgage one's future earnings had not brought financial freedom to the salariat but instead had transformed a sizable fraction of it into the fearful dependents of the moneymen. Judge Dunne spoke for many of the critics of this revolution when he declared:

> The laws of this state, as construed by the Supreme Court, permit a man to assign and mortgage his honor and wages for an indefinite period in the future, thereby establishing a state of peonage, fostering usury, and depriving his wife and family of the means of subsistence. The evil wrought thereby in Cook county has become well nigh intolerable. The legislature should pass a law declaring all such assignments null and void.[102]

Grinding the Tooth of Usury

Necessity cannot bargain to advantage with cupidity.

—Clarence Hodson, Beneficial Loan Society, 1918[1]

Judge Edward Dunne's appeal for legislative action on loan-sharking, quoted at the end of the last chapter, was made in June 1904. In less than a year the judge would be elected Chicago's first progressive mayor. Later he would serve a term as governor of Illinois. But it would not be until after Dunne left office that the state legislature would strike a decisive blow against high-interest lending. In June 1917 Dunne's successor, Governor Frank Lowden, signed the Illinois Small Loan Law, a landmark piece of legislation. Modeled on the Uniform Small Loan Law drafted by the Russell Sage Foundation the previous year, the "Loan Shark Act," as it was called, sought to split the shiver of sharks, taming one breed and exterminating the other. It permitted lenders of small sums to exceed the state's usury limit, but only under stringent regulation and with violators subject for the first time to criminal penalties. This legislation had teeth in it, and its aim was to force the loan sharks to loosen their grip, to end their predatory tactics, and to become reputable lenders to working people. The legislation struck a bargain, legalizing a higher rate of interest for this class of loans but only on condition that the sharks came out from the shadows and agreed to have their sharpest teeth filed.

The enactment of the Uniform Small Loan Law in Illinois and other industrial states at this time was one of the great accomplishments of progressivism in the early decades of the twentieth century. Curiously, however, the story of its formulation and passage never figures in the histories of the Progressive Era. But if Michael Willrich is right that progressivism combined "a pluralistic, issue-oriented politics of social responsibility and an ideological commitment to professionalization, scientific rationalization, and administrative governance," then the Uniform Small Loan Law is a textbook example of progressive public policy.[2] It sought to impose social responsibility and professionalization on those who would lend small sums to working people by mandating a "scientific rate of interest" that was both profitable and fair and by regulating the industry through an activist state administrative agency. This progressivist achievement in Illinois, one of the first states to enact a version of the Uniform Small Loan Law, is all the more striking because progressive reform had usually been stymied in Illinois.[3] Judge Dunne, the most prominent progressive politician in the state, failed as both mayor and governor to enact much of his agenda. City, county, and state politics were fragmented and mired in corruption, but eventually a coalition of progressive reformers was somehow able to push through the swamp of Illinois politics legislation that promised to put an end to loan-shark abuse and to create a new, safe financial product for cash-strapped wage-earners. This was an impressive accomplishment, and the story of how it came to pass is telling.

The achievement was difficult not only because Illinois politics was a swamp but also because the solution proposed to the loan-shark problem was counterintuitive. The public was outraged by the high interest rates charged by the salary and chattel-mortgage lenders, but the reformers proposed to solve the problem by legalizing a rate six times higher than the existing usury cap. It is not surprising that the Russell Sage Foundation and other reform advocates were sometimes accused of being fronts for the loan sharks.[4] The more obvious solution seemed to be to enforce the usury statute, but experience had taught the reformers that the obvious solution was counterproductive. It made things worse, not better, and this was true of many of the other reforms that were proposed. The progressives did not begin with a grand ideology that could teach them how to solve this problem. They groped toward a solution and frequently wandered down paths that turned out to be dead ends. Victory was proclaimed many times, but then the old abuses quickly resurfaced. The story of how the reformers tamed the loan sharks during the Progressive Era is a twenty-year tale of trial and error. Experience and failure taught those who eventually crafted the Uniform Small Loan Law to be modest in their ambitions and to accept practical realities. As Rolf Nugent, the last director of consumer credit studies for the Russell Sage Foundation, later explained, "The test of each new proposal was not whether it would contribute to the removal of underlying causes of the loan-shark problem, but whether it would remedy observed abuses, would contribute further protections to borrowers without restricting the availability or increasing the cost of credit, and would be sustained by the courts."[5] These were the constraints within which the reformers operated, and practice therefore dominated theory. The groping efforts of the shark hunters a hundred years ago, which culminated in the passage of the Uniform Small Loan Law near the end of the Progressive Era, tell a story that offers some valuable lessons for reformers today who find themselves battling a new breed of loan shark—the payday lender.

The Crying Sin of Usury

A usury statute is a price control law.[6] It sets the maximum interest rate that may be charged by a lender for the use of money. One might think that such price control laws would fare poorly in the United States, the land of economic liberty. In fact, however, such laws were the norm in this country until the last decades of the twentieth century, when the federal government preempted state interest rate restrictions in many sectors of the lending industry. Even now, most states still have usury statutes on their books, and these do remain effective in the small-loan market with which we are concerned. This persistence of price controls in the consumer-loan sector made the United States something of an anomaly among the more developed nations. In many countries across Europe "the crying sin of usury" was discarded as a medieval relic during the course of the nineteenth century.[7]

Lendol Calder speculates that the persistence of usury laws in the United States into the twentieth century was a residual of the Victorian hostility to "consumptive" borrowing.[8] But if so, it is curious that usury laws should have been repealed in the native land of Victorianism, Great Britain, around the middle of the nineteenth century. Perhaps the endurance of these laws can be ascribed instead to an earlier Puritan imperative to fashion a "moral economy"; it is striking that usury laws remain in force today most powerfully in the northeastern portion of the United States, where the Puritans first settled. In any case, usury laws are an ancient institution, once pervasive. They are a rudimentary kind of social insurance and an alternative to income-transfer programs. The price cap is meant to prevent risky borrowing and to force households to live within the means of their current income. These credit-constrained households are denied the opportunity to try to smooth consumption over time by borrowing against future income, perhaps because it is thought that the prospect of future income is too uncertain. Limiting the ability of households to contract debt reduces the amount that will be written off if bankruptcy is declared, and this benefits solvent consumers who pay for these losses through higher prices. Usury laws can also prevent the moral hazard of excessive risk taking in societies that try to sustain a minimum level of consumption. Unless coupled with a usury cap, income transfer programs may encourage risky borrowing because some of the losses that result from bad debts will be covered by the more cautious or the more solvent households that pay for welfare provision. Since ancient times the adoption of usury laws has been a way to ensure that "individuals did not reduce themselves to a level of poverty, where they would be burdens on the community."[9]

Christian theology in the high Middle Ages proscribed entirely "payment for the use of money lent"; the legal rate of interest was supposed to be zero.[10] Over time this doctrine was softened to permit lending at modest rates of interest, since productive investments with borrowed capital clearly benefited society. Low usury caps favored secured debts. In case of default, the security could be seized and sold to cover the loan, rather than charging off the loss and forcing other borrowers to pick up the tab. The original usury statutes in the American colonies set a single maximum price stated as an annual percentage rate. This rate applied to all loans, no matter the size, duration, or security. The average cap was 7%.[11] A uniform rate prevented price discrimination between rich and poor. The practical effect, however, was to banish those without security from the legal credit market because lenders were prevented from pricing loans to reflect the greater risk of unsecured or undersecured debt.

Although usury was proscribed, it was not usually treated as a criminal offense in the United States before the twentieth century. Debtors were permitted to plead usury as a defense if creditors brought suit in court to force payment, but the statutes did not classify usury as a misdemeanor or felony that could be prosecuted by the state. If debtors could prove usury had been taken, lenders might forfeit the remainder of the interest due, or some multiple of the principal, but they could not be sent to jail. Unless the defense was mounted, it was assumed that debtors had consented to usury, which was permissible. The courts would not enforce usurious contracts that were brought to their attention, but they also would not permit the recovery of usurious interest that had already been paid. In other words, a court could terminate a contract tainted with usury if the debtor made the request, but it treated past payments as voluntary.[12]

In addition to voiding the contract, the courts in some of the American colonies could impose upon the usurer a fine equal to three times the principal of the loan. This was a deterrent to usury, but during the nineteenth century the penalties for taking excessive interest were softened. In Illinois the remedy was merely forfeiture of the remaining interest due above the maximum legal rate of 7%. The debtor must have already repaid a sum equal to the principal of the loan before usury could be employed as a defense because it was the established doctrine that "he who comes into a court of equity must come with clean hands."[13] As a result, before the passage of the model act in 1917, the law was essentially toothless in the fight against the loan shark. The burden was placed upon the debtor to escape a usurious contract, and that burden would be heavy because a successful defense typically required the services of a lawyer. To fight one shark you had to hire another, and cash-strapped debtors were unlikely to think they could afford this additional expense. In any case, most debtors were unaware of their legal rights and were easily intimidated by the contracts they had signed, which the county "justice shops" stood ready to enforce.

The usury statutes had been devised long before loan-sharking came on the scene and they were ill suited to contend with this new social problem. The law increased the risk to the loan shark somewhat, but the product could be priced to absorb that risk, which was fairly minimal. In Illinois, usury "was practically without penalty, since the moneylender, however unconscionable his bargains, was guaranteed the principal at all events. Moreover, the courts of Illinois had held that interest in excess of the legal rate cannot be recovered after the borrower has voluntarily paid it. This law and the manner in which it was enforced made the position of the loan shark perfectly safe."[14] Though the usury statute was intended to protect borrowers, it actually worsened their plight. Because the courts could nullify the loan contracts, the market was gray, but that grayness only inflated costs for borrowers. To compensate for the risk that the courts might cancel the interest payments, the lender had to charge higher prices. Those prices were high to begin with, because the risk of default was greater with this cash-strapped clientele, and quite a bit of money had to be spent vetting applicants and dunning the deadbeats. The grayness of the market also discouraged investment by reputable firms, thus reducing the competition that might check prices. As a contemporary economist observed, with statutory rate caps "the borrowers are suffering both from the scrupulousness of the honest, who refuse them capital, and from the unscrupulousness of the dishonest, who charge them extra high rates."[15] The laws did nothing to reduce demand for quick cash, but they did restrict the supply of loan capital and increase the costs that lenders passed on to borrowers in the form of higher interest rates. "Social ills were thus often increased rather than cured. Money-lending at high rates being outlawed, the lender would charge even higher rates to compensate for the stigma attached to his business."[16]

In the public mind, usury was a scandal and an outrage. If banks could loan money at low rates, people wondered, why couldn't the salary lenders? The mathematics of lending was not well understood, even by educated people. The going rate for farm mortgages was fixed in the popular mind as the fair price for loans, no matter their size or duration. But mandating that low rate across the board for every financial product had the perverse consequence of increasing the burden many debtors had to bear. Treating salary loans like real estate mortgages only made the former more expensive. As the Russell Sage Foundation came to recognize, "The failure of the public to legalize rates at which lenders could carry on their business was a mistake that cost the borrowing classes dearly."[17]

When applied to consumptive lending, the traditional usury statute was effectively a policy of decriminalized prohibition. As newspaper stories about the plight of loan shark victims multiplied after the turn of the century, it became increasingly clear to observers that this brand of prohibition had failed. The gray market it created seemed to feed the sharks rather than starve them. The cries of the victims swelled, but it is doubtful that the debtors by themselves could have forced progressive legislation through the swamp of Illinois politics. As debtors, these people lacked the resources to mount a campaign of reform. They were broke, harassed, and afraid of losing their jobs if their employers discovered their predicament. Their desperation rendered them passive and notoriously difficult to organize. As George Gisler pointed out, "Obviously the one who suffers the most at the hands of high-rate lenders is the borrower, yet he is almost the only member of society who has done nothing about his plight. No case is known where a group of borrowers (or even a single borrower) have made a fight for themselves."[18] The contrast with the fight against sweatshop conditions in the garment industry is striking. There workers organized in unions and helped to forge the coalition that pressed for change.[19] The customers of the lending sweatshops, by contrast, remained completely atomized. They participated in the campaign against the loan sharks only as the pathetic victims of abuse on whose behalf the progressives fought.

The fight against the loan sharks was spearheaded by a coalition of elites.[20] This coalition was progressive, not populist, which meant that it aimed not to rouse or activate the ordinary people whom it sought to benefit but relied instead on the tools of "expertise, organization, and compromise."[21] Progressive movements favored administrative solutions to the new problems of an industrial urbanism, and this is the sort of solution that the anti–loan shark coalition eventually pushed through. In the front ranks of this coalition came the experts and educated professionals— lawyers, social workers, journalists, foundation scholars, and activists. But they were joined by establishment members of the business community, the owners of the great corporations in Chicago. These men were organized in the Merchants Club and the Industrial Club, elite business groups with clout, respectability, and financial resources. They favored action because the flood of wage assignments had swamped their payroll offices and the harassment of the loan sharks was demoralizing their employees. Salary lending in its current form was bad for business. The bankers didn't like it, either, because loan-sharking tarnished the reputation of lenders. What is more, those quick-cash upstarts violated the usury statute by which the chartered banks had to abide.

The first payday lenders managed to alienate nearly every stratum of society. They victimized working people, including middle-class occupations that were highly visible within the division of labor. With their wage assignments they were able to skip ahead of other petty creditors, like the grocer and the landlord, and collect their debts first. They annoyed the large employers and cost them money by trapping a sizable fraction of the workforce in debt peonage. In the same way they irritated the politicians and the heads of the executive departments in government, whose civil servants were notoriously tied up with the loan sharks. And the triple-digit usurers scandalized the educated professionals, who recognized in the agony of the debtors a social problem that required the intervention of experts. Unwittingly, the salary and chattel-mortgage lenders constructed a grand coalition against themselves, precisely the sort of coalition that carried through progressive reforms in the early decades of the twentieth century. They managed to make themselves hated by nearly everyone. In business and in politics that is always a mistake.

Still, this grand coalition was in the beginning only potential, not actual. Large coalitions are difficult to forge and to sustain because the members are pulled in many directions and there is always the temptation to free ride on the efforts of others. What is more, a coalition can only be formed if there is a common plan of action, but when loan-sharking first came on the scene there was no such plan. Many different remedies were proposed, and only a prolonged period of trial and error created the body of practical experience out of which the consensus reform eventually emerged. Twenty long years separate the first news stories about salary lending from the passage of the Illinois Small Loan Law in 1917. During these years the loan sharks themselves were not inactive. Though not members of the elite business community, the sharks possessed resources of their own, and they had a powerful incentive to block progressive action. They tried to split the reform coalition, buy up politicians, and appeal to the prejudices and misunderstandings in the popular mind.[22] Having been spawned by the traditional usury statute, the loan sharks became its most ardent defenders. Ironically, nobody condemned the "crying sin of usury" more than the usurers themselves and their lobbyists.

The Failure of the Free Market

Many reforms were proposed and many experiments undertaken to address the loan shark problem in the twenty years between 1897 and 1917. But the one solution never seriously contemplated in Illinois, or almost anywhere else in the United States, was the establishment of a free market in small loans. This is surprising, for we tend to assume that the school of laissez-faire was hegemonic in this country at the end of the nineteenth century. This was the Age of Social Darwinism. If government price controls had created the problem, what could be more natural for an American to think than that doing away with the usury statutes entirely might solve the problem? Since prohibition had manifestly failed, why not repeal it and treat the small-loan transaction like any other commercial exchange?

These questions are good, but the fact is that hardly any of the participants in the debate about small-loan reform at this time adopted the standpoint of the untrammeled market. You are much more likely to encounter advocates of laissez-faire today in the argument about payday lending than you would a hundred years ago when the free-market ideology was allegedly so dominant. The economists of that day more readily accepted the argument for regulation and restrictions on free contract than seems true now in the third phase of payday lending. This changed sensibility makes it more difficult for advocates of reform in the twenty-first century to make their case.

The advocates of free-market lending achieved much greater success in Great Britain. The great utilitarian thinker Jeremy Bentham blazed the trail at the end of the eighteenth century with a famous defense of usury. In his pamphlet Bentham exposed what seemed to be a contradiction in Adam Smith's political economy, for, despite his advocacy of the invisible hand, the author of *The Wealth of Nations* had nonetheless justified price controls in the loan market. Bentham shredded this justification, arguing that usury caps could only have perverse consequences for the desperate person whom these laws were intended to protect. According to Bentham, "Preventing his borrowing at an extra-rate, may have the effect of increasing his distress, but cannot have the effect of lessening it: allowing his borrowing at such a rate, might have the effect of lessening his distress, but could not have the effect of increasing it."[23] A usury statute priced some people out of the legal loan market, denying them funds they believed they could employ to good effect, and drove them into the illegal loan market, where the rates were inflated to compensate for the increased risk the lender undertook in breaking the law. In Bentham's view the policy smacked of a misguided paternalism, with legislators setting themselves up as omniscient judges of the borrower's self-interest and imposing a one-size-fits-all interest rate on a complex reality. Lenders and borrowers should be left free to negotiate whatever terms they found mutually acceptable. This policy of noninterference was much more likely to produce the greatest happiness for the greatest number than government-mandated price controls and the inevitable rationing of credit that would ensue.

Bentham's devastating critique percolated through British society for a half century and eventually helped to bring about the repeal of the usury statute in 1854. Great Britain initiated a fifty-year experiment in free-market lending that underwent review just as loan-sharking was emerging as a social problem in the United States.[24] In 1898 a parliamentary commission issued an exhaustive and scathing report on the British system of unregulated money lending. Rates remained high, the lenders engaged in deceptive practices, harsh collection methods were still employed, and many who borrowed became trapped by their debts. The commission found "that in many cases default is inevitable, and that once a borrower has obtained a loan from a money-lender it is extremely difficult for him to get clear of the transaction. The circumstances are generally such as to force him to obtain renewal after renewal at increasingly extortionate rates until he is utterly ruined." This is what the Americans were beginning to call loan-sharking in the 1890s, and it flourished in an essentially free market. The report concluded that "the system of money lending by professional money-lenders at high rates of interest is productive of crime, bankruptcy, unfair advantage over other creditors of the borrower, extortion from the borrower's family and friends, and other serious injuries to the community." Indeed, the commissioners went so far as to claim "that only in rare cases is a person benefited by a loan from a professional money-lender, and that the evil attendant upon the system far outweighs the good."[25]

Two years later, Parliament passed the Moneylenders Act of 1900. This legislation did not reimpose a usury cap, but it did authorize the courts to scrutinize lending contracts and to relieve those debtors who were being victimized by "harsh and unconscionable" terms. The problem with this solution, however, was that the courts found it difficult to determine whether a contract was unconscionable without the benchmark of a usury statute. Debtors remained vulnerable to abuse, and after another quarter century of experimentation Parliament drew up a new Moneylenders Act that imposed more stringent restrictions on the small-loan business. While preserving the practice of judicial review of lending contracts, the legislation clarified that interest in excess of 48% a year created a presumption that the transaction was unconscionable.[26]

The American legal system never warmed to the British solution, which assigned to courts of equity the main responsibility for protecting borrowers. Permitting freedom of contract but then asking judges to decide after the fact whether the bargain was unconscionable seemed contradictory and imposed heavy burdens on the courts. As the *Harvard Law Review* explained, "This statute seems objectionable to the American lawyer in that it permits a court to make over a contract. Moreover, it is too vague and makes uniformity impossible."[27] If freedom of contract did indeed create pervasive abuses, it seemed more appropriate for legislatures to take responsibility and spell out clearly the boundaries of a fair bargain within this sector of the lending business.

The justification for this legislative exercise in boundary setting was that the market in small loans was different from other lending markets. Bentham had no experience with modern consumptive lending. He took as his paradigm productive lending, in which entrepreneurs borrowed capital for their ventures and could be assumed to know their business and to understand the risks of expensive debt. In this market usury caps did indeed seem arrogantly paternalistic and counterproductive. The businessman did not need or want the protection of the law. But Bentham generalized his argument, applying it to every lending transaction that might occur, and he did so without mustering any empirical evidence for his claims. The entire argument was in fact abstract and hypothetical.[28] It simplified reality and made large assumptions. Given those assumptions, Bentham's defense of usury was persuasive. But Bentham was entirely oblivious to the way in which certain financial products could trap the debtor. He had no inkling of the wage assignment as an instrument of security or the short-term, high-interest cash advance that was not amortized. Bentham was right that this kind of product "might have the effect of lessening the [borrower's] distress," but he was wrong in assuming that it "could not have the effect of increasing it." The newspapers in Chicago after 1900 recounted hundreds of stories of loan-shark victims whose distress had been increased by usurious lending. These were the stubborn facts that seemed to refute the free-market solution.

Over time the advocates of regulation, including a number of economists, worked out a multifaceted critique of the free-market thesis. They argued, in the first place, that "under conditions of complete freedom of contract, the small loan field provides an excellent example of imperfect competition."[29] That imperfection resulted from what economists today describe as "information failure," when "one party to a contract is substantially less well informed about some aspect of the contract subject matter than the other party." The advocates of reform maintained that the ignorance of small-sum borrowers was pervasive in an unregulated market, in part because the lenders had an incentive to conceal their charges or to state them in a way that made comparison shopping difficult. Any lender who was scrupulously forthright about the terms of the contract was likely to be undercut by those who boasted falsely of low rates. What is more, those in the market for a small loan were usually loath to shop around because of the stigma attached to the product. They tended to go to the office that was most convenient and accept whatever terms were dictated. This meant the ignorance of these debtors was partly self-imposed but also completely predictable. They did not know enough to make informed decisions about the transaction, and the lenders actively worked to increase this confusion. As Michael Trebilcock observes, "if at least one party inaccurately perceives or evaluates the impact of the exchange on her utility, we can no longer be confident that the exchange will in fact render both parties better off." Rather than being mutually advantageous, an exchange founded on the ignorance of one party is quite likely to result in gain at that party's expense, which undercuts the justification for freedom of contract.[30]

Many advocates of government regulation were quite blunt in their assessment of the capacities of the typical loan-shark victim. They could say, without a blush, that "the typical consumer borrower is pathetically incapable of securing a fair bargain at the outset." They did not shrink from a paternalistic insistence on "protection for the needy borrower against his own ignorance and the pressure of his need." The reformers stated frankly that "these borrowers, despite their numbers, constitute a rather helpless group because of their ignorance, partially the result of carelessness, of the true nature of their obligations under the loan, and ignorance of their legal rights and remedies."[31] Those who entered the quick-cash market were viewed as more like children than the shrewd and rational adults of economic theory. Their impulsiveness, ignorance, and guilelessness made them fit objects of paternalistic intervention. This was the conviction of many advocates of reform, and their willingness to question the competence of the small-loan customers sets them off from most critics of payday lending today. There is now a taboo against disparaging the capacity of people who become entangled in debt. They are depicted as honest victims of greed but not as incompetent consumers who must be protected from their own stupidity. Blunt assessments like this have become even more untenable because of the changed composition of the payday-lending clientele. A hundred years ago both the reformers and the people on whose behalf they fought were overwhelmingly white males. Today, as we shall see, payday-lending debtors are disproportionately female and nonwhite. Advocates of intervention who spoke disparagingly of the capacities of these populations would no doubt be accused of sexism and racism. It would be easy for defenders of free markets to demagogue the issue. Over the course of a century the ideological climate has changed, and the fact that the climate has become more egalitarian does not make the argument for intervention easier. Rather, it makes it harder.

The harsh form of the incapacity argument made by critics of unregulated lending seemed to question the intelligence or rationality of the debtors. There was a softer version of the point, however, that ascribed the vulnerability not to some organic intellectual defect but, rather, to a distortion in the capacity to calculate engendered by the pressing need of these wage-earners. Cash-strapped borrowers suffered from a kind of financial myopia that made them "discount the future at a high rate."[32] Their need for money now was so urgent that they were unable to think clearly about whether they could realistically repay such an expensive debt in the future. This myopia was especially acute when the debt was structured in such a way as to require a large balloon payment at the end of the term. If the debtor could not come up with the lump sum needed to retire the debt, the loan would have to be renewed for additional fees. It would roll over again and again, with the principal growing in size as late penalties accrued, and at every payday the debtor would be confronted with the same dilemma: make the interest-only payment now, which was smaller in size but endless, or pay off the principal in full by sacrificing current consumption. A far-sighted consumer would choose the latter course, but the lenders exploited the intense myopia of the salary debtor that was brought on by the high marginal utility desperate people assign to every extra dollar in their pockets that they can spend right now. A free market that paired clear-sighted profiteers with myopic and exploitable consumers could not produce the mutually advantageous bargains that rendered government intervention unnecessary.

The incapacity induced by ignorance and myopia constituted one class of objections to the operation of the free market in the domain of consumptive lending. The other class of objections focused on a different type of weakness, that stemming from circumstance rather than incapacity. The favorite argument of the advocates of reform was that "borrowers of small sums lack the equality of bargaining power necessary to fair dealing." Even if they weren't ignorant and myopic, the clientele of the loan sharks was said to be too hard up and cash-starved to bargain effectively. Their backs were to the wall, they were desperate to conclude a deal, and so the lenders had them over a barrel. "Necessity cannot bargain to advantage with cupidity," Clarence Hodson declared, nicely summarizing this other objection to the operation of an unfettered market. Just as sweatshop employers could induce desperate proletarians to work for low pay in dangerous conditions, so too could loan sharks induce panicked wage-earners to consent to debt servitude in exchange for a cash advance now.[33]

The assumption of this argument is that money is power. If you have it, you can bargain effectively; if you don't, you are exploitable. Without a cushion of cash to buy you time, according to this view, the market is rigged against you, and this remains true even if competition in the market is intense. Increasing the number of lenders to whom one may apply does nothing to alter the imbalance in assets that gives the lending class leverage in this market. This leverage is all the greater because, "unlike the merchant who offers his wares for cash, the lender has the right to select his customers."[34] The would-be borrower enters the lender's office as a supplicant, and this circumstance further weakens the desperate borrower's already tenuous bargaining position. Every option is bad, and the loan shark lies in ambush to exploit this vulnerability.

This sort of argument implies that the exploitation of debtors is structural. It would occur even if competition was perfect, meaning, even if lenders had no discretion to set prices as they wished. More competition, then, would not prevent gain at the borrowers' expense. Indeed, it might even increase it. Some advocates of reform claimed that there was a "mushrooming of improper lending practices where there are too many lenders. Excessive lending creates more loans on marginal credit which result in harsh collection practices and more personal bankruptcies." Cutthroat competition between loan sharks was unlikely to tame their behavior, because as a rule, "competition makes it difficult for one business institution, be it lender, producer, or merchant, to exercise self-restraint without being assured that the others in his business will follow suit."[35] The sweatshop industry illustrated the problem. It was intensely competitive and, for that very reason, intensely exploitative. Survival was possible only if the employers took advantage of their labor force. The same rule applied in the lending sweatshop: exploit or fail. Given the structure of the situation, the loan shark either had to behave like a predator or had to close up shop. The system itself was the problem, and freedom of contract could not possibly solve it. Structural reform was required. Government intervention had to compensate for the weakness of the borrower in this market and to establish the rules of engagement. Without the visible hand of regulation, it was thought, gain at the expense of the weaker party would be pervasive.

These were the arguments employed by the opponents of Benthamism. It was their conviction that "complete freedom of contract . . . has never produced decent conditions in the small loan field."[36] If consequences should be the test of policy, as Bentham himself taught, then the policy of laissez-faire had to be rejected. In this branch of the lending industry this policy yielded, not the greatest happiness for the greatest number, but gains for the few and losses for the many. And these losses were especially undesirable because those who suffered them were already bad off. Some fraction of them fell into peonage, and it was peonage that sustained the sharks. To free the peons, the free market would have to be constrained and regulated. On this the advocates of reform agreed. But it was not clear to them at the start of their fight with the sharks what sort of constraints were needed. There were many possibilities, but an abstract theory could not answer the question. Thus they groped their way forward along several different paths. Only after twenty years would they arrive at their destination—a regulatory formula that they believed would tame the rehabilitable sharks.

The Intractability of Demand

If demand begets supply, as is true in the small-loan market, then the surest way to starve the sharks is to dampen the demand for quick cash. Just as drug dealers will be put out of business if there are no junkies, the loan sharks cannot survive without the debtors who feed them. One might suppose, then, that the only strategy that could really solve the problem of predatory lending is to address the sources of the demand that attracts the sharks in the first place.

The supposition is not false, but the weakness of this strategy is obvious. Today's drug war illustrates the difficulty. While it is possible to reduce demand to a degree, the desire for drugs seems insatiable. The government has tried both penalties and education, but people still want drugs. They are willing to take risks and to spend quite a bit of money to purchase narcotics.[37] The demand is largely intractable, and so government has devoted most of its efforts to interdicting the supply and to punishing the suppliers whom it can catch. Demand would be even more difficult to reduce in the payday-advance business because no one has seriously proposed criminalizing that demand. As one law book explains:

> Usurious transactions, from the actual or present disparity of condition between the parties, have formed an exception to the general rule, that parties shall be deemed *in pari delicto*, when they intentionally participate in the violation of the law. The theory of the law is, that the borrower's necessities deprive him of freedom in contracting and place him at the mercy of the lender, under such moral duress as to take from him the character of *particeps criminis*.[38]

Asking someone to lend money hardly seems like criminal conduct, so government can't wield the stick in order to reduce the demand that feeds the loan sharks. It cannot treat debtors like addicts, even if the debtors are profligates and wastrels.

The government could try carrots instead, but all of the alternatives would be either politically infeasible or prohibitively expensive. Government could starve the loan sharks very quickly by offering low-cost loans itself, but this would increase demand, not reduce it. Alternatively, the government could try to alter the distribution of income by raising wages or supplementing the incomes of the bottom half of the population, where the sharks tend to swarm. A more equal distribution of income might ease some of the financial strain that consumers in the bottom half experience when inequality increases. But extensive redistribution of income by government would meet vigorous resistance in the United States and, in any case, probably wouldn't have been feasible at the beginning of the twentieth century. The Sixteenth Amendment, permitting the federal government to collect income taxes, was only ratified in 1913, and it would be another quarter century before the first federal minimum-wage law was enacted. The bureaucracy and statistical information necessary to redistribute income on a large scale did not yet exist in the United States. But even if it had existed, this strategy of narrowing the gap between high and low, or constructing a sturdier safety net, would not have eliminated the demand for quick cash entirely. As a representative of the Russell Sage Foundation explained, "Worthy as these objectives are, our empirical evidence clearly demonstrates that the loan-shark problem would outlast their attainment. Wage-earning classes that have the highest incomes and the most regular employment have frequently been the most seriously victimized by loan sharks."[39] Even a more egalitarian America would still have to contend with the problem of the loan shark. Indeed, loan-sharking persisted in a particularly brutal form during the middle decades of the twentieth century, when the distribution of income in the United States narrowed considerably (see Chapter 3).

Convinced that sticks and carrots were too expensive, both financially and politically, the government did almost nothing in its role as regulator to reduce the demand for short-term loans. The only thing it did do was to mandate more frequent paydays for wage-workers. The labor unions often complained about the common practice of paying workers once a month. Delaying payment for wages already earned transformed employees into the creditors of their employers, but because they lacked savings to fall back on, many employees in turn would have to seek credit from the loan sharks to cover them until their wages were paid. Infrequent paydays created the demand for payday loans, and some labor delegates thought "there would be fewer loan sharks in Chicago if employers would establish more frequent pay days rather than waste time on anti–loan shark legislation."[40] A policy like this might nip demand in the bud.

The Illinois legislature did pass legislation in 1891 requiring more frequent paydays, but the State Supreme Court struck down the law two years later as an infringement of the freedom of contract, which it jealously protected. Subsequent efforts were made to craft legislation that could survive judicial review, but it wasn't until 1913 that a satisfactory measure was enacted.[41] This provided for biweekly paydays, but loan-sharking continued to thrive. Despite being paid more frequently, many employees still found it necessary to mortgage future income in order to sustain present consumption or to cover emergency expenses.

This was the only measure adopted by government in its role as regulator to check the demand for the loan-shark product, but government did take more vigorous action to reduce demand in its role as employer. A sizable fraction of the loan-shark clientele consisted of government employees. The decent wages they earned and the greater degree of job security they enjoyed made them ideal customers for the salary lenders. Claims were made that half the workforce in certain departments was indebted to the sharks. The resulting distress and harassment demoralized employees, reduced their efficiency, and imposed costs on the payroll department. The heads of departments felt they had to do something to address the problem, and their gut instinct was to wield the stick. They threatened to suspend or fire employees against whom a wage assignment was filed as a way to discourage the demand for salary loans. Surely employees would become more prudent about household finances if they faced the threat of termination for mortgaging future income.

But the punitive approach failed to reduce demand. The need for temporary financing remained despite the risk of job loss, but now the lender had a more efficient tool with which to extract payment from debtors in arrears. If the borrowers didn't pay up, the sharks could threaten to file the wage assignment and so get employees fired. Instead of reducing demand, the new policy merely increased the leverage of the loan sharks. That is why the salary lenders frequently expressed support for such sanctions. One loan agent, for example, wrote to the chief of police in Chicago and urged him to enforce the policy of a month's suspension for any officer caught assigning wages: "No one will stand for the man borrowing money and not paying it back, much less the money lenders. Now see what an easy thing it will be to stop all this filing of assignments, and how much less notoriety the department and we would get if there was an order issued and an example made." Another company quoted the departmental order in a collection notice sent to patrolmen behind in their payments. The notice went on to warn that "unless you call at our office upon the receipt of this and arrange for settling our account against you we shall file your assignment of salary, which you have executed in our favor." The policy of suspension or termination was intended to coerce employees into getting by without payday credit, but in many cases all that coercive threat actually accomplished was to render cash-strapped employees vulnerable to blackmail by the loan sharks.[42]

Private employers adopted the same policy and the results were exactly the same. Demand for the product persisted but the misery of the debtors was increased. It would take some years before reformers recognized the perniciousness of this policy and counseled employers against it. They tried to explain that firing employees for assigning wages did not starve the sharks but actually fed them. Once they had fallen into debt, wage-earners would submit to endless peonage in order to protect their jobs. They would pay the sharks protection money, in the form of interest-only installments, to keep the secret they could not afford to have revealed.

Neither employers nor government possessed an effective way to weaken demand for the loan-shark product. The only institution that found a way to do so without increasing the misery of debtors was the city's newspapers. Lincoln Steffens called the Chicago press "the best in any of our large cities. There are several newspapers in Chicago which have served always the public interest, and their advice is taken by their readers." Papers like the *Tribune* sought to expose the methods of the sharks to the reading public and to explain to debtors how they could escape the grip of usury. The press also played a vital role in forging the coalition of progressive forces that would press through reforms. As David Nord explains, the aim of the papers was to "socialize" an issue like salary lending, "to help make it part of the reader's political frame of reference."[43]

The papers achieved this effect through a steady stream of scandalized accounts that were punctuated by concentrated campaigns of exposure. The coverage was slanted and uniformly hostile; almost never were the salary lenders or their apologists allowed to present their side of the question. This journalism would likely be deemed unprofessional by today's standards. These businesses were demonized in both news stories and editorials, and the rhetoric could be fiery: "The bloodsucking usurer is a shocking anachronism in this century. There is no shadow of excuse for these vampires who prey upon the weak, the sick, the ignorant, waiting to fatten themselves when accident or mistake trips for an instant those who are traveling close to the edge of misfortune." That fire was said to be fueled by personal experience. "Many reporters, compositors, and pressmen were chronic borrowers. Editorial offices in unregulated states were well aware of the small loan problem, and many newspapermen had paid dearly for their schooling in the ways of the high-rate lender." The problem was concrete and personal, not abstract, and a dispassionate neutrality would probably have seemed biased and inauthentic to these journalists.[44]

The *Tribune*'s first exposé of the loan-shark evil appeared in November 1897, twenty years before the passage of the Illinois Small Loan Law. The article described for readers "the new spider system," and it was accompanied by drawings that illustrated the plight of borrowers caught in the lender's web. Within ten days the paper claimed the article had produced an effect, for the loan sharks were said to have removed their advertisements from the streetcars and other locations to avoid public attention.[45] This would be the pattern over the next two decades: every few years the *Tribune* would publish a spate of articles on the sharks and their victims, and business would reportedly drop. Made aware of the illegality of the transaction, debtors would screw up their courage and insist that their loan papers be returned. The lenders, hoping to avoid bad publicity and the scrutiny of the courts, would comply in exchange for one last fee. Demand would fall, and some of the sharks would quit the business. But the editorial board of the paper recognized that the relief was only temporary:

> There is no doubt whatever that the business of the loan sharks can be abated, if not destroyed—for a time. But when the "tumult and the shouting dies," as it always must in newspaper crusades after the impatient readers have got "thoroughly sick and tired of the whole business," as they usually phrase it in their letters of protest, then the loan sharks will creep back into the city. With the front page full of Roosevelt or the opening of the baseball season, they will feel safe in reopening at the old stand under a new name.[46]

The newspapers could reduce demand for payday advances by exposing the scandal, but scandals have to be hidden before they can be exposed. Neglect is their precondition. Thus, by themselves, the newspapers could not solve the problem of loan-sharking, but they could help to mobilize public opinion in favor of legislative action. They could create that sense of urgency needed to counter the natural sluggishness of the political system.

The most intense crusade against the loan sharks undertaken by the *Tribune* was launched after New Year's Day in 1912. It imitated a similar campaign waged by the *New York Globe* the previous summer. The offensive commenced with an announcement that the paper would no longer accept advertisements from the salary lenders.[47] This was followed by a barrage of articles that revealed the secrets of the sharks and told hard luck stories about their victims. Then, on 4 February, it was announced that an Anti–Loan Shark Bureau had been formed. Eighty reputable attorneys in the city had been enlisted to provide free legal aid for debtors, who could fill out a form printed in the paper and return it to the bureau. In the first week 441 forms were received. Over the course of the campaign, more than 3,000 cases were processed. The paper reported that the average victim helped by the bureau saved $30, or roughly two weeks' wages. At the highpoint of the crusade, one loan shark claimed that demand had been reduced by 80%.[48]

Other Illinois papers waged similar campaigns.[49] And the new medium of film also participated in the exposé. D. W. Griffith made a short film entitled "The Usurer" in 1910 that illustrated the plight of chattel-mortgage debtors. Two years later the Russell Sage Foundation produced the script for another indictment of the "easy loan" business, "The Usurer's Grip."[50] That same year the *Tribune* commissioned a photo play from Essanay Films entitled "The Loan Shark" that dramatized the real-life stories the paper was recounting in its pages.[51] The media seemed to speak with a single voice. There was a lending crisis in America and the moral lines were clear. The debtors were honest folk, hardworking but cursed with bad luck. The lenders, by contrast, were greedy and evil. They preyed on misfortune with hardened hearts and increased the misery of already desperate people. The loan sharks had to be stopped—and in the movies they were. Griffith killed off the usurer in his money vault, where he suffocated in cosmic retribution for the suffocating oppression he had imposed on others. His kindly sister then forgave the debts. The problem had been solved.

But this was no solution to the real loan-shark evil. The films could not convey the structural nature of the crisis. The media was effective in exposing the lenders and in isolating them, but it did not have a permanent solution to the problem. The demand for payday credit was essentially intractable, and that is why the progressives sought instead to transform the supply. Acting in the spirit of Sir Francis Bacon, their aspiration was "that the Tooth of Usurie be grinded, that it bite not too much."[52]

The Grip of the Wage Assignment

The strategy first pursued to grind the tooth of the loan sharks targeted their instrument of security, the wage assignment. This was an obvious target because the lenders used the leverage it afforded to extract payment from debtors, and this leverage was strengthened by the employers' policy of discharging any employee against whom an assignment was filed. That policy had been adopted to undercut demand for the loan shark's product, but the results were just the opposite. Once it was realized that a punitive policy made matters worse, not better, the reformers decided something had to be done about this security behind which the lenders hid.

The first tactic employed was a frontal assault. On several occasions Chicago's city council tried to abrogate the use of wage assignments by ordinance.[53] If employees could not assign their wages, so the theory went, payday lending would lose the security that made debt collection possible, and so it would become impossible. The aldermen were joined in this assault by circuit court judge Edward Dunne, the progressive leader. In 1901 the judge declared the assignment of wages to be unconstitutional because it amounted to involuntary servitude:

> If a laborer or employee in this State can be permitted to mortgage or assign absolutely his whole earning capacity for ten years in advance, he can be permitted upon the same principle to mortgage or assign his earning capacity for life. If this be possible the thirteenth amendment to the constitution of the United States, which declares that "neither slavery nor involuntary servitude shall exist within the United States," would be practically nullified.[54]

However, neither the appellate court nor the Illinois Supreme Court were persuaded by this legal reasoning. Dunne's decision was reversed because the validity of the wage assignment as a contractual instrument was well established in the common law tradition. Employees were held to possess a property right in their future wages, which right they were entitled to transfer as they saw fit, within broad limits. The high court denied "that there is anything intrinsically vicious in an assignment of wages. The assignor, in such cases, simply draws upon his future prospects to supply present needs, which may be of the most urgent and pressing character." The wage assignment was just a mortgage instrument, and to invalidate it now would constitute a massive confiscation of property rights. This is something that this court, with its deep respect for freedom of contract, would not do. The justices could not believe that the "takings" effected by Judge Dunne would really benefit wage-earners as a class, and they quoted the authority of another court to buttress their decision: "It is argued that such contracts are so much against public policy that they ought not to be supported, but we think they are rather beneficial, and enable the poor man to obtain credit when he could not otherwise do it, and that without detriment to the creditors." How, the court wondered, would employees be made better off by stripping them of a valuable asset they could use to secure credit?[55]

That was a good question, but the truth is that many victims of the loan sharks would have been better off if the courts had not awarded them this asset in the first place. That asset consisted in the right to mortgage future income, but mortgaging income that you didn't possess could easily transform a wage-earner into the peon of loan sharks. The high court could not see this, just as Judge Dunne could not see that his decision amounted to an expropriation. This clash of judicial opinions nicely illustrates the paradox of the wage assignment: by awarding working people an asset it consigned a sizable portion of them to penury and servitude.

Having failed in the courts, the advocates of abrogation turned to the legislature. The Bureau of Justice wrote a bill that voided "every assignment, transfer, sale, or hypothecation of wages," but the bill died in committee during the 1903 legislative session.[56] The frontal assault on the wage assignment could make no progress, so the reformers tried instead to re-craft the instrument, building in consumer protections that would prevent this mortgage device from being abused by the loan sharks. A new bill was introduced in 1905 that required assignments to be signed by both spouses, recorded with a justice of the peace, and served on the employer within three days of execution. The instrument was void if it assigned wages more than six months in advance, or if it was "given as security for a loan tainted with usury."[57] Although it did not outlaw the wage assignment, the Dixon Bill, as it was known, rendered the wage assignment useless as security for salary loans. Backed by the Merchants Club, the measure survived the lobbying campaign of the sharks and was signed into law by Governor Deenen on 13 May 1905.[58]

The law went into effect on 1 July 1905, but within a week, complaints were heard that wage assignments continued to flood the payroll offices of large employers. In Chicago Controller McGann wrote, "The law . . . appears to have revived the practice, and we have already received many notices of assignments which will certainly produce the conditions heretofore existing." A month later he again voiced his exasperation: "We are simply swamped with these notices. . . . I don't see why this law was ever enacted. It hurts the city and can't do anybody but the loan agents any good." Two years later, a state senator admitted that the law had failed to achieve its purpose. The loan sharks found ways round its provisions, and so a new bill would have to be introduced.[59]

That effort went nowhere, and then the Illinois Supreme Court struck down the original law in a famous opinion. This opinion was famous (or notorious) not only because of its legal reasoning but also because it was issued twice. The first decision in *Massie v. Cessna* was handed down in October 1908. It ruled the Dixon law unconstitutional because it interfered with the wage-earner's freedom of contract, which the court said was guaranteed by Article 14 of the U.S. Constitution. Taken aback by this sweeping judgment, the reformers petitioned for a rehearing of the case. The motion was granted, new arguments were heard, and the court issued a second opinion the following April. It once again struck down the law, but this time the justices rejected the measure because it applied to salaries as well as wages. The law infringed unnecessarily on "the right of persons earning the higher salaries to assign or transfer their salaries in such manner as they see fit, there being nothing in the public policy of the State requiring or warranting such abridgments of their right."[60] In other words, the high court objected to the statute because it prevented rich people from going to the loan sharks. They didn't need protection from the state, and thus nobody would get it.

The reformers were outraged by the logic. An attorney for the Legal Aid Society declared that "the Illinois decision stands without any possible justification upon legal principles and without a parallel or precedent in any other state." The Maryland Supreme Court later wrote that the "distinction between salaries and wages . . . is in our opinion too refined and delicate to justify us in recognizing it, and it does not appear to have been followed elsewhere." Holding staunchly to an undiluted doctrine of free contract, the Illinois Supreme Court placed a large obstacle in the path of reformers. Hostility toward the court within the legal profession was so high that the Illinois State Bar Association took the unprecedented step of inviting all of the justices to a banquet in Chicago at the end of October. It was an attempt to smooth over hard feelings and to increase mutual understanding between bench and bar.[61]

Even if the court had decided the *Massie* case differently, evidence suggests that the wage-assignment law had failed to grind the tooth of usury. Wage-earners continued to mortgage their salaries to the loan sharks, and the papers continued to print exposés of the carnage. Prohibition and abatement had failed. So now the reformers turned to a new strategy—competition. They would try to beat the loan sharks at their own game.

Remedial Competition

As Robinson and Nugent observed, the switch to competition "represented a change in the tactics of those fighting the loan shark. Exposures, denunciations, repressive legislation, and prosecutions had in only a small degree checked his abuses, and had not in the least eradicated them." The plan now was "to enter the small loan field and to lower the charges of existing lenders and improve the tone of the small loan business generally by competition."[62] If it was true that salary lenders gouged their customers and earned windfall profits, it ought to be feasible to establish a class of low-cost vendors that could drive off the sharks, or at least tame them.

The concept of remedial competition was not new. Philanthropic pawnbrokers, called *monts-de-piété*, had existed since the fifteenth century and provided low-interest loans on the security of a pledge. These European institutions became the model for remedial loan associations in the United States, which began to be formed late in the nineteenth century. The first ones, like the Provident Loan Society of New York, were also pawnshops. Because their aims were philanthropic, these lenders did not try to maximize profits. They set their rates to cover the costs of the business and also to pay a dividend to the stockholders. The concept was known as "philanthropy and 6 per cent." The Merchants Club helped to establish a chartered remedial pawnbroker in Chicago in 1899. The First State Pawners Society made nearly a quarter million dollars in loans its first year, in sums that averaged $14, and charged substantially less than the competition.[63]

As soon as that business was established, the Merchants Club explored the idea of establishing a similar organization that would lend at a somewhat higher rate on the security of a chattel mortgage, but nothing came of this proposal at that time. The idea was revived a decade later by the Legal Aid Society.[64] The chartered association it envisioned would make both chattel-mortgage and salary loans at a maximum rate of 4% a month, well below the going rate among the loan sharks. A bill was introduced at Springfield in 1909 but died in committee. The same thing happened the next year, and a state legislator was investigated on charges of graft. The papers reported that the state's attorney had "uncovered evidence of contributions to the 'jackpot' by loan shark men of Chicago," but the juries refused to convict.[65] The reformers tried again in 1911 with the backing of a powerful coalition of supporters, including the Commercial Club, the Industrial Club, and many church associations. A bill was introduced and compromises were struck, but the legislation was derailed, this time by representatives from the rural districts in the state.[66] As a *Tribune* editorial explained, "The bill encountered in the Senate the violent opposition of men who said that they never would consent to make it lawful for the money lender to exact from the poor man who had no other security than his household furniture or wages such usurious interest."[67] The paper scoffed at these "addle-pated senators," who allegedly were too dumb to understand that blocking the legislation only benefited the loan sharks. But the downstate representatives were just trying to protect their constituents by defending the state's usury cap. They feared that if 48% interest was permitted in the city, it might jeopardize the farm mortgage, which was capped at 7%.

The opposition of rural interests to any revision of the usury statute was one of the great frustrations of the reform movement. The legislative power of the rural districts stymied other progressive causes too. As Robert Wiebe explained, "By a combination of custom, majority rule, and the gerrymander, [state legislatures] served as rural strongholds where the enemies of the city generally held sway. Assistance came grudgingly and sparingly."[68] The problem was especially acute in Illinois, where the agricultural regions "held the balance of power in the General Assembly at Springfield." Conservative in their instincts and suspicious of urban innovations, "downstate interests built a governmental structure that resisted change."[69] This pattern was repeated across the country. In fact, the spread of the Uniform Small Loan Law correlated well with the proportion of a state's population that lived in cities.[70] The more industrial states adopted the legislation first—and the most agricultural states, particularly in the South, never did.

Two years later, another effort was made to charter a remedial loan association. The new bill permitted philanthropists to endow a semipublic salary-lending organization that could make loans as large as $250 at an interest rate not to exceed 3% a month. This time the bill sailed through the legislature, though not without some grumbling from partisans of the traditional usury statute. Referring to this proposal, one legislator claimed, "It was conceived in the Hotel LaSalle, attended by blue points and mallard ducks, washed down by champagne. It is in the interests of bankers who pay 3 per cent a year on small deposits and who under this bill will loan the same money back at 36 per cent a year. For a purpose like this 1 per cent [a month] would be plenty." But the reformers overcame the opposition and the measure was signed into law by Governor Dunne. The First State Industrial Wage Loan Society opened its doors to the public on North Dearborn Street on 10 November 1913.[71]

Five hundred people applied for a loan the first day, but on average only 70% of applicants were approved at what was dubbed the "Poor Man's Bank." Successful applicants had to have been employed for at least a year, have dependents, intend to use the loan for a good purpose, and consent to inform their employers about the debt. During its first full year in operation, the loan society advanced money at 3% a month to 2,000 people, most of whom had been in debt to the loan sharks, and it claimed to have driven four of the illegal lenders out of business. According to the director, "The four loan sharks who quit told me we had provided the only sort of competition they could not stand—money to lend at reasonable rates. And the professional money lenders who remained in the field changed their attitude and made big reductions in their rates."[72]

This last boast was surely an exaggeration, for the survey conducted by the Department of Public Welfare a few years later indicated that high-rate lending continued unabated in Chicago until the passage of the Illinois Small Loan Law in 1917. One loan society with a capital of $50,000 might be able to starve a few sharks, but there were nearly 150 operating in the city in 1916 and they did roughly $11,000,000 in business that year. Across the country there were never more than a few dozen remedial loan societies in existence at any one time, and the credit they were able to extend amounted to only a few drops in the loan-shark tank. As Irving Michelman pointed out, "the idea that the remedial associations would tame the loan sharks by competition was of course fanciful as the associations could not possibly cover the field adequately and borrowers then as now do not necessarily nor even generally seek the lowest cost lender."[73] There was not enough philanthropic money invested to create a serious threat to the survival of the sharks. With their more stringent lending requirements, the remedial associations were essentially skimming the least risky borrowers from the shark-infested waters and rewarding them with lower rates. This strategy could do nothing to benefit the ordinary debtor. Indeed, it might result in higher rates for those who didn't qualify for a remedial loan because the quality of the risk pool left to the sharks declined somewhat. In a for-profit business, riskier customers had to be charged higher rates.

Still, the experiment with remedial competition taught the reformers a valuable lesson. They learned that a reputable lender seeking a modest return on small loans could not succeed at the statutory rate of 7% a year. The First State Industrial Wage Loan Society charged five times that rate, and it could only turn a profit at 3% a month because its average loan was twice the size of the typical debt in the loan shark's portfolio. It had to be exempted from the usury statute in order to make a go at competing with the 10% firms, and this meant a new standard of usury would have to be established in the small-loan market if the strategy of competition were to be extended. Facts would have to be faced: the public would have to accept the idea that 7% a year was not a universal law of fairness in the credit market. Insisting that it was had spawned the sharks. To tame the sharks it would be necessary to give up this shibboleth.

Dividing the Sharks

The acknowledged leader of the remedial loan movement was the Russell Sage Foundation, a fine specimen of the progressive breed of philanthropy. Although its wealthy namesake was reputed to have been a usurer in his day and was himself a staunch advocate of freedom of contract, Russell Sage's widow and heir was determined to put her husband's fortune to good use in the service of progressive causes. Established in 1907 with an endowment of $10,000,000, the foundation's guiding idea was that "a large part of the 'human wants and ills' in America was preventable, and therefore would be prevented if only the facts about conditions and remedies were generally known." Then as now, the organization devoted its income to funding research into social problems and their solution. From the start, one of its main concerns was the loan-shark evil. As the story goes, after her husband's death Mrs. Sage was inundated with letters from loan-shark victims, and the foundation therefore decided to make their plight an object of investigation and constructive action. A department of remedial loans was established at the foundation's New York headquarters and an energetic young economist, Arthur Ham, was appointed its director.[74]

More than any other figure of his day, Ham was responsible for carrying the fight against the loan sharks through to its triumph with the adoption of the Uniform Small Loan Law.[75] A tireless advocate of reform, Ham favored competition and opposed punitive measures. As he saw it, "drastic laws result, not in the discontinuance of the usurious loan business, but in driving it further into the dark. Any attempt to work unnecessary hardship on the lender, to compass him about with unreasonable restriction, has the inevitable result of forcing the borrower to pay a still higher charge for his loan." The loan shark could not be hunted into extinction. It had to be supplanted by a benign alternative: "the remedy appears to lie in attracting honest capital into the salary loan business on a reasonable money-making basis."[76]

The remedial loan societies were the first attempt to attract honest capital into this market, and Ham headed up the National Federation of Remedial Loan Associations. But, as the Illinois experience illustrated, the semi-philanthropic societies lacked the loan funds necessary to undercut the high-rate lenders on a large scale. Credit unions were just coming into existence at this time, their advocacy being another project of the Russell Sage Foundation, but they were too few in number and too small in size to displace the salary and chattel-mortgage lenders. "Morris Plan" banks were also being formed in some cities. These made complicated loans, dressed up as a sale of stock, at an advertised rate of 6% a year, which in fact was rather misleading. The effective rate was about three times greater, though still much less than the loan sharks charged. But this product was pitched to borrowers with higher incomes and for this reason was unavailable to most salary debtors.[77] Clearly the market in consumer credit was expanding and undergoing transformation in the second decade of the twentieth century, but the vast bulk of working capital in this sector remained in the hands of the loan sharks. They were the big fish in the pond, and outside capital from reputable sources would not flow in as long as the sharks remained the dominant species of lender.

But not all loan sharks were alike, and this was the decisive circumstance that made the victory of the reformers possible. Some high-rate lenders secured their loans with a wage assignment while others employed the chattel mortgage. Loans advanced against the latter kind of security tended to be greater in size and made at a somewhat lower rate of interest. The wage-earners who qualified for this type of loan were usually family men with decent incomes who were joined in the debt by their wives. The risk of default for this group was lower, and this is why the rates weren't as high. The sharks in this line of business viewed themselves as more reputable than the salary lenders, and some were looking for a way to legalize their transactions. They knew they served a legitimate need, and some, at least, recognized that they could cut their rates and still make a profit if they were permitted to emerge from the shadows into which they had been driven by the traditional usury statute. It was this fraction of the shiver of sharks that reached out to Ham and the progressives and offered to cut a deal. They would submit to regulation and to a cap on their charges in exchange for a licensed and enforceable monopoly to do business in this market at rates well above those permitted to traditional lenders.[78]

This pact was sealed on 29 November 1916, at a conference in New York. Its fruit was the Uniform Small Loan Law. The pact was negotiated between Ham and members of the American Association of Small Loan Brokers, a trade group that had been formed the previous spring. Among the latter's members were representatives from the two largest chains of chattel-mortgage lenders, Frank Mackey's firm (the future HFC) and Clarence Hodson's Beneficial Finance. Mackey himself had resisted the move, insisting that "regulation will ruin everything," but his subordinates prevailed upon him to yield.[79] Based on the experience of the remedial loan societies, Ham favored a maximum rate of 3% a month, with no other fees allowed, but the lenders insisted they could not make small loans at that rate except in the largest cities. They lobbied instead for a rate of 4%, but in order to seal the pact the two sides split the difference at 3.5% a month, or 42% a year. This became the "scientific" rate of interest touted by the reformers in their fight to get the model law enacted.[80]

Ham himself drafted the text of the Uniform Small Loan Law. In addition to fixing the maximum rate of interest and prohibiting other charges on loans up to $300, the model required lenders to be licensed and bonded; to submit to scrutiny of their books and records by a state regulatory body; to provide borrowers with a written copy of the contract, and receipts for all payments made; to compute interest on the unpaid balance of the loan only, and not to take interest in advance; to take no power of attorney; and to limit wage assignments, if required, in various ways. Violation of the rules voided the debt in its entirety, could result in revocation of the license, and was punishable by a maximum fine of $500 and/or a maximum jail term of six months.[81]

The plan embodied a supply-side strategy. It sought to grind the tooth of usury by transforming the lenders. It brought them out into the open, and issued them a license, but then subjected the licensees to regulatory control. The usury cap was raised considerably for small loans but was not done away with. It was set at a level at which experience demonstrated a decent profit could be earned, but the lenders were required to amortize their loans and to give up the balloon product that had led so many wage-earners into the debt trap. The wage assignment was defanged as a form of security, and full disclosure of the contract was mandated. Everything would be above board and open—no more blank forms to sign, no more note shaving or false advertising. The consumers would be protected, but so would the licensed lenders. The latter had been granted a legal monopoly of the trade, and they had a powerful incentive to report violators of the statute to the regulatory authorities. In this way the licensed lenders would be conscripted into the fight against any loan sharks that refused to be tamed. As one advocate of reform, Raymond Fosdick, put it, "it is only the better sort that will succeed in driving out the worse."[82]

This was the theory of the Uniform Small Loan Law (see Chapter 3 for how the law worked in practice), but before it could be put into practice, the proposal had to run the gauntlet of the political process and win approval from the state governments. This fight commenced almost immediately in Illinois. Less than two weeks after the pact between the Russell Sage Foundation and the American Association of Small Loan Brokers had been forged, the commissioner of the Public Welfare Department in Chicago, Louise Osborne Rowe, convened a conference of the reform forces in the state in order to draft legislation. It was Rowe's department that had commissioned Earle Eubank's exhaustive report on *The Loan Shark in Chicago*, which armed the reformers with detailed information about the workings of the salary-lending business. Rowe invited Ham to present the model law to the conference, and it became the basis for the legislation that was submitted at Springfield the following month. In attendance at the meetings in December was a representative of Frank Mackey's chain, which was headquartered in Chicago.[83]

As House Bill 431 was being introduced in the state legislature, Chicago's city council voted to eliminate Commissioner Rowe's position. An angry group of female supporters attended the meeting and suggested the loan sharks were behind the vote. One informed the council, "There is a rumor afloat that the loan sharks are trying to influence the aldermen against the department on account of a bill Mrs. Rowe intends to introduce at the next meeting of the legislature. We do not believe that an intelligent body of men like yourselves would allow the loan sharks to control your actions."[84] But the aldermen insisted their vote was only intended to save the taxpayers money because Rowe's job was just a sinecure for a longtime crony of Mayor "Big Bill" Thompson.

House Bill 431 was virtually identical to Ham's model law. As it moved through committee only one section was amended, the part that set limits on the usage of wage assignments. The model prevented assignees from collecting more than 10% of a debtor's paycheck, but the Illinois legislation raised the limit to 50%.[85] This was not a fatal weakness, however, because the licensed lenders that would be brought into existence by the law would tend to prefer the chattel mortgage to the wage assignment as their instrument of security.

The advocates of reform assembled an impressive coalition of supporters to lobby for the bill. Its ranks included the Chicago Association of Commerce, the Commercial Club, the Industrial Club, the City Club of Chicago, the Legal Aid Society, United Charities, and the Illinois Committee on Social Legislation, which was a consortium representing dozens of groups across the state. The newspapers endorsed the bill and the reformers issued a pamphlet in February to state their case. Entitled *Smashing the Loan Sharks*, it appealed directly to the state's legislators:

> We ask that you drive the unscrupulous loan shark out of Illinois. . . . We are not coming to you as tearful theorists who imagine they have a God-given mission to perform. We come to you as business men and women talking to people of the same type. We have studied this thing inside and out. We think we know it. We are not hunting jobs for anybody. We are not seeking new ways to make money. We merely want you to cut out a malignant sore that is eating its way in on [a] large element of Illinois' citizens.

The pamphlet then explained the proposed law and warned that the loan sharks would lobby hard against it. They would do so, it was pointed out, because the legislation provided criminal penalties for those who violated the rules, and the loan sharks knew well that "Illinois jails are not very lovely places."[86]

Federal judge Kenesaw Mountain Landis also lobbied for the bill. Named for the Civil War battle in which his father had lost a leg, Judge Landis had been the terror of the loan sharks in Chicago for years.[87] He would hold what the newspapers dubbed "informal loan shark parties" in the bankruptcy court where he presided. Taking a rather sadistic pleasure in his task, Landis commanded the loan sharks to a special table he reserved in his courtroom and asked them to calculate with paper and pencil the interest rate of their loans. Then he would check their math. After one of his famous grillings, a rattled lender exclaimed, "For goodness sake, judge, cancel this claim. I'd rather lose the money than go through such an ordeal again."[88]

His colleagues described him as a "show-boat judge" and "an irascible, short-tempered, tyrannical despot," but the head of the *Tribune*'s Anti–Loan Shark Bureau claimed that "much of our success has been due to the hearty cooperation of Judge Kenesaw M. Landis in the bankruptcy court."[89] In March 1917, Landis took the unusual step for a sitting judge of appealing directly to the legislature for passage of the small-loan bill. But that effort may have done more harm than good because some opponents of the legislation tried to make an issue of Landis himself.[90] On two occasions motions for his impeachment had been introduced in Congress, and the U.S. Supreme Court had overturned a massive fine he levied against Standard Oil in an anti-trust case.[91] Judge Landis was a divisive figure, but the reform bill survived his intervention. A few years later he would resign his post to become the first commissioner of baseball, an office well suited to his temperament.

The Uniform Small Loan Law was under consideration in several different states in 1917, but, according to Robinson and Nugent, "the bitterest fight occurred in Illinois." The measure was nearly tabled in the state house in early May, that motion failing by only two votes. The loan sharks lobbied hard behind the scenes against it, and the reformers also had to contend with the usual objections from those who were scandalized by the idea of 42% interest. As a history of the Russell Sage Foundation explained, "The type of legislation recommended was opposed not only by the high-rate moneylenders who held that untrammeled competition should be trusted to control business, but also by a large part of the public who could see no reason for a higher rate of interest on a small loan . . . rather than the regular legal rate." Sometimes the loan sharks would join with the chorus of those who defended the traditional usury statute. They would decry the 42% rate advocated by the reformers, even though their charges were five or ten times greater.[92]

The battle was hard fought, but in the end the reformers prevailed. The measure passed in both houses by the end of the legislative session and was signed into law by Republican governor Frank Lowden in June. Lowden, a millionaire lawyer and successful industrialist, had ousted incumbent Edward Dunne the previous year. Although reviled as an enemy of organized labor, Lowden subscribed to a kind of "progressive conservatism," and his first months in office were accompanied by more progressive victories than Governor Dunne had achieved in four years.[93] Perhaps this was made possible by the harmony that accompanied America's entry into the First World War in April, but the spring legislative session was actually progressivism's last gasp in Illinois. Its coalitions, always weak, were disintegrating. But progressivism did not pass into history without some accomplishments to its credit. The passage of the Uniform Small Loan Law was one of its more enduring successes.

The Mitigation of Usury

The Loan Shark Act went into effect on 1 July 1917, less than three weeks after it was enacted. It wasn't long before a Chicago loan shark named Stokes was prosecuted for breaking the law. He did not possess a license, but Stokes loaned a salesman $100 at the usurious rate of 10% a month. He was convicted and fined $50, but the case was appealed all the way to the Illinois Supreme Court. Given its past record of support for freedom of contract, the reformers had reason to fear the worst from this court, but in *People v. Stokes* the justices upheld the new law. Without retracting its reasoning in *Massie v. Cessna*, the high court now admitted that "evils exist with respect to small loans which are not common to other loans." Greater regulatory control might well be necessary in this market, and the court found that the new provisions fell within the legitimate police power of the state. Colonel McCormick's newspaper took great satisfaction in the decision, boasting that "a fight that was begun five years ago by the *Tribune* was brought to a successful end."[94]

The Uniform Small Loan Law has been called "one of America's greatest advances in social legislation."[95] Certainly it was one of the more important accomplishments of progressivism in the early decades of the twentieth century. A combination of factors made this breakthrough possible. In the first place, the debtors whom the law was intended to help were numerous, visible, and often sympathetic victims. They were not, for the most part, members of a despised or forgotten underclass but wage-earners in respectable professions—white, male, and middle-income. The papers could tell a good story about these people, that they were down on their luck and then taken advantage of by lenders who were really sharks. The fact that the papers told so many stories of this sort is a second factor that contributed to the success of the reform movement, for they kept the problem visible and were able to mobilize bursts of activity in the fight against the loan sharks. The papers were partisan, demonizing the lenders relentlessly and never really letting them state their case. This one-sidedness created a presumption in favor of reform, and this presumption was further strengthened by the extent and quality of the coalition that wanted change, a third factor. Business, government, labor, and the professions each had an interest in solving the problem. The sharks stood alone, reviled. They had to buy their support or manipulate it. Their only defenders were the courts, and even these deserted the sharks in the end. A fourth factor that facilitated the success of the reform was the appearance on the scene of a credible and energetic leader, the Russell Sage Foundation. It possessed the resources and the drive to coordinate the fight against the loan sharks and it cultivated an aura of expertise and public spiritedness that allayed the fears of legislators, who were being asked to increase the usury cap substantially.

The prejudice in favor of the traditional usury law was the greatest obstacle lying in the path of the reformers, but they were able to overcome it because there were in the ideological climate of the day other prejudices and sensibilities to which they could appeal. This is a fifth factor to be noted. Widespread abhorrence of usury neutralized the argument for free contract in this market, and the reformers were able to frame their case in often starkly paternalistic terms that evoked no backlash. The progressives subscribed to an economics that did not make a fetish of the invisible hand, and this position could be made persuasive to a public that was predisposed to believe that interest rates ought to be regulated by the state. Admittedly, 42% was a hard sell for a public that assumed a fair rate of interest had to be in the single digits. But people could accept a higher ceiling if it was made clear that 42% was actually less than 7% because 7% in theory meant 200% or more in practice.

The reformers understood this math and could explain it to the public because the experience with remedial lending had taught it to them. That experience is a sixth factor that contributed to their success. The semi-philanthropic associations demonstrated that scrupulous lending could not be sustained at the old usury rate. Those experiments pointed the way forward toward the solution embodied in the Uniform Small Loan Law and also represented an effort to meet the for-profit lenders part way. The fact that there were lenders willing to strike a deal and submit to regulation constitutes a final and decisive factor in explaining the success of the reform movement. The lenders did not form a monolithic group, and some were looking for a way to legalize their trade. Their defection split the school of sharks and brought a final, crucial ally into the reform coalition. The defection meant there would be creditors available to put the model law into practice and to supply the demand of wage-earners for small loans in a mutually advantageous way. Without these willing lenders the new law would have amounted to prohibition, but what the progressives sought was domestication.

The passage of the Uniform Small Loan Law rolled back prohibition to a considerable extent in the small-loan market. This was done because total prohibition had been a catastrophe for cash-strapped consumers. It had put them at the mercy of the loan sharks. Through hard experience the progressives had come to adopt the standpoint of Sir Francis Bacon, who once observed that "it is better, to Mitigate Usury by Declaration, then to suffer it to Rage by Connivance."[96] Usury raged by connivance when the law enforced but one low rate. It would be mitigated, the reformers anticipated, by relaxing that rate in the small-loan market. This was the formula that was supposed to grind the tooth of usury, that it bite not too much.

But for this formula to work, the new rate had to be set just right. If it was too low, the connivance would continue; if it was too high, the tooth would still be sharp. The Uniform Small Loan Law did indeed grind the tooth of usury for many consumers. But at the same time it spawned a new breed of loan shark, one more savage than the salary lenders of old.

A Profusion of Species

The black marketeer gets automatic protection, through the law itself, from

all competitors unwilling to pursue a criminal career. The law gives a kind of

franchise to those who are willing to break the law. —**Thomas Schelling,**

Task Force on Organized Crime, 1967[1]

Just as the Uniform Small Loan Law was relaxing the prohibition imposed by the old usury statutes, a new and more famous prohibition was about to be imposed on the liquor industry in the United States. That prohibition, of course, created a black market in the manufacture and sale of alcoholic beverages and gave a powerful boost to organized crime. The Beer Wars in Chicago during the 1920s brought fame and fortune to gangsters such as Al Capone and created a crisis of illegality. The dozen years of Prohibition have become an enduring object lesson in the failure of efforts to criminalize a commodity that people need or want.

But here is the paradox. The Uniform Small Loan Law eased an ancient prohibition in the domain of credit and called into existence a higher-rate industry to fight the loan sharks, yet this relaxation nonetheless generated a black market in small loans that came to be served by organized crime. Somehow the repeal of a prohibition produced the same results we associate with the imposition of prohibition. It is *after* the passage of the Loan Shark

Act, we should note, that the mob entered the cash-advance business. The mob's appearance on the scene gave rise to the enduring image of what a loan shark is: the ruthless thug, operating underground, who will break your leg—even take your life—if you fall behind on your payments. That is the black-market shark, but this predator seems curiously to have been spawned following the success of the Uniform Small Loan Law in establishing a legal, low-cost market in short-term credit.

The aim here is to resolve that paradox. We will begin by charting the development of the personal finance industry, as it came to be known, and by comparing its white market in cash loans with the gray market it displaced. That displacement did not occur all at once. While some of the old loan sharks reformed themselves and became licensed lenders, others remained unlicensed and tried to adapt to the new environment. They evolved new variations of the old product and slipped through loopholes in the net of state regulation. Loan-sharking in its original form continued for quite a while after its obituary had been written. In some states in the South, it never really disappeared before the rise of payday lending. In the regulated states, however, the old loan sharks seem to have died out by the middle of the twentieth century. Without fanfare they vanished from the public record.

But then loan-sharking resurfaced after 1950, at least in the big cities, in its most notorious form. Crime syndicates went into the business of high-rate lending, and later on in this chapter, we will explain why that happened and how these new sharks compared to their predecessors. Although evidence about mob loan-sharking is fragmentary, its reputation for brutality seems to be inflated. The Hollywood depiction that shaped the popular imagination about what loan-sharking is did not correspond exactly to the street-level operations of syndicate payday lending. The resort to violence by these loan sharks was less common than we imagine. And alongside these mobster sharks, there flourished other black-market lenders who had no apparent connection to organized crime and no penchant for violence. Vest-pocket sharks proliferated in populations not served by the personal finance companies, and newspaper accounts sometimes offer us a glimpse of these minnows of the black market in credit.

What we encounter, then, is a profusion of species. Payday lenders in the era of the Uniform Small Loan Law were white, black, and gray. Some were large and corporate, others tiny and local. Some were violent, but most were not. Our aim will be to determine why this proliferation occurred, and what that proliferation reveals about the progressive strategy of regulation. Should we judge the Uniform Small Loan Law to be a failure because it did not extirpate the loan sharks? On the whole, did that law improve the lot of working people or did it make some of them worse off? Arriving at answers to these questions will be helpful when we turn, later on, to the problem of today's payday loan sharks and what to do about them. We must decide whether progressives of the twenty-first century should imitate the strategy of the Uniform Small Loan Law or, instead, treat that piece of legislation as a cautionary tale about what must be avoided in the fight against predatory lending.

Rehabilitated Sharks

In September 1922, the American Industrial Lenders Association held its eighth annual convention at the Hotel Pennsylvania in New York City. In attendance were 350 representatives of the licensed small-loan companies from all across the country. One of the organization's founders, Colonel Clarence Hodson of Beneficial Finance, reported that the industry's loan fund had grown to $50 million and now served 300,000 customers. The convention's announcement bragged about how far consumer lending had come in such a short time: "A decade or so ago . . . the business of money lending was confined to loan sharks whose personalities and practices were universally execrated. Today, however, the profession of money lending has been rehabilitated and placed on a plane as legitimate and respectable as that of ordinary commercial banking."[2]

The last claim would have been disputed, both by the commercial banks and by many members of the public. But the claim about rehabilitation was correct. The Uniform Small Loan Law rehabilitated the cash-loan business, some of whose members had been bona fide loan sharks not that long ago. These old-time sharks had emerged from the shadows of the gray market, reformed their business practices, and submitted to state supervision. In the early years the new licensed vendors called themselves "industrial lenders" in recognition of the working class they aimed to serve. But by the 1930s they would prefer the label "personal finance companies" to describe their sector of the credit industry, and this is the label that would stick.[3]

Immediately after the enactment of the Illinois Small Loan Law there was a shakeout within the shiver of sharks. Some lenders, like Frank Mackey's chain, quickly applied for licenses and began to vend a new product. The businesses that could most easily adapt to the new law were the old chattel-mortgage lenders. Their loans tended to be larger in size and could be made profitably at the legal rate of 42% a year. The salary lenders, by contrast, dealt in smaller sums and served a riskier clientele. Their product was not viable at the legal rate, and many decided to quit the business rather than submit to supervision. But some salary lenders continued to make loans, even without a license. Now, however, loan sharks were subject to criminal penalties. If caught they could go to jail—but not all of them were caught, as we shall see.

At first, regulation produced a contraction in the market. In 1919 the Illinois chapter of the licensed lenders' trade group reported that 45,000 residents of the state were being served by its members. This figure is well below the estimates of the clientele for the old loan sharks in Chicago, let alone the entire state. No doubt many residents were still patronizing unlicensed lenders, but the trade group also claimed that 200 sharks had been driven out of business in the two years since the new law had gone into effect.[4] It would take a few more years before legitimate capital flowed into the market in a greater stream and permitted the licensed lenders to satisfy the existing demand better. Through 1930, the personal finance industry as a whole was reported to have grown at the torrid pace of 20% a year. By 1934, when the industry had matured, there were 406 licensed lenders in Illinois serving more than a quarter million residents. This works out to be roughly one in six urban households in Illinois doing business with the personal finance companies. Similar rates were recorded in other regulated states. A 1938 study put the figure at one in eight families. Another report a few years later claimed that 20% of urban wage-earners had borrowed from this class of lenders during the past three or four years. If Ham's estimates from the pre-reform years are accurate, it means that by the 1930s the personal finance industry was reaching roughly the same proportion of the population as the original loan sharks.[5]

But the personal finance companies constituted just one segment of a consumer credit market that was undergoing tremendous growth and diversification in the first few decades of the twentieth century. While the old remedial loan associations had dwindled, credit unions and Morris Plan industrial banks had proliferated. In the 1930s, commercial banks began to open personal-loan departments to compete in this burgeoning market. There were also installment-sale creditors and auto-loan companies that made it possible for consumers to buy big-ticket items "on time." And the old-fashioned pawnshop endured, catering to those who could not find credit elsewhere. The total cash-loan market in 1936 approached $1 billion, with the licensed small-loan companies accounting for about 30% of the nation's loan balance.[6] Despite the contraction of the Great Depression, the age of consumer credit had arrived.

Prospective borrowers now had many more options to choose from than at the turn of the century, but these different types of lenders did not exactly compete against each other. Instead, they tended to cater to different segments of the consumer market. Affluent households were served by the commercial and industrial banks. These institutions made loans in larger sums at lower rates of interest but only to salaried professionals with good credit and reliable cosigners. The credit unions served working people but were tied to places of business, usually the larger employers. While their rates were low, they asked a lot of questions about what the money was for and supervised borrowers more closely. They served the better risks in the middle strata of the workforce. The pawnshops, by contrast, dealt with a clientele that lived in straitened circumstances and could only get cash by mortgaging a piece of personal property at a big discount.

The personal finance companies did business, for the most part, in the middle half of the income distribution: "that large segment of the population between the poverty line and the commercial bank window." The bulk of its customers were married white men, city dwellers, neither old nor young, and employed in offices or factories. The majority could be classified as working- or lower-middle-class, but a sizable fraction of its clients had better than average incomes. Over time this fraction would grow, especially in states with more stringent regulations. According to a 1970 study of the industry in New York, "The licensed lender clientele today comprises more than escapees from the loan sharks. There is less to differentiate the licensed lenders' customers from those of commercialized banks today than in the past."[7]

This customer profile of the personal finance companies roughly corresponds to the population served by the first loan sharks. That was indeed the aspiration of the reformers: they wanted to meet the legitimate credit needs of working people by calling into existence a regulated, lower-cost industry that would undercut the gray-market sharks. The new class of lenders would become "bankers of the common people" and "the borrowers' first line of defense against the loan shark."[8] As authorized remedial lenders, the personal finance companies were assigned the mission of "stepping into the breaches of our present economic system and making it possible for people in the lower income groups to meet financial emergencies and to maintain a steady purchasing power." The language of public service often figures in accounts of licensed lending in its first decades. This was said to be "a business tinged heavily with the public interest." According to secretary of labor William Doak, the industry had a "public obligation imposed upon it to earn socially clean dollars." That obligation was embodied in the license bestowed upon the lender. That license, the lender was reminded, was "a privilege that carries responsibilities to his community."[9]

As some observers saw it, the Uniform Small Loan Law had transformed the "midget loan" vendors into "semi-public utilities." Their licenses accorded them a monopolistic position within the small-loan segment of the market, and the rates these businesses could charge were fixed by government at a level that was supposed to afford them a decent but not windfall profit. The main difference between the personal finance companies and other regulated utilities was that the former were permitted to engage in price discrimination and to refuse service to prospective customers who were not deemed good credit risks.[10]

The state regulatory bodies established by the Uniform Small Loan Law were charged with the task of supervising the licensees, and they varied considerably in the degree of oversight they exercised and in their regulatory philosophy. In describing its yearly examinations of the licensed lenders, the Pennsylvania Department of Banking noted that "the scope of this examination covers not only the legal aspects of the business but takes into consideration also the moral obligation of the lender to the borrowing public and society in general." This moral obligation encompassed the methods of collection employed by creditors against accounts past due: "The Department will not permit a lender to use harsh and unconscionable collection methods on delinquent borrowers who are unable to pay by reason of unfortunate circumstances." The report went on to note that, while the department had no formal authority to regulate the advertisements of its licensees, it did feel obliged to raise objections about misleading claims. "Advertisements which feature 'easy' payments or 'repayment on easy installments' should be abandoned by licensees," it cautioned. "Little effort is required to borrow money but the repayment of a loan is never 'easy.'" Illinois regulators went further. They did formally proscribe the use of "easy" in the advertisements of lenders under their supervision.[11]

Eventually the personal finance companies would tire of this regulatory paternalism, but in the beginning their trade groups embraced the spirit of public service. The Illinois Association of Licensed Lenders acknowledged as its charge "the protection of the borrowing public against usury and extortion in procuring salary, chattel, and other small loans." These businesses prided themselves on being a different kind of creditor. They assessed an applicant's ability to repay a loan and tried to ascertain whether the money would be used for some constructive purpose. According to a 1940 report of the National Bureau of Economic Research, "It has become customary in the business for lenders to view themselves as consultants to family finance, with the object of fostering community goodwill." Many provided free assistance in preparing family budgets. The personal finance companies tried to cultivate an image of probity. Their aim, they said, was to help households avoid becoming burdened by debt and to learn to use credit responsibly. Indeed, some of the state trade groups went so far as to hire social workers, "whose business it is to cooperate with family welfare societies, to aid borrowers who are in distress, and to see that extreme measures are taken only when there is deliberate intent of fraud on the part of the borrower."[12]

Certainly the new class of licensed lenders did not hand out money indiscriminately, to everyone who requested a loan. All of them rejected sizable numbers of new applicants, in some cases more than half. Household Finance Corporation (HFC), the premier lender in the industry, cut its rates at the end of the 1920s but regularly turned away two-thirds of the people who were interviewed for loans. Many of these applicants were judged to be poor credit risks or wanted to borrow too much money. As a rule, most lenders would limit loans for new customers to one month's pay. If a client did seem credit worthy, the information on the application would be verified by the "outside man" in the office. The personal finance companies also established exchanges, or credit bureaus, to determine whether applicants were already indebted to another lender. "The loan companies," it was said, "make every effort to prevent one man from borrowing from several different companies at once." If the applicant was a married man, his wife would be required to endorse the note to ensure that the couple cooperated in budgeting for the debt.[13]

The vetting process often included a home visit to appraise the value of the client's household possessions, which would be subject to a chattel mortgage. That instrument of security was preferred by the licensed lenders to the wage assignment, which had been hedged in with restrictions by the Uniform Small Loan Law. In Illinois, where a larger proportion of the debtor's wages could be assigned than in other regulated states, the chattel mortgage was still the most common form of security; during the 1930s, two-thirds of the small loans were tied to household possessions. The chattels that were mortgaged rarely equaled in value the cash advanced by the lender and, in practice, were almost never seized in lieu of payment.[14] But the legal right afforded by this lien to haul away the debtor's furniture in case of default gave the lender some leverage in compelling repayment. Over time, however, more and more lenders dispensed with the home visit and the mortgage device and simply treated the transaction as a character loan. This became more feasible as it became harder for debtors in America simply to vanish. Deadbeats could be traced and compelled to pay if there was a signed contract. It wasn't really necessary any more for the lenders to hold hostage their clients' furniture.

The vast majority of customers served by the licensed lenders did pay their debts. However, the rate of delinquency and default was greater for the personal finance companies than for the lending institutions that served more affluent populations. This stands to reason. In Illinois, about 15% of accounts were delinquent in any given year during the 1930s, and roughly one-third of those loans would have to be written off. Bad debts accounted for 21% of the expenses on the ledgers of the small-loan companies. These figures declined modestly over the course of time but remained fairly stable. Other states reported similar statistics. Despite these losses, licensed lending was profitable. Net earnings in Illinois during 1934 amounted to 7.9% of assets. Stated another way, the average loan of $100 generated slightly less than $10 in profit during the course of the year. Like the default rate, the rate of return on assets also declined over time. By 1964 the figure had dipped below 5%.[15]

At first glance it seems puzzling why a loan charging a 42% rate of annual interest should not have been more profitable. The expense of bad debts is part of the explanation, as is the cost of vetting many applicants for small loans and servicing delinquent accounts. But also important is the fact that the nominal rate of interest for this product overstated its effective rate substantially. By law, interest could only be assessed on the unpaid balance of the loan, and since each installment paid down some of the principal, the amount of interest collected also diminished. For example, a $100 loan repaid in twelve monthly installments at the rate of 42% a year actually cost just $24 in interest. The effective rate of interest, then, was only 2% a month, or more than 40% less than the nominal rate.[16] This is one important reason why a $100 loan at the maximum rate of interest generated less than $10 in profit during the course of a year. The lenders, however, found it difficult to explain this math to the public. They were frustrated by the fact that other classes of lenders, like the commercial and industrial banks, were allowed to advertise their charges in a way that substantially understated the true cost. The Morris Plan banks, for example, boasted of 6% loans, but the effective rate was nearly three times as great. While still cheaper than the finance company product, the gap between the two was much less than the statutory rates indicated. The difficulty of finding a uniform way to state interest charges across loan products would bedevil policy makers for decades to come.

The complexity of small-loan math grew in the 1930s, when more states began to establish interest rate tiers. Illinois, for example, shifted from a straight maximum charge of 3.5% a month on loans up to $300 to a new schedule that permitted 3% a month on balances up to $150 and 2.5% on the remaining portion of the debt. Other states adopted even more complicated formulas. The movement toward legislative reductions in the rates lenders could charge was spurred in part by HFC's announcement in 1928 that it was cutting its rate on loans to 2.5% a month. Until that time there had been no real price competition between the lenders. Everyone charged the maximum rate. Competition occurred, instead, on non-price features, like the size of loans or their duration, collection practices, and convenience of hours or location.[17] HFC was able to get away with charging less than its competitors only because it made larger loans to less risky customers. The imposition of reduced rates by state legislatures did nothing to increase price competition between lenders. Indeed, it made it more difficult since there was now less room to maneuver and to engage in price discrimination. The effect of the new rate caps was to increase the average size of loans. These were already bigger than in the days before regulation had been imposed. Nugent calculated that the average loan prior to 1917 was roughly $40; by 1930 the average had grown to $145, an increase much greater than the rate of inflation during that interval.[18] This trend would continue in the following decades. In 1934 more than half the loans originated by licensees in Illinois were for less than $100, but by 1958 that figure had fallen to less than 8%. Adjusting for inflation, the average loan balance in the latter year was about 50% greater than in 1934 and more than three times the size of the average loan in the pre-reform era.

The high cost of small loans was an enduring grievance of the industry's critics. It spurred numerous efforts to impose rate cuts on the licensed lenders. Many people were not convinced that 3.5% a month was the lowest rate at which small loans could be made without calling back into existence the old loan sharks. Indeed, many people believed that 42% or 36% a year was still a loan-shark price, and so they applied the old epithet to the new lenders. New York's mayor Fiorello LaGuardia exclaimed, "To think of 42 percent interest in these days and this age is simply appalling." That, he insisted, "was a rate of interest which makes a typical loan shark appear as a generous philanthropist." Anyone who charged such rates "is not a human being: he is just a slimy hog." LaGuardia did not hesitate to apply the shark terminology even to prestige lenders like HFC. In his last days in office he berated this "loan shark" for tracking down a soldier stationed in Italy and asking him to pay the balance due on his debt. Even in retirement, he continued to complain that "a few individuals who do not want to go out and earn an honest living are accorded legal protection in charging a nefarious, blood-sucking rate of interest."[19] LaGuardia was convinced that a rate of 6% a year was sufficient for any honest business. If the banks could do it, he asked, why couldn't the small-loan companies?

LaGuardia was only the most famous proponent of this view. Plenty of other people also freely applied the "loan shark" label to the firms operating within the bounds of the Uniform Small Loan Law. An advocate for credit unions reminded his audience that "loan shark interest rates run 3½ per cent a month, or 42 per cent a year"; a banking group announced a new campaign "to fight the so-called loan sharks or licensed lenders"; a state senator called for lower rates and predicted that "the day of legal recognition to loan sharks in Illinois is passing"; a state representative attacked HFC and complained that "under a cloak of respectability these loan shark companies extort money from the people and exploit them"; and so forth. For these critics, the legal status of the personal finance companies was irrelevant in classifying this species of lender. As journalist Robert Edwin Pride explained in an eloquent tirade entitled *Loan Sharks of America*, "If a banker were to loan money on a basis other than six per cent per annum he would at once be classified as a usurer, a law violator, and therefore a criminal, but when licensed and bonded loan sharks loan money at a rate of forty-two percent per year they are distinguished gentlemen and illustrious citizens." Pride didn't buy it. He thought the licensed lenders were just "legitimatized loan-sharks."[20]

The two dominant chains of installment lenders, HFC and Beneficial Finance, had come into the world as loan sharks. Pride, like other critics, expressed doubt that "a shrewd money-loan parasite . . . had been converted over night from a vulture into a dove" just because a state agency had issued it a license. Instead, what that license had done was to allow the sharks to grow large. Switching metaphors, Pride described the licensed chain lender as a "gigantic, interlocking, interwoven, intertwining corporate gorilla-like money robot . . . whose hairy paws reached out over the entire nation." Far from being a progressive piece of legislation, Pride thought the Uniform Small Loan Law with its 42% rate was a "pathetically absurd masterpiece of statutory buncombe."[21]

High cost and an unsavory pedigree, then, were two common complaints lodged against the new industry. But there were others. The head of New York City's Legal Aid Society condemned the harsh collection methods employed by some licensed lenders, the seductive radio ads that encouraged unnecessary borrowing, and dishonest practices such as tricking friends of the debtor into signing forms that made them cosigners on the loan. Others agreed that "many unethical procedures and sharp practices are still found . . . which take advantage of the borrower's stupidity or carelessness or both."[22] The sale of credit life or disability insurance was often cited as an example. The product was both unnecessary and expensive, and the lender pocketed a large fraction of the premium as profit. Abuse of the wage assignment was another grievance, especially in Illinois where the instrument was more effective than in other regulated states. At one big streetcar firm in Chicago, an average of 3,400 wage assignments a year were processed in the payroll office during the early 1930s, and the vast majority of those assignments were filed by various types of licensed lenders.[23]

What is more, despite efforts to end the practice, some borrowers were still "doubling up" or getting more than one loan at once from the finance companies. Some lenders didn't assess carefully the borrower's ability to pay or check with the local clearinghouse to see whether an applicant was trying to "pyramid" by using the proceeds of one loan to pay off another. Observers claimed that there was a "mushrooming of improper lending practices where there are too many lenders. Excessive lending creates more loans on marginal credit which result in harsh collection practices and more personal bankruptcies." Licensed lenders were said to suffer from a loan-shark atavism when too many crowded into a single market. To rectify this problem, the fifth draft of the Uniform Small Loan Law added a "convenience and advantage clause" that permitted regulators to ration the number of licenses issued within a local jurisdiction. "Its main purpose was to prevent over-lending and the attendant evils resulting from excessive competition."[24]

"Overlending" could mean that some people were encouraged to borrow when they didn't really need the money. But it could also mean that some customers were lent more money than they could pay back in a reasonable period of time, trapping them in debt. The latter seems to have been the most widespread problem in the reformed industry, but the lenders were only partly responsible for this difficulty. After all, "overlending" could also be construed as "overborrowing." The facts, however, are clear. Studies consistently showed that 40% of all loan contracts were renewals. Before the original loan was paid off, the customer would "flip" or refinance the debt, often getting new cash that would be added to the remaining principal from the old loan contract. The debt, in other words, was extended, and borrowers remained in debt for longer periods of time than the initial installment plan specified. Whereas most loans were supposed to have been paid off within twelve months, the average duration of indebtedness for installment plan customers was actually a bit more than two years.[25] The debts dragged on and the lenders earned more interest.

As I have argued before, debt that endures is the essence of loan-sharking. Loan sharks vend a product that is not meant to be paid off in a timely fashion. Given the facts cited above, it is not surprising that many critics of the personal finance industry classified these creditors as loan sharks. The licensed lenders promised "easy" payments, but it wasn't easy for many of their customers to escape this installment debt. Still, that was not necessarily or entirely the fault of the lenders. Unlike the original loan sharks, the regulated companies never made interest-only cash advances. Their loans were always amortized, and every payment reduced the principal at least a little bit. They did not trick borrowers into balloon products that required a large lump-sum payment at the end. Loans of that sort were sure to trap people with modest incomes in a swamp of debt from which it was nearly impossible to escape without the help of a lawyer. The personal finance companies were required to be more responsible than that, and most of them were. The difficulty was that their clientele behaved in a different way than more affluent consumers did. People who turned to the high-rate lenders were, in the terminology of economists, "rationed" borrowers. They could not get as much credit as they wanted, certainly not from the low-cost vendors. Rationed borrowers tend not to be price sensitive or to shop extensively for the best deal. Convenience matters a lot to them, and what they want above all are low monthly payments. As a 1964 National Bureau of Economic Research report explained, "rationed consumers will prefer a combination of longer maturities and higher finance rates rather than one of shorter maturities and lower rates, while unrationed consumers will have the opposite preference."[26] Easy payments appeal enormously to households in straitened circumstances because these low installments permit them to consume at a higher level in the present.

The fact that such debt is more costly and will last longer does not matter as much since cheap credit is not available to them. The real alternative to easy payments is reduced consumption, which most people try to avoid or to put off if they possibly can.

In renewing loan contracts and extending debt, then, the personal finance companies were responding to consumer preference. To be sure, they were making money too, but these businesses were not raking in windfall profits. If they couldn't flip a sizable fraction of their loans, it is doubtful that many of them could have survived. Indeed, when some states tried to rein in the practice by imposing strict limits on the length of indebtedness, the number of licensees declined precipitously.[27] Profits couldn't be made at 42% a year if the loans were too short. They also couldn't be made if the loans were too small.

If the aim of the Uniform Small Loan Law was to find a path of consumer lending around the debt swamp where the predators lived, it was unable to ensure that this path would be short and inexpensive and that some debtors wouldn't choose the roundabout trail of easy payments. But, after all, that law had only tried to rehabilitate the lenders. It didn't make provision for reforming the rationed borrower.

A Hardy Breed

The Uniform Small Loan Law was supposed to tame the rehabilitable sharks and encourage them to grow. The idea was that this new and privileged species of lender would be so successful in the small-loan market that it would starve into extinction the incorrigible sharks, who would also be hunted by the state's attorneys. Competition plus prosecution would end the scourge of the loan sharks.

Victory in this fight was declared even before it had really begun. A *New York Times* headline in March 1917 proclaimed "Shylocks Have Practically Been Exterminated." It touted the work of the Russell Sage Foundation and claimed that "today a procession of loan shark victims making payments in New York would be lost in the average audience about a suffragette orator on a street corner." The Uniform Small Loan Law had not yet been enacted in either New York or Illinois by this date, but the author was convinced that "the extortioners have all but given up their cruel trade." This was the first in a long succession of victory proclamations issued in the war on the loan sharks, and each subsequent declaration was just as fatuous. The loan sharks had been driven out of business, the reformers claimed, but then some new exposé would reveal that predatory lending in its antediluvian form had survived into the age of regulation. Eventually, by mid-century, it would have to be acknowledged that some of the gray-market sharks had endured the rise of licensed lending, proving that they were "a hardy, agile lot, conditioned by having survived half a century of efforts to eliminate them."[28]

It is not really surprising that the Uniform Small Loan Law failed to extirpate the old-style loan sharks all at once. The new class of licensed lenders could not be called into existence overnight. It took time for legitimate capital to flow into the market, set up loan offices, and rise to the level of the preexisting demand. Wage-earners needed loans now, not in a few years, and if there weren't licensed lenders available they would have to turn to the unregenerated sharks. Letters reprinted in the *Chicago Tribune's* "Friend of the People" column of legal advice attest to the survival of shady lenders into the 1920s.[29] They could not operate openly from storefront offices, but they still found ways to do business. Veterans returning home from the war were "warned against loan sharks, who are said to be securing assignments of the $60 government bonuses to be paid to discharged men." A state insane asylum was discovered to have been infiltrated by loan sharks working in league with the chief clerk. The lenders advanced cash at the rate of 25% a month and took powers of attorney as security for the debt. These were midget sharks, purely local, and doing business on a restricted scale. One result of the criminalization of unlicensed lending was to fragment its operations and reduce the size of each firm. To avoid detection it was advantageous for the sharks to remain small and to move within personal networks. They became vest-pocket lenders, one-man operations, and this had the added advantage of reducing overhead costs. Instead of setting up an office and waiting for trade to come in off the street, these minnows infiltrated the larger workplaces. Some years later Adele Rabino told the story of a petty shark who did business in city hall and the county building: "Investigation revealed that he made small loans to employees of both divisions."[30]

But not all of the surviving loan sharks were small and furtive. Chains of unlicensed firms continued to operate, even in the regulated states, because the salary lenders of old had figured out a way to re-craft their product to evade the reform statutes. Instead of "salary lending," they now claimed to be "salary buying." The concept was said to have been invented in Atlanta early in the twentieth century, and that city remained the hub of the salary-buying chains all the way through the 1940s. If someone inquired at the office about a loan, the agent replied, "We don't loan money; you'll have to sell your wages." The firm claimed to be buying income that had already been earned by the customer but had not yet been paid by the employer. For example, if you made $33 every two weeks, the company would offer to buy this amount of wages from you at a discount of 10%. You received $30 today but had to pay $33 in two weeks. If you couldn't afford to let the salary buyer keep all of your wages on your next payday, you could negotiate a new transaction. For $3 the old contract would be torn up and replaced with a new one. These renewals could go on indefinitely because the buyer did not accept partial payments. You either paid $3 or $33—it was your choice. As a Russell Sage Foundation study pointed out, "The vicious part of the scheme was that the borrower usually did not repay the loan but constantly renewed it every payday, and sooner or later either increased the loan or borrowed concurrently from another salary-buyer, or both."[31]

This product more closely resembled today's two-week payday loan than the salary loan did because the salary purchase was not an installment transaction but a single-payment cash advance, endlessly renewable. Like the payday loan, salary buying functioned for many consumers like an interest-only debt. These wage-earners could not come up with the lump-sum payment of principal that was due every payday and so became trapped by the product. One borrower in Decatur, like countless others across the country, paid his $3 every two weeks for two years, spending $156 on interest for the privilege of receiving a single $30 cash advance. Another man in Chicago started the same way at $3 a payday but then, when money grew tight, sold wages to a second buyer at the same rate, and then a third and a fourth, until he had paid $1,080 in fees over the space of four years. In 1926 it was estimated that one-third of railway employees in the nation were selling their wages to at least two salary buyers simultaneously, using the proceeds of one transaction to pay off another. As these examples make clear, salary buying was loan-sharking in its purest form because "the loan itself is so designed as to handicap repayment."[32]

Although salary buyers had been operating for some time in Chicago, the product only came to the attention of the public in 1926 because of a joint investigation of the state's attorney and United Charities. It was revealed that these wildcat lenders were "operating in a vicious circle, with chains of offices in twenty or more cities." Eight firms were doing a brisk business in Chicago, and most of these concerns seemed to have ties to the Big Four salary buyers based in Georgia.[33] But the exact identity of the owners was often a mystery. Even a branch manager might not know who had hired him or who was collecting the money he sent to a post office box down south. The whole business seemed to be the work of outsiders, a slick southern conspiracy. One loan agent was heard to speak in "a lazy Southern drawl." Salary buying, some said, went "back to carpet bag days following the Civil War, when it was started among the Negroes of the South." Now the scam had migrated north. Its victims were no longer sharecroppers but office clerks and factory hands.[34]

The latest incarnation of loan-sharking employed new variations of old tricks to collect its debts. Instead of sending the old-style bawler-out to make a scene at work, "some of the sharks employed attractive women and girls to intercept borrowers in their offices." They would "appear to have some secret understanding with the victim which led to gossip and sometimes, when the victim happened to be married, to scandal." Others would send strong-arm squads to repossess assets, like the delinquent's car.[35]

Salary buying was definitely a scam, but it wasn't exactly illegal. The first draft of the Uniform Small Loan Law had not contemplated a transaction of this sort and so its provisions were inapplicable. Most courts were not fooled by the claim that salary buying was a purchase, not a loan, but because the product did not fall within the purview of the uniform law, only the usury statute applied. In Illinois the debt could be cancelled if the equivalent of the principal plus 7% had been repaid, but the salary buyer could not be charged with a criminal offense. The Russell Sage Foundation had been slow to recognize the threat represented by the new product, and "by 1925 salary-buying was thriving in two-thirds of the states in the Union and still expanding rapidly." Arthur Ham had stepped down as head of the foundation's remedial loans department in 1917, after the first legislative victories had been won, and it wasn't until 1925 that an energetic successor began to mount an offensive against salary buying.[36] Leon Henderson, who would become FDR's "price czar" in 1940, launched a nationwide campaign against the new breed of loan sharks and urged passage of a revised draft of the Uniform Small Loan Law, which closed the loophole through which the sharks had slipped.[37]

In Illinois several attempts were made to revise the Loan Shark Law to cover salary buying, but success was only achieved in 1933. The reformers blamed the delay on the loan-shark lobbyists, "whose habits are devious and whose ways are dark."[38] They were regularly accused of buying legislators and employing dirty tricks. In the state of Washington, one lobbyist was charged with impersonating an agent of the Russell Sage Foundation and then offering clumsy bribes on behalf of the Uniform Small Loan Law. The idea was to sully the reputation of reformers and to block passage of the statute. In Illinois the sharks set up a dummy organization called the "Protective League" that lobbied Springfield for rate reductions in order to undercut the licensed lenders.[39] One danger of trying to close loopholes in the uniform statute was that it revived criticism of the law by those who had never made their peace with 42%. These critics did not believe the assertion that, "if a law is passed, cutting their interest to 18 per cent, the small operators will be squeezed out and bootleg money lending will spring up all over the state."[40] The loan sharks, however, did think this would happen and that is why they joined the fight for price cuts on behalf of consumers.

Eventually the law in Illinois caught up with the adaptations of the storefront loan sharks and made possible a concerted campaign against them. The statute was revised once again in 1935, adding new provisions from the fifth draft of the Uniform Small Loan Law. In supporting the revision the *Tribune* admitted that "the present Illinois law has not completely succeeded in driving out the loan shark," but it did promise that "the proposed law would eliminate the loan shark entirely." Its passage "would complete the job started by the *Tribune* a quarter century ago of ridding the state of loan sharks."[41] Like other boasts by the reformers, this one was too hasty. But criminal prosecutions did accelerate in the 1930s. In June 1934 a dozen lenders pleaded guilty to violating the statute and had to surrender 2,793 notes worth $50,000. In February 1936 a notorious salary buyer, Carl White, paid a fine and turned over contracts worth $10,000.[42] Stories about loan-sharking in Chicago appeared sporadically thereafter, but the accused always seemed to be vest-pocket sharks.[43] Any reference to salary buying had disappeared by the end of the decade. That trade persisted, however, in the unregulated states. The Bar Association in Atlanta was still locked in a struggle with the salary-buying chains as late as 1949. Indeed, William Simpson documented the existence of old-style loan sharks across the South in the early 1960s, and a shark-like industry hawking "small small loans" flourished in Texas in the 1970s (see Chapter 4 for more about the survival of this sort of operator in the South before the rise of payday lending).[44]

Hauled into court for violating the state's loan statute, Carl White was asked by the prosecutor why he didn't apply for a license. "Under the rate of 3½ per cent a month it is impossible to make any money," he replied. "Why, on a $10 loan that would give me only 35 cents in a month. I can't comply with that and stay open." This usurer made a good point. The maximum rate imposed by the Uniform Small Loan Law made it impossible to lend tiny sums profitably. Personal finance companies made larger loans because that was the only way they could stay in business. Sometimes these lenders did make small loans to new customers in order to expand their clientele, but they did so at a loss and with the expectation that these customers would borrow again and in larger sums.[45] White, by contrast, was trying to make a living by serving those who only wanted to borrow $10 or $20 at a time, and to do this he had to charge more than the statutory maximum.

This one case illustrates a larger point, that the loan sharks and the licensed lenders tended to serve different populations. Abe Fortas recognized the pattern in his empirical study of wage assignments in Chicago: "Comparison of the average amount owed licensed and unlicensed lenders . . . brings home the fact that the two are not competitors, but operate in different spheres." One of his case studies was the Armour meatpacking plant in the Stockyards. Fortas observed, "The income of Armour's employees is so low as to place them, by and large, outside the field of operation of the licensed loan companies." Many of the workers were blacks who had migrated from the South during the past generation, but, according to Fortas, "Negro laborers . . . are not considered a fair risk by money lenders." The personal finance companies didn't make loans under $75, but that was an entire month's wages for the typical Armour meatpacker.[46] The latter definitely needed credit, but he wasn't going to get it at HFC or Beneficial Finance.

African Americans are a good example of a population that was not served by the licensed lenders at this time. Low incomes and racial discrimination were the main reasons. But where the personal finance companies would not do business, the loan sharks plied their trade. Blacks were said to have been the original customers of the southern salary buyers, and when they migrated north to cities like Chicago, African Americans did not escape the predations of the loan sharks. Very little documentary evidence exists, however, about the scale of the problem. In the newspaper stories of this era the victims are almost always white. A few shreds of evidence can be gleaned from the *Chicago Defender*, a paper that served the city's African American community. In April 1920 it excerpted the speech of a bank president, who said that "money loan sharks . . . are doing business in the rear of every saloon." More than three decades later, it was reported that "many Negroes are not eligible to borrow from the licensed loan companies. . . . Consequently, they are forced into the hands of loan sharks and usurers, who obviously operate without the checks of legality and bleed them dry. The number of Negroes so victimized can be counted in the hundreds of thousands." Skip forward another two decades and the *New York Times* can still report that "slum residents are at the mercy of loan-sharks because many blacks and Puerto Ricans cannot borrow money from legitimate sources."[47]

But African Americans were not the only victims of the hardy breed of loan sharks. It was widely recognized that "the salary buyers enjoy a virtual monopoly of lending in the lower [income] brackets and to the more ignorant classes of borrowers." As that merciless critic of the personal finance companies Robert Pride observed, "These institutions . . . take the cream of the business, leaving the less fortunate ones exactly where they were—at the mercy of the outlawed loan shark."[48] After all, some of the licensed lenders rejected more than half their applicants, which left a sizable population of poorer risks still looking for credit. If they couldn't get it from the licensed lenders, let alone the banks or credit unions, where else could they go but to the loan sharks?

According to Evans Clark, this was the fundamental defect in the Uniform Small Loan Law: within its framework "no adequate provision has been made for small salary loans to wage workers." Such loans weren't economically feasible at 3.5% a month, so they remained outside the ambit of the law. But since the demand for these loans persisted, it meant that loan sharks would still have prey upon which to feed. The midget loans and the poorer risks had been left to them. This difficulty was recognized by the last director of the Sage Foundation's remedial loans department. Rolf Nugent acknowledged that "the fixing of any maximum rate in small loan legislation tends, of course, to exclude certain classes of borrowers from the legitimate market for small loans." Some critics of the law thought this exclusion was "uneconomic," but Nugent replied that "there are many people who will make the most burdensome promises for the future in exchange for present purchasing power." To permit the desperate and the myopic to contract debt at higher rates would "merely aggravate the borrower's financial difficulties," causing hardship for him, his family, and the larger community. Poor risks who would consent to rates above 42% a year were all too likely to become trapped by their debts, and Nugent insisted that society must not "tolerate loan contracts that are liable to result in economic peonage." If some wage-earners could not be served by the licensed lenders, he maintained, "alternative means of relief must be furnished and those pressed by necessity compelled to use them."[49]

But alternative means of relief were not furnished—certainly not on anything like the scale that could satisfy existing demand. Indeed, most of the remedial loan societies passed out of existence after the Uniform Small Loan Law was enacted. In 1924, for example, St. Bartholomew's Episcopal Church in New York City announced that it was dissolving its loan association because, the rector said, "the 'loan sharks' have been driven out of business." To be sure, some groups within society did establish self-help organizations on a large scale, but they were the exception. One reason Jews in Chicago were spared the depredations of the loan sharks was that the Jewish Social Service Bureau managed an interest-free loan fund for indigent families.[50] But other segments of the population lacked the necessary solidarity and resources to starve the sharks. Nationwide, Evans Clark estimated that the loan sharks in the late 1920s accounted for 10% of the outstanding small-loan fund and served more people than the personal finance companies. A decade later, Rolf Nugent calculated that the market share of the sharks was roughly the same. While the bulk of this loan-sharking occurred in the unregulated states, Nugent admitted that "a fringe of illegal lending, which can be minimized but not completely eradicated, persists in most industrial metropolises."[51]

This fringe business served the fringe elements of the workforce, wage-earners whose low incomes made them high risks for the personal finance companies. These debtors had not benefited from the Uniform Small Loan Law. Instead, that law seemed to have benefited consumers who earned more and were deemed better risks. They were able to borrow at lower rates than had been available to them in the pre-reform days. This was possible because legal lending was less costly than loan-shark lending but also because the marginal wage-earners were excluded from the risk pool of the licensed lenders. With them out, less debt had to be written off by the personal finance companies and fewer resources had to be devoted to debt collection. Viewed in this way, we can see that unreformed loan-sharking was in some sense more egalitarian than the regime imposed by the Uniform Small Loan Law. Before rates were capped at 42%, more borrowers belonged to the same risk pool. All were charged a high price, and the lower risks paid for the substantial number who had to be dunned or written off. The Loan Shark Law emancipated the better risks from the worse and rewarded the former with lower rates and consumer protections. The latter group, by contrast, was rejected by the new class of lenders and consigned to the backwaters in which the sharks hunted. Their plight wasn't necessarily worsened, since salary buyers seemed to charge the same rates as the old salary lenders, but they were left behind. The Uniform Small Loan Law turned out to be a grand exercise in price discrimination. It represented the great escape of the better risks in the wage-earning class.[52]

When viewed from this angle, the Uniform Small Loan Law does not look quite so progressive. It made some people better off, but not the least advantaged group. Its members remained where they were. Or did they? What if they not only didn't move ahead but also fell behind? What if they stayed where they were, in the swamp, but the predators with whom they had to contend became more savage?

Sharks in the Underworld

And so we arrive finally at the loan sharks of popular imagination—the mob sharks. It took us so long to encounter this species because it only evolved decades after loan-sharking had come on the scene in the United States. The first loan sharks, we have already noted, had no connections to organized crime, and organized crime, in turn, did not emerge out of, or engage from the start in, the business of making small loans. There is no direct path of evolution from the gray-market sharks of the pre-reform days to the gangster moneylenders of later decades.[53] Those gray-market operators became black-market as soon as unlicensed lending was criminalized, but criminalization did not automatically drive bootleg creditors into the ranks of the syndicate. The two could exist side by side, and around them moved a profusion of vest-pocket vendors who were also black-market. The demand was sufficient to accommodate them all.

If we go hunting for the first traces of mob loan-sharking, nothing definite can be uncovered before the 1930s. But Francis Ianni does tell an interesting story about immigrant lending in Italian neighborhoods after the turn of the century. The patriarch of a lineage that would grow into a crime family in the decades to come arrived in the United States in 1902 and soon established an informal bank for his *paesani*. He loaned small sums at a high rate of interest without demanding tangible security: for example, an acquaintance might borrow $2.00 on Wednesday and repay $2.50 on Saturday. If borrowers did not make good on their debts they might be beaten, and there were suggestions that the patriarch was connected to Sicilian Black Hand gangs that specialized in extortion.[54] Operations of this sort must have been widespread in immigrant communities in the early twentieth century and were really just vest-pocket networks of credit. The patriarch would only become a crime boss later on, with the coming of Prohibition and the Mafia takeover of organized gambling. While his crime family did engage in loan-sharking in subsequent decades, that franchise wasn't the same as Giuseppe's *paesani* bank. The one operation did not grow seamlessly from the other, as an extension of intra-immigrant credit networks.

The era of the Dry Law swelled the ranks and the coffers of organized crime enormously, but if you scour the record of the 1920s you won't find any evidence of mobster money lending. Frederic Thrasher's exhaustive study of a thousand gangs in Chicago, for example, makes no mention of loan-shark operations. Frank Nitti, Al Capone's lieutenant and successor, was tied to a loan business in 1930, but this was a licensed firm that may have served as a money-laundering front for the mob.[55] By all accounts, Chicago was not the birthplace of syndicate loan-sharking. If that trade existed at all in the 1930s, it was invisible in the city. "Juice racketeering," as it came to be known later on, did not become a growth industry in Chicago until the 1950s. To find the origins of the mob loan shark we must travel back east, to the boroughs of New York.

Before 1935—and indeed for quite a few years thereafter—the idea of loan-sharking did not imply violence as it does today. That may seem curious to us since the shark is after all a violent creature, but it was the predatory nature of the species and not its physical brutality that was emphasized in the colloquialism's original usage. The "loan leech" might have been a better metaphor to convey the concept of a creditor who won't let go and who bleeds his victims, but then again the leech isn't a predator who mauls, like the shark. In any case, the first loan sharks almost never employed violence to collect their debts. They had other means of coercion, like the wage assignment, the chattel mortgage, and the bawler-out. To be sure, from time to time the newspapers did report some act of physical assault employed by a loan shark to collect a debt, but these were anomalous cases. The methods of extorting payment from reluctant debtors were usually not so crude.

But then, suddenly, in 1935 there appeared on the scene in New York City a kind of loan shark who was a crude and brutal extortionist. In the first weeks of the new year, the *New York Times* began to report on the plight of brokerage house clerks or "page boys," as they were called, who were being charged very high rates of interest for small loans and, if they fell behind on their payments, were beaten by thugs. The fee was exorbitant: 20% a week, or $6 on a $30 loan. The clerks were easily exploitable because their wages were low to begin with, and then their employers began laying them off once every eight weeks during a slow season. To get by, many had to borrow, but the new sharks demanded a heavy price and moved quickly to violence when payments were late.[56]

By the summer, the paper was reporting on gun battles between rival gangs of loan sharks in Brooklyn and the Bronx. They were fighting for territory in a way that was unprecedented for unlicensed lenders, and by October seven men had been killed in the ongoing feud.[57] Then into this carnage there waded a new crime fighter—Thomas E. Dewey—and he would play an instrumental role in bringing this new form of loan-sharking into the light and also in forging the enduring image of the mob loan shark. Dewey, an ambitious young lawyer and future presidential candidate, had been charged with the task of prosecuting racketeers. He was stymied in his efforts until he came across the loan-shark networks, which turned out to be easier to penetrate and to prosecute than other crime rackets. As Mary Stolberg explains, "unlike other racketeers, New York's loan sharks were disorganized, and victims were more willing to testify against individual sharks than they would have been had they been organized by the mob."[58]

Dewey was fortunate that the usury cases proved easy to prosecute because he was under pressure to show results. He grabbed headlines late in October with the arrest of twenty-seven "Shylock mobsters" who were quickly put on trial for violating the loan statute. Within a few weeks all but one had been convicted. In his remarks to the press Dewey identified "the usury racket" as "one of the city's major troubles." He estimated that the loan sharks were earning $5 million a year in interest in the city, and the Sage Foundation thought the real figure might be twice that number. According to Nugent, "The entrance of criminals into the small loan field has occurred within the last two years and most rapidly within the last six months." He speculated that this had something to do with the end of Prohibition: "Many bootleggers, preferring an illegal occupation and supplied with capital from their formerly profitable activities, seem to have found money-lending an opportune field."[59] The scale of this new industry was stupefying. One article claimed that the "Shy racket" employed 2,000 operatives in the city, including "touts" or scouts, and that more than 50,000 New Yorkers were in debt to them.[60]

It isn't clear, however, just how connected the street-level loan sharks were to the city's crime families. This was not a tightly controlled operation, and many freelance lenders may have been lumped in with the syndicate affiliates. The suspects Dewey rounded up were described as "a motley gathering of nondescripts, some of them far more poorly clothed than the witnesses who glowered at them." The fact that the witnesses felt comfortable glowering also suggests, as Stolberg noted, that these were not "made-men" whom an organization would protect. Some of the debtors had been required to sign notes or confessions of judgment, which meant that other means of debt collection than brute force had been contemplated.[61] From this point forward there would often be ambiguity in the news stories about which kind of loan shark had been discovered. An article might suggest a mob connection, but this wasn't necessarily the case. There was plenty of scope for vest-pocket operators.

Dewey's campaign captured headlines for a month, but then he moved on to new exploits. Two years later, when running for district attorney, the Rudy Giuliani of his day claimed to have broken up the loan-shark racket in New York, but the occasional news story suggests otherwise. In March 1939 five men were indicted for running a $6-for-$5 business in Brooklyn that employed "terroristic" methods of collection. The five men were also involved in a gambling operation and used their muscle to extort protection money from small businesses. Two years later, a special prosecutor uncovered a large usury ring in the same borough that was connected to the notorious Murder Inc. gang of Abe "Kid Twist" Reles.[62] Stories of this sort would recur periodically in the years to come but be interspersed with other news reports of loan-shark operations that had no apparent connection to organized crime. In the summer of 1941, for instance, several men were arrested for loaning money on a large scale and at high rates to employees of New York's power utility. They didn't beat up delinquent debtors but filed wage garnishments instead.[63] The idea that crime syndicates ever had a monopoly over the loan-shark trade was a fantasy of future prosecutors, in the tradition of Thomas Dewey, who had an interest in exaggeration.

Through the middle of the century, the mob form of loan-sharking seems to have been restricted to the New York area. The journal *Law and Contemporary Problems* devoted entire issues to the problem of unlicensed lending in 1941 and 1954, but only a single, brief reference in the earlier symposium was made to mob influence.[64] These experts were concerned, instead, with the survival of the old-style loan sharks, especially in the unregulated states. Where the Uniform Small Loan Law had been applied, they insisted, the problem of usurious lending had been solved. The 1954 issue read like an obituary for the loan shark. Its articles claimed that "A Regulatory Small Loan Law Solves the Loan Shark Problem," "Nebraska Has No Loan Shark Problem Today," and so forth. The Kefauver hearings on organized crime a few years earlier also made no mention of a mob loan franchise. Neither did several studies of the Chicago syndicate published in the early 1950s.[65] Even in New York, coverage of thug loan-sharking in the 1940s and 1950s was restricted almost entirely to the waterfront districts. There were plenty of stories about longshoremen who paid 10% of their wages each week to moneymen on the piers with ties to local crime families.[66] But this was not a pure form of loan-sharking because the men had to borrow in order to be selected from the large crowds that formed during the daily "shape-up" outside the warehouses. As a report from the Citizens Waterfront Committee explained, "The men are forced to kick back part of their meager earnings as the price of getting a job."[67] The payments, then, weren't really interest installments on debt but rather bribes demanded by the foremen as a condition of employment. No doubt some authentic loan-sharking occurred on the piers, too, but the press tended to misconstrue the kickbacks as if they were straight Shylock transactions. In fact there weren't as many loan sharks down by the wharves as the public was given to believe.

Hollywood helped to shape these misconceptions. Mob loan sharks began to show up in the movies after Dewey's campaign exposed their existence in 1935. These violent sharks were more colorful and more menacing than the prosaic wage-assignment lenders who were passing from the scene. Their villainy was greater because it combined greed with organized and methodical brutality. The violence of these sharks could be met with a heroic counter-violence of the authorities, and raw struggles like this between good and evil are the bread and butter of the film industry. The archetypal depiction is the 1952 B-flick "Loan Shark." Starring George Raft in the downward phase of his career, the film suggests a vast criminal enterprise in payday lending at twenty industrial plants scattered across some undisclosed big city in America. The mobsters beat and murder with impunity until Raft penetrates their organization, rises through its ranks, and then eliminates the top man in the final scene. That solution to the problem was thoroughly utopian, but the film's account of the factory-level operations of this network matches fairly well what we can reconstruct from empirical sources. But in real life not all of those operations were controlled by the mob, and even the mob crews didn't usually resort to violence as swiftly as the Hollywood villains were wont to do.

If "Loan Shark" was a faithful depiction of organized crime's small-loan operations, then that film scooped the newspapers by nearly a decade. Outside the waterfront districts of New York, there was no journalistic coverage of mob loan-sharking in the big cities throughout the 1950s.

The *Chicago Tribune* ran no stories at all. In hindsight we have reason to believe that syndicate-affiliated loan operations were beginning to form in Chicago during that silent decade, but awareness of their existence burst on the scene only in 1961. In April of that year the *Tribune* began to publish a series of sensational stories about "juice men" who squeezed as much as 20% a week in tribute from their victims and who were implicated in a string of bombings, assaults, and executions. All through the 1960s there was a frenzy of articles about juice lending in Chicago, and that coverage shifted attention away from the vest-pocket operations that continued to flourish in offices and factories. It was in the 1960s that the modern image of what a loan shark is was cemented in the public consciousness. Eventually the authorities could even forget that any other kind of loan shark had once existed or still operated. In its 1970 report on juice racketeering, the Illinois Crime Investigating Commission repeated a canard that circulated at this time about how the colloquialism "loan shark" had been invented. According to the report, "The word 'Shylock' was unintentionally slurred by guttural, illiterate hoodlums. The word came out as 'shark,' thus giving rise to the additional usage of the term 'loan shark.'"[68] This etymology is part of the apocrypha of loan-sharking. It is pure confabulation and betrays a gaping ignorance about the history of high-interest lending.

The pioneer of Chicago's juice racket was reputed to be Sam DeStefano. He wasn't a made-man himself but paid tribute to the city's mob bosses and received protection from them. DeStefano was known as an eccentric and violent man. Dissatisfied with his new car, he decorated it inside and out with grapefruit and drove around town with big signs that said "This is a lemon." DeStefano often represented himself in court and might ask prospective jurors, "Have you ever seen an elephant?" On one occasion he brought a bullhorn into the courtroom and cursed the prosecutors during the proceedings; another time he tossed a roll of toilet paper in the air and likened the mess to a witness's testimony.[69] On the street DeStefano was a feared sadist who tortured men to death. When an associate, William "Action" Jackson, was suspected of cooperating with the authorities, he was lured to a mob hangout, hoisted on a meat hook in the cellar, tormented with an ice pick, cattle prod, and blow torch, beaten with a baseball bat, and finally shot. Another victim was chained to a scorching hot radiator, beaten unconscious, stabbed repeatedly, and then executed. Facing trial for murder in 1973, DeStefano himself was executed on orders from the highest level; he died of a shotgun blast in his own garage.[70]

The Chicago loan sharks had a reputation for being the most vicious in the country. It was said that "they use violence much sooner in the collection process and are more likely to brutalize customers than loan-shark organizations in other underworlds."[71] DeStefano's crews more closely approximated the Hollywood stereotype, but the typical mob loan shark organized his business in such a way as to minimize the resort to violence. In fact, one authority claimed, "most loan-shark transactions are amicably conducted with both parties being satisfied."[72] The client needed cash, which the loan shark provided without asking a lot of questions. The price was high but nobody else would lend the debtor money, so the exchange was mutually advantageous. The debtor was motivated to pay not only because his body was pledged as collateral but also because he wanted to preserve his only line of credit.[73] The creditor, in turn, wanted to avoid the expense of hiring a "nutcracker" to collect the debt. It might cost $100 to have someone break a deadbeat's leg, and with a broken leg it would be hard for the debtor to earn money and catch up on his payments. Imposing a less debilitating penalty usually made more sense. As one "juice man" explained, "a finger deliberately slit open with a razor blade never kept anybody from working, and serves as a constant reminder of next payday." But the best strategy, he insisted, was to select customers carefully and not load them with excessive debt; as he put it, "When business is good in a smoothly-run operation, muscle is seldom needed for collections." Another loan shark agreed: "I tried to run it as a business. I'm not looking to beat up somebody. I want to make money, and the idea is to keep it circulating." As the juice man saw it, "The overwhelming majority of my customers are all for me, the same as when I was in the liquor business during prohibition."[74]

Of course, we shouldn't take the loan shark's word on the matter. The Chicago papers were filled with stories in the 1960s of debtors who were harassed and beaten. One man who fell behind on his payments was suspended from a pipe in the basement of a tavern and savagely beaten. Another was hounded relentlessly, assaulted, and then advised to make his wife turn tricks to repay the debt. The man eventually took his own life.[75] But it is difficult to ascertain how representative such cases are. One of the few empirical studies of a mob-loan-shark operation paints a very different picture from the sensationalism of the newspapers. Based on FBI case files, the study reported that interviews with 115 customers of the loan business turned up only one debtor who had been threatened. None were beaten.[76] Perhaps the sharks in this particular city were unusually placid, but it wouldn't be surprising if the use of force was rare. It wouldn't take many examples to teach the lesson to debtors, and excessive use of force would only scare off business. The economics of violence in the loan-shark market ought to have diminished the resort to corporal or capital punishment.

One of the "Shy" operators quoted above, Joe Valachi, explained that the key to a cost-efficient business was lending to the right sort of people. He preferred fellow hoodlums and avoided businessmen because if the latter had to borrow from a loan shark it meant they were already in desperate straits. "It's the same with working people," he said. "Those are the ones you got to use force with, so I don't bother with them."[77] Valachi's observation highlights a crucial fact about mob loan-sharking: much of it wasn't payday lending, which is the subject of this study. A sizable portion of the business, impossible to specify with any precision, served populations very different from the working and middle classes seeking payday credit.

It was thought that the bulk of the loan capital funneled to the syndicate moneylenders came from the proceeds of illegal gambling, and tapped out gamblers were an important clientele for the mob loan sharks. The latter would hang around the craps games and betting parlors and advance cash at steep rates to losers hoping their luck would turn.[78] Criminals were another reliable source of demand. They needed investment capital to pay bribes to the cops or to post bail when caught. "Milwaukee Phil" Alderisio was a high-ranking mobster in the Chicago Outfit who bankrolled local burglary rings at the rate of 20% a month.[79] Another fraction of the loan fund was let out to small businesses that were starved for capital. These debtors had the advantage of possessing collateral. If the owner couldn't meet his debt payments, the business could be looted by the mob and then burned down for the insurance money. Another advantage of lending to businesses was that they could be used to launder cash or to perpetrate fraud. Over time it was said that the business world became the body of water in which the mob loan sharks preferred to feed. It was richer in opportunities and more cost effective to do business with, because, as banks well knew, the overhead for servicing a few large loans was less than for managing many tiny ones.[80]

As John Seidl notes, "criminal loan-sharking developed first as a small-loan business." The motley crew that Thomas Dewey prosecuted in the 1930s advanced small sums to working people; they were bootleg payday lenders. That brand of mob money lending also flourished after the Second World War and was depicted in the George Raft film mentioned above. But by the 1960s many observers claimed that this old-style loan-sharking was passing from the scene. According to the *Columbia Law Review*, while "the prime victims of the loan sharks were formerly selected from impoverished wage earners, the prey is now found in the middle classes." Larger loans to professionals and businessmen were both more lucrative and safer because they did not fall within the scope of the Uniform Small Loan Law and its criminal penalties. The usury statutes did not apply to business loans.[81] By the end of the decade one observer could claim that the $6-for-$5 factory operations of yesteryear were now "an anachronism bearing virtually no relation to current reality." Later still an FBI official in New York would insist that "organized crime in this region has grown from the traditional concept of giving small loans to poor slobs who are beaten up by the system and need a few hundred bucks to a corporate level of substantial loans to businessmen."[82] Like the personal finance companies and the banks, organized crime increasingly abandoned the payday-loan business as insufficiently profitable. They moved up the income scale to a more lucrative and less troublesome clientele.

In its earlier phases, however, mob operatives did work the factories and office buildings where there was a demand for payday credit. Most of the street-level sharks in the underworld franchises were not formal members of a crime family. They either worked for a lieutenant in the organization or paid a tax in exchange for the right to operate within the family's jurisdiction. Some claimed that the mob exercised a strict monopoly over money-lending concessions, but this seems unlikely.[83] While the numbers racket could only be operated profitably if such a monopoly was established, the same was not true in the domain of payday lending. Each factory might have just one loan-shark ring, but many such rings would be operating across the city and only a fraction were likely to be controlled by the mob. The business was fragmented and each network tiny.[84] Smaller enterprises were less likely to be detected by the authorities but also would have had difficulty growing larger for want of working capital. In her empirical investigation of one crime family, Annelise Anderson identified a dozen mob networks in one city but also several freelance rings. One consisted of two men who served a clientele of 300 and were unmolested by the local syndicate. That syndicate's only stipulation was that each customer should be served by no more than one loan shark to prevent conflicts over debt collection. According to economist Peter Reuter, a cohesive monopoly in this market could only be established if the police actively colluded with a mob organization.[85]

A fascinating account of one of these underworld payday-lending enterprises was published by *Burroughs Clearing House* in 1965. Although the author was not named, internal evidence suggests he was a Chicago juice man. This loan shark had agents in four different factories working on commission and five bookkeepers on salary who managed the accounts. His working capital came from a higher level in the Outfit and he was charged 1% a week for its use. In turn, the juice operator charged 10% a week to the factory workers for a $100 loan. This was not an installment product. As the shark explained, "I don't care when you pay back the principal. . . . Just keep up the interest payments every payday, that's all."[86]

This was one of the bigger networks. Many were single-man operations. Because the overhead was low, the rate of return on capital could be higher than in labor-intensive industries like the numbers racket. In contrast to the bookie, it was pointed out, "the loan-shark does not need a network of controllers, runners and bankers without which the successful policy operator could not operate. The bookmaker requires an office or a wire room and must be generally available at a fixed location with well paid sheet writers and the like on the payroll."[87] Not so the juice man. That's why some thought "loan sharks had the best jobs in organized crime. They needed no office or extensive, incriminating records, no regular employees or overhead, no special equipment or skills. A shark ran his affairs out of his wallet and memory." Invisible as he was, the underworld lender was "seldom bothered by lawmen." Thus "he had no need to bribe them."[88]

Seidl, a graduate student at Harvard in the 1960s, provided an inventory of the mob payday lenders he had uncovered in the course of his fieldwork. One operation served housewives in a waterfront neighborhood in Philadelphia. Another advanced cash at the rate of 20% a week to the staff of a large hospital in Boston. None of the borrowers would cooperate with the authorities in prosecuting the usurer because "they all considered him a friend who was doing them a service for which they were happy to pay the 20 percent." Three loan sharks worked a huge bookbindery in New York City, and a similar ring served the employees of three large newspapers in Chicago. But Seidl sometimes lumped in with these underworld loan operations other networks that were not mob-connected. For example, he cited the case of a clerk in the main post office in Chicago who had been lending money to his fellow employees for four years. The authorities classified him as a "friendly" shark who "discouraged large loans and never threatened borrowers if they defaulted."[89] He was one of the minnows of the black market in small loans who operated in waters not claimed by Sam DeStefano's juice crews.

To gauge the extent of mob loan-sharking, Seidl traveled across New England and made inquiries about illegal lending at police stations, bars, and factories. He found no evidence of underworld credit networks outside the big cities. There were bookies in the smaller towns but no loan sharks, not even where there were large concentrations of factory workers. It seemed that organized crime could establish itself only in the largest markets, where it was possible to escape detection by the authorities. And this observation helps to put in perspective the scope of the money-lending business of crime syndicates. They were said to be doing a billion dollars a year in trade during the 1960s, though the actual figure is anybody's guess.[90] But this business was largely restricted to urban markets, and only a fraction of it was payday lending. Over time this fraction seemed to decline as the mob sharks moved upstream and invested their money in business firms. Stories about old-style underworld rings operating in the factories and offices had disappeared by the end of the 1960s. That kind of lending may still have been in existence, but it had been eclipsed by more lucrative forms of loan-sharking. The bigger fish were now the prey.

One New York loan shark explained why he no longer worked the piers: "I wouldn't put out any money even at 15 per cent [a week] now because operating costs are so high. Half the guys who borrow are on dope and no matter what you do, they aren't going to pay you back because they end up on Rikers Island [in jail] or getting shot by the cops." Even a juice man couldn't squeeze blood from a turnip. His money was now invested with a brokerage firm, he said, "because even if it ain't sure, you don't have all those creeps and bums to work with."[91]

That judgment was harsh. Reuter thought the real reason there was a noticeable decline in loan-shark activity along the waterfront was just the opposite: "some traditional markets, such as small loans to longshoremen, have probably contracted as longshoremen have become fewer and wealthier." Higher wages reduced the demand for payday credit, and so the supply of loan capital had to shift elsewhere. More generally, Reuter argued, "the growing financial wealth of the population over the last three decades, the shift of population from the areas in which loan sharks were most native, and the development of an increasingly variegated set of financial institutions . . . all suggest the possibility that the overall market for loan sharks has declined."[92] Supply-side factors were also relevant. The major crime families were subjected to relentless harassment and prosecution by law enforcement over the years. Then, in the 1970s, many forms of gambling became legalized, depriving the mob of the capital that funded its loan-shark operations. By 1974, veteran crime reporter Bob Wiedrich of the *Chicago Tribune* could taunt the city's old, gray mob. "The tentacles of their criminal cartel," he declared, "have become arthritic."[93] Entrepreneurs like Sam DeStefano had passed from the scene, and new executive talent had not emerged out of the street crews. The Outfit was increasingly a pale shell of its former self. Its payday loan sharks, certainly, had gone into evolutionary decline. Like the salary buyers before them, they passed from the scene without fanfare.

Assessing Progressivism

Toward the end of the 1960s, a group of economists specializing in consumer credit began to push for a loosening of regulation in the small-loan market. They pointed out that the rules imposed on lenders in some states were so stringent that a sizable fraction of the working population was being excluded from the legal market in cash loans. As these economists saw it, "One of the unfortunate aspects of a small loan statute that has restrictive rate ceilings is that it cuts down the availability of loans in poorer areas."[94] High-risk groups could not be served if rates were capped too low. The fact "that consumer finance companies find it necessary to reject about half of all new applicants shows that a significant group of consumers cannot be served under present rate ceilings." To be sure, these scholars admitted, this was not always a bad thing since "some who are refused service in the legal market will postpone their use of credit, and this result may be socially desirable."[95] More debt does not automatically increase well-being in a population. But if the personal finance companies were prevented from doing business in the higher-risk pool, these economists warned, then "the alternative to these regulated lenders could be the brutality of loan sharks."[96]

The brutal loan sharks operated in the underworld. They were experts in extortion. But was it true that a restrictive small-loan law would call into existence the savage sharks? Did low ceilings breed mob lending?

It so happens that a regulatory experiment in Maine at this very time helps to answer this important question. In 1967 the state imposed a strict limit of 36 months on the length of time a borrower could be in debt to a licensed lending company. Renewing the loan partway through its term would not start the clock all over again. The idea was to force debtors to free themselves from the burden of interest payments by ending the practice of rollovers. As it turns out, the new restriction had a devastating impact on the licensed lenders. Many were forced to close their doors, and profits in the industry plummeted. More consumers were turned away by the companies that continued to operate, but the reaction of these would-be debtors was mixed. One in nine former customers felt they were worse off because they couldn't borrow now, but three times as many thought their situation had improved because they were "rid of the burden of the finance company." Having to make do without credit, they discovered, reduced the strain on household finances. But the really significant result of the experiment was that "no evidence of loan sharking was found" after the limit was imposed.[97] The mob did not suddenly fill the vacuum left by the retreat of the small-loan companies.

Underworld loan-sharking was a kind of historical accident. The mob had to be formed first, then provided with cash to lend, before it could enter the credit business. The prohibitions on alcohol and gambling were crucial preconditions without which the juice racket would not have existed. Those prohibitions built the ranks of organized crime and filled its coffers with funds to be invested in new enterprises. Once illegal gambling had been monopolized, loan-sharking was an obvious next step because gamblers formed a ready population eager for credit and willing to pay high rates of interest to get it.[98] The personal finance companies could never service that risk pool, even if their rate ceilings had not been lowered over time, because these businesses didn't have available to them sufficiently harsh methods of collection to extract payment from gamblers in arrears. The mob did. It specialized in extortion, but that expertise was only one element in the mixture out of which the loan-shark racket emerged. The juice crews had to lend first, before they could extort payment, and to be in a position to extend credit they needed both a loan fund and access to rationed borrowers. The numbers racket, while it lasted, provided both.

Mob loan-sharking overlapped during the middle decades of the twentieth century with other forms of loan-sharking that did not employ muscle to compel repayment. But mob loan-sharking was a more diffuse phenomenon than the vest-pocket operations. Mob loan sharks served a variety of populations, and much of the trade could not be classified as payday lending. Unlike the other bootleg vendors, the underworld usurers did not deal exclusively in small sums. Indeed, it appears that over time organized crime abandoned this market and sought out a richer clientele.

Because it had never been restricted in its dealings exclusively to the wage-earning class, there was no necessary reason that it would gravitate to this class just because the demand for payday credit was not being satisfied in the legal market. Where such demand exists loan sharks are likely to appear, but (as we have seen) there are many species of that predator. Most have not beaten delinquents or stuffed bodies into trunks. The loan sharks native to the troubled waters of cash-strapped wage-earners have never been violent in their extortion. It was the underworld interloper that gave all loan sharks this undeserved reputation.

A restrictive small-loan law, then, would not inevitably call into existence the savage sharks. Certainly Illinois' Loan Shark Law did not, for the juice men came on the scene only four decades after its enactment. That law, however, did fail to drive the loan sharks—savage or not—into extinction, as it was intended to do. The sharks survived and evolved and mutated but did not disappear. Why this happened should now be clear. Although the Uniform Small Loan Law relaxed the statutory prohibition on high-rate loans, it simultaneously imposed a prohibition by criminalizing all transactions above the new ceiling. If that ceiling had been higher, there would have been less demand for a loan-shark product, but 42% a year did not yield a sufficient return on smaller sums to make it feasible for the licensed lenders to satisfy this demand. Lowering the ceiling in later years only intensified the problem. As Thomas Schelling pointed out, prohibitions issue a sort of license to the black marketeer because they prevent those firms that want to remain within the bounds of the law from trying to satisfy the demand of risky populations. If those firms can't satisfy this demand, the bootleggers will, and the latter must charge a premium to cover the added expense of servicing a black market.

It is a basic rule of consumer credit that "the higher the rate ceiling, the more marginal the borrowers accepted, and the higher the necessity to provide for bad debts."[99] If the Uniform Small Loan Law had done what was politically infeasible and set the maximum rate at 48% or 60% a year, the licensed lenders could have accepted more applications and there would have been fewer loan sharks. But then more people would have considered the licensed lenders to be loan sharks themselves, and the less risky customers with whom they did business would have paid somewhat higher rates to cover the larger number of bad debts. Either way there would be tradeoffs.

These tradeoffs will concern us more fully in the chapters to come, when we confront the dilemmas of today's payday lending. But even while acknowledging the tradeoffs, it has to be recognized that the Uniform Small Loan Law benefited many more people than it may have harmed. It definitely benefited all those wage-earners who paid (or would have paid) high prices to the old loan sharks but who now did business with the licensed lenders. The legal maximum under the reform law was about one-sixth the rate charged by the salary lenders. While 42% a year sounds like a lot, it is much less than the 240% a year that was the going rate of the gray-market sharks. And this differential actually understates the extent of the savings, because the licensed lenders were permitted to calculate interest only on the unpaid balance of the loan. The effective rate of interest for their amortized product was one-tenth the rate of the interest-only cash advance in which the wage-assignment lenders ensnared their victims. The savings realized by the millions of customers of the personal finance companies were therefore enormous. And in addition to this financial benefit, we must also recognize the large but unquantifiable emotional relief that resulted when debtors could no longer be threatened with job loss through the filing of a wage assignment. Customers of the licensed companies didn't have to skulk about for a loan or live in fear that the debt would be revealed to their employers. No doubt the anxiety of juggling household finances to meet the monthly payment remained for many borrowers, but that anxiety was surely diminished for most compared to the bad old days. The legal small-loan industry was not, as its predecessor had been, an enterprise of extortion. Employers and employees both benefited from that transformation effected by the Uniform Small Loan Law.

The advocates of deregulation were willing to admit that the customers of the new industry brought into existence by this law did "appear to benefit" from the installment product it established, but they wondered "whether it is desirable for the state to deprive one group of consumers access to [legal] cash credit by rate ceilings while permitting more affluent consumers to obtain cash credit." As they saw it, "rate ceilings may allow some better credit risks to pay less in imperfectly competitive markets, but only at the expense of the higher risk borrowers who are excluded from the market."[100] This criticism is almost populist in siding with the worse off over the better off, but it is important to recognize that the beneficiaries of the Uniform Small Loan Law were "affluent" only in a relative way. They weren't some privileged elite but, rather, working people deemed sufficiently credit worthy to be lent money at the rate of 42% a year. If they were "gaining at the expense" of the higher-risk population that couldn't be served at this rate, these beneficiaries stood only one notch higher in the income scale. They had been freed from the burden of covering the higher risks, but the fact that some wage-earners were higher risks than them, due to low incomes and other factors, was not their fault. While the customers of the personal finance companies could not be classified as the least advantaged group in society, they certainly weren't the most advantaged group either. Enhancing their well-being ought to be an important priority of public policy, and the Uniform Small Loan Law achieved that aim. It reduced the burden imposed on many blue- and white-collar workers by the first loan sharks.

But some blue- and white-collar workers failed to gain from the new regulatory regime. The personal finance companies thought they weren't good risks and so refused to do business with them. The licensed lenders couldn't extend credit to these wage-earners and still earn a profit. Some who were rejected didn't borrow elsewhere and thus had to reduce their consumption. That wasn't necessarily a disastrous outcome, as some consumers in Maine discovered, because acquiring more possessions (especially on credit) does not always lead to greater happiness. Others sought out loan sharks, but if the loan sharks with whom they did business were like the vendors of yesteryear, their plight was not worsened but simply didn't improve. The salary buyers charged as much as the old salary lenders, and so did many of the vest-pocket sharks; they also used similar instruments of debt collection—the wage assignment and the garnishment decree—but not the baseball bat or the razor blade. These borrowers were left behind by the Uniform Small Loan Law, but they weren't positively harmed by it. Hence the better risks did not actually gain at their expense since the burdens of this class of debtors were no greater than before.

But there was another class of debtors that did do worse after the new law was enacted. Many who were driven into the clutches of the underworld lenders paid more and suffered worse than they would have if they had been able to patronize the salary lenders of the early twentieth century. This was not invariably the case, however. Many sources insisted that relations between mob lenders and their customers were often friendly. No one ever made that claim about the first loan sharks and their victims. The juice men, as we have seen, did not resort to violence quickly or frequently. And not all of them charged 20% a week, which is a very stiff price and four times the rate of the salary buyers. But many did.[101] A loan this expensive is bound to chain wage-earners to a treadmill of "vigorish," or interest-only payments, that renders the debtor a peon. To become the peon of a juice crew is the sorriest possible lot for somebody who has sought payday credit.

If the Uniform Small Loan Law inflicted losses on anyone, then, it was this class of mob peons. How large this class was is impossible to establish.[102] But it is doubtful that it was as large as the advocates of deregulation imagined. In 1972, when the National Commission on Consumer Finance issued its report, mob payday credit was already dwindling. The loan sharks of the underworld were seeking a richer class of peons with collateral to exploit. They were no more interested in doing business with the high-risk but low-income population than were the banks or the personal finance companies. Thus the savage shark was already passing from the scene at the very moment when its threat was being appealed to as a justification for undoing the regime of the Uniform Small Loan Law. The dying breed was depicted as an ever-present danger. Its historical contingency was not recognized.

Let me conclude this chapter by summarizing the balance sheet of progressive reform: many consumers gained, some did not, and a few actually lost. But those who lost were worse off to begin with, so their losses should count for more. Still, the gainers were not a privileged group, so their gains can't be discounted very much. We are confronted, then, with a dilemma, and that dilemma did not disappear with the passing of the Uniform Small Loan Law. That piece of legislation was on the verge of being cast aside in many states as we approach the 1980s, and its passing would make possible the return of the loan sharks by the end of the twentieth century. But those new loan sharks, the payday lenders, will confront us with a comparable sort of dilemma. We will have to weigh gains and losses in the small-loan market today and decide whether it is better to benefit many if that benefit comes at the expense of the few who are the least advantaged group.

4   The Migration of the Sharks

I tell my people that we are in the collections business, not the payday advance business. If you don't look at it that way, you won't stay in business for very long. —**Bob Srygley, $howmethemoney Check Cashers, 2005**[1]

Loan-shark operations are the sweatshops of the lending industry. Loan sharks sweat their customers, chaining them to their debts and exerting pressure in various ways to keep up the interest payments. Like the garment sweatshop, the loan-shark business is an enterprise of exploitation in which resources are extracted from dependent and often desperate populations. In both trades, the entrepreneurs seem to gain at the expense of working people who lack good options.

The vernacularisms "loan shark" and "sweatshop" came into currency at the same time, at the end of the nineteenth century. Both forms of exploitation labeled by these epithets were attacked by progressive coalitions whose proponents did not believe the free market would automatically correct the abuses that flourished in the absence of state regulation. Unlike the loan-shark victims, however, sweated workers in the garment factories participated actively in the struggle to improve their lot. They formed unions, bargained collectively for better wages, and actively lobbied government for oversight and protections. Progress was slow, and real success in this fight was achieved only during the New Deal, when unions were strengthened and a national minimum wage was established. But by the middle of the twentieth century sweatshops in the garment industry had been driven to the margins. Naked exploitation in the needle trade, it seemed, had become a thing of the past.

Then the sweatshops returned. They became visible in the United States in the 1980s and created a scandal in the 1990s. Thousands still exist today. They reappeared after international trade barriers were reduced, intensifying competition within the industry. It now became profitable for American companies to shift operations abroad and to contract with low-wage shops in developing countries. This competition placed tremendous pressure on domestic contractors to cut labor costs and to evade workplace regulations. An influx of foreign workers provided a ready supply of cheap labor for the sweatshops that made it difficult for the garment unions to organize. Those unions, in turn, had since the 1950s been weakened by capital flight and a less hospitable regulatory climate. Sweatshops proliferated, but the governmental agencies responsible for oversight lacked the resources—and sometimes the will—to detect and sanction violations. Since there was usually no penalty for breaking the rules, competition set off a race to the bottom. To survive in this cutthroat market the sewing shops had to sweat their employees.[2]

This isn't the dynamic out of which a new wave of loan-sharking emerged, however. The loan sharks did indeed return to the market near the end of the twentieth century, at the same moment the sweatshops reappeared, but the resurgence of high-interest lending in the United States was not a byproduct of globalization. It can't be blamed on capital flight, illegal immigration, the decline of unions, or lax oversight. It wasn't the fault of Ronald Reagan. Intensified competition did have something to do with the reemergence of the loan sharks, but not in the direct way that impelled garment contractors to cut corners and exploit their labor force. It wasn't the existing class of licensed lenders that became loan sharks; these businesses did not turn to high-rate lending in order to survive in a more competitive environment. The environment in which they operated was certainly more competitive in the 1980s, as deregulation in the banking sector remade the landscape of the financial industry. But in response to that pressure, the personal finance companies did not regress to their origins and reintroduce a loan-shark product. Instead, they accelerated their decades-long trek up the income ladder and away from the working-class populations that have always been the breeding ground of loan sharks. The finance companies and the banks left these populations behind, and in doing so they opened up the space within which a new breed of loan shark could evolve.

Those new sharks—today's payday lenders—were the accidental invention of what has come to be known as the "fringe banking" industry. It was the check-cashing outlets that devised this product in its modern form. They did so in response to the heightened demand of working people for payday credit—a demand heightened by transformations occurring in American society. We will chart the forces of supply and demand that called into existence this financial product, and then we will see how the new industry evolved. Today's payday advance is a variation of the salary loan that flourished a century ago, but it taps into a wage-earner's income stream in a different place and employs a different instrument to secure the debt. These differences are important, because they permit the payday lenders to antagonize fewer groups as they go about their business. In fact the payday lenders of today are able to operate in symbiosis with banks, which once constituted a staunch opponent of the quick-cash firms.

The differences between salary and payday lending are real but subtle; the similarities are gross and palpable. Many of the abuses perpetrated by the first loan sharks recurred at the end of the twentieth century as payday lending spread across the country. Above all, the new product produced the same debt trap that is the defining trait of the loan-shark business. Debts that were supposed to be short-term stretched on and on and grew in size because the borrowers were unable to pay down the principal. A new generation of urban peons began to form in the states that permitted this kind of lending, though the composition of that class was not identical to the salary debtors of a century ago. American society has changed quite a bit since then, and loan-sharking now has a new face. Its agents are corporate, but the debtors are no longer primarily married white men. Indeed, the customer profile today is almost exactly the opposite.

The Infrastructure of Liquidity

The year is 1983. You are a wage-earner in a clerical position, and your annual household income matches the median for this occupational category, $18,000. That's less than the median family income for the country as a whole, but nobody would say you are poor. Now let's suppose you need $100 right away to cover an emergency expense.[3] Where could you get the money and what would it cost? Of course, if you had savings you wouldn't need to borrow from others. In 1983, 59% of the people in your income range had savings accounts; the median balance was $840.[4] But let's say you belong to the minority and you lack liquid assets. Now where can you turn?

Chances are you have a checking account at a depository institution because three-quarters of the people in your income range do. But your bank won't loan you such a small sum, and you definitely couldn't get the money within thirty minutes of making the request. As a rule, banks at this time don't make loans under $1,000, and their customers have to have good credit and collateral or cosigners.[5] You might have better luck at a credit union, if you belonged to one—but most people don't. Even if you did, the credit union would ask questions, check your credit record, and make you wait to get the money. In states with a usury cap, it would be impossible for these types of lenders to earn any profit on such a small loan. That was especially true in the early 1980s, when the inflation rate was high.

The quickest way to get credit in small sums, then or now, would be to use a credit card. The interest charge would run you about 20% a year on the unpaid balance. But only one in four households in your income range have a bank card at this time, and chances are you don't, because your credit record seems weak. In just a few years, banks will discover the subprime population to which you belong and begin to distribute credit liberally, but at this time the bank card lenders are more cautious. They haven't yet figured out that "troubled debtors have two attractive characteristics, despite their financial precariousness: they do not pay off their debts very quickly, so the interest keeps running up, and they do not argue about high interest rates."[6]

The next place to which you might turn is a personal finance company. After all, that industry was established in the first place to make small loans to working people. But by the 1980s, the licensed lenders have gotten out of the small-loan business. As an executive at General Finance Corporation explained, "We just can't afford to service the low end of the income scale like we used to. The small-ticket items are a thing of the past. They're more expensive to get onto our books, and they're more bankruptcy-prone." Instead, the finance companies have expanded into the home-equity market. They lent larger sums to homeowners on the security of a second mortgage. Many ads in the newspapers said the minimum amount you could borrow was $1,500. It was evident that the licensed lenders no longer had the sense of vocation and public service with which the industry had been endowed in the early decades of the twentieth century. This transformation is symbolized by the retirement of "Friendly Bob Adams," the mascot of General Finance. He had been a fixture of Chicago radio for decades, helping ordinary people out of financial jams. But now the company was trying to project a new image. The executive explained, "We're trying to broaden our segment of the market, looking for people in their 30s and 40s with a substantial job and good income."[7]

So you won't be able to get fast cash from the finance company. But you could from a pawnshop, provided you have a valuable possession to hock. Pawnshops are the original fast-cash business, but the industry went into decline after the rise of licensed lending. That decline began to be reversed in the 1970s, as the finance companies retreated from the small-loan trade. By the 1980s there were more pawnshop lenders than before, especially in the South. But a stigma was still attached to the business, and many people in search of cash tried to avoid this option if they could. The rates were also high—as much as 20% a month—and the sums advanced tended to be small. A $100 loan would have been large for a pawnshop in 1983 and could only be secured with a possession at least twice as valuable. If you didn't keep up the interest payments on the debt, your possession would be sold by the pawnshop.[8]

Another alternative, of course, would be to borrow from family or friends. Lots of people do, and micro-level surveys of consumer behavior confirm that "informal networks play an important role among households in need of income smoothing due to financial shocks."[9] This is especially true in lower-income populations. Studies of distressed neighborhoods in Chicago during the 1990s revealed that three times as many households sought assistance from friends or family as from banks and other lenders in the formal sector.[10] The advantage of this type of credit is that it is usually interest-free. The disadvantage is that the sums advanced tend to be smaller in size and often less than the borrowers desire. What is more, these types of loans place debtors in relations of dependence on people whom they must frequently encounter. Friends and family are likely to ask a lot of questions about what the money is for, and they are well positioned to monitor the debtor's consumption and to nag or criticize. As a result, many cash-strapped people will avoid tapping their informal networks if they possibly can, even if this requires paying a hefty interest charge. One reason why many people in a financial bind turned to payday loans after they came on the scene was that this product allowed them to avoid asking their relations for help. The convenience was worth a lot to them.

If all else failed, you could seek out a vest-pocket lender or mob loan shark for the money. But these high-rate creditors who operated in the informal sector seem to have been on the decline since the 1960s (see Chapter 3). There weren't as many of them as before, hence the odds of encountering one were lower. Much depended on where you lived or worked. There seemed to be plenty in the poorer neighborhoods, and they would continue to operate even after the rise of payday lending. They charged up to 30% a month.[11] But by the 1980s it was no longer the case that you could find a black-market creditor in every factory or office building in the big cities. The mob-connected loan sharks who had survived the onslaught of prosecution now dealt in larger sums and tended to serve a business clientele.

Those were your credit options in most states in 1983. But in the South another class of lenders operated in the formal sector—old-fashioned loan-shark firms that had managed to survive into the modern era and even to win legal recognition for their trade. In Georgia the salary buyers had become licensed "industrial" lenders in the 1950s, pushing a high-rate installment product that was secured with household possessions. The fee structure was complicated, and each loan was encumbered with several useless insurance policies that inflated the price. A $100 cash advance paid back over four months might cost you $168, which works out to be an annual percentage rate (APR) of 121%.[12] Nearly a thousand industrial lenders operated across the state of Georgia in the 1980s, and they would fight hard to drive out the payday lenders when these entered the cash-loan market at the end of the century.

Texas had long been known as "a paradise of loan sharks," so in the early 1960s the legislature decided the best way to deal with the problem was to license the "high-raters." Known as the "small small loan" industry, these vendors made unsecured installment loans up to a $100. You could borrow $30 for one month and pay back $36, which meant the APR was 240%. The $100 cash advance was usually paid back over six months in installments of $22.33. The APR was 109%. Two-thirds of the loans were renewed before the debt was paid off, which meant that the low-income and minority wage-earners to whom these businesses catered were often continuously in debt.[13] The small-small-loan sharks were still in operation at the start of the 1990s when the postdated-check lenders first made their appearance. In the 1970s one of these high-rate firms did business in Flour Bluff as Pay Day Loans.[14]

But financial products like these had not been openly available in Illinois for nearly fifty years. In 1981 the state government repealed the usury ceiling on consumer loans, but high-rate products did not suddenly flood the market. If you needed a cash advance right away, your options were limited, especially if your income was modest and your credit record blemished. You might have to tighten your belt and do without instead of assuming debt. That isn't necessarily a bad thing, and people adopt this strategy all the time when resources are tight. A survey of low-income residents in a Chicago neighborhood revealed that nearly half reduced their consumption in hard times even as they searched for sources of credit.[15] But some expenditures—like fixing a car on which you rely to get to work—pay large dividends and cannot be forborne without incurring heavy costs. Access to credit, even if it is expensive, can increase the efficiency of household finances and enhance well-being over the long run. If credit is unavailable, consumption will be stunted. When the credit constraint is widespread, economic growth will be hampered.

Clearly the demand for quick credit was not fully satisfied in the early 1980s. But the same was true for earlier periods. Demand had always exceeded supply for this service during the twentieth century.[16] The crucial issue is whether that demand had grown in the 1980s. Was there now a greater need for short-term loans than in the past?

There is indeed reason to think that demand was on the rise at the end of the twentieth century. One source of that new demand was the steady erosion in the personal saving rate that began in the middle of the 1980s. After all, people only need quick cash if they lack liquid savings. The trend in the rate of personal saving is well documented: it had been fairly constant for decades in the United States but then began to fall after the economy emerged from recession at the start of the 1980s. The decline was modest at first but then accelerated rapidly during the 1990s. By 2005, according to some calculations, the saving rate had become negative. The last time this had happened was during the Great Depression.[17]

Gross measures such as this, however, are not conclusive. Since the bulk of saving in society is done by the most affluent groups, a decline recorded in the National Income and Product Accounts might reflect changes occurring within the elite that would have no bearing on the demand for small loans. Better evidence can be found in the triennial Survey of Consumer Finances. Over the course of the 1980s, the proportion of families with savings and money-market accounts fell 11%. The amount of cash held in those accounts declined by half when adjusted for inflation. Some of this reduction was due to a shift in savings to the new 401k retirement plans, but funds held in those types of accounts are not as liquid and early withdrawals incur penalties. It seems that family finances were becoming less liquid during this decade. At the same time debts were increasing. The proportion of families with any debt rose, as did the median amount they owed. Credit card debt increased 50% when adjusted for inflation and credit card usage grew among the lower-income strata. The percentage of families behind on their loan payments bumped up, and the debt–income ratio rose across all households. The most burdened third of families experienced the greatest jump in the ratio of their income devoted to nonmortgage debt payments. The increase was even greater among the third of households with the fewest assets. Bankruptcy filings doubled over the course of the decade.[18]

These trends make the 1980s sound like a grim decade. In fact the economy grew significantly after emerging from recession, employment rose, and inflation and interest rates declined. The median net worth of households grew 10% and median financial assets of all types doubled. But the gains made in this decade were not evenly distributed across the population. Income inequality between households ticked up noticeably during the 1980s, with the most affluent decile surging ahead of the rest. Volatility in the labor market also increased, making the flow of the income stream less predictable for many wage-earners. To sustain their level of consumption, households without a cushion of savings increased their debt load, mortgaging future income. Since debt payments are really enforced saving, many households seem to have redistributed their savings portfolio during this decade from liquid assets held in reserve to debt repayment. The advantage of this strategy is that it allows these families to consume more now by shifting saving to the future, though of course they must pay a charge for this service in the form of interest. Financial innovation, including increased access to bank card credit and subprime lending, made this strategy feasible, and one common explanation for the fall in the personal saving rate is the financial revolution set off by deregulation in the banking industry. New products allowed households to tap more easily into formerly illiquid assets. This meant that it was no longer so necessary to horde cash to weather financial shocks. One could borrow instead and devote income to debt repayment, which is just saving after the fact and by other means.[19]

With cash savings on the decline and a greater share of household income committed to debt repayment, demand for short-term credit ought to increase. The expansion of bank card credit could meet some of this demand since cardholders can charge unanticipated expenditures or get a cash advance and repay the debt later. But for those who had reached their credit limit and lacked savings (a growing share of the population), the demand for quick cash would remain. The restricted supply of small loans at the start of the 1980s was a bottleneck in the liquidity infrastructure being constructed by financial deregulation.

Most of the trends that increased the demand for fast cash in the 1980s continued through the end of the century and beyond. The proportion of households that reported saving for a rainy day declined, as did the share of financial assets held in liquid accounts. Credit card usage grew. In 1970 only 2% of households in the lowest income quartile had bank cards; by 1998 that figure had multiplied fourteen times. The percentage of households carrying monthly balances on their cards doubled over this period. Between 1989 and 2004 a number of measures of financial stress increased, including the ratio of debt payments to family income, the percentage of borrowers with a debt–income ratio greater than 40%, and the share of households with payments past due at least 60 days. The bankruptcy rate also continued to rise. This isn't surprising, for "a growing consumer debt burden means a shrinking buffer against financial disaster."[20]

The shrinking buffer of liquid savings, then, was one factor that intensified the demand for short-term credit as we entered the 1980s. The other main factor was the increase in bank fees that began at this time. That trend was also a product of deregulation in the banking sector. What banks were doing—and not doing—decisively shaped the environment within which payday lending emerged. The return of the loan sharks at the end of the twentieth century was to a considerable extent an unintended consequence of the effort to loosen the net of regulation that had constrained competition within the banking industry since the New Deal.

Looking back, it is striking how tightly bound depository institutions had been before 1980. The interest rate they could pay savers was capped, they were not permitted to pay interest on checking accounts, savings-and-loans were allowed to pay higher rates than banks, states were permitted to impose ceilings on the interest rates that could be charged for credit, there were strict rules about where banks could build branches, and so forth. But this regulatory scheme came apart in the 1970s. Low ceilings in states like Illinois caused the credit market to dry up when inflation increased at the beginning and the end of the decade. Mortgages were capped at 8% in the state, and nobody could make money vending the product when inflation was high. As a result, mortgage funds flowed to states with higher ceilings, and people who wanted to buy homes in Illinois couldn't get loans or had to make very large down payments. The same problem plagued the finance companies. The state legislature temporarily lifted the usury cap in 1974. Three years later, it established a floating rate, but the drought in credit returned in 1979 when inflation spiked sharply. To attract funds, savings-and-loans had to pay more than 12% a year on certificates of deposit, but they were only permitted to charge an interest rate of 11% on mortgage money. The phenomenon was known as "disintermediation," and it forced three-quarters of the state's thrifts to suspend mortgage lending.[21]

To cope with the crisis, the state government temporarily set aside the usury cap and allowed the market to set interest rates. Two years later, in 1981, the usury statute was repealed permanently. Roughly one-quarter of the states also deregulated interest rates within their borders at this time. Mainstream economists applauded the reform. Numerous studies published over the previous decade and a half showed that usury limits rationed credit and dampened economic growth.[22] During the debate over the repeal act, one state senator warned, "We're going to see . . . 50-per-cent interest rates if this passes." But an advocate of the measure replied, "Higher rates would help consumers by discouraging them from borrowing beyond their means."[23]

The incentive for states to deregulate interest rates had been initiated a few years earlier by a famous decision of the U.S. Supreme Court, *Marquette National Bank of Minneapolis v. First Omaha Service Corp.* Marquette, as the decision became known, interpreted the National Bank Act of 1864 to mean that interstate banks could export interest rates on their credit cards and loan products from the state in which they were chartered.[24] The ruling created an incentive for bank holding companies to relocate their headquarters to states that did not cap rates. South Dakota seized the opportunity and repealed its statute, as did several other states. The big credit card lenders shifted their operations to these deregulated jurisdictions and then exported the high rates that were permissible there all across the country. The spigot of bank card liquidity was opened wide.

The eclipse of price restrictions on consumer lending, however, did not immediately call into existence a new high-rate, short-term product. More than fifteen years would pass after the repeal of the usury statute in Illinois before payday lending would appear in the state. A more important change was the end of price controls imposed on savings and checking accounts. Regulation Q, as these price controls were known, was phased out in the early 1980s. Savers could now earn the market rate for their funds, but in this new competitive environment customers with small balances in their accounts would have to be charged fees to cover the cost of servicing them.

Regulation Q had prevented price discrimination in banking services. As a result, the big accounts subsidized the small ones. Price deregulation resulted in the tiering of customers and a new fee structure that more accurately assessed the costs borne by banks. Customers with small balances would now have to pay fees to maintain their accounts at depository institutions.[25]

As the *Chicago Tribune* reported, "Some bank customers have been shocked to find, for example, that their bank now charges a monthly fee for accounts with balances of less than $300 or $400 instead of paying interest. Numerous complaints have also centered on the hefty minimum account balances and charges for checking, overdraft and other services now being levied by some banks." A future governor of the state charged that "Illinois is rapidly becoming a state where there is Rolls-Royce banking for the rich and used-car banking for the rest of us." He claimed bank service charges had doubled in the four years since Regulation Q had been phased out. But the bankers replied that they were only responding to market forces: "The basic problem is that folks got many of these services free for so long that it's hard for them to focus on the fact that we've had to adjust the focus and prices to compensate for paying higher interest rates."[26]

The rise in fees drove some people with modest incomes from the depository institutions and into the fringe banking sector. But a checking account is such a valuable service for most consumers that many with low balances are willing to pay a monthly fee. They must manage their money carefully, however, because the cost of bouncing checks is high. Both the bank and the merchant will charge a fee if there are insufficient funds in the account. Those fees also increased during the 1980s. Some banks charged as much as $30 for every bounced check. Overdraft protection was also expensive. This service wasn't construed as a loan and there was no requirement to state the charge as an annual percentage rate, but if the calculation is made, the result is often a triple- or quadruple-digit rate of interest.[27]

Banks were also earning more fee income through their credit card operations. There were substantial penalties for late payment. Later, universal default clauses were introduced permitting the banks to raise the interest rate on balances due when other creditors reported missed payments. These penalties and fees could seriously disrupt household finances for those with modest incomes, and this financial stress increased the demand for short-term credit. If a bill was due but your checking balance was low, you needed a quick infusion of cash to tide you over until payday. Even if the charge for that bridge loan was steep, it could be a better alternative than bouncing checks or triggering a rate increase on your credit card.[28] But in 1983 this type of mini-bridge loan would have been difficult to secure, at least in most states outside the South. A credit card would have been your best bet—if you had one and it wasn't already maxed out.

There is reason to think, then, that the demand for small loans was on the rise in the 1980s. A growing share of households had come to adopt a sort of "just-in-time" strategy of financial management. These households weren't building up an inventory of easily accessible savings on which to draw in hard times but were relying instead on the new liquidity of a deregulated financial industry to smooth consumption and enforce saving through debt repayment. This strategy allowed them to finance more consumption from a given level of income, which wasn't growing in the bottom half of the distribution. But this game also imposed harsh penalties for miscalculation or bad luck. To avoid those penalties it would be helpful if households with no savings could tap into the financial pipeline for short bursts of liquidity. The demand was there—and, as it turns out, so was the infrastructure of supply needed to meet it.

Tapping the Income Stream

The payday loan in all its variations is defined by one essential feature: it taps the wage-earner's income stream in a more direct way than other forms of credit. Payday lenders, old and new, loan money in such a way that they get to skip to the head of the line of creditors when the debtor is sure to have cash. To reduce their risk, which is high, they insist on being paid first.[29] A mortgage payment, by contrast, is due on the first of the month, whether that is the debtor's payday or not. Credit card debt revolves, but its monthly cycle doesn't necessarily end on payday.

There are two obvious places for payday lenders to tap the debtor's income stream. One is at its source, when wages are paid by the employer. This is where the first- and second-generation loan sharks hunted. Salary lenders and salary buyers secured their cash advances with wage assignments, which entitled them to take their cut from the pay packet before it was handed over to the employee. Garnishment decrees accomplished the same result. Many old-style loan sharks also had connections in the payroll office or stood by the cashier's window as employees lined up for their pay. Mob loan sharks on the piers of New York collected the metal chits entitling the longshoremen to wages but then deducted the weekly installment when they cashed the paychecks.[30] The basic idea was to stand between employer and employee, or to threaten to do so, in order to ensure that the debtor didn't spend the money that was owed as interest.

There were two drawbacks to this strategy of diversion, however. The first was that it annoyed employers, who resented being collection agents for loan sharks. Processing wage assignments complicated the task of paying employees and tended to demoralize the workforce. As a result, employers developed a deep antipathy to loan sharks and were willing to join forces with other groups seeking to stamp out predatory lending. The other drawback of trying to tap the income stream at its source was that it could get the debtor fired. Many employers adopted a policy of dismissing employees against whom a wage assignment had been filed. This policy could be exploited by the loan shark to extort repayment, but following through with the threat and actually presenting the wage assignment might very well cut off the income stream of the debtor at its source. Then the loan shark wouldn't be paid, and additional resources would have to be expended to dun the victim or to harass friends and family. Because the first loan sharks had no other place to hunt than at the headwaters of the income stream, they drew a lot of attention to themselves and eventually provoked a broad coalition to mobilize against them.

There was no other place to tap the income stream of wage-earners early in the twentieth century because cash in a worker's pocket rapidly drained away. If you didn't take your cut immediately, the money would be spent. But over the course of time the topography of the wage-earner's income stream changed. Increasingly the money flowed into a reservoir before being released to creditors. That reservoir was a checking account. Hardly anyone in the bottom half of the income distribution had such an account at the start of the twentieth century, but by the 1980s roughly three-quarters of all households did.[31] Though these accounts had become more expensive after deregulation of the banking sector, they remained a convenient and secure place to pool cash before it was spent. If payday lenders could tap the income stream here, they would avoid annoying employers or costing employees their jobs. It might seem there was some risk of annoying banks, which had never liked loan sharks. But (as we shall see) this turned out not to be the case, because the banks could earn fees if household finances were disrupted by other creditors. What is more, banks stood at the very front of the line when it came to being paid, and so they didn't have to fear that loan sharks would cut in front of them. Whereas banks and payday lenders were enemies a century ago, today they have worked out a relationship of competitive symbiosis. Each complains about the high prices the other charges, but each is also positioned to profit from the predations of its rival.

The tool that can be used to tap this reservoir of cash is the postdated check. It can secure a loan, and it is certainly less cumbersome to process than a chattel mortgage, which requires the lender to go to court first and to have in reserve an expensive apparatus for repossession. Better than an IOU or a signature on a contract, the postdated check gives the creditor legal access to the debtor's financial reservoir on a specified date. If that date is payday, the likelihood that there will be sufficient funds in the account is maximized and the lender will stand just behind the bank at the head of the line for repayment. What is more, the postdated check gives the creditor leverage in two different ways. First, it is a legal instrument the fraudulent misuse of which can incur harsh penalties. It is a crime to write a bad check. Second, if the lender presents the check on the appointed day and it bounces, the bank will charge a fee to the account and collect its money as soon as there are sufficient funds. Failure to pay the lender, in other words, will be doubly expensive. The bank is a kind of respectable collection agency that is sure to be paid because it manages the reservoir into which the income stream flows. The swift and certain penalties it enforces give the check-lender leverage to collect its debts. The postdated check is like a hostage that the payday creditor takes. To compel repayment, the lender need only remind the debtor how painful it will be if the hostage is turned over to the bank instead of being ransomed on payday.

There is a kind of genius in this modern version of the payday loan. It is a more efficient way to tap into the income stream. And entrepreneurs from an early date recognized the possibility. The postdated-check loan isn't actually an invention of the 1980s or 1990s, as is often claimed. Ever since the 1930s, lenders have been experimenting with this financial product. But all of these earlier experiments were nipped in the bud or withered away. Only in the 1980s did the breakthrough occur. It is an important question to ask why.

There were two versions of the check loan scheme before the 1980s. One version was patently fraudulent. The lender would require the borrower to write a postdated check for an account that did not exist at a local bank. The borrower might also be asked to sign an affidavit swearing that the checking account did exist and had funds in it. If the client failed to repay the loan, the fraudsters would threaten to go to the authorities with the bad check and press charges. The attorney general of New York uncovered a loan-shark ring employing this method of extortion in 1940. The typical loan of $100 was advanced at the rate of 1% a day. The four men charged in the scheme were said to be doing $100,000 in business each week.[32]

That tactic was still being employed by loan sharks in the South during the 1960s.[33] But it had obvious limitations as a business model because the lender was knowingly soliciting false statements from debtors. The other version of the check-loan product was not fraudulent but it remained illegal. Certain businesses as a sideline would cash postdated checks at a discount, giving less to the borrower than the face amount of the check but holding it until a later date. These bank drafts were written on valid accounts but in which there were currently insufficient funds. The *Tucson Daily Citizen* ran a short article in 1953 about a dry-cleaning business that was making "between paydays" cash advances to airmen at the local military base. If you wanted $20 in cash now, you could write a check for $28 and postdate it to payday. No fraud was perpetrated, but the transaction was construed as a loan and this entrepreneur didn't have the necessary license to extend credit. Even if he did, the rate being charged (40% for two weeks, or 1,040% a year) was grossly usurious and thus illegal (although reportedly less than other airmen were charging for small loans on base).[34]

This sort of business had been going on since the Great Depression. Leon Henderson, the energetic director of the remedial loans department at the Russell Sage Foundation, reported in 1930 that some newfangled loan sharks were "discounting post-dated checks, the rate being from 50 to 75 cents per $100 per day." The main purveyor of this new loan product in the 1930s was a business that performed some of the functions of a bank but did not accept deposits: the commercial check casher. Invented first in Chicago and termed "currency exchanges," these storefront operations set up shop during the great wave of bank failures at the start of the decade. With many banks closed, working people were having great difficulty cashing their paychecks. The currency exchanges stepped into the breach. They charged a hefty fee for the service but gave instant access to the cash. They were also open at more convenient hours and in more convenient locations than banks. Within a few years, more than a hundred currency exchanges were operating in the city but without any oversight. In 1943 a bill was passed placing the industry under state supervision.[35]

Check cashers were soon established in New York City, too, and it was there that some were reported to be holding postdated checks for a fee. The practice violated the state's small-loan law and was one of the abuses that prompted the legislature to license the businesses a year after Illinois had done so. Two decades later, New York's Department of Banking insisted that, "under present conditions, it is fairly reasonable to assume that no check casher with a substantial volume would resort to illegal acts such as making loans."[36] No further trace of the practice by currency exchanges can be found before the 1980s. This experiment in using the postdated check as an instrument of security was snuffed out by state regulation.

But that isn't the only reason the product didn't catch on until late in the twentieth century. To be sure, usury statutes are a serious obstacle to the spread of high-rate loans, especially in states like New York that have a tradition of vigorous enforcement. The repeal of these statutes in many states during the 1980s, as well as the legalization of interest-rate exportation, cleared the way for high-rate lending by licensed businesses. But even where the statutes had not been repealed, licensed businesses started to vend a high-rate product during the 1980s (see below). In some states the rules about usury were rewritten *after* payday lending had taken root, not before. Regulatory barriers were not insurmountable.

A more important reason that the product did not spread earlier was the restricted scope of the check-cashing industry before the 1980s. The business existed in only a handful of cities until the 1970s; Chicago and New York were the hubs.[37] Check lending was prohibited in those places and there wasn't enough geographical dispersion to facilitate experimentation elsewhere. On top of that, the spread of checking accounts into the strata of the population most likely to make use of the check-loan product (the bottom half of the income pyramid) took time and didn't reach the saturation level until the last quarter of the twentieth century. In the early 1960s, for example, only 40% of households in the bottom two quintiles of the income distribution had a checking account at a bank.[38] If wage-earners searching for short-term credit didn't have a checking account, they could not get a check loan.

One last factor of importance concerns the technological infrastructure of the business. Before the spread of computer technology and communication networks, it would have been difficult to manage risk for this product with any precision. The ability to assess creditworthiness instantaneously did not exist. As a result, the default level for the product might have been unacceptably high. The computer and communication revolutions of the 1980s made possible the expansion of the liquidity infrastructure to which payday lending belongs.

The check-cashing stores began to spread out from the Chicago hub during the 1970s. In the 1980s the industry experienced explosive growth.[39]

These businesses benefited from the exodus of low-income households away from the depository institutions that was spurred by financial deregulation. Even though commercial check-cashing is expensive, it can be cheaper than running up fees in a bank account. It can also be more convenient. These fringe banks offer a range of services and products, are open late, and give immediate access to your money. You don't have to wait several days for a check to clear at the bank—the currency exchange provides instantaneous liquidity. For people who live from paycheck to paycheck, that is a valuable service.

Not everyone who frequents the currency exchange is "unbanked" or without a checking account. Many bank customers also make use of the check cashers because the greater convenience is worth the price to them. A survey of households in a low-income neighborhood in Chicago revealed that slightly more than half of those who patronized the currency exchanges also had a bank account. Compared to the unbanked, these consumers were more likely to be married, to own their own homes, to be older and better educated, and to have higher incomes.[40] They were the premium customers of the fringe banks, and some of them wanted a new service. They wanted to cash a postdated check drawn on their own account at the bank. There wasn't enough money in the account right now to cover the check, but payday was only a few days away. These customers were willing to pay a higher fee to get access now to money they had earned but that had not yet been deposited into their bank accounts. One entrepreneur described what happened: "For a while we said no we wouldn't do that, then we started trying it out, found there was a demand for cashing post-dated checks, and slowly gravitated into that, charging an extra 5% or so for the extra risk and service. People loved it."[41]

Thus was born a new financial product. The postdated-check loan was not invented by a single famous person. It seems to have been devised independently in several different places where supply recognized demand. Then others within the network of currency exchanges imitated their competitors. At first the product was just a sideline to the main business of the check casher. It wouldn't be until the early 1990s that stand-alone (or monoline) stores were established just to vend this type of cash advance.

The practice was no doubt occurring for some time before it made its way into the papers. The earliest trace to be found is an offhand reference to the product in a July 1986 article published in the *Minneapolis Star Tribune*. The story was about check-cashing outlets in the Twin Cities, and the reporter noted that the businesses were not all the same: "For example, at Cash Stop, 812 E. Lake, the windows are filled with signs trumpeting 'We cash post-dated checks' and 'No I.D. required.'"[42] Minnesota had a small-loan law at this time that capped interest rates well below what Cash Stop must have been charging, but the owner probably didn't consider the service a loan. In any case, currency exchanges were not regulated by the state until 1989.

The next traces of the product come two years later and are scattered across the country. On the West and East Coasts, military authorities complained in 1988 that check cashers were holding the postdated checks of armed forces personnel and discounting them substantially. The practice came to the attention of the Consumer Affairs Office at Fort Bragg in North Carolina when a soldier was arrested after his check bounced. Check cashers in the Seattle area were making similar loans around the military bases, which are the primordial hunting ground for every generation of loan sharks. On the West Coast the charge was $13 for a $100 loan, but some soldiers couldn't scrape enough together to redeem their checks. Instead, they borrowed from another check casher in order to pay the first. Some were running in circles to three or four of the businesses, which were clustered together. This was the ancient dance of the loan-shark victim.[43]

But the product could also be found in the heartland. The *Kansas City Star* reported in October 1988 that two dozen firms had sprouted up within recent months and were engaged in the trade. One man who owned three check-cashing stores in the city claimed to have come up with the idea a few years earlier, but others thought the concept had been imported from Chicago or California. Most of the state's regulators were unfamiliar with this kind of transaction. When the practice was described to him, one official said, "I've never heard of that." The county prosecutor, who had been filing bad-check charges on behalf of the businesses, was surprised to learn that the checks were postdated. The law didn't apply to that kind of transaction because the recipient knew there wasn't enough money in the account to cover the check. But a sign at one of the stores warned, "Writing a bad check is a criminal offense. We can and will prosecute."[44]

Many people were shocked to discover the interest rates these loans carried. The fees were stated in a different way, but when calculated as an annual percentage rate and disclosed in the contract the number was always triple-digit. Of course, if you paid the loan off right away the APR was meaningless, even deceptive. But some customers weren't redeeming their checks on the due date. Instead, they paid a new fee to keep the currency exchange from depositing the check. Each renewal was like a ransom payment. As the renewals accumulated, the APR became an increasingly accurate measure of the loan's cost. If customers couldn't pay the fee, they were directed to another outlet down the street where a new cash advance could be secured. Part of the proceeds from that loan could be used to pay the first one. In St. Louis there was a cluster of shops in the same neighborhood and the chain debtors would make the rounds. The lenders knew exactly what was going on.[45]

After that, there were news reports about the new product in Oregon, Colorado, and Virginia, and then in Wisconsin and Kansas. In some states the authorities clamped down on the businesses; in others they rewrote the rules to make these loans permissible. For the first five or six years the product didn't have a special name. The transaction was described but not labeled. But then, in 1991, these cash advances began to be referred to as "payday loans."[46] That terminology had been around since the 1930s, but until the last quarter of the twentieth century the "between payday loan" or the "payday advance" designated the smallest cash advances offered by the licensed personal finance companies. The advertisements for these products tried to entice customers into the office with appeals like "$10 for 10 days costs 10¢" or "$50 till payday for 70¢." The rates were based on the statutory maximum of 3% a month for small loans. If any loans this small were made on these terms the businesses would clearly lose money, but one suspects that the loan agents would try to talk anyone who inquired about these tiny single-payment loans into securing a larger installment product. Ads like these ran in markets all across the country until the end of the 1960s, when they disappeared. The finance companies probably gave up advertising "payday loans" as they moved upstream and into the home-equity market. Over the course of four decades, not a single newspaper article appears to have been written about this product, which isn't surprising because loans this cheap could never trap anyone in debt. After the licensed lenders discarded the terminology, it lay dormant until the check lenders latched onto the concept at the start of the 1990s. "Payday loan" better described their product anyway because the check loan, unlike the finance company loan, was timed to mature on the borrower's payday.

At the start of the 1990s, according to one estimate, there were fewer than 200 outlets nationwide offering this new deferred-deposit cash advance.[47] This figure may understate the number of check cashers making such loans at that time, but it is impossible to know for certain. The first stand-alone chain of payday lenders, Check Into Cash, was founded in Tennessee in 1993 by W. Allan Jones. He got his start in the credit-collection business and then recognized the potential of the new product. Over the next dozen years, his chain would spread to more than thirty states. In 2006 the 1,250 Check Into Cash stores did $1 billion in business.[48]

The growth of payday lending in the 1990s was explosive. By the turn of the century, there were roughly 12,000 stores making payday loans, and that number would double again in six years. In 2000, more than 40 million transactions were recorded, generating an estimated $1.4 billion in fees. Payday lending had become the most rapidly expanding segment of fringe banking by the end of the 1990s. Its popularity eventually took business away from the pawnbrokers, whose custom had also been expanding earlier in the decade. Many consumers thought borrowing on a postdated check was a more respectable and convenient way to get quick cash. By 2008, the payday-lending industry claimed to be extending $50 billion a year in short-term credit to 19 million households in the United States. Its fee income from 154 million transactions was $8.6 billion.[49]

If these estimates are accurate, one in six households in the country is now borrowing from the payday lenders.[50] This proportion equals or exceeds the scale of salary lending early in the twentieth century. The loan sharks have indeed returned, but the complex of forces that made possible the resurgence of high-rate lending now is not identical to the dynamic that gave birth to the industry during the Gilded Age. In the nineteenth century, a decisive factor that opened the space within which salary lending would take root was the bureaucratization of work and, in particular, its system of remuneration. Regular paydays and an apparatus to process the payroll efficiently for large concentrations of workers were structural prerequisites of lending on the security of a wage assignment. Once the income stream had been routinized and made predictable, the wage-assignment tool—which lay ready to hand— could be deployed by entrepreneurs specializing in liquidity to tap the flow of cash running from employer to employee. These entrepreneurs offered an advance in anticipation of the next payday, in exchange for a hefty fee. The opportunity they exploited to sweat borrowers was provided them by a prior bureaucratic revolution in the world of work.

The progressive reforms enacted early in the twentieth century were intended to clear the headwaters of the income stream of the loan-shark infestation made possible by this bureaucratic revolution. Those reforms did thin the shiver of sharks where they were enacted, but the hoped-for extinction of the species never occurred. Over time the flow of the income stream shifted, which opened up a new hunting ground for loan sharks further downstream. The crucial transformation that brought back high-rate lending on a large scale late in the twentieth century was the democratization of the checking account, that reservoir built by banks and into which the income stream of most wage-earners flows. As the number of these financial reservoirs multiplied in the bottom half of the income distribution, an opportunity presented itself to a new generation of entrepreneurs specializing in liquidity. Those reservoirs never filled very full, and the banks that maintained them assessed heavy penalties if the water level fell too low. Creditors who could supply sudden bursts of liquidity were well positioned to command a premium price for their service and to turn some of their chronically thirsty customers into addicts. That is exactly what the payday lenders did.

The return of the loan sharks, then, happened not because America regressed a century but because its banking system evolved and deepened and then had its leash unloosened. To a much greater extent than was true at the end of the nineteenth century, payday lending now is facilitated by what banks do and do not do. The depository institutions foster the habitat within which loan sharks feed. Without the checking accounts they police and the bank fees they charge—not to mention the pile of credit card debt they encourage—there wouldn't be a new way to loan shark. The failings of the banks called into existence the check-cashing industry, and those fringe banks in turn figured out how to exploit the deregulation of the depository institutions to tap into the income stream. The two tiers of the modern banking system are bound together, and it is at the interface of these two tiers that a new breed of loan shark now feeds.

The 7-Eleven of the Banking Business

Payday lending came late to Illinois. While a few outlets may have existed earlier, the takeoff began in 1997. This was years after the product had begun to proliferate in other states, including several that bordered Illinois. The delayed start might seem surprising because the usury statute had been uncapped years earlier. There was also a large and well-established check-cashing industry in Illinois, but this industry was more closely regulated than in any other state and the currency exchanges were not free to innovate.[51] It is a striking fact that "deferred deposit" lending first appeared in states that did not license the check-cashing businesses. The product was the invention of an unsupervised market, which did not exist in Illinois. But expansion was rapid once the concept had been imported. In less than three years, the Department of Financial Institutions (DFI) licensed nearly 600 payday-lending outlets. More than a third were located in Cook County. At the peak of this growth, the DFI was processing more than 60 applications a month. Over the next several years 200 more outlets would be opened. The business was fragmented, but most vendors belonged to local or national chains. In 2004, five corporations owned slightly more than one-third of the state's licensed stores.[52]

The distribution of payday-lending outlets tracks population density closely. In 1999 there were no licensees in half of Illinois' counties, most of them downstate and rural.[53] As has always been the case, the quick-cash businesses require large concentrations of wage-earners to thrive. Convenience is one of the main attractions of the product. As one storeowner explained, "We like to consider ourselves the 7-Eleven of the banking business." This means that the shop must be nearby and accessible. According to an industry document, the bulk of a location's customers will be drawn from the surrounding three miles.[54] The best sites are located on high-volume corridors, should be visible from the street, and have plenty of free parking. The lenders often share space in strip malls with grocery stores, discount retailers, and fast-food restaurants. Because the businesses are licensed and legal, they no longer have to be tucked away in the nondescript second-floor offices to which the salary lenders were consigned by their gray-market status.

Within population centers, the distribution of payday lenders is also uneven. They are rarely found in affluent areas but tend to cluster in low- and moderate-income neighborhoods with younger and less educated populations. There is also a strong correlation with concentrations of African American households, even when other factors have been controlled for. One study in Chicago reported that there were twice as many check lenders per capita in black neighborhoods compared to white residential areas. Another population that has been a magnet for the payday lenders is armed services personnel. Until restrictions were imposed, military bases were often ringed with quick-cash shops. From the start, loan sharks have proliferated wherever large concentrations of these government workers can be found. It is a population perpetually short of cash and uprooted from the network of family and friends that might be able to sustain them through financial emergencies.[55]

Like shoe and clothing stores, payday-lending outlets tend to cluster together. Though they compete with each other, all will do more business if customers have several convenient options within close proximity. The neon signs draw in trade from the streets, but many firms also advertise. Benny the Bull, mascot of Chicago's basketball team, promoted the grand opening of several Check Into Cash outlets in 1999. Placards are also regularly displayed in the elevated trains, just like in the days of salary lending. Cards sent through the mail promise "First Payday Loan Interest Free." Some lenders pay cash for good leads. One former manager explained, "I was trained to approach apartment managers and offer them referral fees of $20 for each tenant who came into our store and took out a loan. The sales pitch was that not only would the manager directly earn money off the loan, but that it would help tenants make their rent payments on time." Similar arrangements were made with car dealerships and repair shops, fast-food restaurants, convenience stores, and even local churches.[56]

The outlets range in appearance from seedy to generically corporate. In one of its disclosures, Advance America—the largest payday lending chain in the nation—explains that it designs its centers "to have the appearance of a mainstream financial institution." The stores are supposed to be clean, bright, and unpretentious. The service should be friendly. But it can be difficult to establish any kind of warmth if the transaction must take place through a thick plate of bulletproof glass, as is often the case. Security is an important consideration for these businesses. There is the risk of robbery but also of employee theft. The larger chains establish controls to monitor each store's accounts and use the stream of data flowing into corporate headquarters to decide how much cash must be kept on premises on any given day.[57]

Unless the loan volume is unusually high, most monoline stores will be staffed by one or two employees. These customer service jobs are not high-paying, and turnover of staff can be rapid. One chain reports that more than half of its store managers must be replaced every year, and the attrition rate for assistants is twice as high.[58] The fact that debt collection is central to the work no doubt reduces its appeal. But some employees do find satisfaction in their jobs. One manager said she was well suited to this line of work precisely because she was so softhearted: "I like being able to help people. I can't be a nurse. I couldn't handle that, but this is another way I can help." Another remarked, "You meet so many nice people. We all have troubles in our lives. Sometimes they just need someone to unload on. We joked that we'd put up a sign [stating a charge] for counseling." But other employees expressed doubts about how they made their living. "I think it's usury," one manager told a reporter. "It's like a ball rolling downhill. It's very easy to do this. It's very easy to get trapped in it, and it's very difficult to get out of it."[59]

As you approach a store, the price of the product is unlikely to be displayed in the windows. That's because the law says fees must also be stated as an annual percentage rate. As a lobbyist for the industry admitted, "The APR is high. It's a bad visual, and it's tough to explain away." Even inside the store, the charges are not always stated in a way that facilitates comparative shopping. A nationwide survey in 2001 reported that only a third of the sites visited listed the APR on charts or brochures.[60] Often the number is revealed only near the end of the transaction, when the customer is presented with a contract to sign. By this point borrowers tend to be heavily vested in the completion of the process and are unlikely to be deterred by this new piece of information. But even if the APR was disclosed sooner, it is doubtful that many customers would turn around and walk out of the store. Studies show that rationed borrowers tend to ignore the annual percentage rate of loan products because the number doesn't tell them what they want to know. What they want to know is the dollar cost of their payment, not the interest rate.[61]

Another reason why prices aren't advertised is because each shop tends to charge the same fee as its competitors. If the state sets a maximum rate, prices gravitate to that ceiling. Unlike other lenders, the payday-advance businesses do not engage in price discrimination among their customers. Everybody is consigned to the same risk pool and pays the same high fee. The stores do not compete on the basis of price but instead on nonprice features of the product such as location, hours, and service. As has long been known, the rationed borrowers whom these businesses serve do not have the habit of shopping around for the lowest APR. Instead, these consumers tend to select the outlet that is most convenient.[62]

Because payday lenders are selling convenience, the loan process must be speedy. The first loan sharks took a day to close their loans, but the payday lenders can get customers in and out of the store in less than half an hour, provided they bring the right documents. In addition to filling out an application, borrowers must submit a pay stub, bank statement, proof of address, and photo identification. A social security number must be provided, but the lender will not run a formal credit check. That is one of the attractions of the product because most customers will have impaired credit. If they could get a cheaper loan somewhere else presumably they would, so the credit score would simply confirm that these debtors are subprime or risky. That's why they are here. Traditional credit scoring, then, is not used in the payday-loan underwriting process, which means the transaction will not show up on a standard credit report unless the loan goes into default. This is good if other creditors to whom customers might apply consider the payday loan to be a blot on their credit. The flip side is that if borrowers pay off their payday loans on time, the fact won't be reported to the credit agencies and can't help to boost their credit scores.[63]

Although payday lenders don't access the standard credit score, accurate risk assessment is vital if the business is to be profitable. Personnel are trained to size up new customers with a few basic questions at the start of the transaction, but most chains will also access a fee-based subprime service called Teletrack to verify information and assess creditworthiness. Teletrack was founded at the end of the 1980s, as subprime lending took off; it gathers information from this class of creditors and tracks consumer activity to facilitate rapid risk assessment of new applicants. Within moments, personnel in the store can verify the authenticity of the social security number, determine whether the customer has applied elsewhere recently, has other payday loans outstanding, is in arrears, or has been charged off by another creditor. Lenders can use the Teletrack information to establish their own internal scoring system, which helps managers decide quickly if they should extend credit. The service also facilitates debt collection because skips who apply for new loans elsewhere are immediately reported to creditors hunting for them.[64]

Personnel will also verify that the applicant's checking account is open and will record the current balance. Some lenders will confirm the customer's employment status by phoning work. These checks, while necessary to reduce losses, discourage borrowers from shopping around for payday credit. A lot of inquiries in a short space of time can be embarrassing and might annoy employers. During the application process, additional information will be gathered that can facilitate debt collection in case the loan isn't repaid. References must be provided but aren't used to screen applicants. Instead, they may be contacted if the loan goes into default. The form may also request information about the applicant's automobile, a valuable asset. Some lenders even take physical descriptions of the applicant.[65]

Though payday lenders have the reputation of being the creditors of last resort, some stores will reject a sizable fraction of applications. One chain operating in Texas that disclosed this proprietary information denied credit to 20% of the people who applied. Some states, like Illinois, impose limits on the size and/or number of loans and require lenders to verify customer eligibility through a statewide database. This second layer of verification increases the rate of rejection.[66] States that impose binding caps on fees will also inevitably increase the proportion of applicants that must be denied credit by the payday lenders. Low ceilings force creditors to be more conservative in selecting customers. To reduce their losses from bad debts they must ration credit away from the riskiest prospects.

If an application is approved, the customer will now write the postdated check and be presented with a contract to sign. The check will be dated for payday and is made out for a larger sum than the borrower will receive in cash since the fee is deducted in advance. The contract must state the fee as an annual interest rate, but this sobering piece of information seems to make little impression on consumers so close to finishing the process. Surveys reveal that few borrowers can recall the APR of their most recent loan.[67] Customers are also unlikely to read the fine print in the contract carefully, but the powers bestowed upon the lender are extensive. In case of dispute, the consumer agrees to submit to binding arbitration and to forgo recourse to the courts. As Christopher Peterson points out, the arbitration services to which disagreements must be referred bear an uncanny resemblance to the justice of the peace courts that flourished a century ago.[68] This extrajudicial mechanism tends to put the borrower at a disadvantage. Many contracts also include a garnishment clause and a wage assignment. These methods of debt collection will be employed if the loan goes into default and the postdated check bounces at the bank. If the debtor's reservoir is dry or closed and other collection efforts fail, the lender will return to the headwaters of the income stream and try to collect the debt there.

Before the cash is advanced and the transaction is concluded, some payday lenders will make an appointment with the borrower to settle the debt in person. A phone call the day before payment is due confirms this appointment. Although the lender holds the postdated check as security, most lenders prefer to be paid in cash. Advance America, for example, deposits only 6% of the checks it receives. Of these, three-quarters bounce.[69] If the debt is settled on payday, the postdated check is returned to the customer. If, instead, the debt is renewed for an additional fee, a new postdated check must be provided to the lender. Some payday creditors avoid the hassle of processing paper checks by securing permission to debit the borrower's account electronically.

That's the basic version of the payday-loan transaction, but there are many variations of the process. In states where the product is illegal, some lenders craft the exchange as a sale or a leaseback arrangement. Other lenders don't dispense cash themselves but give the borrower a check or a debit card instead. Internet vendors may not have bricks-and-mortar locations and must therefore process the transactions without any face-to-face contact. Payday lenders that partnered with banks worked out sophisticated procedures to speed money to customers. Consider this arrangement by ACE Cash Express and Goleta National Bank:

> When a potential borrower completed a loan application at an ACE location, ACE transmitted the borrower's data electronically to its former partner Goleta National Bank. If Goleta approved the loan, it opened a bank account in the name of the borrower, and activated a debit card and PIN connected to that account. ACE delivered the card and PIN to the borrower, who could withdraw the funds at the store or at another retail ATM.[70]

According to a regulatory disclosure, this three-party transaction took just twenty minutes to complete.

This speed in processing loans is one of the conveniences for which customers are willing to pay such hefty fees. The money is available right away. It is also provided without intrusive questions about the purpose for which the cash will be used. Although public statements by the payday lenders suggest that most borrowers use the funds to cover emergency expenses, the advertisements for the product often seem to encourage discretionary spending—for a vacation, shopping spree, or night on the town. Customers are allowed to do anything they want with the money, no questions asked. As one borrower explained, "There is no family drama."[71] While friends and relatives may not charge a fee, they still impose costs on borrowers. They can make them pay in a different way. Payday lenders, by contrast, charge more up front for the service of minding their own business. They adopt a libertarian and nonpaternalistic approach to lending money. What they sell, in part, is freedom of choice—but freedom isn't free, as the saying goes.

Drowning in Liquidity

In Illinois, the price of freedom in the days before the state capped fees was $20 for every $100 borrowed over two weeks. That translates into an APR of 521%. A nationwide survey at the turn of the century reported that the average interest rate for the product was 474%.[72] This average is about twice as high as the standard rate charged by the salary lenders early in the twentieth century. It is comparable to the rate that used to be levied by many mob payday lenders operating in the black market. Legalization, it seems, has not made this financial product any cheaper.

Some critics charge that these high interest rates are proof the payday lenders earn windfall profits. But the APR is not a measure of profitability. While the continuous surge of capital into this new market indicates that returns on investment are solid or better, the competition of several hundred payday lenders in the Chicagoland area, for example, ought to check the rate of profit in this industry. Unfortunately, because many of the chains are privately held, information on the income and expenses of the payday lenders is fragmentary. But the annual disclosures of the publicly traded companies probably give us an accurate picture of the trend. The most comprehensive survey to date reports that the average after-tax profit rate of the big chains in 2006 was an unexceptional 7.63%. The profit rate for a comparable set of large commercial lenders was nearly twice as high.[73] Payday lending, then, is not inordinately profitable. Advance America, for example, loaned $4.3 billion in 2007 and served 1.5 million customers at more than 2,800 locations. Its fee income on 12 million payday loans was $710 million, but store expenses consumed three-quarters of that revenue. For every dollar Advance America takes in, it must set aside 20 cents to cover bad debts. Corporate expenses and taxes eat up most of the remaining $170 million in revenue, leaving the company with a net income of $54 million. The profit margin is 7.61%. After paying expenses, Advance America makes just $4.54 on each payday loan it originates.[74]

The interest rate of the product, then, isn't sky high because the vendors make exorbitant profits. There is no relationship between those two numbers. The first loan sharks charged lower rates but kept a larger fraction of their revenue. So do many credit card companies today. A better explanation for the high APR of the product now compared to a hundred years ago is the relative quality of the risk pool that payday lenders serve. Because there were fewer credit options available at the start of the twentieth century, the salary lenders advanced cash to a broader segment of the market. The fact that their customers couldn't get loans at the bank didn't mean all of them were terrible risks. The risk pool serviced by the salary lenders was heterogeneous, and the better risks within their clientele subsidized the poor ones. Once the personal finance industry was established by the Uniform Small Loan Law, the better risks migrated there and were charged lower rates. The average quality of the remaining risk pool to which a new generation of loan sharks catered was lower, and rates therefore had to rise. What the high rates of today's payday lenders indicate is that they do business with a more uniformly subprime population of credit-constrained consumers than did the salary lenders of old. The check lenders operate at the margins of creditworthiness and within a fringe population of consumers to which legal credit has been extended by the financial revolution of the past thirty years.

The fringe status of this population, however, does not correlate automatically with household income. While many payday-loan customers must be numbered among the working poor, the clientele extends into middle-income groups. Unfortunately, the surveys from which a demographic profile of the borrowers might be drawn often suffer from methodological weaknesses and do not always report their findings in a way that facilitates comparison. The organizations in the best position to know this population are the lenders themselves, but they rarely give unfettered access to the data they collect. The Illinois DFI conducted a survey in 1999 at the behest of the legislature and reported that the average annual salary of payday-loan customers was $25,131. That figure was slightly higher than per capita income in the state but quite a bit less than the median income for full-time workers. An average, however, tells us nothing about the distribution of incomes across the population. A few years later, a research firm hired by the payday lenders reported that the median *household* income for borrowers in Illinois was about $32,000, placing that middle customer at the lower end of the second quartile of the state's income distribution.[75] A national survey from this period sponsored by the lenders' trade group but conducted by the Credit Research Center at Georgetown University reported that the middle 50% of payday-loan customers had family incomes between $25,000 and $50,000, a span that corresponded to the second quartile of the national income distribution at that time. This means a quarter of the customers clustered in the bottom quartile and were unambiguously poor, but the most affluent quarter had family incomes above the national median. Some questions have been raised about how representative this sample was, but it is practically the only national survey of payday-loan customers to have been published. Several high-quality surveys in individual states report median incomes for the borrowers falling around the border between the first and second quartiles.[76]

In short, payday-advance customers tend to have below average incomes, but many could not be classified as poor. Not coincidentally, the population also tends to be disproportionately female and minority. On average, payday-loan customers are younger than adults as a whole and are less likely to be married but are more likely to have children to support.[77] A sizable number are single mothers. Over the course of the last century there has been a feminization of payday lending as women have entered the workforce in larger numbers and assumed (or had thrust upon them) responsibility for household finances. The convenience of the payday loan is well suited to the hectic lives of single parents and to the just-in-time strategy of financial management many must adopt in order to make ends meet.

Wage-earners with lower incomes have always been charged a premium for credit. In this particular market, the poor will pay more.[78] But the very high rate imposed on payday-loan customers today results not so much from the fact that they tend to have lower incomes, for many people with small salaries still have access to cheaper credit. If they haven't maxed out their bank cards, for example, the interest rate will be 10 or 20 times cheaper than for the typical payday loan. What really marks out the payday-advance customers and makes them especially risky debtors who must be charged a high rate is the fact that they have not been deemed creditworthy by lower-cost lenders. Their credit records are much more likely to be blemished compared to other wage-earners. For example, according to the national survey cited above, about four times as many payday-loan customers have filed for bankruptcy in the past compared to the general population. Five times as many are 60 days late on debt payments. Three times as many have been turned down for credit during the past five years. Two-thirds have bounced a check. These consumers have higher debt–income ratios than the population as a whole, and three in five have reached the limit on their credit cards. Seventeen out of twenty did not have enough money in the bank to cover the postdated check they gave the lender.[79]

In short, payday-loan customers tend to be the most marginal of debtors, whatever their household incomes might be. Their finances are usually quite precarious, but a lender operating on the fringe of the credit market has agreed to advance cash to them in exchange for the highest legal rate of interest that can be charged. Until the end of the twentieth century, this sort of transaction with this sort of clientele had almost never been legal in the United States. But now the spigot of financial liquidity has been opened to this thirsty population. Although already mired in debt, these cash-strapped wage-earners want additional credit in a hurry, to help them juggle their finances. Having recognized the demand, the payday lenders set about satisfying it with short bursts of liquidity that are billed at a premium rate. After the fact, policy makers in most jurisdictions decided to let the payday lenders continue to operate the spigot that they had opened without asking anyone's permission. Rules—more or less stringent—were imposed on the operation of this new pipeline of liquidity. But, in conformity with the libertarian spirit that prevailed in this era of financial deregulation, it was decided to permit this expensive credit to flow.

And so the industry grew and the outlets multiplied. More and more credit-constrained consumers who owned checking accounts flocked to the payday lenders. In 1990 there probably weren't more than 100,000 people in the country borrowing money on the security of a postdated check, but a decade later, as many as 10 million households a year were getting these expensive cash advances.[80] That population would double again in less than ten years. Obviously many people thought the product could help them out. A survey of customers reported that roughly two-thirds used the proceeds of their loans to cover unplanned expenditures or a temporary reduction in household income.[81] They came for fast cash, and most came back again and again. If Advance America originated about 12 million loans in 2007 and served 1.5 million people, that means the average customer had eight loans during the course of the year. The average duration of each loan was 16.5 days, hence the typical borrower was indebted to this short-term lender for 132 days, or for more than a third of the year. If the loans were spread out evenly over twelve months, the average customer received $2,881 in cash and paid back $3,321, the typical fee being $15.24 for every $100 advanced. But it is more likely that some or all of the loans ran back-to-back, so that the fees accrued on just one—or a few—cash advances. If this average customer were allowed to renew the initial $361 loan seven times in a row, the $440 in fees paid would translate into an annual percentage rate of 337%. The borrower would receive $361 and pay back $801 over the course of four months, including a lump-sum payment due at the end of the cycle.

These are just averages. In practice, some customers had only one loan during the year but others had fifteen or more. Advance America's averages are not unusual. In fact, if the industry's estimates for 2008 are accurate, the 19 million households that patronize the payday lenders will secure an average of eight cash advances during the year and pay $453 in fees. If those eight loans are spread evenly through the year, so that a new fourteen-day cash advance is obtained every six weeks or so, the repeat business could be fairly construed as customer loyalty. It is rather surprising, however, that such a sizable share of the nation's households could be afflicted with so many financial emergencies. Can one in six households really be faced with a new unexpected expenditure every six weeks? Aaron Huckstep's wry observation seems appropriate, that all of these ostensibly loyal customers are "using the product with a frequency that suggests their only 'emergency' is that their bank account is low."[82] But matters are much worse if the eight loans cluster together as one longer transaction instead of eight discrete episodes. In this case, the average household is paying roughly $450 in interest over sixteen weeks in exchange for one $325 cash advance. It would be hard to construe this chain of rollovers as customer loyalty. The transaction seems much more like a debt trap into which households with bad credit and no savings have fallen.[83]

One thing is certain: people who get one payday loan usually get many more in the months that follow. Only a small percentage of customers get one loan, pay it off in two weeks, and then quit. The Illinois DFI survey in 1999 found that the average customer whose file was pulled by state examiners had thirteen contracts listed, which means this typical borrower was indebted to the licensee for at least six months. A survey by Indiana's DFI the same year reported that the average debtor had ten loans during the previous twelve months and that three-quarters of these transactions were rollovers.[84] The industry-funded study conducted by the Credit Research Center disclosed that half of the respondents had seven or more two-week loans during the previous year and nearly a quarter had at least fourteen contracts. Only 15% of this sample of respondents said they had taken out no more than two loans during the previous twelve months. In Colorado the average number of loans in a year was nine, and 20% of the sample had at least sixteen transactions with the same lender. For a chain of stores in Texas the average was also nine.[85] Another study that gained access to proprietary data reported that half of all customers borrowed at least six times in a year, and 30% got a dozen loans or more. At the mature stores, only 14% of customers borrowed just once in twelve months.[86]

This last statistic matches the trend reported by states tracking consumer activity. In Florida and Washington, 17% of customers borrow just once; in Oklahoma 13% do. By contrast, the 10% of customers who are the most frequent borrowers in Florida and Washington get at least nineteen loans during a twelve-month period. In Oklahoma the top 10% get at least twenty-one. According to a 2007 report, 3,646 Oklahomans had more than twenty-six payday loans during the previous fifty-two weeks.[87]

As a rule, the only way you can have more than twenty-six payday loans in a year is to borrow from several vendors simultaneously. Although you've got just one payday, you can get many payday loans. Newspapers offer plenty of anecdotal evidence of this syndrome. A couple in Urbana, Illinois, got their first cash advance to cover the bill for a car repair. Soon they were borrowing from four different lenders simultaneously, paying the interest due on each loan with the proceeds from the last one. They owed $1,440 in principal, but their monthly household income was just $1,178. The lenders weren't troubled that the loans kept rolling over. "They encouraged us to come back," the wife said. "They got to be like friends to us." Another woman in Decatur started with a small loan to fix her car. Eventually she had five loans going at once and was paying $600 a month in fees, making it impossible for her to reduce the principal on any of the loans. "It's almost like an addiction," she told the reporter. "Once you get in there you can't stop. There's always something that comes up. You want to pay them off, but you can't."[88]

A nurse in DeKalb had a similar experience. She thought she could pay back her $600 loan in two weeks, but then her overtime was cut. So she rolled the loan over and paid another $140 to keep the lender from cashing the postdated check for two more weeks. Once she was trapped, she couldn't get free. Over the next two years, she paid more than $10,000 in interest to several different companies. "It's the most horrible thing I can imagine people getting into," she recalled. "It can destroy your life, and you don't realize what's happening until you're in so much trouble you can't see over the top of it."[89]

Some chain debtors are more nonchalant, however. A single mom in Denver who admitted to having "five or six" loans at once told the reporter the money had kept her from being evicted. "It's nice to have it when you need it," she said on the way out of a shop with the proceeds from two new loans.[90]

Anecdotes are no substitute for hard data, but unfortunately there isn't much hard data on the frequency with which payday-loan customers are indebted simultaneously to several vendors. The states that track customer activity closely also limit the number of loans consumers may have; where the limit isn't imposed, data isn't gathered. Also, most empirical studies rely on data supplied by or gathered from individual lenders, but this information can't uncover how many loans any given customer has outstanding at one time with several different chains. One way—not entirely reliable—to ascertain the number is to ask the payday-loan customers themselves. The Credit Research Center did this and reported that about half of its sample admitted to patronizing more than one company. Of that population, one-third said they had paid off one cash advance with the proceeds of another.[91] The true numbers are almost certainly higher, for it seems likely that some respondents would be unwilling to disclose this behavior to a stranger conducting a telephone survey.

Another way to try to gauge the extent of the phenomenon is to examine bankruptcy petitions, for these list all of the creditors from which debtors are seeking protection. In a sample drawn from petitioners filing in Milwaukee County in 2005, 70% of those reporting any payday-loan debt listed two or more such creditors on their schedules. One person listed nine. The median payday-advance debt for this sample was $928, but the median net monthly income of these borrowers was only $1,823, which means that when the petition was filed the typical debtor owed all of the next paycheck to these payday lenders. Samples drawn for other counties across the country where payday lending was lightly regulated reveal similar patterns. In a few cases, the debtors had managed to acquire more than twenty different payday loans before going bankrupt. In these more extreme cases, the cumulative principal owed was several times the debtors' monthly take-home pay. A few examples will illustrate the process by which one paycheck is mortgaged to several payday lenders. One single mother received four different cash advances over the space of five months in 2004. With a monthly income of $1,347 she managed to get $1,855 in payday loans. The first loan for $261 was issued in January; she received the next one for $640 in April; a month later, a third outlet lent her $583; and six weeks before she filed for bankruptcy, a fourth company advanced her $371. But sometimes the loans come all at once. A divorced father with a monthly net income of $1,263 received four different payday loans totaling $2,035 all on the same day in November 2003. One of the loans was for more than his biweekly paycheck. Another couple received nine different advances in the space of eighteen days. Most of the loans were for less than $200, but together they nearly equaled the couple's monthly disability income.[92]

These pyramids of loan-shark debt revealed in the bankruptcy petitions were constructed even though most lenders have access to the Teletrack system, which records the subprime borrowing activity of applicants. In many cases, the creditors must know that their competitors have already secured a claim against the debtor's next paycheck, but they advance cash anyway. While there is no organized cartel, the lenders cooperate to ensure these overleveraged debtors will only be able to pay the interest on their loans. This is why payday-loan outlets tend to cluster together in neighborhoods—to make it easy for consumers to borrow from several at once. The organization of these quick-cash ghettos is one dimension of the industry's business model of convenience.

To test whether payday lenders are responsible in originating their high-cost loans, an Ohio State University law school professor and her research team tried to see how many single-payment loans they could secure in a short space of time. One assistant obtained nine loans in three days. Nearly all of the lenders used Teletrack, and most asked why the applicant needed another cash advance so soon. He replied, "My paycheck wasn't big enough" or "I lost money gambling last night." But, in conformity with the libertarian philosophy that animates this industry, most of the clerks said, "It's none of my business." Only the tenth store to which he applied refused him cash. A short time later he got additional loans from two more outlets.[93]

Drowning in liquidity—that is the plight of many of today's payday-loan customers. A new class of creditors has appeared on the scene and made it convenient, though not cheap, for the growing population of cash-strapped subprime wage-earners to turn their checks into cash despite the fact that they have no money in the bank. For some consumers, this burst of liquidity is no doubt a blessing and worth its high price because it helps them to survive a temporary drought in their family finances. Certainly those customers— roughly one in six—who borrow only once and pay off their debt do not seem like victims of exploitation. The lender has not sweated them; the loan shark did not bite. But the same cannot be said, for example, for the 4,843 consumers in Washington who had more than twenty-six payday loans apiece in 2006.[94] They crammed more than fifty-two weeks of debt into a single year and surely paid far more in interest during this interval than they received in principal. It was to describe exactly this sort of debt trap that the phrase "loan shark" was coined at the end of the nineteenth century, and it seems impossible to avoid the conclusion that the loan sharks have indeed returned, and in large numbers, since the banking system was deregulated.

This new breed of shark has come to infest those particular reservoirs at the end of the income stream in which there does not pool sufficient cash to pay back with interest the emergency infusion of liquidity that has been provided on a rent-or-own basis. This rent-or-own alternative is the camouflage that has always concealed the quick-cash debt trap in all its forms. The payday lender, for example, will let you buy back the postdated check you pledged if you make a balloon payment on your next payday two weeks hence. But if you can't scrape together this ransom money for your check, you have the alternative of renting the lender's forbearance by paying a new fee. That fee will buy the hostage check a two-week reprieve. You can do this several times, but then the lender will want the balloon payment, which you weren't able to accumulate because you had to pay the rent on the postdated check. So now you've got a new financial emergency. You don't want the lender to induce a liquidity crisis in your financial reservoir by delivering the hostage you pledged to the bank. There isn't any money in your account, so the check will bounce, the lender will hound you, and the banker will impose a stiff penalty for having let your reservoir run dry. To avoid this catastrophe, it seems better to deliver another hostage to a new check lender, use the fresh burst of liquidity to pay off the first creditor, and begin the cycle again. This is how a sizable fraction of payday-loan customers flail around and sometimes drown in the tiny puddles of liquidity that can be wrung from postdated checks.

As always, the real art to loan-sharking is not to let too many debtors drown too quickly. The idea is to prolong the interest payments, to encourage renewals and payoffs, by lending enough principal to make it difficult to meet the balloon payment but not so much that the biweekly interest charge on this sum is unmanageable for the debtor. Despite what critics of the industry sometimes say, check lenders do assess ability to pay during the hasty underwriting process. Advance America, for instance, limits the loan size to between 15% and 35% of the applicant's net pay.[95] But having established a maximum limit, the loan agents will encourage the applicant to borrow up to that threshold. This increases the likelihood that the debtor will choose the rent option when the balloon payment is due, and so does advancing more cash to debtors who already have another payday loan. But at some point in the construction of this pyramid of debt, it is likely that the borrower won't be able to rent the lenders' forbearance any more. If the borrower's income stream is disrupted, or a fresh financial emergency strikes, or no more lenders will extend credit, the pyramid scheme of the chain debtor will collapse. Payday lenders must set aside a sizable portion of the revenue they take in to cover bad debts. According to one study, the average ratio of loan losses to total revenue is 15%. Between one-fifth and one-quarter of the typical store's operating costs consists of debt outstanding that must be written off. This works out to be slightly more than 3% of loan volume at the typical chain. In other words, for every thirty loans the business originates, one will not be repaid. This loss rate is not much higher than the figure reported by commercial banks for consumer loans, and it is actually lower than the charge-off rate for credit card debt.[96] But the difference is that the average payday-loan customer secures eight cash advances a year, so at the typical chain every fourth customer will not repay a loan. These debtors will flounder and drown, but in most cases not before they have generated more in fee income than must be written off in principal.

If 25% of your customers will eventually stop making payments, and the other 75% have bad credit and precarious finances, then Bob Srygley is right that the payday-advance business is really a collections business. From the very start you've got to think about how you're going to get blood from these turnips. The application process lays the groundwork; the postdated check you hold gives you leverage; the call you make the day before the loan is due reminds the debtor; but in many cases more aggressive collection efforts must be employed. The delinquent must be phoned at home or at work, and references can be pestered. If this doesn't work, the check can be cashed, though in most cases it won't get your money back. When the check bounces, some lenders will try to get the authorities to file criminal charges. This tactic was more common in the early days of the business, before prosecutors and sheriffs realized what was going on. In Illinois, Nationwide Budget Finance went a step further and mailed letters to delinquents in the name of the state attorney general threatening prosecution for check fraud, but the company was slapped with a lawsuit by the state's attorney and had to shutter all of its stores.[97]

If these collection techniques fail, the next step is to file the wage assignment, provided one was included with the contract. Nationwide Budget Finance also got in trouble with the state for processing blank wage assignments, just like the salary lenders of old. An alternative is to go to court and garnish the debtor's wages. Several chains in Illinois have been very aggressive in collecting their debts through the courts, winning default judgments for sums several times as large as the outstanding principal. One man who owed $150 to a lender plus late fees had his wages garnished for $2,200. Another woman with a $1,000 debt was being harassed by a collection agency for $10,743, most of it for interest that had accumulated over the preceding three years at the loan shark rate of 43% a month. The bill collector said he was just doing his job and didn't necessarily endorse payday lending. "I think the interest is exorbitant," he admitted. "Going there is just committing suicide."[98]

But not everyone who gets one of these high-priced loans commits financial suicide. If most did, the business would wither away. And the business hasn't withered away—on the contrary, it has grown enormously in a short period of time. This fact suggests that the product fills a need within the modern infrastructure of liquidity. If one loan in thirty goes bad and must be written off, we should not forget that the other twenty-nine transactions (or 97%) were completed successfully. One customer in four may eventually default on a loan, but the other three will not. They will pay their debts and move on. Should 75% of payday-loan customers be denied emergency credit because the other 25% cannot manage their finances? Will a new prohibition in the domain of high-priced credit really enhance the well-being of cash-strapped households? Such prohibitions have never extirpated the loan sharks, as we have seen. They merely drive them underground.

Payday lending in its modern form has been a grand experiment in the democratization of credit made possible by financial deregulation. It has given people with modest incomes and weak credit a chance to try to solve their money problems on their own and through legal channels. Given the risk profile of the population, it isn't surprising that some will fail in the juggling act they choose to undertake, but should we ignore the many who succeed because a few spectacularly fail? Surveys of payday-loan customers consistently report that they want the freedom to manage their own affairs. They don't want the product banned. Shouldn't we respect their opinions and try to improve the product rather than attempt to stamp it out?

Perhaps. But can payday lending be improved? Can anyone make money with the product if its abuses are removed? What has been tried and what seems to work?

5 The Slipperiest Fish

It's your job to write the law, it's our job to find the loopholes.

—Tom Ball, Louisiana Check Cashers Association, 1998[1]

One of the profound insights of the discipline of economics is that nearly all human interactions can be analyzed as markets in which the forces of supply and demand operate. The exchanges made between creditors and debtors are one obvious example, but this conventional market is shaped from the start by another that is less frequently recognized: the market for credit regulation. The supplier of this valuable service is the political system, which claims the coercive authority to supervise and constrain economic transactions. Because the rules of the market imposed by policy makers can advantage or disadvantage producers and consumers, it is not surprising that there are intense and competing demands for this service, a service that the various levels of government offer to provide. From the standpoint of economists, the regulatory process is essentially "a political auction in which the high bidder receives the right to tax the wealth of everyone else."[2] Such taxation occurs when market outcomes deviate from the benchmark of economic efficiency.

Since ancient times, the market for consumer credit has almost always been sharply constrained by government. Demand for this regulatory service is often expressed by both borrowers and lenders. But the standard economic models of regulation predict that producers or elite consumers will usually be the high bidder in this auction because their resources, incentives, and small numbers make it profitable for political entrepreneurs to reward them with concentrated benefits. Although the regulations may be framed in terms of the public interest, the constraints they impose on competition make it possible for the beneficiaries to extract rents that would not be possible if the market remained free. Several studies have demonstrated that this was the effect of traditional usury statutes, which reduced the costs of borrowing for established businesses and prevented upstarts from raising the capital necessary to innovate and produce goods or services more cheaply. In these cases, elite borrowers and the political entrepreneurs whom they lobbied gained at the expense of the rest of the population, even though the price controls were justified in the names of consumer protection and economic fairness.[3] In other cases, it was licensed creditors who benefited the most from ostensible consumer protections. A good example is the "convenience and advantage" clause added to a later draft of the Uniform Small Loan Law. This rule permitted regulators to deny licenses to applicants in order to prevent "excessive competition" in local markets. The provision was justified as a way to forestall the return of the loan sharks, but in practice it simply permitted incumbent businesses to extract rents from their consumers in the form of higher prices or reduced service.[4]

This is the demystified, free-market interpretation of consumer protection. But there is a countermodel in the economics literature that shows how the demand for deregulated markets itself can actually reduce economic efficiency in certain settings. If regulatory agencies do not impose rules in markets where producer firms have grown large and powerful, disputes must be adjudicated through the court system, which can be susceptible to subversion. The classic example is the Gilded Age, when corporate abuses went unchecked. According to this analysis, the progressive regulation that supplanted the era of unconstrained markets better allocated costs and reduced the feasibility of subversion by wealthy actors, thus enhancing economic efficiency.[5] A similar conclusion has been reached about the effect of usury statutes in certain contexts. Where inequality is high but impermanent, and growth rates in the economy are low, imposing price ceilings in the credit market can be shown to make everyone better off over the long run. In primitive societies where saving is difficult and the likelihood of being a debtor is great, usury prohibitions can function as an efficient form of social insurance.[6] A free market in credit, by contrast, would allow wealthy lenders in this type of society to extract unproductive rents from debt peons, thus reducing social well-being.

Because there are competing models, we cannot predict with certainty what the effects of regulation will be or who will prevail in this market for the services of government. The ideologies of consumer protection and free markets attempt to legitimate the interests of those who express a demand for regulation, and only sometimes will the satisfaction of one or the other group's demands by the suppliers of credit regulation enhance the well-being of the community as a whole. This chapter treats the regulatory fight over payday lending during the last two decades as a series of market transactions in which the various consumers of regulation have competed intensively for the valuable but limited supply of this service offered by the political system. Interest groups of various sorts have mobilized in order to lobby the politicians, and different coalitions have prevailed in different jurisdictions. The operation of this political market cannot be told in any neat or tidy story. In some states the market in regulation has been cornered by the lenders, in others by the advocates of prohibition. One has reason to suspect that many of the participants in this high-stakes auction are trying to write the rules of the market in such a way as to facilitate the extraction of unproductive rents, even as they appeal in their public statements quite sincerely to the common good. The suppliers of the service, meanwhile, have been cashing in wherever the issue remains in play.

Illinois, our case study, illustrates the last point nicely. The fight over payday lending has continued for more than a decade in the state, and the only unambiguous winners in this endless auction have been the suppliers of the service of credit regulation. The politicians have raked in money and support and given the appearance of being concerned, but no final disposition of the service they supply has been achieved. The problem is that the commodity they offer—the net of regulation—is full of holes. Each new model is introduced with much fanfare, but almost immediately the sharks find gaps through which to squirm. Then the bidding in the political auction is reopened, and new contributions flow in. An analysis of the Illinois experience might lead one to conclude that the most egregious and unproductive rent-seekers in the market for payday-loan regulation are the suppliers of this shoddy service themselves.

All Markets Are Local

Long ago, before the British colonies formed the United States, credit regulation was delegated to the intermediate jurisdictions of the political system. Each colonial legislature fashioned its own rules about credit pricing, the philosophy being that local conditions shaped in relevant ways the market for money. This same decentralized philosophy survived the split with Great Britain and has endured to the present day, though the federal government does play a larger role in credit regulation in the twenty-first century than it did in the eighteenth. Over time the scope of state jurisdiction in the regulation of credit markets has become more restricted, but the content of those rules has at the same time become more diverse, at least in the domain of consumer credit. The original thirteen states each had a usury statute, and the maximum permissible rates were clustered together in the single digits. Specific rules governing credit transactions were minimal. Today there are many more rules, of course, and the philosophies that underlie each set are strikingly different. In no division of consumer credit is this variance greater than in the regulation of payday lending.

No Uniform Small Loan Law has been written yet to govern payday credit. The rules vary enormously, and with one exception, there is no obvious pattern in the distribution of this variance across the country. Some states prohibit these transactions while others permit them with little regulation. Most states fall somewhere in between these two extremes and, for that reason, have more complicated sets of rules. The size of the state, its wealth, or the extent of its poverty does not predict where each state falls on the continuum of payday-lending regulation. The ideological leanings of voters or legislators also do not seem to matter. Payday lending is not a red state/ blue state issue. What does matter is geography and history. The older a state is, the more likely it is to have written the rules of consumer credit in such a way as to make payday lending impossible. Of the territories that formed the original thirteen states in the Union, only Rhode Island, Delaware, Virginia, and South Carolina tolerate triple-digit interest rates in consumer-credit transactions. Maine, New Hampshire, Vermont, Massachusetts, Connecticut, New York, Pennsylvania, New Jersey, West Virginia, Maryland, the District of Columbia, North Carolina, and Georgia have each adopted rules that make payday lending illegal, though the creditors continually search for ways around these regulations and sometimes just ignore them. New England today is a nearly payday-loan-free zone. There isn't a comparable cluster of low-ceiling states anywhere else in the nation. In fact, only one state west of the Mississippi—Oregon—has legislated rules that have driven off most of the check lenders. The case of payday lending seems to offer powerful support to the idea that political culture and the history that shaped it matter a lot in explaining the variance of regulatory regimes.

As of 2010, fourteen states plus the District of Columbia have opted for prohibition with regard to payday lending. Ten of these jurisdictions never permitted such expensive cash advances, and the other five rescinded rules that had once made payday lending legal. The lynchpin of prohibition is a low statutory ceiling for credit transactions. The maximum permissible interest rate for small loans must be pegged at a level that makes for-profit payday lending impossible. These double-digit rates range from a low of 18% (Vermont) to a high of 60% (Georgia) and are mostly relics from the era of the Uniform Small Loan Law. The magic number for advocates of prohibition is 36%, but there seems to be little awareness today of how rates like this were chosen in the first place. Just as 6% was the prejudice a century ago, 36% has become the prejudice of opponents of payday lending at the start of the twenty-first century. This percentage could not be described now as it was in the 1930s as the "scientific rate of interest." Instead, it is simply the inflation-adjusted equivalent of the ancient British usury ceiling—the new just price for credit. The original English settlers brought the idea of a "just price" with them to the New World, and somehow it has survived and remained powerful in most of the territories they originally occupied.

At the opposite extreme are a half dozen states that have eliminated price ceilings for credit. In these jurisdictions, payday lenders may charge whatever the market will bear. These states and a few others, including Illinois, deregulated interest rates after inflation surged at the end of the 1970s. In a few cases, the repeal of the usury statute was effected to attract investment by the banking industry. Surprisingly, even though payday lending was legal in these states from the beginning, none of them was the birthplace of the product. Instead, the check loan emerged first in markets where high-interest cash advances were illegal. In the 1990s, a dozen states had no price caps for small loans, but after the rise of payday lending half of this cohort subsequently reimposed rate ceilings. Illinois is a special case, because it eventually set a maximum price for one kind of small-loan product but not for another, thus leaving a loophole through which the sharks immediately passed. The six remaining states where rates continue to be unrestricted are distinguished by the fact that each has a population below the national average. Wisconsin is the most populous of the group. It is also the state with the most minimal rules. Having never passed a law to regulate the product, Wisconsin does not restrict the price of credit, the size of loans, the minimum or maximum terms, the number of times one may roll over a loan, or the number of loans one may have at once. It is as close to a pure free market in payday loans as is ever likely to exist.[7]

The largest number of states—thirty as of 2008—belongs to the middle category of regulation. In these states, payday lending is legal but hedged in with price caps and other restrictions. In many of these jurisdictions the high-rate consumer loan was illegal when it first appeared on the scene. The check cashers began to vend the product without asking for permission since they did not consider the transaction to be a loan. It was a "delayed deposit" or a "deferred presentment," not a formal extension of credit. Regulators and the courts did not find this distinction persuasive, but legislators in many states decided the demand for this technically illegal product was such that it warranted statutory authorization. The first state to pass a law recognizing the transaction was Missouri, in 1990. The next cluster of statutes was adopted by the Show Me State's neighbors—Kentucky, Kansas, Nebraska, and Iowa. From the heartland, legal recognition spread in all directions but occurred more rapidly west of the Mississippi, far from the territories settled by the original British colonists.

Nebraska was the first state to impose a formal price ceiling for the product through legislation. Its maximum permissible fee is $15 for every $100 loaned, which translates into an annual percentage rate of 391% if the term of the loan is fourteen days. About a third of this intermediate category of states expresses the price ceiling in this way, as dollars-per-dollars. This is probably the easiest formula for borrowers to understand, though some consumer advocates complain that it deceptively understates the true cost of the loans compared to the annual percentage rate (APR).[8] Still, compared to the more common way of expressing the fee (as a percentage of the check), the dollars-per-dollars formula is preferable from the consumer's point of view. Many states limit the fee to 15% of the face amount of the postdated check, but the APR for a fee calculated in this way is higher than if the fee is set at $15 for every $100 borrowed. This sounds false, but consider an example. If I write a check for $100 and the fee charged is 15%, I receive $85 in cash because the fee is deducted in advance. But the $15 fee I will pay for this two-week loan is actually 17.65% of the $85 I received in cash, which means the APR for this transaction is 460%. In a $15-per-$100 transaction, by contrast, a check written for $100 will entitle me to $87.25 in cash. The APR for this transaction is 15% lower even though $15 per $100 seems identical to 15% of the face amount of the check. Requiring lenders to calculate the fee only as an annual percentage rate would eliminate this confusion, but no state does so, and the rationed borrowers who patronize the payday lenders would probably not find this way of expressing the costs helpful or clear. The dollars-per-dollars formula is more straightforward and less expensive, and more states have opted to express the price ceiling in this way in recent years.

The range of ways in which the maximum price is stated in legislation is rather dizzying and probably has less to do with local conditions than with the balance of power between the various interest groups that contend in this policy arena. Some states have adopted sliding scales while others mandate a dollar fee plus a percentage of the check. In others still a lesser or greater of two alternatives is provided. In 2008, Virginia enacted the most complicated formula on the books. It permits licensees to "charge and receive on each loan interest at a simple annual rate not to exceed 36 percent," plus "a loan fee in an amount not to exceed 20 percent of the amount of the loan proceeds advanced to the borrower," plus "a verification fee in an amount not to exceed $5 for a loan."[9] This scheme seems designed to confuse consumers. Because the price ceilings are so variegated, it is difficult to identify an average or median for this middle category of states. But the typical maximum APR for a two-week loan seems to be in the neighborhood of 450%, which works out to be roughly $17 for every $100 loaned. For this category of states, the price ceilings are lowest in Florida and Minnesota and highest in Montana, Missouri, Wyoming, and Virginia.

A usury limit is only one facet of the rules devised to govern the payday-loan transaction in states where it is permitted. Over time the regulations have become more extensive, in the name of consumer protection. The statutes can limit the amount that may be borrowed, the number of times a loan may be renewed, and the number of loans running simultaneously. The rules may require various kinds of disclosures in addition to stating the annual percentage rate in the contract, which is mandatory according to federal law. Some states also establish "cooling off" periods between loans, requirements to pay down some of the principal with each renewal, voluntary repayment plans for those who have rolled over loans several times, credit-counseling requirements or options, and the use of a statewide database to verify compliance with the law. There are also the usual sorts of rules about licensing, annual reports, regulator examinations, and penalties for infractions. The agencies charged with overseeing the industry usually have discretion to write additional rules, such as whether payday lenders may sell other kinds of products like lottery tickets.

New Mexico adopted its first law governing payday lending in 2007.[10] The industry had operated legally in the state for fifteen years because there was no usury statute and the legislature had failed numerous times to pass a law imposing restrictions on the trade. It took a long time for the deadlock to be broken, but the resulting piece of legislation benefited from years of experimentation in other states. The New Mexico law offers an example of the latest thinking in consumer protection for states that have decided to legalize payday lending. In addition to the usual rules about licensing and annual reports, the statute authorizes the regulatory agency to police advertising and also requires it to provide the legislature with a statistical report each year analyzing the loan transactions. The rules set a maximum fee of $15.50 per $100 loan, plus an additional 50¢ fee to cover the costs for maintaining a database verifying compliance with the law. The minimum term for the loans is fourteen days and the maximum is thirty-five. Customers may borrow no more than 25% of their gross monthly income, whether from one lender or several simultaneously. Customers have a right to rescind the loan without charge within one business day and may not be assessed a prepayment penalty. Loans may not be renewed or paid off with the proceeds of a new cash advance. Consumers who cannot pay back their loans must be offered an extended payment plan. The lender may not take collateral for the loan except the postdated check and may not act as a broker for a third party in order to evade the rules. Consumers must not be sold insurance policies as part of the transaction or charged a fee to cash a check if the proceeds of the loan are provided in that form. No wage assignments, confessions of judgment, waiver of rights, or powers of attorney may be taken in the contract, which must state clearly the annual percentage rate of the loan and, like any other disclosures required by the regulatory agency, must be provided in English or Spanish, at the borrower's discretion. Finally, the lender is required to abide by fair debt-collection practices, must not threaten criminal prosecution to collect on the loan, and may only charge a modest fee if the postdated check bounces.

These rules seem ironclad, but so have many others before them. Time will tell whether the rules contain holes through which predators may slip. The laws governing payday lending have grown more extensive in the regulated states precisely because the creditors and the attorneys they employ have proved themselves so adept at constructing subterfuges. An ever more finely woven net of regulation has had to be devised because the lenders have never been creatures of the statute. The sharks came first, and regulators have been trying ever since to constrain them. By contrast, the Uniform Small Loan Law created a whole new class of lenders, imbued from the beginning with a spirit of public service, that was called into existence by the state and for some decades cooperated with the state as a remedial and semi-public enterprise. Nothing comparable has been effected in the domain of payday lending since the rise of the check lenders. These businesses from the start have subscribed to a different philosophy that conceives of the loophole as the gateway to free enterprise.

The Search for a Safe Harbor

What the different consumers of credit regulation demand depends in part on what they already have. When the check lenders first began to extend credit, their operations were illegal in most jurisdictions across the country. But rules in a book matter only if some agency is willing and able to enforce them, and in many states the regulatory climate was lax. Check cashing did not require a license in some places, and the authorities were not always aware of what was going on. Attitudes varied, too, about whether the product was harmful, and different units of government could work at cross-purposes. But in other places, the attorneys general were vigilant and enforced the rules vigorously. In Virginia, for example, the state shuttered the handful of check lenders that were operating in 1992 and went to court to recover the usurious interest that had been paid by customers.[11] The first thing, then, that the payday lenders wanted in jurisdictions where the product was illegal was a mild regulatory climate that would permit them to do business while they sought legalization through the legislative process. In Alabama the attorney general had ruled back in 1994 that payday lending violated the state's Small Loan Act but the businesses continued to operate anyway. In 1998 the banking department finally ordered the lenders to cease and desist, but the check-cashers association went to court and negotiated a consent decree that permitted them to extend credit while they tried to push a bill through the legislature.[12] It was another five years before such a bill became law, and despite losses in the courts, the payday lenders were never forced to comply with the existing usury statute.

Tolerance was better than prohibition, but what the lenders really wanted was a safe harbor within which to vend their product. They needed the courts to recognize and enforce the contracts into which they entered with consumers, especially since their business model would require them to haul many debtors into court to compel repayment. The lenders also wanted a predictable environment in which they could do business and plan for the future. Ideally, the safe harbor carved out by legislation would contain few nets to constrain freedom of contract and would be lightly patrolled by the authorities. But more regulation was usually preferable to the uncertainties and risks of the gray market in which most of the lenders operated in the early days of check lending.

In a dozen states, the safe harbor craved by the new breed of loan sharks already existed because price caps had been eliminated back in the days of hyperinflation. But even here the regulatory agencies still had discretionary authority to write rules impacting the business, and legislators, of course, might yield to the demand of consumer-protection advocates or other interest groups and impose burdensome restrictions. In these jurisdictions the aims of the lenders were mostly defensive, to protect the hospitable waters they already enjoyed. In the 1990s Illinois belonged to this most favorable category of states.

The specific demands of the payday lenders varied, then, depending on the regulatory environment in which they had to operate. But their overarching demand was uniform: they wanted a free market in cash advances. Born in an age of deregulation, this new business and its entrepreneurs subscribed to an essentially libertarian philosophy that rejects in principle the idea that government should regulate prices or write the terms of voluntary contracts. Those kinds of restrictions weren't imposed in other markets, and the payday lenders thought it was unfair to single out their business and subject it to a heavy-handed regulatory scheme that had been discredited in other sectors of the economy. As a spokesman for the Illinois Small Loan Association insisted, "The government has no business telling consumers how much they can have in a loan [or] what the terms of that loan should be. Nobody is telling somebody with a credit card how many charges they can make."[13]

The strategy and demands of the payday lenders today are starkly different from the lobbying efforts of the first loan sharks who operated a century ago. Given the ideological climate at the start of the twentieth century, it would have been entirely futile for the bootleg lenders then to have appealed to the creed of freedom of contract in order to defend their interests. This is surprising to us, for we tend to assume that the ideology of economic liberty was hegemonic in the late nineteenth century. But in the domain of credit this was not true. The idea that government should regulate the price of credit and proscribe usury was widely accepted, even in the Gilded Age. Double- or triple-digit interest rates were a scandal and treated as *prima facie* evidence that the lender had taken unfair advantage of the borrower. The victim manifestly had been cheated and government ought therefore to intervene. Where this interpretation of high-rate lending was accepted, an argument for freedom of contract would have fallen on deaf ears. It could not defeat the accusation of exploitation. The first loan sharks, therefore, had to reach their goal of protection by a more devious path. Since they couldn't defeat the prejudices of the day, they played on them. When the reformers lobbied for the Uniform Small Loan Law, the loan sharks attacked the higher rate the law permitted for licensed lending as a moral outrage. They formed front organizations and published pamphlets in defense of the traditional usury statute. Their strategy was to keep the statutory rate low so that the new class of lenders favored by the progressives would not be able to undercut their prices and steal away customers. Thus, whatever their personal views on the question might have been, the public ideology of the salary lenders was moralistic. They condemned usury as roundly as any traditionalist and disparaged their progressive opponents as duplicitous loan sharks.[14]

Today's payday lenders proceed in an entirely different fashion. While some of the Internet entrepreneurs seem resigned to operating in the gray or black market of cyberspace, the bricks-and-mortar vendors have fought vigorously for legalization. They are not ashamed of what they do, and they do not accept the ideology of consumer protection. Markets should be free and government should be small. Excessive regulation only reduces competition, but unconstrained competition offers consumers all the protection they need. As one lender explained, "The market will determine what consumers are willing to pay. The market is already doing that job as numerous non-competitive payday lenders have shuttered their doors. Competition has served us well in the past, and I'm sure it will continue to do so in the future."[15]

As the payday lenders see it, the ideology of consumer protection is hopelessly paternalistic. It treats people who want a cash advance as if they were incompetent children rather than responsible adults. "People are grown-ups," one spokesperson for the industry insisted. "They are able to make their own decisions. How much of a nanny does the government have to be?"[16] This rhetorical maneuver is effective because it presents the payday lenders as the advocates of their customers. In fighting against burdensome regulations they are fighting for the freedom of working people to make their own financial decisions. The ideology is very egalitarian. It gives the benefit of the doubt to wage-earners who want fast cash and it paints as elitist the consumer-protection advocates who would take their freedom away. As an executive with Check Into Cash explained, "It's the folks who look at it from an ivory tower and don't like the decisions our customers are making. There are hard-core consumerists in this country who don't want people doing with their money what they wouldn't do."[17] The consumer-protection advocates don't have to borrow against their next paycheck, it is said, and they seem to have contempt for anybody who does. They have no qualms about imposing restrictions on a population to which they do not belong but would never accept government meddling in their own affairs. "Nobody in the state government that I'm aware of is going to tell somebody how much they can charge at Nieman Marcus on their credit card," one lobbyist complained. "Why should a customer of a payday loan business be told by the government how much they can and cannot borrow?"[18]

But it is worse than that, the industry's advocates say. The policies of the self-styled consumer protectionists are not only paternalistic, they are perverse; although they claim their regulations will benefit the borrowers, the opposite is the case. "These laws have unintended consequences," a spokesman for the industry explained. "This will be hurting the very people it's supposed to help."[19] Price caps, for example, reduce the supply of credit to those who need it the most. These consumers do not benefit from the low prices but actually suffer. No one can afford to lend to them, so they must do without or—worse still—bounce checks or pay late fees. These consumers end up paying for the protections imposed on their behalf by arrogant elites.

The payday lenders press this consumerist ideology at every opportunity. They also invest resources to demonstrate how closely their views match those of the people they serve. They have funded surveys that regularly show large majorities of their customers favor unfettered freedom of choice. When asked whether payday-advance companies provide a useful service, 92% of their customers say yes. When asked whether the government should limit the number of payday advances one can get in a year, 69% say no. The only restriction of freedom this population favors is the one from which consumers appear to benefit: when asked whether government should limit the fees charged by the payday lenders, 75% say yes.[20] But perhaps some of the customers would change their minds if they realized that price ceilings that bind inevitably reduce the supply of credit.

And the payday lenders have done more than this. They have sought to mobilize their clientele as an interest group in the fight over regulation. They have gathered signatures on petitions and organized referenda in defense of financial choice. They have encouraged their customers to phone legislators and to write letters to the newspapers. In Illinois, the main lobbying group for the industry flooded a public forum on payday lending with angry customers who feared the politicians were going to take away their source of credit. When Governor George Ryan tried to explain the rules he proposed to implement, he was shouted down by the crowd. "Let me have the choice to spend my money the way I want," one woman insisted. "I'm not stupid." Another woman told the regulators, "My cash company helps me and you're considering regulations to try to take that away from me." The room became so raucous that the police arrested several of the protesters, who had been provided with printed signs by the lenders and ferried to the forum in stretch limousines.[21] This sort of spectacle of popular support had never been organized by the salary lenders, who were forced to lobby behind the scenes and through dishonest arguments because they were unable to mobilize in the progressive era around the ideology of freedom of choice.

The strength of this ideology is that it depicts the lender and the borrower as sharing a common interest in their mutually advantageous exchange, but it can also write off any problems that arise from this exchange as resulting from a failure of personal responsibility. If debtors roll their loans over again and again, it is either their choice or their mistake. They should be free to do as they please but must also bear the consequences for their choices. "Responsible adults must meet their obligations," a *Tribune* editorial insisted. "But provided customers are adequately informed about what those obligations are, they and these companies should be free to go about their business. People need money quickly for a short period of time for all kinds of reasons—and there should be a way for them to get it. It would be a travesty if, to protect those who aren't responsible, the do-gooders closed off this source of cash for the rest."[22] A *Sun-Times* columnist was blunter. Tired of the sob stories told by the advocates of consumer protection, she didn't mince words: "Deadbeats are griping about being gouged again. They borrowed money from payday loan stores without having to put up collateral, and when it's time to repay, they complain that the interest rate is too high." If they had been responsible adults, they would have set aside money for a rainy day. But they didn't, so now these debtors must pay. As she saw it, "Most people who fall into this predicament have only themselves to blame." They were free to choose and now they must be free to fail.[23]

Industry representatives are rarely as harsh as the editorialists who support them. Every now and then, however, a candid manager would admit, "Anyone who takes out a loan from us for a year is a nitwit."[24] But the usual strategy is to deny that problems exist or, when such denials are no longer believable, to insist that self-regulation could solve them. In 1999 the emerging national chains formed the Community Financial Services Association of America (CFSA), which lobbies on behalf of the industry and also touts its "best practices." Today more than half of all payday-lending outlets are represented by CFSA. The best practices to which members commit themselves include a right of rescission, a limit on rollovers, and an extended payment option. The association has also drafted model legislation incorporating these provisions. In 2005, CFSA sponsored a pilot project in Chicago to boost the credit scores of participating customers by offering to report their transactions to a credit bureau.[25] The idea was to build goodwill by showing that payday lenders don't want to trap their customers in a subprime ghetto of credit. The organization has also conducted an advertising campaign to encourage consumer responsibility. Its cautionary notice reads: "Payday advances should be used for short-term financial needs only, not as a long-term financial solution. Customers with credit difficulties should seek credit counseling."

Most of the national chains belong to CFSA, but the organization has also exposed rifts within the industry. Two of the larger companies withdrew from the association when it imposed a limit on rollover transactions, though one of these chains subsequently rejoined.[26] Many local and regional chains have never belonged to the national association, and in some states, including Illinois, they have vigorously opposed CFSA legislation, which they believe is skewed toward the interests of the biggest firms. This fissure within the industry has been exploited by the advocates of reform. They have imitated the success of the original progressives, who cut a deal with one fraction of the loan sharks and isolated the other. But the local lenders have been resourceful in defending their interests. They are organized, too, and every bit as shrewd and slippery as the national chains. They understand how to make their demand effective within the market for credit regulation.

Demand becomes effective when it is backed by purchasing power. The fuel of purchasing power is money. To the auction for credit regulation the payday lenders have brought a fat purse. Since 2000, they have contributed more than $2 million to the coffers of politicians in Illinois, more than in any other state.[27] This has been possible because Illinois does not cap the amount that donors may contribute. The system is known in the state as "pay to play." The contributions have been made by the competing national and state trade groups, individual corporations, and executives and lobbyists. The money has been scattered around widely, with three out of four legislators receiving cash donations from lender sources in recent years. Members of the Illinois house and senate financial institutions committees have been especially favored. The aim of the contributions is to buy goodwill but also obstruction. As one observer pointed out, "They want to be left alone. . . . They're perfectly happy with the status quo, and anything that doesn't draw attention to them makes them happy." Donors of this sort were said to be very popular with legislators. "It's far easier to kill [a piece of legislation] than it is to pass something in Springfield. So if there's someone willing to hand out checks in exchange for killing stuff, that's far easier than giving out checks in exchange for passing stuff."[28]

The biggest recipient of the industry's largesse was Governor Rod Blagojevich, who was recently impeached for corruption. During his six years in office Blagojevich raked in hundreds of thousands of dollars from the lenders. The gush of money into his campaign was furious in 2005, as a reform bill moved through the legislature. The trade group representing the smaller chains and the independents desperately wanted to defeat the measure, which they claimed would put them out of business. So they organized a fundraiser for Blagojevich in the spring. The governor spent an hour chatting with the lenders and listening to their concerns while collecting tens of thousands of dollars in contributions. But a few weeks later, he nonetheless signed the reform bill, which had been backed by CFSA. A spokesman for the local group was bitter. "We should have saved our money," he said. "It was an exercise in futility, because nothing was really accomplished."[29]

This episode points up the difference between a political auction and the more ordinary kind. In a political auction you must pay whether you win a concession or not. The contributions are made piecemeal, without any guarantee that the investment will pay off. But the game is played over many rounds, and a loss in one can be recouped later on. Defeats are rarely permanent, and victories are often ephemeral.

The Coalition of Altruists

According to an industry-funded survey, only 17% of payday-loan customers express an unfavorable opinion of the industry.[30] The rate of dissatisfaction with banks in this population is only slightly lower than it is for payday lenders. What is more, the fraction of this sample with a favorable opinion of the check lenders is substantially greater than it is for banks. But if so, it is a puzzle why there has been so much demand expressed for consumer protection from this product within the market for credit regulation. The banks are less popular, yet nobody is trying to shut them down or to impose low price caps on their products. Why would a business three-quarters of whose customers express satisfaction with their most recent experience face such a difficult regulatory climate?

One possibility, suggested by this survey's data, is that payday-loan customers are a bifurcated population. While two-thirds of them report a favorable view of the industry, one-sixth of them are hostile to the payday lenders. This industry's negative rating is higher than those recorded for any other industry about which consumers were surveyed—except the credit card companies, the only credit providers about which this sample expressed more dissatisfaction than satisfaction. It might be the case, then, that the payday lenders produce serious antipathy in a minority of the population with which they do business even as they provide what is perceived to be a valuable service by the majority.

It might also be the case that one specific component of the payday-advance transaction that is widely disliked—its high fees—could also account for the intensity of the demand for credit regulation that has been expressed over the last decade. In the industry-funded survey cited above, fewer than half of the respondents expressed satisfaction with the cost of the loans.[31] In another industry-funded survey, three-quarters of the customers said they supported government action to limit the fees.[32] The sky-high interest rates of the payday-loan product, then, might be the widely shared grievance that has provoked a consumer backlash against the industry.

But opinions by themselves are not an effective source of demand in any market, including the one for credit regulation. The fact that some consumers are unhappy with the product they purchase does not guarantee that their dissatisfaction will register in the political system or extract from political entrepreneurs a share of the limited supply of regulation that they can provide. Needs or wants are not necessarily demands to which producers might respond. This is especially true with regard to payday lending, for the consumers of this product never make their appearance at the political auction for credit regulation as an autonomous and organized constituency. They possess no union or consumer federation of their own. Unless mobilized by other interest groups, payday borrowers today—as in the past—have remained passive and fragmented. No matter how miserable their plight might be, they have never possessed the capacity to coalesce or enter the political arena on their own initiative. Scattered and without resources, these debtors have been inert until some external force has enlisted their aid in the fights that have been waged on their behalf. Lenders and consumer advocates both claim to speak for those who have mortgaged their checks. The one can produce satisfied customers to buttress its claims, the other can produce pitiful victims of abuse, but the debtors themselves do not form a cohesive class. They are an object, not a subject. They are a heap of sand or an invisible gas.

If they needed protection, these consumers could not protect themselves. Hence others have entered the market for credit regulation on their behalf. The lenders claim that their interests and the interests of the debtors from whom they profit are identical. The protection they seek for their customers is protection from excessive regulation. Why the lenders do what they do is easy to understand. But the motivation of the self-styled consumer-protection advocates is more puzzling. Most of the organizations that have mobilized against the payday lenders are nonprofits. They aren't in the business of business. They also aren't debtors themselves. Why then would they expend resources on behalf of a population to which they do not belong and from which they seem to derive no profit?

For the sake of the common good, the advocates might reply, and because gain at the expense of others is wrong. Justice does matter, and it ought not to be sacrificed simply because entrepreneurs have found a new way to make money. Taking unfair advantage of people is exploitation, and that is a wrongful way to gain. Such forms of cheating shouldn't be tolerated, even if they expand the market and create new jobs. Payday lending is predatory lending, it is said, and decent societies don't permit predators to devour helpless victims.

These are what philosophers call deontological arguments, concerned with duties and justice, but the advocates of consumer protection also appeal to consequentialist considerations. High-rate lending should be curbed or prohibited, they claim, because the costs exceed the benefits. It drives some debtors into bankruptcy, prevents better creditors from being repaid, and increases the demand for government assistance. Consumers, taxpayers, and businesses must pick up the tab for the costs that payday lending imposes on the community. The lenders obviously gain from these transactions, but everybody else loses.[33]

This second argument is an argument from self-interest. It says that most of us would be better off if subprime lending on the security of a postdated check was more strictly regulated. But one could wonder whether the anticipated gains for the reform advocates justify the expenditure of resources that they must bear in order to prevail in the auction for credit regulation. If the benefits of regulation are diffuse but the costs required to produce them are heavy, why would anyone but a hopeless altruist agree to shoulder that burden—especially when success is by no means guaranteed?

Perhaps the world produces more quixotic altruists than a strictly economistic calculation would predict, but perhaps it is also the case that the ideology of consumer protection obscures the material interests that impel groups to enter the market for credit regulation in opposition to the payday lenders. Beneath the universalistic claims, in other words, there might be a more narrow self-interest. This would certainly be the case if the consumer-protection advocates were actually also direct competitors of the payday lenders in the market for credit. Then the demand for protection would seem more like an effort to corner the market and to capture customers, from whom rents could be extracted with the connivance of the political system.

There are indeed egregious examples of this kind of anti-competitive rent seeking in the fight against payday lending. The successful movement to prohibit payday lending in Georgia furnishes the clearest case. Among the various groups that lobbied against high-rate check lending were the state's licensed industrial lenders, a thousand strong and well connected. Descendants of the original loan sharks, these storefront vendors pushed an installment product that competed directly with the payday creditors. Although their rates were capped at 5% a month, the statute by which they were governed permitted the industrial lenders to load each contract with three or four worthless insurance policies, or a bogus auto-club membership.[34] This had the effect of doubling the bill for these small loans, which were secured with the debtors' possessions. The product could trap borrowers in the same way as the payday loan did, but this did not stop consumer-protection groups from forming alliances with the industrial lenders in order to impose restrictions on the creditors with whom the latter competed.[35] In 2004, payday lending was definitively prohibited in the state, but it is hard to view this victory as a principled blow against usurious exploitation. It looks, instead, like a fight between two breeds of the loan shark in which claims of consumer protection were exploited as camouflage for naked self-interest. Some evidence suggests that consumers in Georgia since 2004 are actually worse off than they were before because they have fewer credit options.[36] A half million residents each year are said to cross the border to neighboring states in order to get the payday loans from which the regulators have decided to protect them.[37]

This is a transparent case of business protectionism exploiting the movement for consumer protection to achieve its self-interested aims. Other variations of this pattern are more subtle and complicated. One of the most forceful advocates for prohibition of payday lending within the ranks of the consumerist movement is the Center for Responsible Lending (CRL), which is based in Durham, North Carolina. It has published a stream of research and position papers on payday lending since its founding in 2002. The center has also lobbied vigorously for legislative action in various states. Although CRL is a nonprofit, nonpartisan research and policy organization, it does have the backing of groups with a material interest in curbing payday lending. CRL was founded by Self-Help, a community-development financial institution formed back in the 1980s. Self-Help, in turn, operates a credit union. The chief executive of that financial institution is also the head of CRL, which represents the interests of the credit-union industry, said to engage in "responsible lending."[38] Credit unions are always not-for-profit, but they are not disinterested institutions. They are in the business of making loans, like the payday lenders, and in recent years some have begun to market lower-priced alternatives to the deferred deposit, as we shall see. Like the industrial lenders, then, they are competitors too. This is not to say that CRL and other credit-union affiliates are "just as bad" as the payday lenders or that they seek their own interest at the expense of consumers. After all, it might turn out that their interests and the interests of consumers are identical. But CRL and other ostensibly nonpartisan groups are nonetheless connected to and serve certain tangible, material interests. Recognizing this can help us to understand why groups that fight in the name of consumer interest expend resources on behalf of a heap of sand. They do so, in part, because there are potential customers in that heap. Recruitment of these customers would be facilitated if payday lending was hampered by government regulation and if credit-union products were subsidized by taxpayers.

Once we begin to look, this web of self-interest becomes more visible in the camp of consumerism. Representatives from financial institutions, including banks and credit unions, serve on the boards of directors of several of the nonprofits that have campaigned for tighter regulation of payday lending. The Woodstock Institute, for instance, is a research and policy organization like CRL that is based in Chicago. It has published a series of reports over the years on payday lending in Illinois, and its representatives are frequently quoted in newspaper stories on the industry. Executives from several depository institutions sit on the institute's board, including one executive whose federal credit union markets an alternative to the payday loan. Heads of several establishment lenders can also be counted among the directors of Chicago's Metropolitan Family Services, which belongs to a coalition of forces in the state that is lobbying for payday credit regulation.

This coalition calls itself the Monsignor John Egan Campaign for Payday Loan Reform. It is named in honor of Father Jack Egan, a Catholic priest at Holy Name Cathedral in Chicago who in the last years of his life helped to mobilize the initial opposition to payday lending.[39] The Egan alliance is diverse, and some of its member organizations have no direct stake in constraining competition from the payday lenders, as the credit unions and banks do. At the heart of this coalition is Citizen Action/Illinois, the state chapter of USAction, which describes itself as a grassroots progressive organization fighting for social justice. The main backers of this group are organized labor, including the Service Employees International Union, the American Federation of State, County, and Municipal Employees, and the Communication Workers of America. These labor unions do not compete with the payday lenders in the credit market but, instead, represent the interests of their members and other working people who may be tangled up with the loan companies or gouged by their high prices. In this fight they are an authentic consumer advocate, but groups like this also have a more generalized interest in supporting restrictions on business. Such restrictions can reduce the resources of their opponents, facilitate labor organization, and create jobs for unionized civil servants. Since employees of the payday lenders are not covered by collective-bargaining agreements, organized labor has no incentive to maximize growth in that industry. To the contrary, its interests are better served by challenging the ideology and policy of freedom of contract to which the payday lenders subscribe. This specific fight, ostensibly about consumer protection, should also be seen as one battle front in the encompassing conflict between the beneficiaries of free markets, on the one hand, and the beneficiaries of protectionism, on the other.

Many who have never done business with the payday lenders and who would seem to have no personal stake in the outcome of this regulatory tussle might nonetheless have an interest in supporting projects of restriction. College professors, for example, work for nonprofit institutions, public or private, and benefit from government investment and redistribution. It isn't difficult to convince most of them that government ought to do something about payday lending because they are predisposed to believe that government action is beneficial. For them, it is. Lawyers, too, readily enlist in this fight because more government regulation is unlikely to deprive them of work. They write the rules, enforce them, and litigate on their basis. The profession makes its living by identifying social problems the solution to which requires their services. So do the other helping professions. When the clients whom they serve have credit problems with the payday lenders, their instincts and their interests will tend to draw them toward strategies of regulatory intervention. This tendency will be reinforced by the fact that it is the most egregious cases that are likely to come to their attention. They see the business at its worst, when customers come to them for help. Their judgments are *ex post*, not *ex ante*, as the economists would say. The legal aid lawyers, social workers, credit counselors, and priests who lobby for consumer protection do not encounter in the course of their work the satisfied customers. Those people do not require their help and so remain invisible to the advocates of intervention.

The coalition of the restrictionists, then, is self-interested too. It doesn't consist of selfless altruists after all. But the interests of those who form this alliance are more heterogeneous than is the case with the advocates of free enterprise. Some opponents of the payday lenders have a narrow interest in restricting the competition while others have a broad interest in enhancing the project of regulation. But whether the opponents' interests are narrow or broad their interests are usually obscured, because the consumers on whose behalf the opponents speak are not their debtors (yet). Their advocacy for that reason seems disinterested, but this is one of the illusions in the show of advocacy. If the advocacy was genuinely disinterested, it seems unlikely that its demands would ever appear or be made effective in the market for credit regulation.

The coalition that has pressed for tighter regulation of payday lending has been dominated by not-for-profit institutions—research centers, credit unions, social service agencies, and church groups. Absent from its ranks, for the most part, have been organizations representing the for-profit business community. The chambers of commerce and the business alliances have not played a central role in pressing for reform. Compared to the fight against the loan sharks a century ago, the contrast is striking. The commercial and manufacturing clubs then helped to spearhead the campaign for passage of the Uniform Small Loan Law in Illinois and other states. But in the movement to curb check lending today the establishment business associations rarely participate. The payroll offices of the large employers are no longer flooded in the same dramatic way with the wage assignments that were the principal instrument of security of the original salary lenders. If their employees are harassed by the high-rate lenders, that harassment is usually less visible within the workplace now. The payday lenders have other methods available to collect their debts. They don't rely so centrally, as the salary lenders and buyers did, on the payroll department as a collection agency. As a result, business groups today don't have the same powerful incentive to expend resources in the market for credit regulation on behalf of restrictionism. Indeed, in many places, the payday lenders belong to the local chambers of commerce, which would be loath to turn against member businesses. The outlets have proliferated rapidly, renting space in strip malls and empty corner storefronts. They create jobs and draw foot traffic into neighborhoods. As one chamber of commerce leader in Arizona explained, "They grew overnight. They must be being used. It is a state-licensed, legitimate business, and if lower-income consumers make use of and need them, that's their business." But then he added, "The socio-economic question is how good is that for the community at large? I can't answer the question."[40] The spread of payday-lending stores didn't exactly seem like an indicator of economic health in the communities where they sprouted, but would that health improve if the local business alliances lobbied to keep these vendors out? Payday lenders aren't dirty bookstores, after all, though some of the critics of the industry might place both kinds of businesses in the same category. The payday lenders are alternative financial-service providers, and credit is completely mainstream now. Hence the business groups tend to be agnostic. They don't lobby for or against the industry. Payday lending isn't their fight.

Because the business community has not entered the market for credit regulation as an organized force, the coalition of restrictionists is significantly narrower now than it was in the heyday of progressivism. It isn't as balanced and establishment. That coalition also lacks a central coordinating agency with the hegemony once exercised by the Russell Sage Foundation in the fight for the Uniform Small Loan Law. The CRL and the CFA play a prominent role in mobilizing support for regulation or prohibition, but neither group possesses the same stature or the scale of resources once commanded by Arthur Ham and the Sage Foundation's remedial loans department. The enormous endowment of that institution freed its representatives from the appearance of being dependent upon partisan material interests that might have undercut the disinterested and scientific authority with which it claimed to speak on the small-loan problem. The fact that the Sage fortune was earned in business only strengthened the authenticity of its pronouncements. The national organizations that fight against payday lending today, by contrast, seem more obviously partisan. They are interest groups and transparently left of center. As a result, the suppliers of credit regulation now are unlikely to be overawed by their judgments. They are one lobby in a sea of lobbyists, and the only thing these consumerist groups might have to offer to politicians are votes, not campaign contributions. Whether they can deliver more votes in this political auction than the other side can deliver cash donations is an open question. But the legislators who are the arbiters of credit regulation are unlikely to treat the self-styled consumer-advocate groups as oracles of science. They have stakes in the fire, just like the payday lenders.

Given the smaller size of the coalition that fights for restriction of payday lending today and the scale of resources mobilized by their opponents, it is a little surprising that they have managed to achieve anything at all. This is especially true in states such as Illinois where the rules in place when payday lending came on the scene were permissive. In these states the restrictionists had a more difficult task. They could not simply defend the status quo. They had to impose limits on freedom of contract in the face of a determined opponent. In politics, as in war, defense is easier than offense. The few can block the many from introducing change. To prevail, the many usually need more than just numbers on their side. They must be organized; it also helps if the forces they're fighting are themselves disorganized.

The Producers of Regulation

In the market for credit regulation, politicians function as both producers and consumers. Collectively they control the supply of this service, but individually, politicians can express a demand for government action from the very body to which they belong. They are lobbyists too, in other words, but political entrepreneurs don't always have to get the bills they're lobbying for passed in order to gain credit from their constituencies. Plenty of pieces of legislation are introduced by their sponsors but never have a prayer of becoming law. In statehouses across the country innumerable payday-loan reform bills—many of them quite hollow or quixotic—have been sent to committee after the obligatory press release is issued and then promptly disappear into oblivion. Just as there is a show of advocacy, there is a show of legislation too. But in the show of legislation the aim is not to appear disinterested. The legislator fights on behalf of particular interests or, at least, must give the appearance of wanting to wage that fight. Perception matters as much as results.

Government is fragmented. It operates at different levels, in different jurisdictions, and is divided into branches, each with its own complicated internal structure. Party lines, in turn, cut across these divisions, further fragmenting the process of producing regulatory change. The system isn't built for speed or efficiency. Although many constituencies petition government for legislative or executive action, the process can satisfy only a small fraction of the demand. There isn't enough time in a legislative session to pass more than a handful of the many bills that are introduced. Once some piece of legislation is ratified in a particular policy area, the likelihood that it will be addressed again by the legislature in the near future is low. The issue will move off the agenda for some time as other constituencies press for the restricted supply of attention that governmental bodies can accord to any given policy question. Whether the problem is solved or not, it will be treated as if it has been fixed by the besieged class of political entrepreneurs.

For a product like the payday loan, the first layer of government to which complaints are usually addressed are the local authorities. Payday lenders are neighborhood institutions, and in urban communities the neighborhood is the bailiwick of the alderman or city councilor. In Chicago it was the aldermen who first registered concerns with payday lending after the industry burst on the scene at the end of the 1990s. Alderman Toni Preckwinkle, from the 4th Ward on the city's South Side, was an early and outspoken critic of the check lenders. "Almost a year ago, when this business came to my ward, and I learned about it, I was horrified," she told a press conference in 1999. "The more I learn about payday loans, the more horrified I become."[41] The alderman regularly berated the vendors as predators or loan sharks and claimed they were "chewing up" the poor in her blighted neighborhood.[42]

But there is only so much that these frontline representatives in the larger political system can do about a problem of this sort when they encounter it.

Credit regulation is not the province of city government. Jurisdiction has been assigned instead to the state and federal governments. City councils cannot impose usury caps on their own initiative or regulate the substance of loan contracts. But local governments are permitted to enforce certain rules, for example, governing advertising inside the stores. Chicago's Department of Consumer Services sued a payday-lending chain in 1999 for deceptive business practices when the company failed to disclose the annual percentage rate of its product in placards and brochures.[43] Local officials also have discretion not to enforce rules, such as those governing bad checks. In the early years of payday lending many of the businesses turned to local prosecutors and sheriffs when they couldn't collect on their debts. They filed check-fraud complaints in order to coerce repayment from delinquent debtors or to win triple damages in municipal court. In one district of Dallas the lenders reportedly filed more than 13,000 criminal complaints during the course of a year.[44] But, increasingly, local authorities declined to apply the bad-check laws to such cases. After all, the creditors knew there were insufficient funds in the account when they accepted these bank drafts as collateral, and in writing the checks, most borrowers had no intent to defraud.[45] Once they became familiar with the transaction, many prosecutors exercised their discretion not to press charges, and state legislatures later revised the statutes to prevent this misuse of the bad-check laws. Local governments resisted the effort to conscript them as collection agents for the payday lenders.

But local jurisdictions are not permitted to outlaw the product, even if its predations are felt most powerfully in their neighborhoods. The city councilors are consigned to the role of consumers of credit regulation instead of its producers. They must lobby the higher authorities who have been accorded the right to decide. Playing that role, Alderman Preckwinkle tried to force the hand of the state agency charged with credit regulation—the DFI—by suing it in 1999 for alleged administrative improprieties. She claimed that the DFI, which was closely associated with the industry in this early phase of its existence, had broken the law by permitting the payday lenders to accept postdated checks as collateral for their cash advances.[46] That suit failed, so the alderman tried a different tack. She turned to one of the few powers possessed by local governments that can thwart the payday lenders: zoning regulation. City councils write the rules about where businesses may be located and the process through which they must go to win approval. Preckwinkle pushed a measure through the city council requiring new payday-loan shops to get a special use permit. This certificate could only be obtained after a public hearing at which community residents and other interested groups could register their objections about the proposed business.[47]

Many other local communities have adopted similar measures over the past decade. In some jurisdictions, zoning laws regulate how close new outlets may be to existing stores or to residential areas. The aim is to reduce the clustering of payday lenders, which might encourage customers to borrow from several vendors at once, and also to prevent the appearance of urban blight. By reducing in some degree the convenience of the product such regulations might weaken demand, but they also reduce competition between the lenders, which seems unlikely to benefit consumers.[48] Either way, the probable impact of zoning rules is minimal once payday lenders have already established themselves in a community. The new rules are typically adopted after the clustering has already occurred, hence what they really accomplish is to freeze the status quo. The tool of zoning regulation, which is practically the only instrument available to local officials, is too weak to restrict supply or to undercut demand. Thus the main battles over payday lending must be fought outside local communities, even if they experience most directly the effects of this brand of borrowing. Local governments are only petty producers in the market for credit regulation.

The main suppliers of this service are the state governments. The state legislatures write the rules, and one or more agencies in the executive branch enforce them. In Illinois, like many other states, the agency charged with supervision of nondepository lenders is the Department of Financial Institutions (recently renamed the Department of Financial and Professional Regulation). The DFI licenses the payday lenders, monitors their business practices, and processes consumer complaints. When check lending arrived in Illinois in the second half of the 1990s, consumer-protection advocates complained that the DFI had been captured by the industry. The agency formed a task force in 1998 to write rules governing the product, but its ranks were filled with industry representatives. Opponents of the business demanded a seat at the table, but the DFI disbanded the commission instead.[49] The agency didn't see the need for additional regulation at this stage but preferred to emphasize consumer education. As a spokesperson explained, "We're working to get the message out that short-term loans, especially payday loans, are not a bad tool if people use them as they were intended to be used, which is as a stopgap measure when people are experiencing a short-term financial crunch."[50] But in less than a year, the DFI had decided that education by itself would not end abuses in the industry. The agency had issued a rule limiting loan renewals to three, but the lenders evaded it by writing new contracts when the limit had been reached. This maneuver, the spokesperson acknowledged, did not technically violate the agency's rule, but it effectively "gutted" the DFI's "effort to protect consumers from continual loan rollovers and spiraling debt."[51] In frustration, the department turned to the state legislature and asked it to pass a law regulating the transaction.

Several bills were introduced in the Illinois house and senate at this time. One sought to impose a rate cap of 36%, which would have killed off the industry. As lobbyists for the payday lenders liked to point out, "You couldn't even pay the light bill, let alone pay rent, salaries and other overhead associated with a business" with rates this low.[52] A $200 cash advance at the rate of 36% a year would earn less than $3 in interest over two weeks. The lenders therefore mobilized to block this bill, fielding a force of thirteen registered lobbyists—including former legislators, judges, and prosecutors—and distributing hundreds of thousands of dollars in campaign contributions.[53] Their efforts were successful, for the bill remained bottled up in committee. The other piece of legislation did not impose a rate cap but limited rollovers and required borrowers to pay down some of the principal each time they did renew a loan.[54] Other restrictions were also included in the bill, but it fell a few votes short in the senate during the spring 2000 legislative session.

But this wasn't the end of the matter. Unable to push rules through the state legislature, the sponsors of the senate bill did succeed in enacting a resolution that called on Governor George Ryan and the DFI to invoke the agency's rule-making authority to impose the regulations they had proposed. The advocates of reform were aggrieved because they had made a major concession to the lenders by not including a rate cap in the measure that was defeated. The chief sponsor complained, "It doesn't matter what you put in front of this industry—it's too much. They want to have the unfettered right to do what they're doing." In August 2000, the DFI issued a set of rules based on the senate bill but including additional measures such as the establishment of a database to monitor compliance with the regulations.[55]

Before the rules could go into effect, however, they had to be vetted by the legislature's Joint Committee on Administrative Rules, a bipartisan oversight panel with the authority to block or alter the DFI proposal. That committee was chaired by state senator Barack Obama, a man whom nobody at this time would have guessed would be elected the 44th president of the United States. Obama's committee was lobbied vigorously by the payday lenders, who claimed that the new rules would shut down the industry. Although he favored the DFI regulations, Obama said the intensity of the lenders' opposition prompted him to request a delay in enacting the rules. "The concern among some people," he told a reporter, "was that the department [DFI] did not negotiate in good faith with the industry, that the rules are too draconian."[56] Obama thought a few minor changes might mollify the opponents on the committee. "In a complicated legislative process like this, you've got to be mindful that it takes some time to put regulations like this together," he said. Advocating the bipartisan consensus style of government he would later tout in his run for the presidency, Obama claimed that he was "optimistic that we're going to end up with some rules that will allow these payday loan company owners to operate profitably, but at the same time curb the egregious abuses that we've been seeing in some neighborhoods."[57] Obama was not a strict prohibitionist at this time.[58] A few weeks later, however, the committee voted eight to one to block the DFI from enforcing the new rules for six months. Although he chaired the panel, Obama was absent from the meeting when the vote was taken. The lone legislator to oppose the majority was Lisa Madigan, who would be elected attorney general in 2002.[59]

The provision in the DFI rules most vehemently opposed by the industry was said to be the state database that would monitor compliance with the regulations. The lenders complained that customers were worried about identity theft and didn't like the idea of the government tracking their financial decisions. Legislators sympathetic to the industry pressed the DFI to negotiate on this provision, but the Ryan administration refused to budge.[60] Florida was the first state to establish such a database, in 2001. Illinois would eventually contract with Florida's vendor to deploy this compliance tool in the state, but it took another five years for this innovation to become politically feasible.

The committee chaired by Obama could only delay the DFI rules, which would take effect after six months unless the legislature passed a joint resolution rescinding them. An effort to pass such a resolution was mounted by the industry's supporters during the spring 2001 legislative session, but it faced an insurmountable obstacle in the person of House Speaker Michael Madigan, the father of Lisa Madigan. He used his clout to bottle up the resolution in the House Rules Committee until the deadline for action passed.[61] A year after the legislature had called on the executive branch to impose rules on checking lending (because the legislature was unable to muster the majority needed to pass a bill of its own), those rules were now set to take effect—because the subterfuges of the opponents of reform were outmatched by the subterfuges of the advocates of reform. For the producers of regulation, subterfuge often seems to be the essential art.

The DFI rules were to go into effect on 1 August 2001. Industry spokesmen warned that the new regulations, which imposed no rate cap, would drive many lenders bankrupt and cost the state jobs. They went to court and won a temporary restraining order blocking enforcement of the rules, but this bought them only a three-weeks' reprieve.[62] By the end of the month it was no longer legal in Illinois to roll loans over again and again or to pay off one cash advance with the proceeds of another.

But these restrictions applied only if the term of the loan was thirty days or less. The new regulations did not govern extensions of credit of longer duration or installment loan products, which remained largely unconstrained within the state. And so, almost immediately after the new rules went into effect, the payday lenders in Illinois re-crafted the terms of their cash advances, now extending credit for a minimum of 31 days. The standard charge for these one-month loans was $45 for every $100 advanced, which was the equivalent of an annual percentage rate of 530%. Loans of this duration could be renewed indefinitely, and the requirement to pay down one-quarter of the principal each time did not apply. In the year after the DFI regulations went into effect, only 3% of the cash advances extended by the payday lenders fell within the purview of these rules. Nearly three-quarters of the 31-day loan contracts written in 2002 were rollovers, and the DFI reported that it was "quite common for borrowers to have multiple payday loans outstanding with several different payday loan companies." The average check loan was paid off after 78 days—frequently with the proceeds of a new cash advance—and cost the debtor $112 for every $100 that had been borrowed. To make matters worse, the database that was supposed to monitor loan activity was never commissioned by the DFI.[63]

So much effort had been expended in 2000 and 2001 to weave a net of regulation for the payday-lending market in Illinois, but no sooner had this net been deployed than the loan sharks slipped right through its gaping hole. All of the industry's claims about bankruptcy and closing up shop seemed in retrospect like misdirection. There had never been any threat to the check lenders if these particular rules were enforced; they only entailed the nuisance of redesigning their product to evade the rules. But if the loan sharks seemed disingenuous, the reformers seemed hapless. They had not asked themselves what the lenders would do if their restrictions were enacted. They had not tried to think like a shark. This is a little surprising, for many of the partisans of reform had practiced law for a living. They were supposed to be trained to anticipate their opponent's next move. But the lenders, it seems, had hired the keener legal minds.

And so Illinois remained part of "the wild, wild west" in payday lending, as a new director of the DFI observed. "We're the largest state that doesn't regulate this industry," he complained.[64] New bills were introduced in the legislature in 2002 and 2004, but none of these reform measures made it to the floor for a vote.[65] Having drawn heavily on the scarce supply of political attention in previous years, the effective demand for regulatory action that could be mobilized by the advocates of reform was slight, even though the problems that had called into existence a progressive coalition in 2000 and 2001 had not disappeared. The reformers had had their chance. It would not be until 2005 that a serious effort was launched to push the issue back onto the political agenda.

The groundwork for a renewed push was laid the previous year, when the advocates of reform entered into negotiations with representatives of the national organization of payday lenders, CFSA, which is dominated by the largest chains in the industry. CFSA sat down with key legislators and leaders from the Egan Coalition and hammered out a bill that both sides could support. The legislation capped fees, limited loan size, restricted renewals, established a database to monitor compliance, and included an extended repayment plan.[66] If enacted, the bill would mandate the tightest set of restrictions short of prohibition imposed on the industry to that point. Part of the CFSA's motivation in yielding these concessions was the desire to head off the prohibitionists—who wanted to impose a cap in the vicinity of 36% that would make it impossible to extend short-term credit on the security of a postdated check. The possibility that a prohibitionist bill might make its way through the legislature had risen considerably because the Democratic Party controlled all of the branches of the state government going into the 2005 legislative term. Rod Blagojevich, elected governor in 2002, had vowed during his campaign to clamp down on the industry. "They prey on the poor and the elderly," he had told an audience at Jesse Jackson's Rainbow PUSH headquarters. "It isn't just wrong, it's immoral. We're going to change that by putting caps on interest for payday loans and [requiring] full display of information on the going rate."[67] With solid majorities in both houses of the legislature, Blagojevich would be in an excellent position to fulfill that campaign pledge in 2005.

But CFSA may have had another motive in forming an alliance with the advocates of reform. Lobbyists for the Illinois Small Loan Association (ISLA), the trade group of the local chains and the independents, charged that CFSA had conspired to write the rules in the reform bill in such a way as to drive the local competition out of business. The rate cap had been set well below the going rate for payday loans in the state and could be skirted by the national chains, which would export higher rates from unregulated states through national banks with which they had forged alliances. "What's really happening," the ISLA president complained, "is that the CFSA is using the Egan group as their front. It's attempting to put us out of business." The same tactic had been employed in other states, he claimed. "This is the civil war within the industry."[68]

As was the case back in 1917, when the Uniform Small Loan Law was passed in Illinois, it was this "civil war" within the industry that made it possible for the reformers to push through the Payday Loan Reform Act during the spring 2005 legislative session. The lenders were divided against themselves, neutralizing each other's campaign contributions, and the reformers could point to the support of CFSA to demonstrate that their bill was a reasonable compromise. Dire warnings about imminent bankruptcy by the local lenders weren't as believable this time. It seemed like they were crying wolf. "We're hearing the same arguments we heard before," the director of Citizen Action/Illinois said dismissively. "'We're going to go out of business. We can't do this, yadda, yadda.' These guys from ISLA just want to keep doing business as usual, it's clear."[69]

As always, the toughest battle the reform coalition had to fight was getting the bill out of committee. The ISLA lobbied hard for changes but remained dissatisfied with the draft when it came up for a vote in the House Committee on Financial Institutions. "It's been a moving target to make ISLA happy," the bill's sponsor reported. "My impression is they just want to delay and don't want the bill at all."[70] Despite intense pressure, the bill made it out of committee by the slimmest of margins but was then passed unanimously by the house in April 2005. The senate followed suit the following month, and Governor Blagojevich signed the bill into law in June. "This is what happens," one of the bill's supporters exulted, "when government works as it's supposed to."[71]

The Payday Loan Reform Act (PLRA) of 2005 was a great victory for the reformers—at least on paper. But when the law went into effect at the end of the year, the same thing that had happened before happened again. The new rules applied to loans with a term of 120 days or less, so many lenders switched immediately to a five- or six-month installment product that skirted the rules. In many cases these new installment loans were simply a series of shorter payday loans strung back to back. The installments were interest-only and the debtor had to make a lump-sum payment of the principal at the end of the loan term. The interest rates were still very high, and the lenders continued to haul large numbers of delinquent customers into court to collect damages several times the face amount of the loan.[72] As the date approached for the new rules to take effect, the Department of Financial and Professional Regulations issued a warning to the licensed lenders that it would apply the statute to all of their loan products. "Does it look like a duck? Does it quack like a duck?" the agency's head asked.[73] If so, the new limits would apply. Fines were issued nearly every day after the law went into effect, but then the lenders went to court and won a restraining order against the state. They pointed out that installment loans were covered by a different statute that did not impose the burdensome limits the state was enforcing. The court confirmed their interpretation, which meant the Department of Financial and Professional Regulations would have to go back to the legislature and request that a new bill be sent forward. "Sometimes I wonder," the leader of the Egan Coalition rued, "if we shouldn't have just banned payday loans to begin with."[74]

Because of this newest loophole in the net of regulation, the number of short-term loans logged into the state's database declined after 2006. Consumers were steered to the new installment products, which became more expensive after PLRA went into effect. Sensing that the legislature would not be hospitable to a new bill introduced so soon after it had passed the last one, in July 2006 the governor tried to push new regulations covering the longer-term loans through the Joint Committee on Administrative Rules. But the committee—no longer chaired by Barack Obama—voted overwhelmingly to reject the rules.[75] Hence the reformers would have no alternative but to return to the general assembly and begin the process all over again. A new campaign was launched in 2008, but this time the reform coalition was narrower because CFSA did not support the legislation. Worse still, the traditional installment creditors—who had been lightly regulated for years—joined forces with the payday lenders to lobby against the bill. The installment finance companies did not like the check lenders but also thought it was unfair to impose regulations designed for a different product on theirs. "They ruined the viability of an act that was perfectly OK before," one industry executive complained. In other states, as we have seen, these two types of lenders could work against each other, but in Illinois circumstances compelled them to join forces. With this enlarged coalition, reform opponents were able to keep the new bill from reaching the house floor for a vote.[76] As a result, a sizable and growing fraction of the small-loan business remained essentially unrestricted ten years after the check lenders first began to extend credit in Illinois.

Dividing the Ocean into Lakes

The Illinois case confirms what has always been true—that the loan sharks are the slipperiest fish in the sea of consumer credit. They are difficult to regulate, in part because the cash they lend at high prices can be packaged in different ways. If the state imposes rules that make one quick-cash product less profitable, the lenders can shift rapidly to a different product not constrained by these regulations. As a newspaper editorial in Oregon observed, "Trying to control predatory lenders is like playing the Whack-a-Mole game at the local arcade. Smack down one mole with your mallet and, sure enough, another pops up somewhere else. Then another. And another."[77]

The effort to regulate the check lenders in Texas offers a fine example of this game of Whack-a-Mole with the loan sharks. One breed or another of the loan shark has plied its trade from storefront outlets in Texas for at least a century. The check lenders first surfaced in the state in the early 1990s and operated alongside the "small small loan" finance companies, which were permitted to extend credit at an annual rate of 100% or so. But the new payday lenders couldn't make money with their short-term loans at that rate, so they either flouted the law or devised subterfuges like the "lease-back" transaction, in which the creditor allegedly purchased one of the debtor's possessions and then sold it back for a fee. After numerous prosecutions and further evasive maneuvers by the check lenders, the Texas Finance Commission eventually legalized the product but set the maximum permissible rate below the level most vendors thought was viable.[78] To evade the new rules, the payday lenders formed alliances with out-of-state banks and used their federal charters to import whatever interest rate the market would bear. This ruse worked until the federal authorities eventually clamped down on these "rent-a-bank" arrangements; then the lenders exploited an old provision in the statutes and recast themselves as "credit service organizations," or brokerages, arranging credit transactions for a high fee but not technically loaning money themselves. The validity of this arrangement has been upheld by the courts, and so Texas has the distinction of being a state in which there are plenty of payday loans but hardly any licensed payday lenders.[79] It nicely illustrates James White's observation that "the usury laws on the books of most states are only a *trompe l'oeil*, a 'visual deception . . . rendered in extremely fine detail'." Because they are full of holes, the payday-loan statutes in Texas, Illinois, and other states create "the illusion that local legislatures are guarding their constituents from high rates, but they are not."[80]

As the Texas case reveals, one strategy adopted by the payday lenders in their effort to evade state regulations they find excessively restrictive has been to insist that the market in consumer credit is an ocean and not a set of isolated lakes. Interest rates, they have claimed, can be imported across state lines without restriction in the free-trade zone that is the United States, as long as the lender has a connection to the jurisdiction from which the higher rates are being exported. That is the rule in interstate banking enshrined in the Marquette decision of 1978, which ushered in a new era in deregulated credit, and the payday lenders have tried to have that rule applied to them by forming alliances with federally chartered banks. These banks (often tiny) would claim to be the source of the credit extended to the customer who borrowed from a payday-advance outlet. The outlet itself insisted that it was merely acting as a broker on behalf of the bank—as a middleman but not the underwriter. As a result, none of the state rules governing payday lending were said to apply to this credit transaction because the cash had been exported across state lines from an unrestricted jurisdiction. These "rent-a-bank" arrangements were first forged in the late 1990s.[81] Later some Internet lenders cut out the bank affiliation and simply claimed to be doing business with their customers in an unregulated state or off-shore. In cyberspace the state lakes of consumer credit disappeared into a boundless and ungoverned ocean, the paradise of loan sharks.

State regulators reject the theory that cyberspace is extraterritorial. Vendors operating through the Internet must respect their rules, they insist, because what matters is not the physical location of the lender but the legal residency of the debtor. The courts have accepted this argument, but that does not mean it is easy to compel the loan sharks of cyberspace to cease and desist. West Virginia has tried to enforce its prohibition vigorously in recent years, but of the Internet lenders one official acknowledged, "We can't even get an address to sue them." Shell companies conceal the identity or location of the vendors and some operate in foreign countries or from tribal jurisdictions. State regulators in Illinois imposed a huge fine on an Internet predator in 2007 but were unable to collect any of the money.[82] Like the loan sharks of old, this new breed closes down one site but then starts doing business the very next day at another address and under a different name.

The shell games of the Internet lenders are hard to defeat but nonetheless patently illegal. The "rent-a-bank" subterfuge, by contrast, was successful in removing payday lending from the legal jurisdiction of the states, at least for a time. The submergence of the state lakes in the open waters of a national market in consumer credit had the authority of a Supreme Court decision to sanction it. For several years those payday lenders that had forged alliances with national banks were able to bypass the rules imposed by state governments, until the federal authorities intervened. The Federal Deposit Insurance Corporation (FDIC), the Office of the Comptroller of the Currency (OCC), and the Office of Thrift Supervision (OTS) each became concerned about the business practices of the federal banks they regulated that were cooperating with the payday lenders. These depository institutions were "franchising the bank's attributes" in order to facilitate and to profit from high-rate, high-default payday lending.[83] While the cash advance technically came from the bank, the payday lender had solicited the customers, selected them, then immediately bought back the loans issued in the name of the bank so that the payday lender could deploy its infrastructure to collect on the debt. In late 2000, the OCC and the OTS issued an advisory letter to the banks they supervised urging them "to think carefully about the risks involved in such relationships, which can pose not only safety and soundness threats, but also compliance and reputation risks."[84] Getting mixed up with loan sharks, in other words, seemed like a problematic business practice for federally chartered banks.

From this first, understated, warning the regulatory agencies moved toward more aggressive action over the next few years, because several of the smaller chartered banks refused to take the hint and exit from this line of business.[85] Under threat of losing their federal charters, several notorious banks were forced to sever their alliances with the national payday-lending chains. One of these notorious charter-renters was Eagle National Bank, located in Pennsylvania. Eagle had allowed the revenue it derived from its alliance with Dollar Financial to become the single largest source of income on its balance sheet. According to the OCC, "Eagle had effectively turned over the management of the bank's main business to a third party, and then virtually ignored how that business was being conducted."[86] The depository institution had allowed itself to become an appendage of the payday lender so that the latter could evade state regulations. This was viewed as an abuse of its charter, and Eagle was therefore compelled to uncouple itself from the high-rate lender. Other recalcitrant banks after the turn of the century were also strong-armed out of the payday-loan business by federal regulators.

In Illinois several smaller banks tried to enter into relationships with the payday lenders because the state had no usury statute, making their federal charters valuable. Brickyard Bank, headquartered in Lincolnwood, agreed to underwrite cash advances for Check n' Go in North Carolina and Texas, states with restrictive small-loan statutes that could be preempted by these rent-a-bank arrangements. Check n' Go also sought approval to acquire the tiny Bank of Kenney, whose most valuable asset was the federal charter it had been issued. But the regulators defeated these efforts to exploit the doctrine of preemption. The Illinois Office of Banks and Real Estate ordered Brickyard to increase its reserves to match dollar-for-dollar the amount it underwrote in risky payday credit. This restriction undercut the bank's incentive to rent its charter to high-rate check lenders doing business in other states, and so Brickyard soon terminated its alliance with Check n' Go.[87]

Increased pressure by regulators eventually rebuilt the dikes that were meant to separate the ocean of consumer credit into fifty lakes. After years of evasion and legal wrangling, in 2005 national chains doing business in North Carolina and Texas were forced to discontinue the subterfuge of renting federal charters. While banks could still provide lines of credit to the payday lenders (and frequently did so), they had to operate at arm's length and could not join forces with the check lenders to skirt state rules. The payday lenders, in turn, were compelled to figure out how to do business within the parameters of each state's statutes—at least, if they wanted their contracts to be legally enforceable. In states such as North Carolina, with a low usury ceiling, check lending was not viable and the payday lenders finally had to close up shop. In Texas, by contrast, the lenders found loopholes within the statutes through which they could squirm. That was the situation in Illinois too. ISLA, in its fight with CFSA, had charged that the reform bill of 2005 would starve its businesses but would not apply to the national chains, which had formed alliances with federal banks to evade the rules. But by the time the PLRA went into effect the rent-a-charter era had come to an end, and yet none of the payday lenders had starved to death. This new net of regulation had a giant hole in it, which permitted lenders to charge whatever rate the market would bear without having to exploit the doctrine of exportation. Likewise, most of the fifty lakes in which the loan sharks were now confined remained hospitable waters for high-rate lending.

Let me conclude by putting the story told here in perspective. Long before there were any payday lenders, Chief Justice John Marshall observed that "the ingenuity of lenders has devised many contrivances by which, under forms sanctioned by law, the statute may be evaded."[88] Creditors, as a breed, have always been slippery and clever. Competition forces them to be shrewd. It is in their interest to probe the net of regulation that seeks to constrain them, searching for gaps in the coverage through which they might pass. That they are able to find such gaps more quickly than legislators can close them should not surprise us, for "in the race between regulation and market innovation, market participants have stronger incentives than regulators to change, and market participants face substantial incentives to test the boundaries of the regulatory framework."[89] The search for profit makes creditors single-minded. The producers of regulation, by contrast, are usually pulled in different directions by irreconcilable demands. In states such as Illinois, the equilibrium point in the market for credit regulation has converged on a regulatory net that is extensive and expensive but also shoddy in its construction and full of holes.

The fact that the net is shoddy, however, does not necessarily mean it is dysfunctional or that it fails to maximize the well-being of the group as a whole. After all, this regulatory net might be sufficiently restrictive to keep out the worst predators but not so tight in its weave that it prevents mutually advantageous forms of high-rate lending. Although the statute has not achieved all that the advocates of consumer protection desire, this result should disappoint us only if it is indeed true that a more lightly regulated market in payday credit is worse for society than a tightly constrained market. In many other markets the opposite is true—less is often more. Too much regulation thwarts innovation and can produce perverse consequences, making disadvantaged groups worse off than if the regulators hadn't tried to protect them at all. Where regulation is counterproductive, we should be grateful when entrepreneurs find loopholes through which to squeeze. Being slippery in such circumstances is a virtue, not a vice.

If the good of society is our aim, then consequences decide the question. We must weigh the balance of costs and benefits engendered by the various alternatives. Would we be better off if payday lending were prohibited, or would such a policy only make things worse? Let us now review the evidence available to us about the consequences of payday lending and its regulation.

Culling the Shiver of Sharks

I was glad the loans were there for me, but I believe they contribute to the delinquency of adults. —B. C. Pennington, Oklahoma City payday loan customer, 2005[1]

From the beginning, loan sharks have thrived wherever military personnel congregate. The first salary brokers were said to have gotten their start in the bivouacs of the Union army, advancing cash to officers who had run through all their pay. Ever since, payday lenders of one sort or another have swarmed near the gates of military bases, scenting there the tangled mixture of desperation and profligacy that is like blood in the water to a shark. Modest pay doled out at regular intervals—the wages of Uncle Sam— has always drawn to it predatory lenders offering quick cash now in exchange for balloon notes that are difficult to repay. Sensing vulnerability, dealers in small sums have taken advantage of the financial myopia that has been a chronic disability within the ranks of the U.S. Armed Forces.

This has been one of the favorite feeding grounds of the loan sharks, in peacetime and in war, for a century and a half. But then suddenly something surprising happened. Just as federal banking regulators had finished dividing the ocean of payday credit back into lakes, putting an end to the charter-renting arrangements that had allowed check-lending chains to circumvent state usury statutes, another branch of the federal government, with the Military Lending Act, began filling in the portions of those state lakes that surrounded military bases. In August 2006 the Department of Defense released a report documenting the extent of payday lending among personnel of the armed forces.[2] It cited evidence that military personnel were three times as likely as civilians to have borrowed from the check lenders, and that 20% of active-duty service members were currently indebted to payday-advance vendors. A mammoth *Ohio State Law Journal* article the previous year had mapped the thick clustering of payday-lending shops around military bases across much of the United States.[3] Pentagon officials warned that high-rate lending was undercutting the military readiness of the armed forces in a time of war. Congress was therefore urged to pass legislation capping the maximum permissible interest rate for cash advances to military families at 36% a year. That measure, known as the Talent-Nelson Amendment, was attached to a Defense appropriation bill and sailed through Congress in October 2006.[4] It preempted all state statutes governing consumer credit for this particular class of federal employees and essentially created an archipelago of shark-free islands across all of the states where payday lending had not already been prohibited.

Suddenly, and without the protracted fight that inevitably ensues when efforts to restrict payday lending are launched in the state legislatures, the federal government established what had never seriously been contemplated before: a national usury ceiling. That ceiling, to be sure, applied to but one class of citizens. But it represented a precedent, as advocates of high-rate prohibition quickly recognized. If military personnel had to be protected from the predations of loan sharks, why should ordinary consumers be treated any differently? Didn't they need protection too? Why did the government insist that consumers show military identification before being allowed to wade ashore on the shark-free chain of islands that had been established by the Talent-Nelson Amendment?

This was a point made by none other than Barack Obama in one of the policy papers issued by his campaign during the 2008 presidential contest. As a state senator, Obama had endorsed rules that placed no rate cap on payday lending. Eight years later, however, Candidate Obama came out in support of the military's new low ceiling for consumer credit, but then he went one step further. "We must extend this protection to all Americans," Obama said, "because predatory lending continues to be a major problem for low and middle income families alike."[5] The usury rate ought to be 36% for everyone, across all of the states, he maintained. The military had shown the way.

Campaign statements like this might not have counted for much in ordinary times. But the sudden collapse of the financial system in the United States during the last months before the November 2008 election suddenly made reforms on this scale seem well within the realm of possibility. If credit deregulation had brought about the crisis, as many observers claimed, then perhaps the era of financial laissez-faire, during which check lending had been spawned, was about to come to an end. To many, the idea that unconstrained consumer credit always furthered the common good no longer seemed so plausible. Subprime debt, of which payday lending is one variety, had become thoroughly unpopular.

This appeared to be a moment of danger for the slipperiest fish. The forces of prohibition were on the march. They had cast a net around the population of soldiers and sailors—one through which sharks could not squirm. In Oregon, New Hampshire, Ohio, and the District of Columbia, opponents of payday credit had also pushed through low caps that forced many lenders to shutter their doors. In Arizona and Ohio, voters rejected decisively ballot initiatives sponsored by the payday lenders that would have exempted their credit products from statutory restrictions. As the national credit crisis deepened, many state representatives also promised to introduce new bills in the coming legislative session that would restrict or render infeasible high-rate lending. In Congress, Illinois senator Dick Durbin vowed to press for the 36% rate cap to which Barack Obama had committed himself during the 2008 campaign. "Within blocks of my home in Springfield, Illinois," Durbin said, "there are payday lenders charging interest rates of two and three hundred percent of the value of the loan. These excessive rates are often hidden and can have crippling effects on those individuals who can afford it least. Congress must enact protections against predatory lending. America's working families depend on it."[6]

Prohibition had become popular. But might it not also have, in Durbin's words, crippling effects on those individuals who can afford it least? Would outlawing high-rate debt actually improve the lot of credit-constrained consumers? Or would imposing a low ceiling actually make them worse off? Might not further regulation be preferable to outright prohibition? Or what about creating an alternative supply of cheaper credit to undercut the payday lenders through competition? Wouldn't it be better to starve the sharks by introducing a benign alternative than to try and drive them away with regulatory nets and prosecutorial spears?

I will try to answer these questions by reviewing the evidence available to us about the consequences of these different courses of action. Prohibition, restriction, competition—these are our alternatives. Suppose we were in a position to impose the policy that is best for society as a whole and, in particular, for those households that currently make use of payday credit. What would it be sensible for us to do?

Domesticated Sharks

Since most states today restrict rather than prohibit payday lending, let us begin by reviewing what we know about the consequences of these restrictions. After all, if loan sharks could be domesticated through regulation, prohibition would be unnecessary. At the start of 2010, more than two-thirds of the fifty states permitted check lending and issued licenses to vendors. The level of restriction imposed by these states differs considerably. Some, like Wisconsin, tolerate nearly free markets in payday credit while others, like New Mexico, constrain these transactions sharply. In the freest markets, little is known about the consequences of payday lending. The newspapers publish anecdotal evidence of abuse from time to time, but it isn't clear how representative these cases are. For every customer who seems trapped by payday credit there might be ten or twenty others who are satisfied with the product but whose stories are too dull to report. The regulatory agencies in the states with the freest markets do not issue statistical reports each year about trends in the industry or the consequences of payday lending. While they do confirm that the average customer enters into a number of loan contracts during the course of a year, their reporting is spotty. By contrast, states with more restrictive statutes tend to gather and disclose more information about these transactions. Some have contracted with a private vendor, Veritec Solutions, to establish a database that ensures compliance with their statutes. The annual reports they issue are the best source of information we have about the consequences of restriction.

What these annual reports reveal is that none of the more restrictive statutes has managed to put an end to the debt recidivism that is the main grievance of the prohibitionists. If "payday advances should be used for short-term financial needs only, not as a long-term financial solution," as the industry's cautionary notice warns, then there is abundant evidence that many consumers are misusing the product, even in states that try to limit these loan transactions. Florida, for example, was the first state to impose comprehensive restrictions on payday lending. The statute, signed into law in 2001, limited cash advances to $500; capped the interest charge at the comparatively low rate of 10% of the cash advanced, plus a modest verification fee; prohibited lenders from extending credit to applicants who already had another payday loan; prevented renewals by requiring debtors to wait twenty-four hours before getting a new loan; entitled borrowers to enter into an extended payment plan if they could not pay off their loan in full; required check lenders to provide information about credit counseling; made it illegal for the businesses to take wage assignments, powers of attorney, and so forth; and established the first real-time online database to enforce compliance with these rules.[7] It was an impressive piece of legislation, cutting edge. The database requirement made it feasible to put an end to the debt pyramids that so many payday-loan customers construct for themselves by borrowing from several lenders simultaneously—except perhaps for residents who lived near the border with other states. They could cross the state line to get additional loans without being detected, and there is nothing the state government can do to stop them.

Each year since 2002, Veritec Solutions has issued a report entitled "Florida Trends in Deferred Presentment" that summarizes the previous twelve months' transactions. The reports reveal that Florida's restrictive statute has not prevented transaction volume in the payday-lending market from rising steadily year after year, at the rate of 15%. In the most recent reporting period, 6.2 million payday loans were issued, roughly one for every household in the state. And though Florida caps the fee at a rate that lenders in Illinois and other less restricted states claim would drive them out of business, the number of payday-loan outlets in the state has risen steadily, from nearly 1,000 in 2002 to more than 1,400 seven years later. The proportion of independents and local chains in this population has not declined over time.[8]

During fiscal year 2009, 5.1% of Florida's adult population took out at least one payday loan. This represents a maximum penetration rate of one in nine households in the state. The average two-week loan was $384 and it cost $41 in fees. Calculated as an annual percentage rate, the charge was 278%. The average customer borrowed not just once but 8.4 times during the year, which means that the typical individual was in debt to the check lenders the equivalent of four months out of twelve. This average conceals, however, the true pattern of transactions, which is bifurcated. Roughly one in six customers borrowed just once during the year; four in ten borrowed no more than four times. But this 40% of the customer pool accounted for just 10% of the loan transactions logged by the payday lenders. By contrast, the 40% of heaviest users had ten or more loans during the year and averaged fourteen. They received three-quarters of the loans closed by the payday lenders. More than 120,000 residents were extended credit at least sixteen times during the year, and these recidivists accounted for more than one-third of the loan transactions. They were the most loyal customers of the payday lenders.

What this data reveals is that the customer base of the check lenders is heterogeneous. A large minority (roughly 40%) uses the product lightly and does not become trapped by these balloon loans, but another 40% borrows chronically. A Freedom of Information request by the Center for Responsible Lending uncovered the fact that 39% of all repeat loan transactions in Florida occur within seventy-two hours after the previous extension of credit has been paid off. Only one in seven of these subsequent loans is closed more than two weeks after the previous debt has been retired.[9] In other words, the loans tend to cluster and are effectively renewals, despite the cooling-off period imposed by the state. Once somebody has secured one payday loan, the chances are high that this customer will get another very soon. In fact, more than 20,000 people who borrowed in Florida during fiscal year 2009 were indebted to the payday lenders the legally maximum number of days during those twelve months. Despite the industry's cautionary warning, these consumers were permitted to use this expensive product not for short-term financial needs only but as a long-term financial solution.

The trends are nearly identical in all of the states that report this information. Oklahoma also uses the Veritec database but its statute is less restrictive than Florida's. The Oklahoma rules permit customers to borrow from two lenders at once, and in any given month, 20% of debtors do. As a result, the average customer in the Sooner State got one more loan during fiscal year 2009 than borrowers did in Florida (9.3 versus 8.4), while a somewhat smaller share of the total pool got through that year with four loans or less (33.5% versus 37.7%). Because Oklahoma borrowers can have two payday loans at once, the most egregious recidivists are allowed to accumulate prodigious numbers of loans during the course of a year. In Florida it is very difficult to rack up more than two dozen loans in twelve months because of the cooling-off period, but in Oklahoma 5.7% of borrowers (6,365 individuals) logged at least twenty-four loans in fiscal year 2009. A total of 488 people had forty cash advances or more during those twelve months.[10]

Statistical reports for Michigan and Washington State tell the same story.[11] Roughly 40% of borrowers are sparing in their use of the product but anywhere from 20% (Washington) to 40% (Michigan) of payday debtors get a dozen loans or more during the course of twelve months. In Michigan, an astonishing 7.9% of customers (24,000 people) received at least thirty loans during fiscal year 2007. It seems impossible not to conclude that these consumers are trapped by the product. Nobody in their right mind would gladly borrow once, twice, or three times a month from payday lenders charging triple-digit interest—and yet we know that large fractions of their customers do borrow this frequently in every state that monitors loan activity. The situation must be at least as bad in the states that don't track loan usage or impose restrictions, unless we assume implausibly that people with more freedom to do as they please will borrow less. But why do the recidivists borrow so frequently? How can anyone be trapped by a $300 cash advance? The sums are so small, and the interest rate is fixed. A payday loan isn't like a subprime mortgage with a teaser rate. That financial product did trap many homeowners during the great housing bubble of the early twenty-first century when the interest rate reset at a higher level, after the introductory period had expired. Then the monthly payments swelled but the borrowers might not be able to refinance the loan or sell the house. They were trapped by a mortgage they couldn't afford and couldn't get rid of. But payday loans don't work that way, as a rule. While some lenders do entice custom into the shop with teaser rates, in most cases the fee is set at the statutory maximum and does not vary. You receive $300 today and you owe $348 in two weeks. Once you've paid off the loan you can borrow again, but the payment is fixed. If you can't afford to fork over $48 to the payday lender every two weeks, why not pay off your current loan and then quit? You won't be trapped if you don't go back.

The solution seems simple: pay off your debt and don't borrow again. But what the data reveals is that some payday-loan customers can manage their money in this way while an equally large population cannot. Both groups are short $300 this week and lack lower-cost alternatives. Each borrows $300 for two weeks with a postdated check at the stiff annual percentage rate of 417%. In two weeks, when payday arrives, the first group pays off the debt and moves on—or perhaps rolls over the loan once or twice and then quits for good. But the other group is in a more serious bind. These customers were short $300 two weeks ago and, after paying off the debt, are now short $348. They aren't going to make it to the next payday, and so they borrow·

again. Only now they need more money because the previous loan cost $48. So perhaps they will borrow from a second lender in order to pay off the first. Perhaps the first lender will even suggest this option.[12] After all, there's another cash advance center just down the street. The process is quick and easy. You can have the money in fifteen minutes. . . . And so it goes. As one observer put it, with payday loans "you start out with a piece of ice, and it becomes a snowball, and then you have an iceberg."[13]

Even though the payday loan, the credit card, and the subprime mortgage are different financial products, the psychological processes by which significant numbers of borrowers become trapped by these debt instruments are identical. The field of behavioral economics has documented the existence of widespread cognitive biases that these products are designed to exploit.[14] To begin with, people generally suffer from an optimism bias; they underestimate the probability that bad things will happen to them. For example, we know that roughly half of all marriages will fail, but hardly anyone enters into the relationship thinking their union won't last. If more people were realistic, more would draw up prenuptial agreements. Then when bad things do happen, people are usually slow to react. They may lose a job but assume they will find a new one quickly. As a result, too many fail to adjust consumption to the new level of income, which increases their debt burden. What is more, many individuals are "hyperbolic discounters," enjoying the pleasures of the moment but underestimating the costs they will pay in the future for the choices they have made. Smokers and junk-food junkies are the paradigmatic examples. They suffer from a weakness of will that entrepreneurs stand ready to exploit.

These cognitive anomalies do not figure in the neoclassical models of rational economic behavior but they have been shown to explain the pricing strategies of high-cost lenders.[15] Credit card companies, for example, often charge no annual fee, or they offer low introductory rates to attract new customers, but then they impose higher rates for long-term debt and load their contracts with expensive fees. While many users will pay off their cards every month, more customers end up carrying a balance or making late payments than anticipated they would at the outset, and it is these revolvers who will be the main source of profit for the lenders. Bank card companies that do not price their products in this way in order to take advantage of consumers who suffer from overconfidence or myopia would be at a competitive disadvantage in the marketplace. They have a powerful incentive to exploit these weaknesses, but the fact that the market selects these particular pricing strategies does not mean the strategies maximize well-being. As more than one observer has pointed out, "the biased competition in the credit card market is welfare reducing."[16] It redistributes resources from disadvantaged agents to those who are already well-off, and thus it can exacerbate social problems. The behavioral approach to economics has demonstrated what the neoclassical paradigm could never grasp—that in certain cases "financial innovation reduces welfare by providing 'too much' liquidity."[17]

Payday lending illustrates the point: wage-earners who can borrow twenty or thirty times a year on the security of a postdated check have too much liquidity. Debt on this scale and at these prices must be welfare-reducing. But no set of restrictions passed by the state legislatures over the last decade has put an end to the patterns of serial borrowing documented above. In no state where the data is reported do we find limited and responsible use of this credit predominating over patterns of chronic indebtedness. No regulatory formula has been discovered yet that would permit only occasional and emergency use of payday credit, but prevent the chains of debt that large numbers of customers fashion for themselves through naiveté, overconfidence, myopia, or weakness of will. Indeed, it is doubtful that payday lending would be financially viable if such a scheme could be devised. As a former store manager observed, "This industry could not survive if the goal was for the customer to be 'one and done'."[18] Even a rule like "no more than four" would kill the business, because it is the serial debtors who generate the profit.[19] Loan volume at the typical store would plummet if customers were not allowed to borrow more than once a quarter or once every two months. Prices would have to rise to make up for the lost revenue of the recidivists, but prices higher than those already charged by the check lenders would scare away many of the better risks who don't become trapped by the product. On this key point the Center for Responsible Lending is right: "loan flipping is the foundation of the payday loan business model."[20]

Lobbyists for the payday lenders vigorously challenge this assertion, but every now and then insiders will acknowledge what the Veritec data inescapably demonstrate. "We're in a good business," an Illinois lender cheerfully admitted to a reporter. "Our customers keep coming back regardless."[21] An executive at Cash America was more explicit: "the theory in the business is you've got to get that customer in, work to turn him into a repetitive customer, long-term customer, because that's really where the profitability is."[22] That theory, of course, applies to most commercial ventures. But when your product is an emergency cash advance billed at a premium price and pitched to a population with bad credit, it is problematic to be encouraging the kind of repetitive business on which payday lending thrives. It means your business product is essentially the debt trap. Former store employees sometimes confirmed this observation. A district manager for a national chain, who had quit the day before, told a press conference:

> Of course, we train our sales staff to keep customers dependent, to make sure they keep re-borrowing, whether in the form of a renewal, or a back-to-back transaction, forever, if possible. . . . The repeat borrower is vital to our business model. It is the basis for bonuses. It is the basis for store payroll budgets. We create complicated metrics with deliberately obscure names like "unique customer count" to disguise—even to our staff—the fact that we're in business to create repeat customers.

Another of these disgruntled whistleblowers was equally frank:

> The secret to the success of the payday loan is its deceptive design. Specifically, we made the process very simple and easy at the front end to get people into the loan. But at the back end, we made it very difficult for customers to get out of the loan. It became a situation where our borrowers were like indentured servants, but with indefinite terms of servitude.
> My goal as a payday loan employee is to keep that customer in the loan for as long as I can. That customer adds to my "customer count," which is what my bonus depends on. And the way I do this is to loan him more money than he can realistically pay back in just two weeks, when the loan is theoretically due. If it were just a two-week loan, my store would not have been profitable and I would have been out of a job.[23]

All of the consumer protections implemented thus far and intended to prevent chronic indebtedness have collided with and failed to tame the impulse of payday lenders to encourage repeat business as much as possible. The lenders must do so, because their profits and their survival depend on cultivating a clientele that has difficulty managing its finances. They live off the repeat customers. You can prevent debtors from borrowing from more than one check lender at a time, which is desirable, but many will still return to the same shop again and again. You can force customers to wait a day or two after paying off a loan before getting a new one, but a large fraction will come back as soon as they are allowed and borrow again at high rates. You can require disclosure of the annual percentage rate of the product, but this will not deter the recidivists from borrowing so frequently that the APR becomes an accurate and meaningful measure of the loan's expense. You can post cautionary messages about the proper use of the product, but they will have no more effect than the warning labels on cigarette packs that go unheeded. You can compel lenders to offer information about credit counseling, but hardly any of those who could really use it will take the initiative and follow through.

In 2003, Oklahoma went a step further and required debtors who tried to secure a sixth loan within ninety days after applying for the first to receive credit counseling from an authorized provider before more cash could be advanced to them. The experiment was a fiasco, because the counseling services were swamped with requests from irate customers. They phoned right from the loan shops and demanded the certificate that would entitle them to borrow again. "The difficult part for us," a counselor explained, "is that they don't really want to get credit counseling. They just want to get the next loan. A lot of times they will take their anger out on us."[24] When a new payday-loan bill was passed by the legislature in 2004, this provision was dropped from the measure.

Some states have established extended payment plans that consumers may request if they find it difficult to retire their debt. In Florida, for example, borrowers are entitled to ask for a sixty-day grace period during which new fees will not accrue and the debtor can repay the loan in installments arranged by a credit counseling service. In fiscal year 2009, however, only 0.35% of payday-loan transactions logged by the state were enrolled in the extended payment plan, despite the fact that 28.6% of customers borrowed a dozen times or more during the year.[25] In Michigan the majority of loan transactions that occur in any given month qualify the debtors to participate in the state-mandated repayment plan, but only a miniscule fraction of consumers take advantage of the option.[26] A former manager at a national chain explained why so few recidivists enroll in these plans:

> Well, we instruct our staff not to tell customers that the option exists. Customers are supposed to discover it referenced on the back of the CFSA brochure that is handed to them quarterly along with their privacy statements. . . . Then they have to ask for an extended payment plan the day before their loan is due. If they ask on the due date, they do not qualify. And they can only get one of

these a year. Moreover, we train our staff to discourage borrowers who ask for
the option from exercising it.[27]

The prospect of not being able to borrow again from this lender or any
other is a powerful deterrent for those who consider taking advantage of the
extended payment plans. They may lose their only source of credit if they
exercise this option.

Only Colorado has had notable success with its repayment plan, which
went into effect in 2007. The statute requires lenders to provide consumers
with a separate form describing the option, which the borrowers must sign
and may keep. According to the state's attorney general, half of the 80,000
customers eligible to take advantage of the program did so during the last
six months of 2007. The option was credited with leveling off demand for the
payday-loan product, which in previous years had grown at the rate of 25%.
Some lenders had even established their own cooling-off period to prevent
customers from becoming eligible for the extended payment plan.[28]

That trend is promising, but Virginia went a step further. The new law passed
in 2008 presented debtors applying for a fifth loan in six months with a choice:
either enroll in an extended payment plan or wait forty-five days after paying
off the fifth loan before being eligible to borrow again. A statewide database
would enforce compliance with the rule. Whichever option is chosen, the cycle
of debt would be interrupted for every serial recidivist, unless they crossed
state lines to a less regulated jurisdiction or borrowed from an unlicensed
Internet lender. But the response of the state's payday lenders was telling and
predictable: as the date for implementation of the new rules approached, many
applied for permission from the State Corporation Commission to offer an
open-ended credit product not covered by the payday-loan statute. Customers
would be billed once a month and charged a fee for this revolving line of credit
equivalent to a 400% APR.[29] As always, when confronted with consumer
protections that threaten to deny it access to the richest sources of revenue, the
slipperiest fish in the sea of consumptive credit will hunt out gaps in the net of
regulation through which it can slip.

This is the paradox of regulation: the restrictions with which the payday
lenders can live do not prevent large fractions of their customer pool from
borrowing again and again, and any restrictions that might minimize this
chronic indebtedness will either drive the payday lenders out of business or
compel them to re-craft the product if they possibly can in order to evade
the limits. No state yet has figured out how to domesticate the sharks; some

don't even try. And there is good reason to think that such domestication is impossible, because the product isn't financially viable for the lenders if it is required to be financially viable for all of the debtors. There is no money to be made if many customers don't misuse the product. This is why some observers have decided that prohibition is necessary. Expressing skepticism about additional consumer protections, a disillusioned former manager explained, "I think the bad outweighs the good. What they do is totally within the law. But they don't really want you to pay it back."[30]

The Consequences of Prohibition

In the classic case of prohibition, the government proscribes a good or a service that gives people pleasure because that way of gaining pleasure is thought to cause even more pain, both for the pleasure-seeker and for society as a whole. The Eighteenth Amendment, for example, prohibited the manufacture, sale, or transportation of intoxicating beverages in the United States because widespread drunkenness produced many antisocial consequences. The pleasures of drink caused the pain of family breakup, child neglect, domestic violence, lost productivity, profligate spending, illness, and early death. Hence banning the substance was expected to further the common good by reducing these evils.[31]

The proscription of high-rate lending, however, is a different kind of prohibition. No debtor derives pleasure from agreeing to pay exorbitant interest. This counts as a pain or disutility that is endured in order to gain access to ready money, which buys the debtor pleasure. In this case the pleasure-seeker calculates that the instrumental pain will result in gain, whereas in the other case, there is an expectation of gain without pain. In both cases, however, when government opts for prohibition it does so because it believes the pleasure-seekers have miscalculated; they have underestimated the pain that results from their effort to gain. But the miscalculation of the one who endures pain in order to gain is tragic in a way that the other miscalculation is not. As a rule, we think that sacrifice is virtuous whereas self-indulgence is not. But a sacrifice that produces more pain than gain seems particularly worthless. The one who profits from that loss will likely seem more odious to us than one who merely facilitates a short-sighted self-indulgence.

These considerations might explain why interest-rate caps are the oldest prohibition, or at least the most enduring. Most societies the world over and throughout human history have imposed a ceiling on the price moneylenders could charge that is pegged at the level where it was thought the calculus of pain exceeded whatever gains might result from high-rate lending. Any price above that level is designated usury, which is a misuse of money. Payday lending is best prohibited in this way, by capping the legal rate of interest at a sufficiently low level such that expensive short-term cash advances are not financially profitable. It would be fruitless to ban a specific product, like the check loan, because the lenders can simply repackage their credit in a different form to evade this prohibition, as we have seen them do. To be effective, the prohibition must target the interest rate of the product and not the product itself. Advancing cash against the security of a postdated check is not the problem with payday lending; the problem is the triple-digit interest rate that traps too many borrowers. If government enforces a rate in the double digits, the myriad of high-priced products that the ingenuity of lenders might invent will disappear from the legal market.

For those who advocate prohibition today, an annual percentage rate of 36% is the favored ceiling. That is a relic from the 1930s, when some states reduced the original cap established by the Uniform Small Loan Law, which permitted lenders to charge 3.5% a month on the unpaid balance of small loans. The easiest way to effect a prohibition on high-rate lending now would be to extend the protections of the Talent-Nelson Amendment, which covers military personnel and their families, to the population as a whole. This national usury cap would supersede state regulations or, perhaps, set the upper bound below which states might experiment. An annual percentage rate of 36%, it should be noted, would put an end not only to payday lending in its current form but to other types of high-priced credit, like the installment loans that flourish across the South (which we have encountered in previous chapters). The subprime market in credit today is crowded with products whose effective annual interest rate exceeds 36% a year. Some of the products of the depository institutions, such as overdraft protection, would also exceed this threshold if regulators required them to calculate their fees as an annual percentage rate.

The best reason to prohibit high-rate lending is if its social costs exceed its benefits by a wide margin. In particular, if expensive credit makes many people who are already bad off worse off than they would have been if they had not had access to it, then the case for prohibition is quite compelling. The only way it might be defeated is if some other sizable group that is also bad off would be made even worse off by prohibition than those who are harmed by the legality of expensive credit. In other words, to decide whether prohibition is justified or not, we must determine which option helps the least advantaged group the most. While the distribution of gains and losses for other groups in society is not irrelevant in our assessment, a policy option that makes bad off people worse off than they have to be has a powerful strike against it. Our default rule should be to minimize deprivation, measured both by the number of people who suffer it and by the intensity of their suffering. In some cases we will face tragic choices, when a relative few are made worse off by an option that improves the lot of many more who experience deprivation. Unfortunately, high-rate prohibition is one of these tragic cases.

On the face of it, the choice might seem easy. We know that even restricted access to expensive credit will trap many debtors. People who borrow from payday lenders a dozen times or more during the course of a year seem trapped by their debt, or they are misusing the product in a way that must reduce their well-being. No apologist for payday lending has yet told a plausible story about how serial debt on this scale makes people better off. What is more, we know that wherever payday credit is permitted, sizable numbers of customers will renew their loans again and again or pay off one cash advance with the proceeds of another. If a dozen loans a year is the benchmark of abuse (and this figure is really too high), then in the more heavily regulated states at least one in five customers will qualify as abused and abusive debtors. Legal access to too much liquidity, it seems, has increased their deprivation. If so, prohibition would improve the situation of this least advantaged group.

But this assessment meets with two kinds of objections from those who defend payday lending. In the first place, some object to the paternalism of a policy that second-guesses the choices of adults who are more likely to know what is best for them than a consumer protection advocate or elite legislator. Even if this many loans is a bad idea, it would be better to let people learn from their own mistakes than to impose on them a one-size-fits-all strategy like prohibition. In this way we encourage self-reliance. In the second place, the opponents of prohibition argue that this policy has perverse consequences. While it may prevent some from borrowing "too much" (whatever that might mean), prohibition also cuts off access to those who do not misuse the product. The data reveals that there are plenty of borrowers who make light use of this credit. They don't become hooked, but preventing them from borrowing against a postdated check might deny these responsible customers access to vital emergency funds. Prohibition would make them worse off than before, especially if it drives some into the black market for credit. That is where the worst predators lurk.

The first objection can be more easily dispensed with than the second. If consequences are the arbiter of the question, then paternalistic policies cannot be rejected in principle.[32] Taking away people's freedom to do as they wish might well make them better off, all things considered. Seatbelt laws illustrate the point. Such laws are fundamentally paternalistic (indeed, they are not a soft but a hard kind of paternalism), and yet the balance of costs and benefits is tipped lopsidedly in favor of such self-regarding restrictions. People lose little by being forced to buckle up, but they gain a lot when the restraints save their lives. The same calculation applies to those who are trapped by payday credit. A usury prohibition prevents them from borrowing from a licensed vendor at a high rate but spares them the misery of peonage. Since the sizable minority of customers who become trapped by their debt are financially myopic, paternalistic prohibition protects them from their own cognitive disability. Even as staunch an opponent of paternalism as John Stuart Mill admits that

> it is a proper office of public authority to guard against accidents. If either a public officer or any one else saw a person attempting to cross a bridge which had been ascertained to be unsafe, and there were no time to warn him of his danger, they might seize him and turn him back without any real infringement of his liberty; for liberty consists in doing what one desires, and he does not desire to fall into the river.[33]

A usury statute, likewise, cuts off access to the too-convenient bridge loans that are so treacherous for the short-sighted population of customers who are tempted to cross the dire straits of financial emergency along this path. They do not want to plunge into those straits, but we know that many will if they are allowed to start across this private for-profit toll bridge.

But by this logic—an advocate of payday lending might reply—people should be prevented from crossing many other bridges. Excessive optimism, short-sighted miscalculation, and weakness of will afflict many consumers who never borrow on the security of a postdated check. People with charge cards buy too many things and people with poor diets eat too much junk food. If government is going to take away our freedom for our own good, shouldn't it also prohibit credit cards and fast food? Why don't the benefits of restriction outweigh the costs in these cases too?

Because there is a crucial difference. People who buy too many things on credit or who overeat do gain benefits, even if they underestimate the costs of the pleasures they take. By contrast, someone trapped by payday debt quickly ceases to benefit at all from the repeat transactions in any positive way. If I have to keep paying the same 20% fee every two weeks on the initial cash advance I renew, the only pleasure I gain from the renewals is the purely relative pleasure of avoiding even more pain by defaulting on the debt. This benefit is negative, not positive, because it is only a lesser evil. But if I charge too much at the shoe store, at least I will have lots of nice shoes to console me when the bill comes due. Debt peons have no such consolation. They have positive costs and negative benefits, which makes their plight more sympathetic. These miscalculators do not seem overindulgent, at least not after they've paid the tenth or twentieth fee. Instead, they must be positively miserable. All the pleasure in the transactions accrues to one party, who takes advantage of the other's awful choices. The exploitation in this case seems much worse than the shoe store's exploitation of the shopaholic. In the latter instance the calculus of pleasure and pain is not so lopsided in its distribution as to justify the hard paternalism of a prohibition.

A prohibition that is legitimate and effective ought to make many people who once had access to the good or the service thankful they no longer do. Most prohibitions that have been imposed or that we could imagine would fail this test, either because former consumers would regret the loss they suffer or because the prohibitions had failed in practice to shut off the supply. By this test, the prohibitions of drugs and alcohol must be deemed failures, probably on both counts. Usury prohibitions might fail the second test (we will return to the problem of black-market credit later), but there is some limited evidence that suggests many chronic debtors are in fact relieved to have lost the freedom to borrow at high rates. Before the prohibition was imposed, they might have sided with the majority of debtors who typically express support for unfettered freedom, but after the fact many might see things differently. I cited a survey conducted after Maine imposed sharp limits on installment lending in the late 1960s (see Chapter 3). Three times as many former customers said they were better off without the credit, because now they were "rid of the burden of the finance company."[34] More recently, the Center for Community Capital conducted focus groups with payday-lending customers who lost access to this credit when North Carolina enforced its prohibition. The sample was small and the Center had a partisan ax to grind, but the responses of these mostly chronic debtors confirmed that they were grateful the option no longer existed. "Thank you, Jesus! Yes! Now I can't do it anymore!" one of these naïve hyperbolic discounters exclaimed. Most felt that it was too easy to borrow but too hard to repay this debt. "Every two weeks I have to run down and get another [loan] before they close," one man explained. "It became a part of my life, until I realized I was paying $45 every two weeks. Then it started to come to me."[35] Focus groups with current payday-loan customers in California reported similar perceptions. "It was easy the first time," one said, "but man-o-man when you try to get out, you get stuck on a merry-go-round."[36] Paternalistically prohibiting people from choosing to start an expensive ride they cannot stop seems justifiable unless we make a fetish of free choice.

So much for the first objection. The second, however, is more powerful. It says that prohibition of payday lending is perverse. Though well intentioned, the policy actually makes the least advantaged group worse off, or more precisely, in its attempt to help one group of borrowers, prohibition harms another. It prevents those who borrow responsibly from payday lenders from gaining access to this credit, which can help them solve financial emergencies. Without the credit, they will be worse off than before. For example, if the car these wage-earners use to get to work needs repairs, payday credit could solve their problem. Prohibition, by contrast, might cost them their source of income if they can't scrape together the funds needed to pay for the work. The loss of credit will make these responsible borrowers worse off than they have to be. While payday advances are expensive, these debts can pay large dividends if used appropriately, as a source of emergency credit. For this class of debtors, the benefits of the product may exceed the costs by quite a bit.

This last assertion is true. We can think of realistic cases in which paying a triple-digit interest rate enhances well-being. The payday lenders say that many of their customers use the product strategically to avoid bouncing checks or overdrawing their bank accounts. Since the imputed annual interest rate of these overdraft products is frequently five or ten times as expensive as the typical payday loan, borrowing against a postdated check could save bank customers short of funds a lot of money. The steep cost of payday credit might also be worth it for renters threatened with eviction or for people without health insurance who need medicine. In a survey of payday-loan customers, 31% said they used the cash advance to cover an emergency expense.[37] If the cash infusion helps them weather this financial crisis, the cost will usually have been worth it.

Predictably, journalistic exposés of payday lending rarely recount stories of this sort, about people who benefited from their use of the product. In states where payday lending is prohibited, no paper publishes counterfactual accounts of cash-strapped wage-earners who could have made good use of the product if it was permitted, though there must be many such cases. Several recent studies by economists, however, do offer evidence that high-rate lending can or does benefit many consumers. An experimental computer simulation of financial decision making conducted at the Economic Science Institute demonstrated that households in straitened circumstances were significantly more likely to survive to the final period of the exercise when subjects had access to payday loans. As long as these hypothetical households borrowed less than eleven times in thirty months against a postdated check (and the great majority of participants did), they more effectively managed their financial resources when faced with unpredictable shocks to the household budget.[38] A study of the welfare effects of access to payday lending in California in the months following natural disasters detected evidence that communities where this expensive credit was readily available registered lower rates of home foreclosure, mortality, and treatment for substance abuse.[39] A study of households expressing uncertainty about their future income determined that unrestricted access to payday credit reduced the likelihood these consumers would pay bills late.[40] Another regression analysis found that more residents bounced checks, filed for bankruptcy, or complained about debt collectors after prohibition was imposed in two southern states.[41]

At most, what this handful of studies demonstrates is that payday lending in the aggregate is beneficial across certain dimensions of well-being. Other studies purport to show the opposite. An analysis of military data revealed that, where payday loans were available before the Talent-Nelson prohibition went into effect, more young recruits were ineligible for reenlistment because of poor job performance and financial difficulties.[42] A study based on the proprietary data of a Texas payday-lending chain suggested that use of the product increases the likelihood of filing for bankruptcy.[43] A regression analysis of banking data across states determined that availability of payday lending increases the rate of involuntary account closure due to excessive bounce activity.[44] A regional study that controlled carefully for other effects concluded that ready access to check lending increases the probability of family hardship and difficulty paying bills.[45] Another project employing the same methodology to isolate the effects of payday lending showed that banks increase the price for some of their products, such as overdraft protection, where payday credit is available.[46] A survey of payday-advance customers in the Pacific Northwest disclosed that half of them still bounced checks despite their use of the product and that three-quarters also paid some bills late. When access to the product was restricted in Oregon, there was no increase in these trends, as one would expect if the payday lenders were right that customers use the product strategically to avoid late fees and bounce activity.[47]

As is usually the case, the economists can't agree among themselves. One set of studies indicates that availability of payday credit is beneficial in the aggregate while the other set shows the opposite. Which set readers find persuasive often depends on what they want to believe. But even if we dismiss the research that shows payday lending makes things worse, we cannot conclude from the other body of evidence that prohibition of payday lending harms the least advantaged group. This is because the trends reported in these papers are aggregates. The papers claim to show that more people are helped by the product than hurt, but they can't show that the ones who are helped would have a lower level of well-being if they did not have access to the product compared to people who are trapped by their debts because they were permitted to borrow at a high rate. Indeed, there is good reason to think that the consumers who use the product effectively to smooth consumption and to weather financial shocks are better off to begin with than those who borrow repeatedly. There is also good reason to think that those who make light use of the product could more easily find credit substitutes if check lending were prohibited. They would not be hurt much if they could not access the product, and any reduction in welfare they experienced due to prohibition would not be as severe as the losses inflicted on those who inevitably misuse payday credit when it is available. This assumption would be refuted if a research project studied only the heavy users and still found aggregate gains in well-being where payday lending is unrestricted. But no such project has yet been carried out. Most of the papers that conclude payday lending is beneficial blithely ignore evidence that large numbers of consumers borrow repeatedly. Several papers claim to prove that a debt trap doesn't exist because the aggregate measure of well-being on which the authors focus increases, as if their regression analyses could refute the hard evidence generated by the state compliance databases—that many payday advance customers borrow serially and construct for themselves long chains of debt out of postdated checks. Empirically, there is no question that payday credit traps many customers. To prove that prohibition is genuinely perverse, the advocates of payday lending must demonstrate that the trapped customers are not as bad off as the people who would make good use of the product if it were available to them but are denied access to high-rate cash advances. It is hard to see how this could be possible, unless prohibition drives would-be check-loan customers into the clutches of a worse predator, in the black market. (The prospect of that kind of perversity will be taken up in the next section.)

Just as there is no question that payday lending entraps many customers, there is also no question that many customers gain by having access to this expensive credit. It is also possible that more people gain than lose when check lending is permitted, though the evidence is ambiguous. Careful studies point in opposite directions. But it is surely the case that the customers who gain tend to use the product less, and those who lose tend to use it more. No study has yet demonstrated that well-being increases with each renewal. But this inverse relationship between use and benefit suggests that the distribution of gains and losses is regressive. Those who use the product sparingly are probably money losers for the payday lenders, which means the recidivists are subsidizing the population that gains the most from access to the product. It is the serial debtors who generate the profits for the lenders; the borrowers who get just one cash advance and then quit do not pay their way. The latter therefore gain at the expense of the repeat customers, but the repeat customers are the ones who are most likely to be made worse off by having access to the product. In other words, there is a redistribution of resources from the worse off to the better off—from the trapped to the untrapped. Now that is perverse.

This is why prohibition might be the best option. No scheme of regulation yet devised has put an end to the debt trap laid by payday credit. Where the product is available, some are made better off because payday loans help them to solve short-term financial problems, but other borrowers dig themselves into a hole. They are made worse off than before, and the price they pay subsidizes the gains of those who make good use of the credit. While the gainers would be worse off if they couldn't borrow this expensive credit, it is doubtful that any losses they incur would make them worse off than those who are trapped by the debt. The latter still count as the least advantaged group. Since this group does not constitute a tiny fraction of the customer pool in any jurisdiction for which reliable data is available, it is hard to write off their losses as a price worth paying to generate large gains for the population that is better situated. Where payday lending is legal, it is the strong who gain at the expense of the weak. If this is so, prohibition of this service is warranted. The sum of gains and losses, properly weighted, is negative.[48]

But this calculation is incomplete. It assumes that prohibition is successful—that capping interest rates dries up the market for expensive credit. But this has never been true in practice. Prohibition always drives some consumers into the black market. They will seek out bootleg lenders, who must charge premium prices in order to compensate themselves for the risks of illegality. If prohibition revives a black market in credit, why wouldn't the debtors drawn into that market count as the least advantaged group? Shouldn't the losses they will suffer count for more than the losses endured now by any who are trapped by payday credit?

Ancient Sharks and Modern Pirates

Advocates for payday lending sometimes boast that the industry starved black-market loan-sharking into extinction. The claim is false, however. Mob payday lending passed from the scene before check cashers began to extend credit in the 1980s (see Chapter 3). The money-lending operations of organized crime that survived into the era of financial deregulation dealt in larger sums and catered to a completely different clientele—business owners, gamblers, and fellow hoodlums. Hence modern payday lending could never have been a substitute for that usurious trade. The juice men of the syndicate long ago gave up trying to extort small sums from the wage-earning class.

The rise of check lending probably did diminish the market for vest-pocket sharks (a species as old as money), but it never managed to kill off these little fish. Brief glimpses of this usually invisible trade can sometimes be snatched from the murky depths of today's underground economy. A critic of payday lending, Michael Stegman, reports a conversation he had with the owner of a check-cashing chain in a state where expensive cash advances were prohibited. This man claimed the neighborhood loan shark made his appearance every Friday afternoon outside the busiest store, where wage-earners came to cash their paychecks. The shark charged 20% every two weeks, which is a little less than the going rate for a payday loan in unrestricted jurisdictions like Wisconsin.[49]

This example might illustrate the payday lenders' point, that black-market sharks endure wherever check lending is prohibited. But consider the story told by Sudhir Venkatesh, a sociologist who spent years moving through the underground economy in Chicago around the turn of the twenty-first century. Despite the fact that payday lending flourished across the city at this time, Venkatesh counted seventeen vest-pocket sharks in the impoverished neighborhood where he lived. All of these men lent money on the side, not as a full-time occupation, and they had political connections that shielded them from police interference. The moneylender in the movie *Barbershop*, which is set in Chicago, is a caricature of this kind of loan shark. The clientele for the trade described by Venkatesh consisted of shop owners or people not employed in the formal economy. They were charged 20% or 30% a month (which is cheap for a payday advance), and the lenders arranged things so that the larger loans were repaid in installments. In case of default, the sharks either seized assets or turned to violence. According to Venkatesh, in this neighborhood a dozen debtors a year were beaten for failure to repay their debts.[50] While licensed payday lenders never resort to such violent methods of debt collection, this example demonstrates that the existence of high-priced credit that is legal does not automatically starve the black-market sharks.

The fact should not surprise us, because payday lenders do not hand out money to everyone who walks through the door. Something like one in five applicants is rejected at the typical store, and many others might never apply for these loans if they belong to the 10% of the adult population who do not maintain a checking account. Sizable numbers of people in this country make their living within the informal sector of the economy, which would disqualify them from accessing credit in the legal market. Even payday lenders cannot afford to service this marginal population. Black-market sharks could be the only source of credit for them.

This is why unlicensed lenders continue to do a brisk business in immigrant enclaves, even in the age of payday lending. In New York City and elsewhere, Dominican shopkeepers borrow from *prestamistas*, vest-pocket sharks who charge as much as 5% or 10% a week for business loans. They extend credit when banks won't and deliver the cash more quickly and in person. But these are not payday loans, and the debt must be secured with assets, which may be seized if the borrower cannot keep up the payments. *Prestamistas* are not violent sharks. "We're not going to break any legs," one of these lenders told a reporter for the *New York Times*, "but we have taken property back."[51] These businessmen would not consider a postdated check sufficient security to risk extending credit to cash-strapped wage-earners who couldn't offer anything more tangible to be repossessed.

Examples like these demonstrate that there will always be sharks, whether payday lending is permitted or not. Even the freest economy, unless it does away with the rule of law, will generate a black market in credit that operates beneath it. But the size of the underground economy where the bootleg vendors ply their trade will vary depending on the restrictiveness of the formal sector. Low ceilings above should enlarge the caverns that always exist underground. The experience of credit markets in Europe seems to illustrate this trend. A comparative study by a research institute advocating financial deregulation found greater recourse to illegal lenders in France and Germany, where credit regulation is stricter, than in the United Kingdom, where high-risk consumers are served by the subprime "home credit" industry.[52] Agents of these ancient moneylenders on a weekly basis go door-to-door in low-income areas and collect the installment payments due for these small loans.[53] There is no such comparable industry in France or Germany, where rate caps and other restrictions ration credit-impaired households out of the legal market. As a result, there is a fringe of gray- or black-market lenders that cater to risky debtors. In Germany, *ohne Schufa* (or "no credit check") brokers hawk expensive installment loans in the classified ads and have an unsavory reputation for threatening borrowers who fall behind on their payments. The product they vend bears an uncanny resemblance to the high-priced installment loans that still flourish across the South of the United States and in other jurisdictions where the salary brokers of yesteryear convinced legislators to issue them licenses. In Germany, the minimum amounts that may be borrowed from this class of lenders are rather large, which means this credit isn't exactly a substitute for payday lending.

Even in Britain, where the credit market more closely resembles our own, the black-market sharks have not been starved into extinction. Vest-pocket entrepreneurs operate in dangerous neighborhoods where the home-credit agents fear to tread, lending small sums to people on the dole. In a survey of low-income households, 3% of respondents admitted to having borrowed from this source. This works out to be 0.44% of the total British population.[54] In Germany, the proportion of low-income consumers who acknowledge borrowing from usurers is three times as great as in Great Britain.[55] But we should note that *ohne Schufa* brokers aren't the same as the black-market creditors who survive in Britain's slums and the German lenders don't seem as thuggish. What is more, because income inequality is greater in Britain than in Germany, the fraction of the total population that goes underground to borrow may not be much larger in the latter than in the former. If the statistics reported by these surveys are accurate, it is doubtful that more than one in a hundred Germans borrows from illegal lenders.

Is that ratio lower in the United States, where subprime credit flourishes? It is impossible to say. Is the rate of borrowing from illegal lenders higher in the northeastern portion of the United States, where low usury ceilings have thwarted the payday lenders? There is no evidence for such a conjecture. Scour the press from the prohibitionist states and you will not find stories about vest-pocket sharks beating debtors who have gone into default. While mob usurers are still prosecuted in states like Massachusetts and New York, they have not been accused of lending small sums at high rates to working people, like the juice crews of old. That historically contingent trade has never been revived, even where credit rationing occurs.

If there has been a growth in black-market lending in jurisdictions that restrict or prohibit payday credit, it is occurring not on the street or around the factory gates but in cyberspace, where Internet lenders are being spawned. Many state regulators have complained about the growth of illegal lending on the World Wide Web, especially among companies that do not maintain a bricks-and-mortar presence. The shadiest enterprises not only flout state credit laws but sometimes engage in outright fraud, cleaning out applicants' bank accounts after gaining electronic access or collecting fees in advance for loans that never materialize. The worst of the Internet fraudsters are pirates who masquerade as loan sharks, offering to extend credit at high rates, then duping their hapless marks and making off with whatever cash they can steal. Some of these pirates are based in foreign countries and may have connections to crime syndicates there. Other operators, only slightly less unscrupulous, engage in old-fashioned loan-sharking within the new domain of the Internet. These entrepreneurs will deposit credit electronically in a customer's bank account, but the fees charged are high even for a payday loan—often 25% or more every two weeks. The transaction will be arranged in such a way that renewals are automatic and not easily discontinued. The interest payment might be debited electronically at regular intervals until the borrower makes a request in writing and before the due date to pay back the principal. Otherwise the debt will roll over continuously. Contacting the lender is made difficult because the site from which customers initiated the application isn't necessarily the creditor's site. Borrowers might be bounced from one location to another, none of which lists a phone number, or the lenders might switch Web addresses without notifying customers.[56] The businesses hide in the shadows until the debt goes into default. Then aggressive methods of debt collection are employed. Empty checking accounts might be debited repeatedly to run up penalty fees or to enlist the banks' help in exerting pressure on the debtor. Those in arrears will be harassed with phone calls at home and at work. "They'll say, 'If you don't pay by 5 p.m., we'll have you arrested,'" one prosecutor claimed. "Consumers get so scared they send them the money."[57]

These are the same tricks that were employed by unregulated loan sharks a hundred years ago, but now they occur in the shifting maze of the Internet. Since state governments insist that consumers who borrow money through their computers must be accorded the protections of the laws in the jurisdiction where they reside, extensions of credit that violate these rules ought to be classified as black-market. If so, quite a bit of illegal lending is occurring today in the United States. According to a consulting firm that tracks the payday-advance industry, roughly $7 billion in short-term credit was extended through the Internet in 2008. This figure represents 14% of the total market for this product.[58] Many of the mainstream lenders operating on the Internet do abide by state regulations, so most of the Web lending isn't black-market, but a sizable fraction is. Still, there isn't any proof that more of this brand of illegal lending is occurring in the states that effectively prohibit payday credit. While regulators in those states are more aggressive in prosecuting the rogue firms and in warning consumers about the dangers of Internet lending, this doesn't mean the problem is greater in these states. Some industry insiders claim that the type of people who borrow from Internet lenders is not the same as the type that patronize storefront outlets. If true, there isn't necessarily an inverse relation between these two types of vendors. The existence of many bricks-and-mortar shops, in other words, is no guarantee that illegal Internet lending is curtailed in the states without low rate caps. The only jurisdictions where we have good reason to think the black market is very small are the ones with the fewest restrictions, like Nevada and Wisconsin. What would count as black-market lending almost everywhere else will often be perfectly legal in the states with the freest markets in payday credit. Because these states are so permissive, the blacker sharks will look white in the light of their laws.

From this quick review of illegal lending today we can deduce six propositions. First, there will always be black-market sharks. It is a fantasy to think the species will ever be extirpated completely. Second, these sharks exist even in states that permit payday lending. Until the check lenders give cash to everyone who wants it, there will always be some demand for black-market credit. Third, the largest volume of illegal lending now occurs through the Internet, where furtive sharks and brazen pirates bilk consumers with usurious or fraudulent payday-advance products. Fourth, black-market creditors today, as in the past, do not necessarily employ violent methods of debt collection. If they operate over the Internet, the illegal lenders can harass or steal, but they are in no position to beat. Fifth, the fees that underground lenders charge today are often no greater than the going rate for legal payday loans. The Internet sharks seem to charge the highest rates, probably because their default rate is also very high. And sixth, it is probably the case that prohibition increases the number of illegal lenders in a jurisdiction, though by how much we do not know. Some consumers who would borrow at high rates if credit were available in the legal market will reduce consumption instead, rather than search for black-market sources of cash when prohibition is enforced. Hence, it is quite doubtful that there is perfect substitution between legal and illegal supplies of credit.

If the sixth proposition is true, then prohibition will inevitably drive more consumers into the underground economy in search of the credit they cannot find in the legal market. How many more will do so we cannot say. But the vital question is whether these new patrons of black-market sharks should count as the least advantaged group in our assessment, and if so, whether the added deprivation they suffer outweighs the benefits that accrue to consumers who are protected by credit prohibitions. Many might assume that the answer is yes to both parts of the question, but the analysis we have offered should make us more cautious (see Chapter 3). Not all who turned to black-market creditors after the enactment of the Uniform Small Loan Law were made worse off by this prohibition. For many, the practices of the second generation of loan sharks to which they were subjected were no worse than those of the first. While these consumers failed to gain, they did not lose when the new prohibition was imposed. What is more, there is ample evidence that large numbers of households had their lot eased by the cheaper credit brought into existence by the Uniform Small Loan Law. Their deprivation was reduced, perhaps to such an extent that the gains this much larger population experienced more than matched the losses suffered by the smaller fraction of debtors that fell into the clutches of the worst of the black-market sharks. For it cannot be denied that some who were rationed out of the legal market in small loans paid more and suffered greater abuses at the hands of usurers with mob affiliations. These terrorized debtors became the least advantaged group in this policy area and were worse off than the victims of the first loan sharks, who were almost never beaten or threatened with physical harm.

Because hard numbers are lacking, a precise calculation of gains and losses isn't possible for that earlier prohibition. But this isn't a problem if we accord absolute priority to the least advantaged group. Then we would prefer the option that raises the bottom as high as possible. If we apply this rule to the case of the Uniform Small Loan Law, knowing what we know now, we would be forced to reject that progressive reform because it made some debtors worse off than they would have been if salary lending had not been criminalized in the first place. Better to pay 20% a month to the gray-market salary lender and be harassed by a wage assignment than pay 40% a month to the black-market juice crew and live in fear for your life. If all that matters is the well-being of the least advantaged group, then we should always prefer the freer market to the one that is more restrictive. The more restrictive market always opens up more space below, in the underground, for the worst sort of predators to multiply.

This conclusion is rather paradoxical, because strict priority for the least advantaged group is the rule likely to be favored by liberals and egalitarians, not free-market conservatives. But according absolute priority to the least advantaged group in the domain of credit policy will compel us to prefer the option that shrinks the black market as much as possible, on the plausible assumption that the underground economy is the breeding place of the worst predatory lenders. Any other policy option seems perverse if our aim is to maximize the minimum. Prohibition of payday lending must therefore be rejected.

This conclusion will be convincing, however, only if the interests and well-being of every other group above the bottom counts for nothing in our assessment. The option that maximizes the minimum might very well reduce aggregate well-being by quite a bit or positively increase the total quantity of deprivation in a population, which also seems perverse. Then we would be helping a few but harming many. If we unleash the payday lenders, fewer debtors will be mauled by the most vicious sharks, but many more who are also not well-off will fare worse because the government refuses to protect them. This larger population will be fed upon by a species that is less savage but more numerous than the breed that hunts in the underground. Both policy options cull the shiver of sharks but in different ways. Prohibition reduces the total quantity of sharks but breeds a more vicious species. Deregulation, by contrast, tends to crowd out the worst predators (without, however, killing them off entirely) by encouraging the propagation of many more sharks whose methods of feeding are less brutal and more refined. It is a trade-off between quantity and quality.

Since perversity is inevitable in the domain of credit policy, which option is less perverse than the other? If our aim is to minimize deprivation, the choice is clear: prohibition is the lesser evil. It prevents more cash-strapped wage-earners from falling into the debt trap laid by the payday lenders. Most of these consumers will be better off if the government protects them from the myopia from which they suffer and which the lenders exploit in order to gain at their expense. They won't be allowed to access the risky bridge loans through which too many plunge into dire financial straits. Unfortunately, some who are turned back by legal barriers will then seek out riskier paths in the underground. They might end up worse off than before, though not for want of government trying to protect them. The pit these most reckless debtors fall into might be a little deeper than the legal traps laid by the payday lenders, but both traps are harmful, and one can be guarded against. Stories about people who build debt pyramids for themselves out of the credit extended to them by licensed payday lenders do not differ in any significant way from the stories that are told about debtors being mauled by the black-market sharks of the Internet. Neither customer will be beaten, but both will be harassed if they can't pay back their debts. Both will be bled dry by exorbitant interest rates, which can only increase their deprivation. Saving many people from this unfortunate lot seems desirable, even if a relative few will inevitably make themselves still more miserable by going underground. At least the government set itself in opposition to these traps. In the least restrictive states, the government issues licenses to debt trappers as if no harm was being done. This seems like a dereliction of duty.

The case for prohibition of payday lending, then, can be sustained even in the face of the perversity objection. It is a tougher call, however, because the ratio of winners to losers changes when we include black-market effects in our calculation. Prohibition harms credit-constrained consumers at the top and the bottom of the distribution of well-being even as it benefits the broad strata in-between. But we would feel more confident about the legitimacy of prohibition if we could increase the ratio of gain to pain produced by this policy. That result would be achieved if we could imitate the strategy of the Uniform Small Loan Law, which did not merely prohibit. It also created a new source of cheaper credit. Could something similar be done now at the start of the twenty-first century?

The New Remedial Lenders

The Uniform Small Loan Law could be classified as a creative prohibition. It not only banished a product from the legal market but also called into existence a cheaper substitute that was hedged in with consumer protections. Because the anti-loan-shark law raised the usury ceiling for small loans by a factor of six or seven, it created space for a new installment product to be introduced into the credit market that was less costly than the illegal salary loan by a factor of five or six. The idea was to drive the loan sharks into extinction through competition, licensing a cheaper alternative that would not be abusive to consumers. While the strategy was not ultimately successful, because the predators survived and evolved, there can be no doubt that this creative prohibition benefited many more consumers than it might have harmed. Millions of wage-earners gained access to cheaper credit because of the success of the Uniform Small Loan Law.

Unfortunately, the prohibition that would result today if the usury limit was rolled back uniformly to an annual rate of 36% would not be creative. The reduction in the legally permissible rate of interest would ration many credit-constrained consumers out of the market, because no licensed lender could afford to advance them cash. If companies are not willing to extend credit to these wage-earners today at 36%, then prohibiting businesses from charging more than this rate will do nothing to satisfy the demand that remains. The only thing this purely restrictive prohibition will accomplish is to increase the share of total demand that goes unsatisfied in the legal market.

This last claim, however, must be qualified. When licensed check lenders are driven from the market through a restrictive prohibition, some of their former customers will reduce their demand for credit by tightening their belts. They will cut costs or delay consumption. Some will find these sacrifices painful, but others may discover that doing without can increase their well-being. Evidence was cited previously that consumers who have been rationed out of credit markets sometimes express relief when they are forced to live within their means. Perhaps their reaction is a case of sour grapes, but it wouldn't be surprising if some who demanded expensive credit when it was legal discovered that they were better off demanding less and getting by with what they have. Other rationed consumers will cut their demand by tapping funds they had been holding in reserve while they borrowed at high rates. Rational maximizers, of course, would have drawn upon such pools of savings to begin with, since it seems foolish to borrow at 400% a year if your savings account pays you less than 4%. But many human beings are not rational maximizers, and survey data shows that sizable numbers of payday-loan customers had savings they could have tapped instead of borrowing.[59] If they aren't allowed to borrow at high rates any more, some of the savers might reduce their demand for credit and draw upon the cash reserves they have been hoarding.

Restrictive prohibition, then, in some degree will reduce demand for credit as well as the supply. Some of the demand that remains will be satisfied in the underground economy, but another portion will be met with legal sources of credit. This last claim may seem implausible to us. Who would lend money to subprime consumers, we may wonder, if lenders cannot charge subprime rates? But the truth is that cheaper sources of credit are often available to these consumers, even when payday lending is legal. Many who borrow against the security of a postdated check could have asked family or friends for the money, which would be interest-free. They choose not to do so because of embarrassment or fear of becoming personally dependent. But if payday loans are not available, some consumers will decide to pay the personal price of indebtedness and tap their informal networks for cash. Others will pay the search costs of time and effort in order to find cheaper sources of credit if the convenience of payday lending is no longer available. Many subprime consumers could qualify for less expensive forms of credit even now, if they bothered to try. They could apply for an installment loan, a new credit card, or an overdraft line of credit at the bank. They could open an account at a credit union, which may offer low-cost loans. These options would be cheaper, but many consumers in our 7-Eleven culture are willing to pay a premium for convenience. If the convenient option of payday lending is no longer available, some fraction of the subprime population to which those businesses cater would expend the effort to find legal sources of credit that would save them money.[60]

For all of these reasons, we can expect that only a fraction of payday-loan customers will turn to black-market sources of credit if a restrictive prohibition is imposed. The other fraction will reduce its consumption, draw on savings, or find alternative sources of legal credit. But to reduce demand for usurious debt still further, it would be desirable to expand the pool of low-priced and responsible credit available to the subprime class of consumers. This cannot be done by calling into existence a brand new industry on the model of the personal finance companies that were licensed by the Uniform Small Loan Law, for there is no virgin territory left to us that might be cleared by a relaxation of the usury statute. Restrictive prohibition kills off lenders; it does not create them. But new regulatory policies applied to the existing class of depository lenders could increase the credit options of rationed consumers, thereby reducing the black-market effects of restrictive prohibition. Any rollback of the usury ceiling ought to be coupled with new efforts to meet the legitimate credit needs of households that are risky and subprime. Fortunately, in recent years efforts have been made to fashion new and cheaper lending products for wage-earners with problematic credit.

The nonprofit credit unions have been the innovators in this field. The North Carolina State Employees' Credit Union (NCSECU) introduced a Salary Advance Loan product (or SALO) in 2001 as an alternative to payday lending. This single-payment cash advance charges an annual interest rate of around 12%, with the balance due debited automatically on payday from the borrower's direct-deposit account. Borrowing $300 for thirty days costs about $3, which is nearly $100 less than the typical payday loan. The low price, however, encourages repetitive usage. About 70% of the government workers who take advantage of the SALO program borrow every month. That rate of debt recidivism is much higher than for any payday loan, but the interest charge is so low that the product is a better deal than most credit cards. Concerned about the chronic usage, management tried to require the serial borrowers to attend financial education classes, but many of these customers found the rule burdensome and returned to the payday lenders. Later, NCSECU conditioned its cash advances on participation in a savings program. SALO customers were required to deposit 5% of the principal from each loan in an interest-bearing account so they could accumulate sufficient savings to avoid having to borrow before every payday.[61]

Other credit unions have experimented with different products. The North Side Community Federal Credit Union in Chicago created its Payday Loan Alternative (or PAL) in 2002. This six-month installment product charges an annual percentage rate of 16.5%, plus a fee to establish the account. Borrowers with very low credit scores are required to take financial education classes. But PAL—like SALO and the other credit-union alternatives to payday lending—fails to bring in enough revenue to cover costs. The North Side program is subsidized as a community service by grants from big, for-profit banks. If these loan products attract new customers who establish long-term relationships with the credit unions, they can be viewed as a loss-leader. But the default rate for North Side's PAL has been high, which would discourage other nonprofits from following its lead.[62]

One credit-union product that does pay its own way is Prospera's

GoodMoney Payday Loan. Based in northeastern Wisconsin and working in cooperation with Good Will Industries, Prospera Credit Union offers two-week payday loans at the rate of $9.90 per $100 borrowed, which is less than half the price charged by for-profit check lenders in the state. Located right inside Good Will stores, the Prospera booths encourage applicants for payday advances to consolidate their debts in lower-cost installment loans or to sign up for automatic savings programs that can help them budget for the future. Rollovers are permitted, however, and nearly 40% of GoodMoney customers borrow seven times or more during a twelve-month period. What is more, nothing prevents these debtors from using the proceeds of their GoodMoney loans to pyramid with more expensive cash advances. What this particular product seems to demonstrate is that the only way to compete effectively with the payday lenders is to mimic them. Prospera has cut the cost somewhat for short-term loans, and it does encourage better financial habits, but this nonprofit must still charge a triple-digit rate of interest to cover its costs. Its experiment offers clear proof that two-week or one-month loans could never be viable if the usury limit were reduced to 36%.[63]

Recognizing this reality, the Federal Deposit Insurance Corporation (FDIC) has recently begun to encourage the depository institutions it regulates to experiment with consumer-friendly installment products that could compete effectively with the payday loan. In 2007 it organized a Small-Dollar Loan Pilot Project to spur innovation and test alternative concepts in the field. Participating institutions were told to craft cash advances that would be paid back over more than one paycheck cycle and capped at an annual percentage rate of 36%. Underwriting was to be expedited so as to compete with the convenience of the payday loan, but customers were also to be encouraged or required to save money regularly so they wouldn't need to borrow at high rates in the future. Ideally, these new products would pay for themselves, but if they didn't, the losses could be justified as a way to build relationships with underserved populations that might be transitioned into other viable products like mortgages and consumer loans, as their credit improved. Banks and credit unions were enticed to experiment in this subprime sector of the credit market with the promise of earning regulatory credit for their community service.[64]

Early reports on the program, however, were not encouraging. In the first three months of 2008, the thirty-one participating chartered institutions only managed to make 1,523 loans—less than what a couple of the nation's 24,000 payday advance outlets might originate in a comparable period of time. What is more, the average amounts being lent were twice the size of the typical payday loan, and repayment was spread over an interval twenty times as great. The alternatives, in other words, aren't exactly comparable to the payday advance and probably appeal to a different segment of the market. Bounce protection programs are a closer approximation to the short-term check loan, but this product is usually more costly than payday credit.[65] Because banks and credit unions earn a substantial fraction of their fee income from bounced checks and bounce protection programs, they have a disincentive to provide low-cost alternatives to the payday loan.[66] While they might take business away from the check lenders, the banks and credit unions will also undercut demand for the bounce products from which they derive much revenue. It is hard to believe that most banks will ever have a sufficient motivation to try to capture business from the payday lenders—unless compelled by regulators to forgo the profits that can be made by charging high fees when account balances turn negative. In an age of deregulation, the two industries are symbiotic. They profit from each other's exploitation of the same cash-strapped clientele.

There is a frequently repeated myth that banks once used to lend small sums to working people but then got out of that business, after which the loan sharks emerged. But in this study we have seen that, from the beginning, the banks have never engaged in this trade. The usury statutes prevented them from doing so during the heyday of the salary lenders, and later the personal finance companies were assigned the task of serving credit-constrained consumers. The banks were allowed to target a different segment of the market. But with the coming of deregulation in the 1980s, the banks did discover the wage-earners who live from paycheck to paycheck and have trouble making ends meet. What the banks discovered about this population, however, is that it is a lucrative source of fee income. It is these people who routinely overdraw their accounts and can be penalized for doing so. They will be charged a fixed fee that is debited from the next deposit when the banks elect to cover these overdrafts. If the regulators required the depository institutions to treat these extensions of credit as short-term loans, the typical rate of interest charged would be astronomical. Once the banks were allowed to lend in this new and surreptitious way, the payday lenders entered the market with a cheaper (albeit still expensive) product. They set themselves up as the new remedial lenders—the poor man's bank of today. But if we want the banks and the credit unions to seize that role back from the payday lenders, policy makers will have to recognize that today's deregulated banks are loan sharks too. They enrich themselves at the expense of the subprime population of consumers in which the payday lenders also hunt, and no effort to undercut the check creditors will work until the abuses of the banks are brought to an end. Their covert usury must be recognized and proscribed.

The unfolding credit crisis of today presents regulators with the perfect opportunity to right these wrongs, if they are so inclined. With so many deregulated banks having lent themselves into insolvency, a thoroughgoing reorganization of these chartered and publicly insured entities is appropriate. They could be compelled to engage in responsible lending.[67] This would mean charging reasonable rates for overdraft protection, which is effectively an extension of credit. Suppose the depository institutions were not permitted to charge more than an annual interest rate of 36% when accounts are overdrawn? This would force the banks to substitute overdraft lines of credit for bounce protection programs as the default product when new accounts are opened. The former are much cheaper than the latter, but many banks today automatically enroll customers in the more expensive option. Account holders have to take the initiative to apply for the less expensive line of credit, and it isn't surprising that many don't. They need a nudge.[68] If regulators changed the default option, the cost savings for many consumers would be enormous and should reduce significantly the demand for payday credit. It would be like extending NCSECU's salary-advance product to all bank customers automatically (though probably at a somewhat higher rate of interest). Consumers would still have an incentive not to overdraw their accounts, but if they did, the small sums they borrowed would cost substantially less than the fees imposed by bounce protection programs or the payday lenders. The resulting loss of fee income to the banks could be justified as the price depository institutions pay for the privilege of being publicly chartered and publicly insured.[69]

The quickest way to reduce the demand for payday credit, in short, would be to compel the depository institutions to become the new remedial lenders. Make them offer cheaper, convenient, short-term credit by expanding access to the overdraft lines of credit that already exist. The credit unions could scarcely resist that imposition, given their public charge, and the banks shouldn't be allowed to either. They bear some responsibility for the growth of payday lending and its abuses. The heavy fees the banks charge drive many consumers to the check lenders, where they become trapped. Because banks have never been compelled to act in a remedial capacity, the United

States has been plagued since the Civil War with swarms of loan sharks. Reducing that scourge will require the participation of the banks, whose public role in our financial system has been made painfully evident by the current credit crisis. The opportunity ought to be seized to enlist them in this fight, by filling the vacuum created by a new prohibition with cheaper payday credit. If they did enlist, the ratio of winners to losers produced by credit prohibition would be increased significantly. Deprivation would be reduced. The result would be a creative prohibition, on the model of the Uniform Small Loan Law. It might even be more effective than that progressive reform, because the banks would be compelled to join the fight. Perhaps the lesson we should learn from the last 150 years is that if banks aren't made part of the solution they will be part of the problem. This is especially true today, when the banks all too often behave like sharks. They have been allowed to become the worst usurers.

The Rehabilitation of Usury

This is the case for prohibition. If consequences decide the question and if our aim is to minimize deprivation, then interest rates ought to be capped. This policy would help more people than it would hurt, especially if it were coupled with progressive banking reform. Fewer people would be trapped by expensive debt. Fewer would be taken advantage of. Exploitation would be reduced. To be sure, the policy wouldn't create utopia. Prohibitions never do. But there would be less misery in the land. The vulnerable would be better protected, from themselves as well as from others.

Admittedly, prohibition—even when creative—produces losers as well as winners. Some would have to make do with less credit; some would have to search harder for cheaper sources; others would have to suffer the embarrassment of asking friends or family for a loan; some who couldn't find credit in the legal market would go underground or click their way into cyberspace. These consumers might be better off if credit was deregulated, but their gain would cost even more pain. It does so now. More people are made worse off than they have to be when debt traps are legal. The fact that some going down this dangerous short-cut don't fall into a hole is scarcely justification for permitting lenders to entrap the rest. Debt trapping ought to be prohibited.

If there was some easy way to figure out which prospective debtors would become trapped and which would not, then wholesale prohibition would not be necessary. But *ex ante* we do not know. This is why a usury limit is imposed. It draws the line at the level of interest above which we have good reason to think losses will exceed gains. Today progressives want to make 36% a year the boundary of usury, reviving the benchmark that was established by an earlier generation of progressives. Several states have imposed limits in that neighborhood, and others may soon follow suit, but a federal statute would preempt these efforts and extend the protection all across the country, even in states where the issue is not in play. In an era when consumer credit is truly a vast ocean, a federalist approach to interest-rate regulation seems antiquated. The enormous variation in laws governing the small-loan field today cannot be justified by local circumstance. There is nothing so unique about Wisconsin that requires it to maintain a free market in payday credit when none of its neighbors does. The variance is better explained by the relative strength of the interest groups in each state and by accidents of history. When some states prohibit payday lending but their neighbors do not, prohibition is weakened. Residents living near the border are drawn across it into loan-shark territory, and the limited evidence available to us indicates that financial difficulties grow worse when payday loans are near. An effective prohibition ought to be national. It ought to set the upper bound below which states would be free to experiment.

The concept of usury sounds medieval. In the age of deregulation it became an antiquated term. But it ought to be revived, at least in the domain of small loans. Usury proscribes a misuse of money. When money is laid as a trap, this is a misuse. Then lending becomes predation. The predatory lenders are loan sharks. While we will never be rid of them entirely, public policy can cull the shiver of sharks. Today, a new creative prohibition would have that effect. It has a better chance of reducing the sum total of deprivation in society than the policy of credit deregulation does.

We stand today amid the wreckage of the credit revolution. Its excesses have become visible. All are suffering from those excesses, even if they did not participate in them. Perhaps we're now prepared to learn what most other peoples the world over have known, that allowing borrowers to consent to exorbitant interest does not further the common good.

The View from the Shark Cage

Blows sharp the keen autumnal wind.

Its clutch is at the throat.

They now repent

Whose money's spent.

The loan shark has their note.

—Anonymous, *Edwardsville Intelligencer,* 1908

I got my first payday loan recently. I didn't need the money, but I wanted to experience what I've been writing about for the past eighteen months. I suspect that most of the participants in the debate about payday lending, including the lenders themselves, have other credit options and do not need to mortgage a check in order to secure a cash advance. Their views on the subject have not been shaped by a bout of indebtedness to this type of lender. I admit that mine haven't been, either. I have good credit and could easily borrow from a less expensive source. But I wanted to compare what I've learned about payday lending during the course of my research with a personal experience. The exercise was rather artificial, I'll concede, because necessity did not drive me into this market. It was like studying the shark from inside a cage: I knew I was safe because I wasn't exposed. But it was still worthwhile to blow a bit of cash on the fee so that I could see for myself what tens of thousands of wage-earners experience each day when they step through those doors.

I chose the outlet closest to where I live, in a city of 100,000 people that lies just across the border from Illinois, in Wisconsin. As I noted previously, Illinois' neighbor to the north is arguably the least restrictive state in the nation when it comes to regulating payday credit. Lenders are permitted to charge what the market will bear, and they may renew loans as often as they like. In the community where I live, the telephone directory lists nineteen different outlets. The one I visited is located downtown and on the edge of a minority residential neighborhood.

The building was small and made of brick. There were a few spaces along the side for cars to park. Directly behind the store was a beauty parlor. The structure was located along a busy thoroughfare and was sandwiched between a gas station and a car lot. A simple neon sign advertised its trade.

This store was a branch of a national chain. The corporation had another outlet located three miles away. The site I visited advertised just two products: the payday loan and a prepaid credit card. Business was slow the day I got my cash advance. The lobby was empty when I arrived around noon, and no other customers entered the store during the twenty minutes it took for me to complete the transaction.

The office was not large. The public area was divided by a counter with three teller stations. There were a few small offices in the back, but the doors were closed and the lights switched off. The front wall was glass and a few chairs were lined along it, facing the counter. A table stood off to the side with a rack of brochures. Unlike a check-cashing outlet, there was no thick pane of glass dividing customer from employee. The space was neat but casual and not as stuffy as a bank lobby. The floor was carpeted and the light was soft. The appearance wasn't seedy. The furnishings suggested that the business was reputable but unpretentious. The soothing color scheme was designed to put customers at ease.

As soon as I entered the store I was greeted by the lone clerk, an African American male in his late twenties. He was pleasant but not loquacious. I told him I wanted to borrow $300 but had never gotten a payday loan before. He asked a few quick questions to determine whether I was eligible to apply. Was I currently employed? Did I have an open checking account? Did I have picture identification? Once I had satisfied these requirements,

he began to take down my information on the application form. I was a
little surprised that I wasn't asked to fill out the form myself. It created the
impression that the lender was in charge and that what I wrote might not be
trusted. But I will admit that the clerk had neater handwriting than I do, and
that it was probably more efficient for him to fill in the blanks because he
knew exactly what information was required. Because the initial application
process consisted of the clerk asking questions and me giving answers, he
could more easily judge whether I was being truthful than if I simply wrote
down some information and presented it to him. In this initial phase of the
transaction, the lender gathered information about where I lived, how I could
be contacted, where I was employed, how much I was paid and when, which
bank I maintained a checking account with, and what my current account
balance was. I was also asked to name three "references," but the term was a
euphemism. These people were not contacted during the application phase
in order to attest to my good character. They would only be phoned later, if I
failed to pay back my debt. They were people who could be harassed or used
to embarrass me if I shirked my obligation. Taking names was a not so subtle
way of binding me to the lender.

Once the application had been completed, the clerk asked me to sign it
and to affix my thumbprint in the lower right-hand corner. A small inkpad
was available for that purpose. Never once in my adult life had a potential
creditor asked for this form of identification. It strengthened the impression
that the lender thought I might not be a trustworthy person. Once that task
was completed, the clerk began to verify the key pieces of information on
the application. He phoned the home number I had given him to verify that
it was connected and belonged to me. Then he phoned work and got my
voicemail message, which was sufficient to verify that I was employed where
I claimed to be. Next he phoned an automated system to verify my bank
balance, which required me to enter the pin number for the account. I had
established a new, basic checking account a couple of months previously for
this very purpose, because my regular account requires me to keep a hefty
balance to avoid incurring monthly fees. I thought it would look strange
to borrow $300 from a payday lender if I already had much more in my
account than that sum. My new checking account charged a $5 monthly
fee and limited how many checks I could write each month, but it did not
require a minimum balance. When I applied for the payday loan I had only
$184.81 in the account. I had brought a recent bank statement along with
me that day but it wasn't required to complete the transaction.

Once those three phone calls checked out, the clerk entered my information into the computer. He told me there was one more step in the verification process that had to be completed, which I assumed was a credit check through the Teletrack system. This service assigns a score based on payment history in the subprime market. It more accurately assesses risk for this clientele than the mainstream credit-rating agencies.[1] I asked the clerk if my payday-advance transaction would show up on a standard credit report. He told me it wouldn't unless I defaulted.

While the clerk entered my information into the computer, we chatted briefly. He mentioned that a friend of his was going to attend the university where I work. The friend had taken some time off before going to college, and I said that was a good way to recharge one's batteries and earn some cash. But the clerk disagreed. He had started college but then dropped out. Now he would like to go back to school, but he said he felt stuck. I got the impression that he thought this was a dead-end job or that the pay wasn't very good. Given the high turnover rate reported by some of the national chains, many other employees seem to have drawn a similar conclusion.

In a couple of moments the computer accepted my application for a cash advance. I was told that I was eligible to borrow the maximum amount, $1,000. I said I just needed $300 and the clerk didn't press me. But one of the documents I signed with my contract asked me to confirm that the clerk had offered me a larger sum than I'd requested. If I hadn't been told that I could borrow more, I was instructed to call a toll-free number. The implication of the document was clear. I was being encouraged to borrow as much as the lender was willing to advance. If I was hard up, as most payday-loan customers are, I might easily have accepted the offer, but borrowing the maximum amount would surely increase the likelihood that customers will refinance the loan on payday rather than pay it off. That is how the lender is going to turn a profit on the loan.

While the printer behind the clerk generated the loan contract, I filled out the check I would leave as collateral for my cash advance. I was instructed to date the check for that day, not payday, and the amount I filled in included the principal plus the fee. Because Wisconsin is a deregulated state, you might assume the fee I was being charged for this loan would be lower than in regulated states like Florida or New Mexico. In most markets, after all, government regulation inflates costs for the consumer. But the payday-credit market is unusual. Because it is so free in Wisconsin, I paid more to borrow $300 than I would have paid in a regulated state. This isn't necessarily because payday lenders earn a higher rate of profit in Wisconsin. The healthy competition of many lenders ought to check that rate. The real reason I paid more is because the lenders almost certainly approve more loans to marginal applicants in Wisconsin than in the restrictive jurisdictions and thus have to write off more bad debts. My inflated fee covered part of these losses as well as the greater costs that had to be borne to dun those who were late to pay or had defaulted. In this respect, then, the pricing in the free-market states is progressive: the solvent are required to carry the insolvent. In the regulated states, by contrast, fewer marginal applicants are approved because the fee is capped. The solvent pay less there, because it is not profitable to lend to the soon-to-be insolvent.

The fee structure for this company's credit product was posted on the wall opposite the door. For every $100 borrowed until payday, the fee was $22. My $300 cash advance cost me $66. If the term of the loan was fourteen days, the annual percentage rate this lender charged was 573%. But I had applied for a loan just eight days before payday. When I was presented with the contract to sign, the Federal Truth-In-Lending Statement printed on the first page listed the yearly rate as 1003.75%. There was no doubt this was an expensive cash advance. If I had borrowed the same sum with the credit card in my wallet, the interest charge on my next bill would have been less than $5. Measured by the APR, this payday loan was fifty times more expensive.

I was struck at the time—in a way that I had not been before—by the fixed nature of the payday-loan fee. Whether I borrowed eight days before payday or fourteen, the charge was the same. The clerk did tell me that if I paid back the loan early, a portion of the finance charge would be rebated to me, but it is doubtful that many customers earn the rebate since they won't be paid again until the loan is due. The fixed nature of the payday-loan fee indicates that the interest the lender pays to borrow the loan fund from investors or banks is only a tiny fraction of the costs associated with extending this type of credit. Most of the costs, like rent and wages, are fixed and do not vary with the term of the loan. My eight-day cash advance could only have been slightly less costly to underwrite than the more typical fourteen-day loan, which was why I was charged the same amount as another customer who had an extra week to make use of the cash.

The contract was three pages in length. Like most customers, I only glanced at the fine print before signing. The first page listed the loan terms, the second page explained the details, the third page was devoted entirely to the arbitration agreement. The pages were stacked so that only the signature lines of the bottom two sheets were exposed. While I was signing the contract, the clerk scheduled an appointment with me to repay the loan. I was to return to the office on payday early in the evening and to bring cash. I would buy back my check rather than compel the lender to deposit it. I was told that if I didn't want to pay back the whole sum, then I could refinance the debt for a new fee, and if I wanted, pay down just a portion of the balance. The clerk did not ask me what the money was for or why I needed it. If he was astonished that someone who earns as much as I do had to borrow from a payday lender, he concealed his surprise effectively. His manner was matter-of-fact.

Once the papers were signed, I was given a copy, together with a half-dozen colorful brochures. One advertised the prepaid credit card, another told me how to register for an online newsletter, a third explained the company's service, the fourth touted one of the lender's charitable causes, the fifth was a guide from the industry's Community Financial Services Association, and the last provided information about credit counseling. All of them were tucked inside a glossy folder. The clerk counted out my cash, and we were done. The transaction was as smooth and efficient as I had expected it would be.

The thought that struck me at the time, however, was what a mismatch there is between this product and the clientele to whom it is being pitched. As a tenured professor, I could afford the fee and would have no difficulty paying back the principal. Indeed, I didn't actually spend any of the $300 I received that day and simply returned the same bills to the clerk the following week when my debt was due. For me a short-term, single-payment loan represented no obstacle. But it is also true that no one who made as much money as I or who had good credit would borrow on such terms. The product seemed way overpriced. The irony is that the only people who are willing to pay this much are the very ones who can least afford it. They have to have bad credit or no savings. Their finances have to be stretched far too thin. The lender knows this and doesn't really trust the clientele that apply for this kind of cash advance. It is necessary to check what applicants say right there, phoning home and phoning work. It is necessary to take the names of friends and family who can be harassed if payments are late. It is necessary to fingerprint these debtors. The transaction is obviously deemed risky, but the lender is willing to accept this risk in exchange for an exorbitant fee. The old adage, that the poor pay more, is entirely accurate. The credit-poor definitely pay more at the payday-loan store.

I was reminded of a law review article I had read about the "duty of suitability."[2] After the Great Depression, the authors explained, the Securities and Exchange Commission had imposed this obligation upon brokers to regulate their dealings with clients, who despite being affluent were recognized as vulnerable to being taken advantage of by deceptive or high-pressure sales tactics. Stock brokers are obligated to ensure that the products they sell are appropriate to the circumstances of each client. One might think acknowledgment of such a duty is even more urgent in the domain of subprime lending, given the greater vulnerability of these consumers to exploitation in comparison to the typical investor. But it was clear to me when I had completed my transaction that the payday lender had not imposed upon itself a duty of suitability to match its expensive credit product to the circumstances of each debtor. This loan was appropriate for someone with my income and credit score, but it wouldn't be for someone whose finances were precarious or who didn't have a good record of paying back debt on schedule. The libertarian ideology of free choice and personal responsibility with which the lenders continuously defend themselves seems disingenuous when you experience firsthand how little confidence they have in their customers. These businesses know very well that most of the people to whom they are extending credit pay late, are in arrears, or have defaulted on other obligations. Their rhetoric strikes a populist chord, as if they have faith and believe in second chances when others don't. But in practice, these creditors have no faith in the reliability of their debtors and are positively counting on the fact that many who apply for these loans don't pay them off right away and are caught short again and again. Unsuitability is the essence of their business model. They are hawking a demanding form of credit—the short-term, single-payment loan—to a clientele that is least fitted to assume this level of financial responsibility, given its current resources and past credit record. They are, in effect, offering an American Express extension of credit to a subprime population.

The likely outcome of this deliberate mismatch was illustrated for me when I returned to the shop the following Friday to pay back my debt. I had received a phone call the day before reminding me of the appointment I'd scheduled the previous week. No other creditor to whom I'd owed money had ever done such a thing before. The payday lender wasn't going to give me the benefit of a doubt; there was no presumption of innocence or personal responsibility. Since I commute a long distance by train, I was a little worried that I might be delayed and fail to get to the store before it closed. I wondered what would happen then. But my train was on time and I arrived at the shop when I said I would. Another man entered the office just before me and the clerk settled his account first. Because the lobby was small, it was impossible not to overhear their business transaction. The man was a trucker and said he had been on the road for seventeen hours straight. He had been worried, as I had been, that he might miss his appointment that evening. The man seemed familiar with the whole process and told the clerk he wanted to refinance part of his current loan. He paid the $88 fee that was due for his $400 debt, plus another $200 in principal, and wrote a new check for $244. The $200 he had not paid back had now cost him $88 to borrow, assuming the man hadn't already refinanced the debt two weeks earlier. He mentioned to the clerk that his wife also had a payday loan and would be in to pay off some of the principal in the near future. One got the impression the couple was pyramiding loans together, trying to play catch-up in the fast-paced game of payday lending. Perhaps the two were on the verge of clearing their debts, but one unforeseen expense or a sudden drop in income would likely put them behind once again.

The trucker was a recidivist, as I've dubbed the repeat customers; in the lingo of the credit card companies he was a revolver. His fees may have subsidized my loan if it's true that the check lenders don't turn a profit from those who borrow just once (or are "one and then done"). I was there to settle my debt, and our business was quickly concluded. I signed a "buyback" agreement, which made it clear that what I was doing was buying back the check I'd left as collateral the previous week. It hadn't dawned on me before, but what I'd done the previous week was essentially pawn a check, which was now returned to me uncashed after being stamped "PAID" in red ink. My bank would never know what had been done. Presumably neither would my other creditors, since the payday lender did not report the transaction to a credit bureau. But a whole new class of creditors did suddenly begin to phone me at home (perhaps by coincidence) and offer to help me consolidate my debts, pay off my credit card bills, or advance me the tax refund I was owed. The lender also began to email me, ostensibly to offer consumer tips about how to save money. But the messages also encouraged me to "apply now" for a new cash advance over the Internet. The fee being charged for this product was $25 for every $100 advanced. For a fourteen-day loan, the disclosure said the APR was 651.79%.

I decided to pass on that offer, however. It might have been fun to pyramid several loans, except that I would have to pay the fees, which were exorbitant. It was hard to justify spending so much more money for whatever additional insight I might gain into payday lending. And so I withdrew from this financial underworld, having entered it as an interloper and in an artificial way. I had felt the bite of the interest, the most shark-like quality of the transaction. But the experience also confirmed an impression I had gained in the course of my research that the shark had never really been the right metaphor for this class of lender. We think of sharks as remorseless and brutal predators, but this isn't how I experienced the payday lender. I liked the clerk with whom I dealt and there was nothing sinister about the office I visited, or the promotional materials I received, or the contract I signed. It was just business, very corporate and banal. What borrowing from the loan shark illustrated for me was the banality of exploitation. The lender was clearly taking advantage of people without good options, offering them a credit product that at this moment might seem mutually advantageous but which for a predictably large fraction of its myopic clientele would only exacerbate their plight. They would become trapped by what they owed, paying the biweekly rental fee again and again because they couldn't scrape together enough cash to get ahead of the debt. The lender would live off those renewals, gaining at the expense of wage-earners who wouldn't be here if they didn't have bad credit. The lender wasn't so much a shark—whose methods are blunt—but a debt trapper, a more subtle kind of exploiter. That was the better metaphor. The government had decided to license debt trapping because not everyone who took the bait became ensnared. These exploiters are shrewd enough not to victimize every customer. They have worked things so that not only they but a fraction of their clientele will also gain at the expense of the recidivists. Resources are redistributed from the relatively weak to the relatively strong.

That's what's wrong with exploitative transactions.[3] The redistribution of resources is invariably regressive. As the saying goes, the rich get richer and the poor get poorer. If the aim of public policy is to improve the lot of the least advantaged group, as I think it should be, then tolerating exploitation will always be problematic—but so will doing away with it, insofar as the trade is mutually advantageous here and now. The trucker who was trapped might very well object to the case I made for prohibition of payday lending (see the Chapter 5). Why shouldn't he be allowed to borrow on any terms he sees fit? Why should the government reduce his credit options? What is he supposed to do if he needs a cash advance right away? These are valid questions.

It is true that, in the short run, the trucker is better off being exploited than not. At this particular moment, his alternatives to borrowing at a stiff price probably seem even worse. But the same is true for the sweatshop worker, who would rather be taken advantage of than forgo the opportunity to work. The case of sweatshop exploitation, however, also suggests why prohibition in the domain of high-priced credit is more justifiable, for in accepting an exploitative offer the sweatshop worker gains in a positive way compared to the alternatives. Sweated labor, as unpleasant as it may be, presumably pays more or one would never agree to do it. But in the case of the payday loan, what prohibition would prevent is the opportunity to contract the most expensive sort of debt there is. One loses the chance to go deeper into the hole. No doubt some will manage the increased level of risk successfully and improve their lot, at least a little bit, but there is also plenty of evidence that a population of equal size or greater but more vulnerable in its circumstances will be rendered worse off in the months to come. These debtors will not be able to escape from the deeper hole into which they've been allowed to stumble. Since we cannot easily determine who will become trapped and who will not, prohibition simply bars this path beyond the point where we think the losses will exceed the gains. We can do so all the more easily because we have good reason to believe that the ones who would have gained if the path were clear are sufficiently strong that they will have other decent options even if this one is closed to them. They won't be put out very much. They will simply be forced to trade the convenience of a payday loan for a lower price they can probably find if they extend their search.

Perhaps another shark metaphor will help to make the point. A usury threshold is like a line of buoys that prohibits swimmers from venturing into deeper, shark-infested waters. No doubt a libertarian will complain about the restriction, but the rest of us will think that the loss of freedom imposed by this restriction pales in comparison to the other losses that will result from an extension of freedom in this domain. If a swimmer complains that he needs to fish on the other side of the line in order to survive, we would still be justified in enforcing the prohibition as long as we have good reason to believe that some sizable fraction of those who strike out into such deep waters will be mauled by the sharks. The justification is the weighted sum of gains and losses. In the sea of consumer credit, plenty of evidence exists that the weakest swimmers are being taken by the sharks. The fact that the sharks don't take every swimmer scarcely counts as a compelling reason not to establish a buoy line. What matters is that many are being mauled now and that society is worse off when it tolerates this form of regressive redistribution. The exploiters gain not only at the expense of the weak but also at the expense of everyone else, who will be expected to clean up the mess. Better to prohibit the trade than to put ourselves out, after the fact, by expending resources to heal the victims of this exploitative subterfuge.

As I have tried to show in this work, the exploitative subterfuge we call loan-sharking was an invention of payday, a relatively recent innovation in the history of remuneration. Without the recurring payday and the bureaucratization of compensation that makes it feasible, there never would have been any loan sharks. That breed of financial exploiter was spawned in the income stream that flows from employer to employee, but over time, the shape of that stream has shifted. Payday lending in the twenty-first century is not identical to payday lending in the nineteenth. I have tried to chart the course of that transformation and to describe the various species of predators that have hunted in this stream. In the beginning they were black or gray, but late in the twentieth century some managed to become white. Their exploitation was legalized, but the form and results were not much different from what they were a century earlier. The key to loan-sharking is not a violent method of debt collection, which isn't necessary at all to the trade and has been the exception rather than the rule. The key, instead, is the short-term, single-payment loan, a financial product that is both expensive and unforgiving. When pitched to wage-earners who are short of funds and without good credit, the product invariably forms a debt trap into which many will fall. They will renew their loans again and again or pay off one with the proceeds of another. For the most vulnerable, the debt becomes interest-only, worsening their plight rather than improving it. Scarce resources are siphoned off to enrich the predatory lender, and social problems are intensified rather than reduced.

Those are the consequences of loan-sharking in every generation, but I have also tried to show that the trade is complicated. The product does not trap every debtor. Some do gain by paying a lot for an emergency extension of credit. And prohibiting the trade does not necessarily make it disappear. Criminalization tends to make the lenders worse and their product more expensive. It will deepen the trap for some rather than dismantle it. Prohibition always engenders black-market effects, though these vary with time and circumstance. The mob shark is not an ever-present threat. The juice men of the 1950s and 1960s are unlikely to return even if a new prohibition is enforced in the twenty-first century. But that new prohibition will work best and impose fewer costs if it is creative rather than merely restrictive. Fostering low-cost alternatives to payday debt is the best way to extinguish the loan sharks. The strategy has worked before, and it could work again. But for it to work, the depository institutions must be enlisted in the fight. They must be transformed into responsible lenders. From the beginning, their failure to play this role has opened up the space within which the loan sharks have bred. Unless the obligation is imposed upon them, we have no reason to think the predators will disappear. They certainly won't disappear if banks are permitted to behave, as they do now, like predators with class.

But we shouldn't deceive ourselves. There will be sharks always. This type of financial exploitation will endure. Policy makers, however, can either foster it or undercut it. Often they do both at once. But what they ought not to do is to pretend that by licensing the trade they make loan-sharking disappear. That maneuver will make loan-sharking corporate and mainstream, but it will do little to reduce the incidence of debt trapping in the subprime population. Legalization only gives loan-sharking a legitimacy it doesn't deserve.

Notes

Introduction—The Evolution of the Shark

1. Robert Kelso, "Social and Economic Background of the Small Loan Problem," *Law and Contemporary Problems* 8 (1941): 22.

2. M. R. Neifeld, *Neifeld's Manual on Consumer Credit* (Easton: Mack, 1961), 387–89.

3. Donald Tyree, *The Small-Loan Industry in Texas* (Austin: University of Texas Press, 1960), 59; Ira Cobleigh, *How and Where to Borrow Money* (New York: Avon Books, 1964), 109.

4. Findley Weaver, *Oklahoma's Small Loan Problem* (Oklahoma City: Bond Printing, 1938), 21.

5. Charles Gates, "The Social Worker in the Service of the Small Loan Business," *Annals of the American Academy of Political and Social Science* 196 (1938): 223.

6. Dennis Telzrow, "Present and Future of the Payday Advance Industry" (presentation at the annual conference of the Community Financial Services Association of America, Las Vegas, Nevada, March 6, 2008), 10–11; Bob Driehaus, "Some States Set Caps to Control Payday Loans," *New York Times*, 8 September 2008.

7. While there is no full-length study of payday lending in its modern form, valuable discussions of the product can be found in these publications: John Caskey, *Fringe Banking: Check-Cashing Outlets, Pawnshops, and the Poor* (New York: Russell Sage Foundation, 1994); Christopher Peterson, *Taming the Sharks: Towards a Cure for the High-Cost Credit Market* (Akron: University of Akron Press, 2004); Brett Williams, *Debt for Sale: A Social History of the Credit Trap* (Philadelphia: University of Pennsylvania Press, 2004); John Caskey, "Fringe Banking and the Rise of Payday Lending," in *Credit Markets for the Poor*, ed. Patrick Bolton and Howard Rosenthal (New York: Russell Sage Foundation, 2005), 17–45; James Scurlock, *Maxed Out: Hard Times, Easy Credit, and the Era of Predatory Lenders* (New York: Scribner, 2007); Jose Garcia et al., *Up to Our Eyeballs: How Shady Lenders and Failed Economic Policies Are Drowning Americans in Debt* (New York: New Press, 2008).

8. Robert Mayer, "Payday Loans and Exploitation," *Public Affairs Quarterly* 17 (2003): 197–217.

One—The Origin of the Species

1. Guy Blake, "The Validity of Laws Regulating Wage Assignments," *Illinois Law Review* 5 (1911): 343.

2. H.T.C., "From Our Correspondent. No. VII," *New York Evangelist*, 14 October 1837.

3. James DuBois and Gertrude Mathews, *Galusha A. Grow: Father of the Homestead Law* (Boston: Houghton Mifflin, 1917), 29.

4. "In Suffering and Want," *Chicago Tribune*, 24 October 1888; "For the Good of the Service," *Chicago Tribune*, 2 August 1900.

5. "Landis Leads Triple War on Loan Sharks," *Chicago Tribune*, 17 December 1916; Earle Eubank, *The Loan Shark in Chicago* (Chicago: Department of Public Welfare, 1916), 9.

6. David Caplovitz, "Consumer Credit in the Affluent Society," in *Consumer Credit Reform*, ed. Clark Havighurst (Dobbs Ferry: Oceana, 1970), 5.

7. Clarence Wassam, *The Salary Lending Business in New York City* (New York: Charities Publication Committee, 1908), 12.

8. Rolf Nugent, *Consumer Credit and Economic Stability* (New York: Russell Sage Foundation, 1939), 72.

9. "Sharks in the City Hall," *Chicago Tribune*, 16 October 1900; "Healy Goes After Chase," *Chicago Tribune*, 8 November 1896.

10. "Union Advances Money for County Pay Vouchers," *Chicago Tribune*, 2 February 1903.

11. "No Pay; Canteen Missed," *Chicago Tribune*, 17 July 1901.

12. Clarence Hodson, *Money-Lenders, License Laws, and the Business of Making Small Loans* (New York: Legal Reform Bureau to Eliminate the Loan Shark Evil, 1919), 53; "6% Honor Loans to Chicago Wage Earners Coming," *Chicago Tribune*, 31 December 1916; "How 250,000 Chicagoans 'Raise the Wind,'" *Chicago Tribune*, 31 March 1907 (one reporter).

13. Wassam, *Salary Lending Business*, 20.

14. "Says Loan Sharks Prey on Teachers," *Chicago Tribune*, 5 December 1908; "Teachers Talk of Loan Sharks," *Chicago Tribune*, 15 November 1903 (quote).

15. In *Chicago Tribune*, "Join against Loan Sharks," 18 September 1907; "How 250,000 Chicagoans 'Raise the Wind,'" 31 March 1907; "Bars Policemen from the Races," 12 May 1901.

16. "In Jail from High Living," *Chicago Tribune*, 4 May 1909.

17. "Clerks Risk All in Speculation," *Chicago Tribune*, 5 May 1901.

18. Wassam, *Salary Lending Business*, 21; "For the Good of the Service," *Chicago Tribune*, 2 August 1900.

19. *Daily News Almanac and Book of Facts*, 18th edition (Chicago: Chicago Daily News, 1902), 29; Hodson, *Money-Lenders*, 12, 30; "6% Honor Loans to Chicago Wage Earners Coming," *Chicago Tribune*, 31 December 1916.

20. "Join against Loan Sharks," *Chicago Tribune*, 18 September 1907; "How 250,000 Chicagoans 'Raise the Wind,'" *Chicago Tribune*, 31 March 1907.

21. "Sharks in the City Hall," *Chicago Tribune*, 16 October 1900; "Street Cleaning Shakeup Begun by Richard T. Fox," *Chicago Tribune*, 4 August 1905.

22. Wassam, *Salary Lending Business*, app. 27; Hodson, *Money-Lenders*, 13. See also Lendol Calder, *Financing the American Dream: A Cultural History of Consumer Credit* (Princeton: Princeton University Press, 1999), 118.

23. "To Control Loan Sharks in Illinois," *Charities and the Commons* 21 (1908): 407–8; "'King of the Loan Sharks' now Goes After Housewife's Savings," *Chicago Tribune*, 21 April 1912.

24. *Daily News Almanac*, 414.

25. Jeffrey Williams and Peter Lindert, *American Inequality: A Macroeconomic History* (New York: Academic Press, 1980), 105.

26. Heather Boushey and Christian Weller, "Has Growing Inequality Contributed to Rising Household Economic Distress?" *Review of Political Economy* 20 (2008): 1–22; Markus Christen and Ruskin Morgan, "Keeping Up With the Joneses: Analyzing the Effect of Income Inequality on Consumer Borrowing," *Quantitative Marketing and Economics*

3 (2005): 145–73. See also Matteo Iacoviello, "Household Debt and Income Inequality, 1963–2003," *Journal of Money, Credit, and Banking* 40 (2008): 929–65.

27. "Notice to the Public," *Chicago Tribune*, 6 February 1856.

28. "William H. English," *Chicago Tribune*, 6 July 1880; "Ten per cent a Month," *Wellsboro Agitator*, 16 March 1886.

29. "The Custom House," *New York Herald*, 5 May 1869; "Salary Brokers," *New York Times*, 16 September 1874; "Salary Brokerage," *New York Times*, 19 September 1874.

30. Louis Robinson and Rolf Nugent, *Regulation of the Small Loan Business* (New York: Russell Sage Foundation, 1935), 36–42.

31. Ibid., 43.

32. Bureau of Justice of Chicago, annual reports published by Hornstein Brothers in Chicago, *First Annual Report* (1889), 9; *Fifth Annual Report* (1893), 5; *Ninth Annual Report* (1897), 4; *Fourteenth Annual Report* (1902), 6.

33. Bureau of Justice of Chicago, *Thirteenth Annual Report of the Bureau of Justice of Chicago* (Chicago: Hornstein Brothers, 1901), 4. The *Tribune's* first exposé of the "new spider system" of salary lending noted that "this particular kind of loan business is comparatively of recent origin." See "Usurious Financial Spiders who Entrap Borrowers in Their Short Loan Webs," *Chicago Tribune*, 7 November 1897.

34. "Lawsuit Reveals 'Savings Bank' as Loan Shark's Lair," *Chicago Tribune*, 18 February 1912; Earle Eubank, *Loan Sharks and Loan Shark Legislation in Illinois* (New York: Russell Sage Foundation, 1917), 5; "Court Order Ends 6 Years' Tribute to Loan Sharks," *Chicago Tribune*, 3 May 1912.

35. Eubank, *Loan Shark in Chicago*, 14.

36. In the *Chicago Tribune*, "Loan Sharks Put under Hard Test by Judge Landis," 24 February 1912; "Loan Shark Has New Way to Hide," 4 March 1912; "Mystery Woman, Loan Shark Tool, Tells Own Story," 15 March 1912; "Social Lion's Mother Backs Loan Octopus," 2 December 1916.

37. Calder, *American Dream*, 118; Herman Kogan, *Lending Is Our Business: The Story of Household Finance Corporation* (Chicago: Household Finance Corporation, 1965), 9–18.

38. "Loan Mortgage Called 'No Good,'" *Chicago Tribune*, 5 March 1910.

39. "Loan Shark Hires Women to Weave Web about Him," *Chicago Tribune*, 7 February 1912.

40. "Banks Join Fight on Loan Sharks, Refuse Accounts," *Chicago Tribune*, 13 February 1912.

41. Kogan, *Lending Is Our Business*, 48; "Help for Slaves of Loan Sharks," *Chicago Tribune*, 17 September 1907; "How 250,000 Chicagoans 'Raise the Wind,'" *Chicago Tribune*, 31 March 1907.

42. Irwin Ellis, "How the Loan Sharks of Chicago Prey upon the Unfortunate," *Chicago Tribune*, 3 September 1911; Eubank, *Loan Shark in Chicago*, 9–12.

43. Arthur Ham, *The Campaign against the Loan Shark* (New York: Russell Sage Foundation, 1912), 1; Irwin Ellis, "The Loan Shark in Search of Prey," *Chicago Tribune*, 25 February 1912.

44. Wassam, *Salary Lending Business*, 24; Robinson and Nugent, *Small Loan Business*, 61; Peter Shergold, "The Loan Shark: The Small Loan Business in Early Twentieth-Century Pittsburgh," *Pennsylvania History* 45 (1978): 205.

45. Robinson and Nugent, *Small Loan Business*, 62.

46. Eubank, *Loan Shark in Chicago*, 12–13; "See Loan Sharks in Chosen Refuge," *Chicago Tribune*, 3 March 1912.

47. "Voice of the People," *Chicago Tribune*, 20 March 1912.

48. Eubank, *Loan Shark in Chicago*, 15.

49. *Chicago Tribune*, 18 September 1892, 19 December 1897, 27 January 1900.

50. "Twelve Teachers Wake Up," *Chicago Tribune*, 9 February 1902.

51. "Usurious Financial Spiders who Entrap Borrowers in Their Short Loan Webs," *Chicago Tribune*, 7 November 1897; Robinson and Nugent, *Small Loan Business*, 39.

52. Irwin Ellis, "The Loan Shark in Search of Prey," *Chicago Tribune*, 25 February 1912.

53. Wassam, *Salary Lending Business*, 18; "Money Is Easy, People Are Not," *Chicago Tribune*, 21 September 1902; W. Martin, "His First Offense," *Chicago Tribune*, 21 July 1907.

54. Wassam, *Salary Lending Business*, 27, 50; Eubank, *Loan Shark in Chicago*, 16; "Living on Loans: Confessions of a Shark's Tout," *Chicago Tribune*, 23 October 1910; Irwin Ellis, "The Loan Shark in Search of Prey," *Chicago Tribune*, 25 February 1912.

55. In the *Chicago Tribune*, "Calls Loan Shark a Curse," 30 March 1911; "Aids Loan Sharks, Loses Job," 10 March 1906; "Barrett Blames Fear of Sluggers," 29 July 1905.

56. In the *Chicago Tribune*, "Street Work Will Continue," 10 November 1900; "Kipley in a Group Picture," 16 November 1900; "Mayor Orders an Investigation," 3 November 1900; "Bad Day for the Loan Sharks," 21 November 1900; "Grand Jury in Shark Scandal," 22 November 1900; "Legal Aid Man Shark's Heir," 4 July 1912; "Says He Told Ludwig of Deal," 24 November 1900; "Political Jobs Do Not Pay," 7 October 1906.

57. Eubank, *Loan Shark in Chicago*, 12; "Loan Shark Hires Women to Weave Web about Him," *Chicago Tribune*, 7 February 1912.

58. Grace Clarke, "Pretty Girl Loan Sharks Prey on Poor of City," *Chicago Tribune*, 28 May 1905.

59. "Lawyer Punched by Woman Loan Shark Manager," *Chicago Tribune*, 17 February 1912.

60. Wassam, *Salary Lending Business*, app. 1; Irwin Ellis, "How the Loan Sharks of Chicago Prey upon the Unfortunate," *Chicago Tribune*, 3 September 1911.

61. Eubank, *Loan Shark in Chicago*, 21–22; in the *Chicago Tribune*, "'Clearing House' of Loan Sharks Detective Agency," 6 February 1912; "Loan Sharks in 'Council of War'," 2 March 1912; Irwin Ellis, "Beating the Loan Sharks," 28 January 1912; "Mackey to Fight Usury Case," 4 March 1910; "'Ku Klux' of Loan Sharks Grips Chicago," 9 December 1916 (quote).

62. In the *Chicago Tribune*, "How 250,000 Chicagoans 'Raise the Wind'," 31 March 1907 (quote); "Hooked the Loan Shark," 7 May 1899; "Loan Shark Waits Yet," 27 March 1904; "Teaches Friends to Evade Debt," 16 October 1908.

63. Wassam, *Salary Lending Business*, 66–67; Shergold, "Loan Shark," 210; Irwin Ellis, "The Loan Shark as a Home Breaker," *Chicago Tribune*, 21 January 1912 (quote); Eubank, *Loan Shark in Chicago*, 17.

64. A. Fortas, "Wage Assignments in Chicago: *State Street Furniture Co. v. Armour & Co.*," *Yale Law Journal* 42 (1933): 526, 533–34; "Loan Shark Pays Damages of $700," *Chicago Tribune*, 15 February 1912 (quote); *Mallin v. Wenham*, 209 Ill. 252 (1904).

65. David Gallert, Walter Hilborn, and Geoffrey May, *Small Loan Legislation: A History of the Regulation of Lending Small Sums* (New York: Russell Sage Foundation, 1932), 181–84, 187 (quote).

66. Fortas, "Wage Assignments in Chicago," 539.

67. "Refer Electric Light Order," *Chicago Tribune*, 9 October 1900; Irwin Ellis, "How One Employer Benefited by 'Knifing' the Loan Shark," *Chicago Tribune*, 10 March 1912; Fortas, "Wage Assignments in Chicago," 535–36.

68. "Usurious Financial Spiders who Entrap Borrowers in Their Short Loan Webs," *Chicago Tribune*, 7 November 1897.

69. In the *Chicago Tribune*, "'Foiled Again,' or, Controller Kerfoot and a 'Loan Shark,'" 1 August 1900; "Mrs. Kerfoot Calls Police," 30 March 1901; "Will Forestall Moneylenders," 31 July 1900; "Big Unpaid Water Tax," 30 May 1901.

70. "Loan Sharks Find Plan for Collecting Blocked," *Chicago Tribune*, 31 August 1901; "Teachers Owe the Loan Sharks," *Chicago Tribune*, 6 October 1903.

71. Irwin Ellis, "How One Employer Benefited by 'Knifing' the Loan Shark," *Chicago Tribune*, 10 March 1912.

72. In the *Chicago Tribune*, "Salary Loan Men Face New Enemy," 6 November 1908; "Take Loan Shark King Again," 3 August 1913; "Links Insurance and Loan Shark," 23 January 1914; "Mystery Woman, Loan Shark Tool, Tells Own Story," 15 March 1912; "O, No; He Never Gets Interest," 17 August 1916 (quote).

73. "Loan Shark Hires Women to Weave Web about Him," *Chicago Tribune*, 7 February 1912; "Usurious Financial Spiders who Entrap Borrowers in Their Short Loan Webs," *Chicago Tribune*, 7 November 1897.

74. "Help for Slaves of Loan Sharks," *Chicago Tribune*, 17 September 1907.

75. Irwin Ellis, "How the Loan Sharks of Chicago Prey upon the Unfortunate," *Chicago Tribune*, 3 September 1911.

76. "Usurious Financial Spiders who Entrap Borrowers in Their Short Loan Webs," *Chicago Tribune*, 7 November 1897.

77. Kogan, *Lending Is Our Business*, 11.

78. "Shows Woes due to Loan Sharks," *Chicago Tribune*, 5 March 1911.

79. "Busts a Secret Loan Shark Aid," *Chicago Tribune*, 13 March 1912; Irving Michelman, *Consumer Finance: A Case History in American Business* (New York: Frederick Fell, 1966), 75.

80. Wassam, *Salary Lending Business*, 81; "Loan Shark Feeds on Woman's Fears," *Chicago Tribune*, 7 December 1911.

81. In the *Chicago Tribune*, Irwin Ellis, "Do Not Sign This Document," 4 February 1912; "Tests Sharks' Chain System," 13 April 1912; "Money Leeches Scar on State: Jail 'Em–Landis," 9 March 1917 (quote).

82. "$1,000,000 a Year to Chicago's Frank Jay Mackey and His Brother Loan Sharks," *Chicago Tribune*, 13 March 1910.

83. Arthur Ham, *The Chattel Loan Business* (New York: Charities Publication Committee, 1909), 29; Eubank, *Loan Shark in Chicago*, 19–20; "Mackey Agents Drive Woman Insane, Report," *Chicago Tribune*, 4 December 1916; Irwin Ellis, "Do Not Sign This Document," *Chicago Tribune*, 4 February 1912. See also Forrest Halsey, *The Bawlerout* (New York: D. Fitzgerald, 1912).

84. John Ross, "Harpooning a Loan Shark: How to Escape Uninjured," *Chicago Tribune*, 18 February 1906; Harry Olson, "Goodbye to Constable," *Chicago Tribune*, 25 November 1906; Michael Willrich, *City of Courts: Socializing Justice in Progressive Era Chicago* (Cambridge: Cambridge University Press, 2003), chs. 1–2.

85. "Dine and Evoke Chicago Spirit," *Chicago Tribune*, 15 January 1905.

86. "Railroads Fight Wage Garnishee," *Chicago Tribune*, 14 August 1910.

87. In the *Chicago Tribune*, "How 250,000 Chicagoans 'Raise the Wind'," 31 March 1907; Fredi Barrison, "On the Trail of the 'Bad Debtor': Adventures of a Skip Locator," 30 July 1911; Irwin Ellis, "Beating the Loan Sharks," 28 January 1912; "Fake Accidents Loan Shark Trick," 11 April 1911.

88. "Loan Shark Hires Women to Weave Web about Him," *Chicago Tribune*, 7 February 1912.

89. Oscar Leinen, "A Wolf at the Stock Yards," in *Told out of Court* (Chicago: P. G. Smyth, 1909), 175; Hodson, *Money-Lenders*, 20.

90. In the *Chicago Tribune*, "$1,000,000 a Year to Chicago's Frank Jay Mackey and His Brother Loan Sharks," 13 March 1910; "Some One Yelled Jake, and What a Licking Jake Got!" 2 November 1918; "Death Releases Sharks' Victim," 1 June 1912 ("dead beat"); "Landis Leads Triple War on Loan Sharks," 17 December 1916 ("pine box").

91. Mark Haller and John Alviti, "Loansharking in American Cities: Historical Analysis of a Marginal Enterprise," *American Journal of Legal History* 21 (1977): 125; Ham, *Chattel Loan Business*, 23; "Loan Shark Charged with Working Trick for Money," *Chicago Tribune*, 23 December 1911 (quote). For another example of the use of fraud in the course of collecting debts, see, in the *Chicago Tribune*, "Tell How Lawyer Gets 100 Percent," 21 December 1911; and "Shark Gets Grip on Families of Eastland Dead," 29 July 1915 (lender posing as relief agent).

92. Robinson and Nugent, *Small Loan Business*, 59–60.

93. "In a Minor Key," *Chicago Tribune*, 7 June 1904.

94. "'Jackpot' Blocks Model Loan Bank," *Chicago Tribune*, 1 March 1912.

95. Robinson and Nugent, *Small Loan Business*, 64; Ham, *Chattel Loan Business*, 10.

96. "Loan Shark Suit Aimed at Mackey," *Chicago Tribune*, 26 February 1910; "Loan Mortgage Called 'No Good'," *Chicago Tribune*, 5 March 1910.

97. "Loan Shark Net Catches Clerks," *Chicago Tribune*, 7 March 1911; Judge Edward F. Dunne, "Assignment of Wage Slavery," *Chicago Tribune*, 26 June 1904 (quote).

98. "Loan Mortgage Called 'No Good'," *Chicago Tribune*, 5 March 1910; "Loan Men's Books Reveal Profits," *Chicago Tribune*, 24 February 1909; Wassam, *Salary Lending Business*, 41–42.

99. In the *Chicago Tribune*, "Students Sorry for Prisoner," 16 February 1904; "Driven to Crime by Loan Sharks," 16 September 1907; "Walsh Clerk Check Forger," 21 September 1907; "Ruined by Loan Sharks," 13 December 1905.

100. In the *Chicago Tribune*, "Danger in Assigning Wages," 29 March 1903; "Justice Courts Scored by Bureau of Justice," 20 January 1905; "Mackey Agents Drive Woman Insane: Report," 4 December 1916; "Hounded by 'Loan Sharks' Young Man Tries Suicide," 9 November 1904.

101. "Usurious Financial Spiders who Entrap Borrowers in Their Short Loan Webs," *Chicago Tribune*, 7 November 1897. As Rolf Nugent observed, "A society which is highly integrated, which assumed responsibility for providing decent standards of living and adequate nourishment for children, and which recognizes the relationship between economic pressures and crime, cannot tolerate loan contracts that are liable to result in economic peonage." See Rolf Nugent, "The Loan-Shark Problem," *Law and Contemporary Problems* 8 (1941): 13.

102. "Judge Attacks Loan Sharks," *Chicago Tribune*, 8 June 1904.

Two—Grinding the Tooth of Usury

1. Hodson, *Money-Lenders*, 5.

2. Willrich, *City of Courts*, xxxviii.

3. Thomas Pegram, *Partisans and Progressives: Private Interest and Public Policy in Illinois, 1870–1922* (Chicago: University of Illinois Press, 1992); Kenneth Feingold, *Experts and Politicians: Reform Challenges to Machine Politics in New York, Cleveland, and Chicago* (Princeton: Princeton University Press, 1995).

4. George Gisler, "Organization of Public Opinion for Effective Measures against Loan Sharks," *Law and Contemporary Problems* 8 (1941): 185, 188; Robert Edwin Pride, *Loan Sharks of America* (Philadelphia: Harper Stokes, 1940), 45–46.

5. Nugent, "Loan-Shark Problem," 11–12.

6. Richard Hynes and Eric Posner, "The Law and Economics of Consumer Finance," *American Law and Economics Review* 4 (2002): 168–207.

7. W. M. Harrison, "Foreign Usury Laws," *Journal of the Society of Comparative Legislation* 1 (1899): 215–36.

8. Calder, *American Dream*, 123.

9. Edward Glaeser and Jose Scheinkman, "Neither a Borrower nor a Lender Be: An Economic Analysis of Interest Restrictions and Usury Laws," *Journal of Law and Economics* 41 (1998): 1–36; Eric Posner, "Contract Law in the Welfare State: A Defense of the Unconscionability Doctrine, Usury Laws, and Related Limitations on the Freedom to Contract," *Journal of Legal Studies* 24 (1995): 283–319; and Kenneth Avio, "An Economic Rationale for Statutory Interest Rate Ceilings," *Quarterly Review of Economics and Business* 13 (1973): 61–72.

10. Thomas Aquinas, *The Political Ideas of St. Thomas Aquinas*, ed. Dino Bigongiari (New York: Free Press, 1997), 147–58.

11. Franklin Ryan, *Usury and Usury Laws* (Boston: Houghton Mifflin, 1924), 25–27.

12. B. Schneider, "Usury as Related to Illinois Law," *John Marshall Law Quarterly* 4 (1938): 489–503; Benjamin Horack, "A Survey of the General Usury Laws," *Law and Contemporary Problems* 8 (1941): 36–53.

13. Ryan, *Usury and Usury Laws*, 25.

14. Ibid., 129.

15. Arthur Hadley, *Economics: An Account of the Relations between Private Property and Public Welfare* (New York: G. P. Putnam's Sons, 1904), 142.

16. Gallert, Hilborn, and May, *Small Loan Legislation*, 53.

17. Robinson and Nugent, *Small Loan Business*, 73.

18. Gisler, "Organization of Public Opinion," 183.

19. Pegram, *Partisans and Progressives*, 68–69.

20. Haller and Alviti, "Loansharking," 135.

21. Pegram, *Partisans and Progressives*, 11. See also Robert Wiebe, *Businessmen and Reform: A Study of the Progressive Movement* (Cambridge: Harvard University Press, 1962), and *The Search for Order, 1877–1920* (New York: Hill and Wang, 1967).

22. John Kilgore, "Legislative Tactics of Unregulated Lenders," *Law and Contemporary Problems* 8 (1941): 173–82.

23. Jeremy Bentham, "Defense of Usury," in *Jeremy Bentham's Economic Writings*, ed. W. Stark (London: George Allen and Unwin, 1952), 1:138. For Adam Smith's justification of usury laws, see *An Inquiry into the Nature and Causes of the Wealth of Nations* (Chicago:

University of Chicago Press, 1976), 1:378–79.

24. Dorothy Orchard and Geoffrey May, *Moneylending in Great Britain* (New York: Russell Sage Foundation, 1933), chs. 3–4.

25. House of Commons, *Report from the Select Committee on Money Lending* (London: Her Majesty's Stationery Office, 1898), iv–vi. See also Thomas Farrow, *In the Money-Lender's Clutches* (Westminster: Yeoman, 1895).

26. Orchard and May, *Moneylending in Great Britain*, 115–48.

27. "The Uniform Small Loan Law," *Harvard Law Review* 42 (1929): 692.

28. George Bogert, "The Future of Small Loan Legislation," *University of Chicago Law Review* 12 (1944): 15.

29. Nugent, "Loan-Shark Problem," 12.

30. Michael Trebilcock, *The Limits of Freedom of Contract* (Cambridge: Harvard University Press, 1993), 102–3. See also Clyde Phelps, "Monopolistic and Imperfect Competition in Consumer Loans," *Journal of Marketing* 8 (1944): 382–93; Theodore Yntema, "The Market for Consumer Credit: A Case in 'Imperfect Competition,'" *Annals of the American Academy of Political and Social Science* 196 (1938): 79–85.

31. Charles Kelly, "Legal Techniques for Combating the Loan Sharks," *Law and Contemporary Problems* 8 (1941): 90; M. R. Neifeld, "Institutional Organization of Consumer Credit," *Law and Contemporary Problems* 8 (1941): 23; Robert Stone and Jack Thomas, "California's Legislature Faces the Small Loan Problem," *California Law Review* 27 (1939): 289.

32. William Simpson, *The Small Loan Problem of the Carolinas* (Clinton: Presbyterian College Press, 1941), 79.

33. F. B. Hubachek, "The Development of Regulatory Small Loan Laws," *Law and Contemporary Problems* 8 (1941): 109; Hodson, *Money-Lenders*, 5.

34. Nugent, "Loan-Shark Problem," 12.

35. Neifeld, *Neifeld's Manual*, 96; Hubachek, "Regulatory Small Loan Laws," 129.

36. Robinson and Nugent, *Small Loan Business*, 245.

37. Robert MacCoun and Peter Reuter, *Drug War Heresies: Learning from Other Vices, Times, and Places* (Cambridge: Cambridge University Press, 2001), chs. 2, 8.

38. James Webb, *A Treatise on the Law of Usury* (St. Louis: F. H. Thomas Law Book, 1899), 15.

39. Nugent, "Loan-Shark Problem," 13.

40. "Labor Has Work for Merriam Men," *Chicago Tribune*, 20 December 1909.

41. Earl Beckner, *A History of Labor Legislation in Illinois* (Chicago: University of Chicago Press, 1929), 128–29.

42. "Charge Forgery to Loan Agents," *Chicago Tribune*, 30 August 1901; "Street Work Will Continue," *Chicago Tribune*, 10 November 1900.

43. Lincoln Steffens, *The Shame of the Cities* (New York: Hill and Wang, 1957), 192; David Nord, *Newspapers and New Politics: Midwestern Municipal Reform, 1890–1900* (Ann Arbor: UMI Research Press, 1981), 128. See also Matthew Gentzkow, Edward Glaeser, and Claudia Goldin, "The Rise of the Fourth Estate: How Newspapers Became Informative and Why It Mattered," in *Corruption and Reform: Lessons from America's Economic History*, ed. Edward Glaeser and Claudia Goldin (Chicago: University of Chicago Press, 2006), 187–221.

44. "A Lesson from Massachussets," *Chicago Tribune*, 30 December 1911; Robinson and Nugent, *Small Loan Business*, 120.

45. "Usurious Financial Spiders who Entrap Borrowers in Their Short Loan Webs," *Chicago Tribune*, 7 November 1897; "Ellinwood Held for Perjury," *Chicago Tribune*, 16 November 1897.

46. "Tribune Bureau Formed to Fight City Loan Sharks," *Chicago Tribune*, 4 February 1912.

47. Michelman, *Consumer Finance*, 124; "Loan Sharks," *Chicago Tribune*, 23 December 1911.

48. In the *Chicago Tribune*, "Tribune Bureau Formed to Fight City Loan Sharks," 4 February 1912; "One Week's Work of the Anti-Loan Shark Bureau," 12 February 1912; "Dr. T. M. Buckley Faces Exposure," 25 February 1916; "Anti–Loan Shark Bureau still Fighting Usurers," 29 December 1912.

49. James Meachan, "Rockford After the Loan Shark: Example Set for the Small City," *Chicago Tribune*, 15 May 1910; "'Sharks' Hold 3,000 in Joliet," *Chicago Tribune*, 14 February 1912.

50. The film was re-released in 2007 by the National Film Preservation Foundation in its collection *Treasures III: Social Issues in American Film, 1900–1934* (Chatsworth: Image Entertainment, 2007). The film includes a valuable commentary by Lendol Calder.

51. "The Loan Shark Photo Play in Story Form," *Chicago Tribune*, 10 March 1912.

52. Francis Bacon, *The Essayes or Counsels, Civill and Morall*, ed. Michael Kiernan (Oxford: Clarendon Press, 2000), 127.

53. "After a New Charter for Chicago," *Chicago Tribune*, 13 September 1898; "Seek Safety on Trains," *Chicago Tribune*, 19 July 1904.

54. "Knocks Out Loan Sharks," *Chicago Tribune*, 27 April 1901.

55. *Mallin v. Wenham* 209 Ill. 252 (1904).

56. In the *Chicago Tribune*, "Bureau of Justice Plans to Stop Pay Assignments," 12 November 1902; "Blow at 'Loan Sharks'," 22 January 1903; "Fight on Rules again Delayed," 29 January 1903.

57. "Assignment of Wages," *Laws of the State of Illinois*, 44th General Assembly (1905), 79–80.

58. In the *Chicago Tribune* in 1905, "Assignments of Wages," 14 January; "It Is 'Gas Day' at Springfield," 18 January; "Has a New Referendum," 1 February; "Still Use Rod on Pupils," 6 April; "Loan Shark Bill up to Governor," 6 May; "Joker Is Found in Theater Acts," 14 May; "In Loan Shark's Clutches," 30 July.

59. In the *Chicago Tribune*, "'Loan Shark' Evil Reviled," 7 July 1905; "Street Cleaning Shakeup Begun by Richard T. Fox," 4 August 1905; "Cigaret Smoking Student in Peril," 7 February 1907.

60. *Massie v. Cessna* 239 Ill. 352 (1909). See also Blake, "Regulating Wage Assignments."

61. Blake, "Regulating Wage Assignments," 349; Maryland Supreme Court quoted in Gallert, Hilborn, and May, *Small Loan Legislation*, 41; "Bench Meets Bar," *Chicago Tribune*, 31 October 1909.

62. Robinson and Nugent, *Small Loan Business*, 80.

63. Cheryl Danieri, *Credit Where Credit Is Due: The Mont-de-Piété of Paris, 1777–1851* (New York: Garland, 1991); John Glenn, Lilian Brandt, and F. Andrews, *The Russell Sage Foundation, 1907–1946* (New York: Russell Sage Foundation, 1947), 1:136 (quote). In the *Chicago Tribune*, "Cheap Loans for the Needy," 11 April 1898; "Move for

Cheap Loans to Needy," 15 January 1899; "To Remedy Loan Evils," 21 October 1900.

64. "Try New Weapon on Loan Sharks," *Chicago Tribune*, 29 October 1908; "Loan Men's Books Reveal Profits," *Chicago Tribune*, 24 February 1909.

65. "Burke Calls Chicago Men," *Chicago Tribune*, 1 August 1910; "'Jackpot' Blocks Model Loan Bank," *Chicago Tribune*, 1 March 1912.

66. In the *Chicago Tribune* in 1911, "Would Curb 'Loan Sharks'," 20 January; "'Loan Sharks' Hit in ApMadoc Bill," 3 March; "Favor Anti-Loan Shark Bill," 14 April; "Bills Die in Committee," 12 May.

67. "The Foolishness of Some Legislators," *Chicago Tribune*, 22 May 1911 (quote); Irwin Ellis, "If Not Your Salary, the Loan Shark May Get Your Home," *Chicago Tribune*, 3 March 1912.

68. Wiebe, *Search for Order*, 176.

69. Pegram, *Partisans and Progressives*, 9.

70. Robinson and Nugent, *Small Loan Business*, 137. See also Bruce Carruthers, Timothy Guinnane, and Yoonseok Lee, "The Passage of the Uniform Small Loan Law" (paper presented at the annual meeting of the American Sociological Association, New York, 11 August 2007).

71. In the *Chicago Tribune* in 1913, "Hull Bill Curb on Loan Sharks," 20 February; "Anti–Loan Shark Bill Wins," *Chicago Tribune*, 25 April (quote); "Loan Bank Draws 500 on First Day," *Chicago Tribune*, 11 November.

72. In the *Chicago Tribune*, "Loan Sharks' Foe Forges to Front," 28 December 1913; "Loan Society Routs 4 Sharks," 16 January 1915 (quote); "'Poor Man's Bank' in New Quarters," 6 November 1915.

73. Eubank, *Loan Shark in Chicago*, 9–10; Glenn, Brandt, and Andrews, *Russell Sage Foundation*, 1:138; Michelman, *Consumer Finance*, 114–15.

74. Glenn, Brandt, and Andrews, *Russell Sage Foundation*, 1:5. See also Michelman, *Consumer Finance*, 28–44, 86, 112.

75. Calder, *American Dream*, 124–35; Michelman, *Consumer Finance*, 45–85.

76. Arthur Ham, *Remedial Loans: A Constructive Program* (New York: Russell Sage Foundation, 1912), 4–5, 11.

77. Robinson and Nugent, *Small Loan Business*, 90–94; Michelman, *Consumer Finance*, 148, 198.

78. Robinson and Nugent, *Small Loan Business*, 104; Calder, *American Dream*, 133.

79. Kogan, *Lending Is Our Business*, 25.

80. Elizabeth Anderson, "Experts, Ideas, and Policy Change: The Russell Sage Foundation and Small Loan Reform, 1909–1941," *Theory and Society* 37 (2008): 271–310.

81. Gallert, Hilborn, and May, *Small Loan Legislation*, 90–94.

82. Raymond Fosdick quoted in Ham, *Remedial Loans*, 12.

83. "'Ku Klux' of Loan Sharks Grips Chicago," *Chicago Tribune*, 9 December 1916; "Support Bill Curbing Rates of Loan Sharks," *Chicago Tribune*, 15 December 1916.

84. "Aldermen Drop Dr. Brushingham and Mrs. Rowe," *Chicago Tribune*, 18 January 1917.

85. *Laws of the State of Illinois*, 50th General Assembly (1917), 553–56.

86. Hodson, *Money-Lenders*, 92, 95. The Illinois pamphlet is an appendix in Hodson's book.

87. J. Spink, *Judge Landis and Twenty-Five Years of Baseball* (New York: Thomas Cromwell, 1947).

88. In the *Chicago Tribune*, "Money Lenders Flock to Court," 6 August 1915; "Landis' Harpoon Puts Great Fear in Loan Sharks," 25 April 1916; "Landis Smites and Gets Back Pound of Flesh," 27 February 1918 (quote).

89. Spink, *Judge Landis*, 20, 26; "Dr. T. M. Buckley Faces Exposure," *Chicago Tribune*, 25 February 1916. See also Richard Cahan, *A Court that Shaped America: Chicago's Federal District Court from Abe Lincoln to Abbie Hoffman* (Evanston: Northwestern University Press, 2002), 52–59.

90. "House Passes Bill to Close up Loan Sharks," *Chicago Tribune*, 23 May 1917.

91. Spink, *Judge Landis*, 8, 20.

92. Robinson and Nugent, *Small Loan Business*, 118; "House Passes Bill to Close up Loan Sharks," *Chicago Tribune*, 23 May 1917; Glenn, Brandt, and Andrews, *Russell Sage Foundation*, 1:144.

93. Pegram, *Partisans and Progressives*, 196–202. On Dunne's career, see Richard Morton, *Justice and Humanity: Edward F. Dunne, Illinois Progressive* (Carbondale: Southern Illinois University Press, 1997).

94. *People v. Stokes* 281 Ill. 159 (1917); "Loan Shark Law Is Upheld by Supreme Court," *Chicago Tribune*, 20 December 1917.

95. Kelso, "Small Loan Problem," 22.

96. Bacon, *Essayes*, 128.

Three—A Profusion of Species

1. Thomas Schelling, "Economic Analysis and Organized Crime," in *Task Force Report: Organized Crime* (Washington, D.C.: U.S. Government Printing Office, 1967), 117.

2. "Money Lenders See Problem in Strikes," *New York Times*, 21 September 1922. These figures, like many of the others cited in this chapter, should be treated with skepticism. Hodson, for example, also claimed that the small-loan business in America amounted to $140,000,000 annually, but this figure is probably grossly inflated.

3. Charles Hardy, *Consumer Credit and Its Uses* (New York: Prentice-Hall, 1938), 17. See also Calder, *American Dream*, 137, 148.

4. "200 Loan Sharks Driven Out by 'Poor Man's Bank,'" *Chicago Tribune*, 27 April 1920.

5. Rolf Nugent, "Small Loan Debt in the United States," *Journal of Business of the University of Chicago* 7 (1934): 17; Illinois Department of Insurance, *Analysis of Reports: Annual Report* (Springfield: Division of Small Loans, 1934), 5–7; Hardy, *Consumer Credit and Its Uses*, 20; William Foster, "The Personal Finance Business under Regulation," *Law and Contemporary Problems* 8 (1941): 154.

6. Nugent, *Consumer Credit*, ch. 13.

7. Stone and Thomas, "California's Legislature," 289; John Chapman and Robert Shay, *Licensed Lending in New York* (New York: Columbia Graduate School of Business, 1970), 20. See also Louis Robinson and Maude Stearns, *Ten Thousand Small Loans* (New York: Russell Sage Foundation, 1930), 39–67.

8. Willford King, *The Small Loan Situation in New Jersey in 1929* (Trenton: New Jersey Industrial Lenders Association, 1929), 94; Foster "Personal Finance Business," 154.

9. Maryland Administrator of Loan Laws, *Annual Report* (Baltimore: The Administrator, 1939), 7; Hubachek, "Regulatory Small Loan Laws," 129; "Doak Asks War on Loan

Sharks by Finance Men," *Chicago Tribune*, 24 October 1931; James Sullivan, "Administration of a Regulatory Small Loan Law," *Law and Contemporary Problems* 8 (1941): 150.

10. Evans Clark, *Financing the Consumer* (New York: Harper and Brothers, 1930), 232 (quote); Rolf Nugent, "Three Experiments in Small-Loan Interest Rates," *Harvard Business Review* 11 (1933): 38.

11. Pennsylvania Department of Banking, *Report on Small Loan Companies* (Harrisburg: Department of Banking, 1935), 7, 18; Neifeld, *Neifeld's Manual*, 484.

12. Kogan, *Lending Is Our Business*, 35; Ralph Young, *Personal Finance Companies and Their Credit Practices* (New York: National Bureau of Economic Research, 1940), 69; William Trufant Foster, *Loan Sharks and Their Victims* (Dallas: Public Affairs Committee, 1940), 20. See also Adele Rabino, "The Small Loan Law and Its Application in Illinois" (master's thesis, Northwestern University, 1942), 56.

13. Young, *Personal Finance Companies*, 55, 73; King, *Small Loan Situation*, 22, 87. See also Robinson and Stearns, *Ten Thousand Small Loans*, 28.

14. Illinois Department of Financial Institutions (hereafter DFI), Division of Consumer Finance, *Analysis of Reports: Annual Report* (Springfield: DFI, 1934), 8; King, *Small Loan Situation*, 22; Clark, *Financing the Consumer*, 60.

15. Illinois DFI, *Analysis of Reports* (1934), 7–8; Illinois DFI, *Analysis of Reports: Annual Report* (1964), 2–6.

16. Clark, *Financing the Consumer*, 117.

17. Rabino, "Small Loan Law," 24; Kogan, *Lending Is Our Business*, 48; M. R. Neifeld, *Personal Finance Comes of Age* (New York: Harper and Brothers, 1939), 87.

18. Nugent, "Three Experiments," 37; Robinson and Nugent, *Small Loan Business*, 177–80.

19. Charles Corzelle, *The Small Loan Racket* (South Bend: Mirror Press, 1934), 107–8; "Six Commissioners Resign City Posts," *New York Times*, 12 November 1945; "LaGuardia Renews Small Loans Fight," *New York Times*, 26 January 1947.

20. Peter Edison, "Federal Credit Union System Is a Success, Costs Nothing," *Edwardsville Intelligencer*, 8 May 1953. In the *Chicago Tribune*, "Bankers Unite for New Fight on Loan Sharks," 3 July 1928; "Loan Shark Foe Favors Pool's 2 per cent Plan," 13 March 1925; Perry Wood, "Asks an Inquiry on Lobbyists in State Assembly," 5 June 1931. Pride, *Loan Sharks of America*, 60, 74.

21. Ibid., 74, 70, 59. See also Corzelle, *Small Loan Racket*, 7, 10.

22. "Loan Evils Scored by Legal Aid Chief," *New York Times*, 9 September 1937; Rabino, "Small Loan Law," 120.

23. F. B. Hubachek, "Progress and Problems in the Regulation of Consumer Credit," *Law and Contemporary Problems* 19 (1954): 19; Fortas, "Wage Assignments in Chicago," 539–40.

24. Rabino, "Small Loan Law," 130–56. Quotes are from Neifeld, *Neifeld's Manual*, 96; Hubachek, "Progress and Problems," 17.

25. Clark, *Financing the Consumer*, 11; Robinson and Stearns, *Ten Thousand Small Loans*, 123; National Consumer Finance Association, *The Consumer Finance Industry* (Englewood Cliffs: Prentice-Hall, 1962), 61, 65; Young, *Personal Finance Companies*, 48–49.

26. F. Thomas Juster and Robert Shay, *Consumer Sensitivity to Finance Rates: An Empirical and Analytical Investigation* (New York: National Bureau of Economic Research, 1964), 2.

27. George Benston, "An Analysis of Maine's '36 Month Limitation' on Finance

Company Small Loans," in National Commission on Consumer Finance, *Technical Studies* (Washington, D.C.: U.S. Government Printing Office, 1975), 2:22.

28. Frank White, "Shylocks Have Practically Been Exterminated," *New York Times*, 25 March 1917; Hubachek, "Progress and Problems," 9.

29. For example, see the "Friend of the People" column in the *Chicago Tribune* on 18 February 1919, 5 April 1923, 3 March, 16 June, 6 October 1926.

30. In the *Chicago Tribune*, "Red Cross Gives Jerry a 'Lift' to Job in Home Town," 7 March 1919; "'Loan Sharking' by Employees in Dunning Bared," 12 October 1923; "Trace Outside Money in Asylum Loans Scandal," 13 December 1937. Rabino, "Small Loan Law," 96.

31. Robinson and Nugent, *Small Loan Business*, 157–58; "Line Forms in Salary Buyers' Offices on Working Men's Pay Days," *Decatur Herald*, 12 April 1929; "Workers Prey of Decatur 'Sharks'," *Decatur Herald*, 11 April 1929; Robinson and Nugent, *Small Loan Business*, 158 (quote).

32. "Workers Prey of Decatur 'Sharks'," *Decatur Herald*, 11 April 1929; "Licensed Lenders Aid State Fight on Loan Sharks," *Chicago Tribune*, 9 April 1926; Robinson and Nugent, *Small Loan Business*, 158; Weaver, *Oklahoma's Small Loan Problem*, 21 (quote).

33. In the *Chicago Tribune*, "Grand Jurors Will Fish Soon for Loan Sharks," 8 April 1926; "Licensed Lenders Aid State Fight on Loan Sharks," 9 April 1926; "More Victims Reveal Loan Sharks' Tactics," 13 April 1926; "Salary Buyers under Attack as Loan Sharks," 27 January 1927.

34. "Salary Sharks Threaten Girl in Loan Exposé," *Chicago Tribune*, 28 January 1927; "Workers Prey of Decatur 'Sharks'," *Decatur Herald*, 11 April 1929. See also Victor Meador, *Loan Sharks in Georgia* (Washington, D.C.: American Bar Association, 1949), 5.

35. "Blackmail Hinted at Loan Inquiry," *New York Times*, 14 March 1928 (quotes); "Loan 'Sharks' Aid Helps Prosecution," *New York Times*, 18 March 1928.

36. Robinson and Nugent, *Small Loan Business*, 158–60 (158).

37. "Sage Foundation Pledged to War on Loan Sharks," *Chicago Tribune*, 20 September 1927; "A Few Questions and Henderson Bows to a Lady," *Chicago Tribune*, 26 November 1941. The fourth draft of the Uniform Small Loan Law, issued in 1923, closed the salary-buying loophole. See Gallert, Hilborn, and May, *Small Loan Legislation*, 96.

38. Percy Wood, "Asks an Inquiry on Lobbyists in State Assembly," *Chicago Tribune*, 5 June 1931.

39. Foster, *Loan Sharks and Their Victims*, 25, 21.

40. "Bill to Reduce Interest Called Boon to Sharks," *Chicago Tribune*, 12 March 1925.

41. "Pass the Small Loans Act," *Chicago Tribune*, 21 March 1935.

42. "12 Plead Guilty to Violations of Small Loan Act," *Chicago Tribune*, 12 June 1934; "Loan Shark Pays Fine of $100 and Gives up Notes," *Chicago Tribune*, 12 February 1936.

43. "City Hall Loan Shark Victims to Be Quizzed," *Chicago Tribune*, 21 July 1939; "Fine Loan Shark $100; Must Give up $2,800 in Notes," *Chicago Tribune*, 18 August 1939.

44. Meador, *Loan Sharks in Georgia*; William Simpson, *America's Small Loan Problem with Special Reference to the South* (Columbia: University of South Carolina, 1963); Thomas Durkin, "A High Rate Market for Consumer Loans: The Small Small Loan Industry in Texas," in National Commission on Consumer Finance, *Technical Studies*, 2:1–99.

45. "Nab Loan Shark on Complaint of 480% Interest," *Chicago Tribune*, 15 September 1931 (quote); Benston, "Maine's '36 Month Limitation'," 17.

46. Fortas, "Wage Assignments in Chicago," 543–44.

47. "Binga State Bank Stockholders Meet," *Chicago Defender*, 24 April 1920; "Usurers and Loan Sharks," *Chicago Defender*, 10 September 1955; Nicholas Gage, "Organized Crime in City Bleeds Slums of Millions," *New York Times*, 27 September 1970.

48. Kilgore, "Legislative Tactics," 174; Pride, *Loan Sharks of America*, 52.

49. Clark, *Financing the Consumer*, 33; Nugent, "Loan-Shark Problem," 13. See also Robinson and Nugent, *Small Loan Business*, 174.

50. "St. Bartholomew's Has No Needy Now," *New York Times*, 29 July 1924; Rabino, "Small Loan Law," 6–7.

51. Clark, *Financing the Consumer*, 30; Nugent, *Consumer Credit*, 401; Nugent, "Loan-Shark Problem," 10.

52. National Commission on Consumer Finance, *Consumer Credit in the United States* (Washington, D.C.: U.S. Government Printing Office, 1972), 136; Durkin, "High Rate Market," 56.

53. Haller and Alviti, "Loansharking," 126.

54. Francis Ianni, *A Family Business: Kinship and Social Control in Organized Crime* (New York: Russell Sage Foundation, 1972), 66–67, 96.

55. Frederic Thrasher, *The Gang: A Study of 1,313 Gangs in Chicago* (Chicago: University of Chicago Press, 1936). See also John Landesco, *Organized Crime in Chicago* (Chicago: University of Chicago, 1968), and John Lyle, *The Dry and Lawless Years* (Englewood Cliffs: Prentice-Hall, 1960). "Nitti, Capone's Manager, Unable to Furnish Bail," *Chicago Tribune*, 1 November 1930.

56. In the *New York Times* in 1935, "Loan Shark Inquiry Hears More Charges," 12 January; "Two Held in Drive on 'Shark' Lenders," 16 January; "Loan-Shark Drive Sends 2 to Prison," 2 February; "Ousted Page Boys to Picket Exchange," 16 March.

57. "Ex-Convict Slain in Street: 2 Seized," *New York Times*, 6 July 1935; "Thug Found Shot near Art Museum," *New York Times*, 16 October 1935.

58. Mary Stolberg, *Fighting Organized Crime: Politics, Justice, and the Legacy of Thomas E. Dewey* (Boston: Northeastern University Press, 1995), 95–96. See also Thomas Dewey, *Twenty against the Underworld* (Garden City: Doubleday, 1974), 180–83.

59. Dewey and Nugent quoted from "27 Arrested as Usurers in Sudden Move by Dewey to Break up Vast Racket," *New York Times*, 29 October 1935.

60. John Harrington, "Loan Sharks Facing Many-Sided Attack," *New York Times*, 10 November 1935.

61. In the *New York Times* in 1935, "Usury Suspects Held in High Bail," 30 October; "Usurer Convicted, Another Pleads," 15 November; "Usury Convictions Rise to Nineteen," 28 November.

62. In *New York Times*, "Dewey Says He Ended Loan Shark Racket," 17 October 1937; "Loan Racket Laid to 2 in Brooklyn," 9 March 1939; "Reles Loan Racket Is Exposed by Amen," 25 January 1941. See also Burton Turkus and Sid Feder, *Murder, Inc. The Story of "the Syndicate"* (New York: Farrar, Straus, and Young, 1951), 121–24.

63. "Held as Loan-Shark, Thief," *New York Times*, 21 June 1941; "2 Held as Usurers in Edison Building," *New York Times*, 24 July 1941.

64. Jackson Collins, "Evasion and Avoidance of Usury Laws," *Law and Contemporary Problems* 8 (1941): 55.

65. Virgil Peterson, *Barbarians in Our Midst: A History of Chicago Crime and Politics* (Boston: Little Brown, 1952); Alson Smith, *Syndicate City: The Chicago Crime Cartel and*

What to Do about It (Chicago: Henry Regnery, 1954). On the Kefauver committee investigation, see John Seidl, "'Upon the Hip': A Study of the Criminal Loan-Shark Industry" (PhD diss., Harvard University, 1968), 124.

66. In the *New York Times*, "Two Union Men Held as Pier Loan Sharks," 16 October 1941; "Ex-Stevedore Is Held in Bail as Loan Shark," 30 May 1947; "3 Seized in Brooklyn as Pier Loan Sharks," 8 May 1949; "New Drive Opened on Dock Rackets," 29 October 1950; "20 Dock Workers, 15 with 'Ghost' Jobs, Seized in Brooklyn," 23 December 1952.

67. Citizens Waterfront Committee, *The New York Waterfront: A Report to the Public of New York City* (New York: Citizens Waterfront Committee, 1946), 27. See also Allan Raymond, *Waterfront Priest* (New York: Henry Holt, 1955), 29; Colin Davis, "'All I Got's a Hook': New York Longshoremen and the 1948 Dock Strike," in *Waterfront Workers: New Perspectives on Race and Class*, ed. Calvin Winslow (Urbana: University of Illinois Press, 1998), 135, 138.

68. Illinois Crime Investigating Commission (hereafter ICIC), *Juice Racketeers* (Chicago: ICIC, 1970), 6. See also Stephen Fox, *Blood and Power: Organized Crime in Twentieth-Century America* (New York: William Morrow, 1989), 359.

69. In the *Chicago Tribune*, "Tells World He Doesn't Like His New Auto," 29 January 1950; "$100 Fine Paid by DeStefano in Rockford Case," 9 November 1962; "Bickley Rips Ward in DeStefano Case," 9 May 1964; Robert Davis, "DeStefano Keeps Court Circus Rolling," 11 March 1972.

70. In the *Chicago Tribune*, Bob Wiedrich, "Boasted of Killings, Beatings," 7 July 1973; Robert Nolte, "Paint Particles on Foreman's Body Tied to DeStefano Home," 8 September 1972; George Bliss, "Mobster DeStefano Believed Victim of an Underworld Double Cross," 22 April 1973.

71. Seidl, "Upon the Hip," 82. On criminal loan-sharking in Chicago, see also Haller and Alviti, "Loansharking," 148–53.

72. "Loan-Sharking: The Untouched Domain of Organized Crime," *Columbia Journal of Law and Social Problems* 5 (1969): 97. See also Carl Simon and Anne Witte, *Beating the System: The Underground Economy* (Boston: Auburn House, 1982), 234.

73. Peter Reuter and Jonathan Rubinstein, *Illegal Gambling in New York: A Case Study in the Operation, Structure, and Regulation of an Illegal Market* (Washington, D.C.: U.S. Department of Justice, 1982), 183.

74. "The Confessions of a 6-for-5 'Juice Man'," *Burroughs Clearing House* 49 (April 1965): 41, 95; Peter Maas, *The Valachi Papers* (New York: G. P. Putnam's Sons, 1968), 159–60.

75. "Juice Victim Tells of Beating," *Chicago Tribune*, 15 May 1964; Bob Wiedrich, "Death Frees Juice Victim from Terror," *Chicago Tribune*, 5 May 1966.

76. Annelise Anderson, *The Business of Organized Crime* (Stanford: Hoover Institution Press, 1979), 66.

77. Maas, *Valachi Papers*, 160.

78. As Selwyn Raab observes, "Loan-sharking is the symbiotic partner of gambling operations." See *Five Families: The Rise, Decline, and Resurgence of America's Most Powerful Mafia Empires* (New York: St. Martin's Press, 2005), 313.

79. Sandy Smith, "How Syndicate Banked Police Graft Loans," *Chicago Tribune*, 25 February 1960.

80. Reuter and Rubinstein, *Illegal Gambling in New York*, 175.

81. Seidl, "Upon the Hip," 126; "Syndicate Loan-Shark Activities and New York's

Usury Statute," *Columbia Law Review* 66 (1966): 167–69 (167). See also State of New York, Temporary Commission of Investigation, *An Investigation of the Loan-Shark Racket: A Report* (1965), 16.

82. Fred Cook, "If You Are Willing to Put up Your Body for Collateral," *New York Times*, 28 January 1968; Selwyn Raab, "Loan-Sharking Inquiry Gives Officials New Insights into Organized Crime," *New York Times*, 17 August 1984.

83. "Loan-Sharking," 94; Lawrence Kaplan and Salvatore Matteis, "The Economics of Loansharking," *American Journal of Economics and Sociology* 27 (1968): 246; "Loan-Sharking," 93; ICIC, *Juice Racketeers*, 9.

84. Anderson, *Organized Crime*, 64; Peter Reuter, *The Organization of Illegal Markets: An Economic Analysis* (Washington, D.C.: U.S. Department of Justice, 1985), x, 10, 23.

85. Anderson, *Organized Crime*, 65–66; Reuter, *Illegal Markets*, 17, 33.

86. "Confessions of a 6-for-5 'Juice Man,'" 40. See also Bob Wiedrich, "'Juice' Loan Victims Live in Terror," *Chicago Tribune*, 8 June 1964.

87. Anderson, *Organized Crime*, 72–73; New York, *Loan-Shark Racket*, 14–15 (quote).

88. Fox, *Blood and Power*, 359. See also "Loan Sharking Is Top Racket, Probers Told," *Chicago Tribune*, 15 May 1968.

89. Seidl, "Upon the Hip," 100–103; "Ex-Mail Clerk Is Sentenced in Loan Racket," *Chicago Tribune*, 2 June 1966. See also John O'Brien, "Ex–Post Office Clerk Named as Loan Shark," *Chicago Tribune*, 21 January 1966.

90. Seidl, "Upon the Hip," 97–100; "Syndicate Loan-Shark Activities," 167. See also Joseph Fried, "U.S. Draws a Portrait of a Loan Shark," *New York Times*, 27 October 1980; Ronald Goldstock and Dan Coenen, "Controlling the Contemporary Loanshark: The Law of Illicit Lending and the Problem of Witness Fear," *Cornell Law Review* 65 (1980): 132; Simon, *Beating the System*, 237.

91. Ianni, *Family Business*, 99.

92. Reuter, *Illegal Markets*, 37.

93. Bob Wiedrich, "The Old, Gray Mob," *Chicago Tribune*, 21 April 1974.

94. Chapman and Shay, *Licensed Lending*, 103.

95. Robert Johnson, "Conclusions for Regulation," in *The Consumer Finance Industry: Its Costs and Regulation*, ed. John Chapman and Robert Shay (New York: Columbia University Press, 1967), 145.

96. National Commission on Consumer Finance, *Consumer Credit in the United States*, 157.

97. Benston, "Maine's '36 Month Limitation'," 33–46, 59.

98. Virgil Peterson, "Chicago: Shades of Capone," *Annals of the American Academy of Political and Social Science* 347 (1963): 36.

99. Chapman and Shay, *Licensed Lending*, xviii.

100. National Commission on Consumer Finance, *Consumer Credit in the United States*, 136, 104–5.

101. On the typical rates charged by mob loan sharks, see Seidl, "Upon the Hip," 40–41. But Anderson's study based on FBI case files indicates that some loan-shark rings charged rates identical with those of the old salary lenders and buyers. See Anderson, *Organized Crime*, 65.

102. In the city that was the site of her case study, Anderson estimates that mob loan sharks provided just one-tenth of 1% of all consumer credit, or an average of 43¢ per

inhabitant. If this estimate is accurate, juice lending was a marginal phenomenon in the small-loan market. See Anderson, *Organized Crime*, 66.

Four—The Migration of the Sharks

1. Quoted at Teletrack, "$howmethemoney," at http://www.teletrack.com/successes/show.html.

2. On the return of the sweatshops, see Edna Bonacich and Richard Applebaum, *Behind the Label: Inequality in the Los Angeles Apparel Industry* (Berkeley and Los Angeles: University of California Press, 2000); Ellen Rosen, *Making Sweatshops: The Globalization of the U.S. Apparel Industry* (Berkeley and Los Angeles: University of California Press, 2002).

3. If we adjust for inflation, $100 in 1983 would be worth $213 in 2009.

4. Robert Avery, Gregory Elliehausen, and Glenn Canner, "Survey of Consumer Finances, 1983," *Federal Reserve Bulletin* (1984): 687–88.

5. Deborah Rankin, "Getting a Loan when You're Jobless," *New York Times*, 4 April 1982. See also Paula Nelson, *Where to Get Money for Everything* (New York: William Morrow, 1982), 42.

6. Teresa Sullivan, Elizabeth Warren, and Jay Westbrook, *The Fragile Middle Class: Americans in Debt* (New Haven: Yale University Press, 2000), 24.

7. Michael Edgerton, "Firm Dumps Friendly Bob, Goes Upscale," *Chicago Tribune*, 3 June 1981. See also Lynn Drysdale and Kathleen Keest, "The Two-Tiered Consumer Financial Services Marketplace: The Fringe Banking System and Its Challenge to Current Thinking about the Role of Usury Laws in Today's Society," *South Carolina Law Review* 51 (2000): 623–25.

8. On the pawnshop trade in the United States, see Caskey, *Fringe Banking*.

9. Sherrie Rhine and Maude Toussaint-Comeau, "The Use of Formal and Informal Financial Markets among Black Households," *Consumer Interests Annual* 45 (1999): 148. See also Maude Toussaint-Comeau and Sherrie Rhine, "Access to Credit and Financial Services among Black Households" (working paper, Consumer and Community Affairs Division, Federal Reserve Bank of Chicago, June 2000).

10. Philip Bond and Robert Townsend, "Formal and Informal Financing in a Chicago Ethnic Neighborhood," Federal Reserve Bank of Chicago, *Economic Perspectives: A Review* (July 1996): 7.

11. For an account of neighborhood loan sharks in a Chicago ghetto, see Sudhir Venkatesh, *Off the Books: The Underground Economy of the Urban Poor* (Cambridge: Harvard University Press, 2006), 140–41, 399–400.

12. Tracy Thompson, "Insurance Sales by Loan Firms Criticized as 'Biggest Ripoff '," *Atlanta Journal*, 9 January 1989.

13. Tyree, *Small-Loan Industry in Texas*, ix; Texas Legislative Council, *The Small Loan Business in Texas through 1961* (Austin: Texas Legislative Council, 1961). See also Durkin, "High Rate Market."

14. Kirk Ladendorf, "Poor Caught in Debt Cycle of Cash, Credit," *Austin American Statesman*, 6 May 1990; *Wallace P. Woodruff et al. v. Lillie O. Bryant et al.*, Court of Appeals of Texas, 558 S.W. 2d 535 (November 1977).

15. Bond and Townsend, "Formal and Informal Financing," 7.

16. Indeed, credit rationing is the equilibrium outcome in the cash-loan market

because lenders could not satisfy the demand of risky debtors without incurring large losses and scaring off reliable customers with the lenders' high interest rates. See Joseph Stiglitz and Andrew Weiss, "Credit Rationing in Markets with Imperfect Information," *American Economic Review* 71 (1981): 393–410.

17. Massimo Guidolin and Elizabeth La Jeunesse, "The Decline in the U.S. Personal Saving Rate: Is It Real and Is It a Puzzle?" *St. Louis Federal Reserve Bank Review* (2007): 491–514.

18. Arthur Kennickell and Janice Shack-Marquez, "Changes in Family Finances from 1983 to 1989: Evidence from the Survey of Consumer Finances," *Federal Reserve Bulletin* (January 1992): 1–18.

19. Thomas Piketty and Emmanuel Saez, "Income Inequality in the United States, 1913–1998," *Quarterly Journal of Economics* 118 (2003): 1–39; Jacob Hacker, *The Great Risk Shift* (Oxford: Oxford University Press, 2006); Markus Christen and Ruskin Morgan, "Keeping Up With the Joneses: Analyzing the Effect of Income Inequality on Consumer Borrowing," *Quantitative Marketing and Economics* 3 (2005): 145–73; Guidolin and La Jeunesse, "Personal Saving Rate," 510. See also David Laibson, "Golden Eggs and Hyperbolic Discounting," *Quarterly Journal of Economics* 112 (1997): 446.

20. Arthur Kennickell, Martha Starr-McCluer, and Brian Surette, "Recent Changes in U.S. Family Finances: Results from the 1998 Survey of Consumer Finances," *Federal Reserve Bulletin* (January 2000): 5–6, 8; Thomas Durkin, "Credit Cards: Use and Consumer Attitudes, 1970–2000," *Federal Reserve Bulletin* (September 2000): 625–26; Sullivan, Warren, and Westbrook, *Fragile Middle Class*, 23 (quote).

21. "Report 75% of S&Ls Halting Mortgages," *Chicago Tribune*, 26 October 1979.

22. For a summary of these objections, see Thomas Durkin, "An Economic Perspective on Interest Rate Limitations," *Georgia State University Law Review* 9 (1993): 821–38.

23. Larry Sandler, "State Senate Ok's End of Interest Rate Limits," *Chicago Tribune*, 24 June 1981.

24. *Marquette National Bank of Minneapolis v. First Omaha Service Corp.*, 439 U.S. 299 (31 October 1978).

25. Sarkis Khoury, *U.S. Banking and Its Regulation in the Political Context* (Lanham, MD: University Press of America, 1997), 44, 50.

26. William Gruber, "Banks Feel Heat over New Fees," *Chicago Tribune*, 22 September 1985.

27. "Costs Bounce Higher on Bad Checks," *Chicago Tribune*, 20 April 1987; Owen Asplundh, "Bounce Protection: Payday Lending in Sheep's Clothing?" *North Carolina Banking Institute* 8 (2004): 349–76.

28. Sheila Bair, *Low-Cost Payday Loans: Opportunities and Obstacles* (Baltimore: Annie E. Casey Foundation, 2005), 7.

29. Regina Austin, "Of Predatory Lending and the Democratization of Credit: Preserving the Social Safety Net of Informality in Small Loan Transactions," *American University Law Review* 53 (2004): 1248.

30. "Ex-Stevedore Is Held in Bail as Loan Shark," *New York Times*, 30 May 1947.

31. Kennickell and Shack-Marquez, "Changes in Family Finances," 5.

32. "Loan Shark Ring, Interest at 365% Bared by Arrest," *New York Times*, 16 March 1940. See also Joe Birkhead, "Collection Tactics of Illegal Lenders," *Law and Contemporary Problems* 8 (1941): 86; Rabino, "Small Loan Law," 98.

33. Texas Legislative Council, *Small Loan Business*, 29; Simpson, *America's Small Loan Problem*, 61. See also Neifeld, *Neifeld's Manual*, 394.

34. "Makes Loans, Cleaner Held," *Tucson Daily Citizen*, 13 November 1953.

35. "Hillquit Denounces the 'New' Tammany," *New York Times*, 29 June 1930; "Find Currency Exchanges Enjoy Thriving Trade," *Chicago Tribune*, 26 October 1937; George Tagge, "Bill Licensing Check Cashers Passes House," *Chicago Tribune*, 4 June 1943.

36. Edward Condlon, "Cashing of Checks Faces Safeguards," *New York Times*, 19 March 1944; Irving Wolf, "The Licensed Check Cashing Industry in New York City" (MBA thesis, Pace University, 1975), 25 (quote).

37. Caskey, *Fringe Banking*, 34.

38. Dorothy Projector and Gertrude Weiss, *Survey of Financial Characteristics of Consumers* (Washington, D.C.: Board of the Federal Reserve System, 1966), 11.

39. Caskey, *Fringe Banking*, 62–64.

40. Rhine and Toussaint-Comeau, "Formal and Informal Financial Markets," 150.

41. The story is told in Ronald Mann and Jim Hawkins, "Just until Payday," *UCLA Law Review* 54 (2007): 862.

42. R. T. Rybak, "At Times, It's a Gamble for Check-Cashing Stores," *Star Tribune*, 17 July 1986.

43. Jason Brady, "Check-Cashing Services Put Off-Limits," *Fayetteville Observer*, 8 April 1988; Jim Erickson, "Check-Cashing Stores Multiply," *Seattle Post-Intelligencer*, 21 November 1988; "Hearing Probes Check-Cashing Services," *Seattle Times*, 27 July 1989.

44. Joe Stephens, "Postdated Check Firms May Violate Usury Laws," *Kansas City Star*, 23 October 1988.

45. Phil Linsalata, "Borrowers Call Shops 'Con Game,'" *St. Louis Post-Dispatch*, 25 December 1989.

46. The earliest use I've found of the label "payday loan" to describe the postdated-check cash advance was in the classified ads of the *Atchison (Kansas) Globe*, in December 1991. The lender, Mr. Money, was located across the Missouri River in Kansas City.

47. John Caskey, "Payday Lending," *Financial Counseling and Planning* 12 (2001): 1.

48. See Check Into Cash, "About Check Into Cash Chairman and Founder W. Allan Jones," http://www.checkintocash.com/allan.htm.

49. Consumer Federation of America (hereafter CFA), *Rent-a-Bank Payday Lending: How Banks Help Payday Lenders Evade State Consumer Protections* (Washington, D.C.: CFA, 2001), 6; Caskey, "Rise of Payday Lending," 17, 26–28; Telzrow, "Payday Advance Industry," 10–11.

50. Other sources report smaller rates of usage. In a 2005 nationwide survey, 2% of adults admitted getting a payday loan within the last twelve months. See Edward Lawrence and Gregory Elliehausen, "A Comparative Analysis of Payday Loan Customers," *Contemporary Economic Policy* 26 (2008): 304. A 2001 study claimed that 5% of the U.S. population had borrowed at least once from a payday lender. This works out to be roughly one in eight households. See Michael Stegman and Robert Faris, "Payday Lending: A Business Model that Encourages Chronic Borrowing," *Economic Development Quarterly* 17 (2003): 14.

51. Alicia Kolaian, "Appendix B: A Survey of the Regulatory Structure Governing the Check-Cashing Industry," in *Economic Profile of the Check Cashers' Industry* (Albany: New York State Banking Department, 1991), 11.

52. Illinois DFI, Consumer Credit Division, *Short Term Lending: Final Report*

(Springfield: DFI, 2000), 10; Michael Stegman, "Payday Lending," *Journal of Economic Perspectives* 21 (2007): 172.

53. Illinois DFI, *Short Term Lending*, 11–12.

54. Jim Erickson, "Check-Cashing Stores Multiply," *Seattle Post-Intelligencer*, 21 November 1988 (quote); Steven Graves, "Landscapes of Predation, Landscapes of Neglect: A Location Analysis of Payday Lenders and Banks," *Professional Geographer* 55 (2003): 310.

55. Graves, "Landscapes of Predation," 311; Mark Burkey and Scott Simkins, "Factors Affecting the Location of Payday Lending and Traditional Banking Services in North Carolina," *Review of Regional Studies* 34 (2004): 201; Mark Flannery and Katherine Samolyk, "Payday Lending: Do the Costs Justify the Price?" (working paper, FDIC Center for Financial Research, June 2005), 13; Uriah King et al., *Race Matters: The Concentration of Payday Lenders in African-American Neighborhoods in North Carolina* (Durham: Center for Responsible Lending, 2005); Assaf Oron, "Easy Prey: Evidence for Race and Military Related Targeting in the Distribution of Payday Loan Branches in Washington State" (working paper, Department of Statistics, University of Washington, 2006); Mark Skeric, "Payday Loans Target Blacks, Study Says," *Chicago Sun-Times*, 11 March 2003; Steven Graves and Christopher Peterson, "Predatory Lending and the Military: The Law and Geography of 'Payday' Loans in Military Towns," *Ohio State Law Journal* 66 (2005): 653–832.

56. Raymond Coffey, "Even Benny In On Payday Loan Act," *Chicago Sun-Times*, 23 March 1999; Coalition for Responsible Lending, "Payday Lending Industry Insiders Tell All: Unsavory Details Emerge about the Debt Trap and Much More" (press release, 11 September 2007).

57. Advance America, Cash Advance Centers, Inc., "U.S. Securities and Exchange Commission Form 10-K" (2007), 6–7, 28.

58. Ibid., 27.

59. Joe Stephens, "Postdated Check Firms May Violate Usury Laws," *Kansas City Star*, 23 October 1988; John Lucas and Bob Okon, "Fast Loans," *Aurora Beacon News*, 20 December 1998; Alex Berenson, "'Fringe' Banking Hot despite Bite," *Denver Post*, 5 May 1996.

60. Diane Hellwig, "Exposing the Loansharks in Sheep's Clothing: Why Re-Regulating the Consumer Credit Market Makes Economic Sense," *Notre Dame Law Review* 80 (2005): 1597; Garrett Ordower, "Fast Cash Is Anything but 'Easy Money'," *Aurora Beacon News*, 28 April 2002; CFA, *Rent-a-Bank Payday Lending*, 14.

61. Michael Bertics, "Fixing Payday Lending: The Potential of Greater Bank Involvement," *North Carolina Bank Institute* 9 (2005): 139–140. See also Peterson, *Taming the Sharks*, 131–33; Juster and Shay, *Finance Rates*.

62. Robert DeYoung and Ronnie Phillips, "Strategic Pricing of Payday Loans: Evidence from Colorado, 2000–2005" (working paper, Networks Financial Institute, Indiana State University, August 2006), 1; Flannery and Samolyk, "Payday Lending," 10.

63. Richard Brooks, "Credit Past Due," *Columbia Law Review* 106 (2006): 994–1028.

64. Paige Skiba and Jeremy Tobacman, "Measuring the Individual-Level Effects of Access to Credit: Evidence from Payday Loans," *Federal Reserve Bank of Chicago Proceedings* (2007): 280–301.

65. Peterson, *Taming the Sharks*, 131–34; Gary Wisby, "Devine Sues Loan Company," *Chicago Sun-Times*, 10 September 1999; Creola Johnson, "Payday Loans: Shrewd Business or Predatory Lending?" *Minnesota Law Review* 87 (2002): 63.

66. Skiba and Tobacman, "Individual-Level Effects." See also Bair, *Low-Cost Payday*

Loans, 19. The larger chains seem to reject a higher proportion of applications.

67. Lawrence and Elliehausen, "Payday Loan Customers," 308.

68. Peterson, *Taming the Sharks*, 236.

69. Advance America, "Form 10-K," 9, 40.

70. Michael Barr, "Banking the Poor," *Yale Journal on Regulation* 21 (2004): 151.

71. Center for Community Capital (hereafter CCC), *North Carolina Consumers after Payday Lending: Attitudes and Experiences with Credit Options* (Chapel Hill: CCC, 2007), 14. See also Hellwig, "Loansharks in Sheep's Clothing," 1585.

72. Illinois DFI, *Short Term Lending*, 4, 26; CFA, *Show Me the Money! A Survey of Payday Lenders and Review of Payday Lender Lobbying in State Legislatures* (Washington, D.C.: CFA, 2000), 7.

73. Aaron Huckstep, "Payday Lending: Do Outrageous Prices Necessarily Mean Outrageous Profits?" *Fordham Journal of Corporate and Financial Law* 12 (2007): 203–32. See also Flannery and Samolyk, "Payday Lending," 10–11.

74. Advance America, "Form 10-K," 5, 48.

75. Illinois DFI, *Short Term Lending*, 26; Io Data Corporation (IDC), *Illinois Payday Advance Customer Study* (Salt Lake City: IDC, 2002), 35.

76. Lawrence and Elliehausen, "Payday Loan Customers," 305. For a similar result, see also Cypress Research Group (CRG), *Payday Advance Customer Satisfaction Survey* (Cleveland: CRG, 2004), 12; Paul Chessin, "Borrowing from Peter to Pay Paul: A Statistical Analysis of Colorado's Deferred Deposit Loan Act," *Denver University Law Review* 83 (2005): 405–6; Skiba and Tobacman, "Individual-Level Effects"; Applied Management and Planning Group (hereafter AMPG), *Department of Corporations Payday Loan Study* (Los Angeles: AMPG, 2007), 66. 77. Lawrence and Elliehausen, "Payday Loan Customers," 305–6. Surveys regularly report that 60% or more of payday-loan customers are female.

78. David Caplovitz, *The Poor Pay More: Consumer Practices of Low-Income Families* (New York: Free Press, 1963).

79. Lawrence and Elliehausen, "Payday Loan Customers," 306–7. Additional statistics from this survey are reported in Gregory Elliehausen and Edward Lawrence, *Payday Advance Credit in America: An Analysis of Customer Demand* (Washington, D.C.: Credit Research Center, 2001), 36, 42–46. See also Stegman and Faris, "Payday Lending: A Business Model," 18.

80. CFA, *Rent-a-Bank Payday Lending*, 6.

81. Lawrence and Elliehausen, "Payday Loan Customers," 309.

82. Huckstep, "Payday Lending," 220.

83. A comprehensive survey in California found that 70% of customers who had more than one loan in 2006 were in debt to the payday lenders continuously rather than intermittently. See California Department of Corporations (CDC), *California Deferred Deposit Transaction Law* (Los Angeles: CDC, 2007), 13.

84. Illinois DFI, *Short Term Lending*, 26; CFA, *Show Me the Money!* 8.

85. Lawrence and Elliehausen, "Payday Loan Customers," 310–11; Chessin, "Borrowing from Peter to Pay Paul," 410, 412; Skiba and Tobacman, "Individual-Level Effects."

86. Flannery and Samolyk, "Payday Lending," 12.

87. For data on payday loan transactions in Florida, see Veritec Solutions, *Florida Trends in Deferred Presentment* (Jacksonville: Veritec Solutions, 2005), 11; for Oklahoma, see Veritec Solutions, *Oklahoma Trends in Deferred Deposit Lending* (Jacksonville: Veritec

Solutions, 2007), 8; for Washington, see Washington State DFI, *Payday Lending Report, 2006* (Olympia: WDFI, 2007), 4.

88. Debra Pressey, "Payday Loan Industry Proliferating," *Champaign-Urbana News Gazette*, 11 November 1998; Susan Reidy, "Consumers Find No Quick Fix for Debt," *Decatur Herald*, 9 February 2001.

89. Melissa Wahl, "Surge Puts Payday Loans under Scrutiny," *Chicago Tribune*, 7 May 2000.

90. Alex Berenson, "'Fringe' Banking Hot despite Bite," *Denver Post*, 5 May 1996, 1.

91. Lawrence and Elliehausen, "Payday Loan Customers," 311. In a California survey, one-third of payday-advance customers reported borrowing from more than one lender simultaneously. Most said they did so because they needed more money than the $300 limit imposed by the state. See AMPG, *Department of Corporations Payday Loan Study*, 52.

92. Robert Mayer, "One Payday, Many Payday Loans: Short-Term Lending Abuse in Milwaukee County" (working paper, Department of Political Science, Loyola University Chicago, April 2005), 5–6.

93. Johnson, "Payday Loans," 63.

94. Washington DFI, *Payday Lending Report, 2006*, 4.

95. Bair, *Low-Cost Payday Loans*, 20–21.

96. Flannery and Samolyk, "Payday Lending," 16. But Stephens Inc., an industry consultant, estimates that the average figure is at least 20%. See Telzrow, "Payday Advance Industry," 19; Chessin, "Borrowing from Peter to Pay Paul," 408.

97. Gary Wisby, "Devine Sues Loan Company," *Chicago Sun-Times*, 10 September 1999, 22; Marla Donato, "Firm to Close Its Payday Loan Stores," *Chicago Tribune*, 22 December 1999.

98. Woodstock Institute, *Hunting down the Payday Loan Customer: The Debt Collection Practices of Two Payday Loan Companies* (Chicago: Woodstock Institute, 2006); Steve Neal, "Ban Payday Loan Sleaze," *Chicago Sun-Times*, 16 April 2001; Cheryl Reed, "The 'Wild, Wild West' in Loans," *Chicago Sun-Times*, 15 August 2004.

Five—The Slipperiest Fish

1. Peter Shinkle, "'Payday' Loans Difficult to Regulate," *Baton Rouge Advocate*, 27 December 1998.

2. Sam Peltzman, "Toward a More General Theory of Regulation," *Journal of Law and Economics* 19 (1976): 212.

3. Efraim Benmelech and Tobias Moskowitz, "The Political Economy of Financial Regulation: Evidence from U.S. State Usury Laws in the Nineteenth Century" (working paper, National Bureau of Economic Research, January 2007); Peter Temin and Hans-Joachim Voth, "Interest Rate Restrictions in a Natural Experiment: Loan Allocation and the Change in the Usury Laws in 1714," *Economic Journal* 118 (2008): 743–58.

4. Miller Uptown, "An Economic Appraisal of Convenience and Advantage Licensing by Small-Loan Statutes," *Journal of Business* 25 (1952): 249–63.

5. Edward Glaeser and Andrei Schleifer, "The Rise of the Regulatory State," *Journal of Economic Literature* 41 (2003): 401–25.

6. Glaeser and Scheinkman, "Neither a Borrower nor a Lender Be."

7. Kelly Noyes, "Get Cash until Payday! The Payday-Loan Problem in Wisconsin,"

Wisconsin Law Review (2006): 1627–81.

8. Christopher Peterson, "Usury Law, Payday Loans, and Statutory Sleight of Hand: An Empirical Analysis of American Credit Pricing Limits," *Minnesota Law Review* 92 (2008): 1110–64.

9. Va. Code Ann. § 6.1–444 et seq.

10. N.M. Stat. Ann. § 58–15–32 et seq.

11. David Ress, "State: Check-Cashers Charge Illegal Rates," *Newport News Daily Press*, 26 November 1992.

12. Jeff Amy, "Payday Lenders, Regulators Clash in Court," *Mobile Register*, 15 December 1999.

13. Douglas Holt, "Fight to Regulate Payday Loans Not Over," *Chicago Tribune*, 5 December 2000.

14. Kilgore, "Legislative Tactics."

15. Bob Wolfberg, "Payday Loans," *Chicago Tribune*, 20 June 2000.

16. Cheryl Reed, "The 'Wild, Wild West' in Loans," *Chicago Sun-Times*, 15 August 2004.

17. Natalie Boehme, "I'll Gladly Pay You Tuesday…," *State-Journal-Register*, 23 September 1998.

18. Dave McKinney, "Ryan Endorses Loan Limits," *Chicago Sun-Times*, 13 September 2000.

19. John Chase and Josh Noel, "State Sets Limits on Payday Loans," *Chicago Tribune*, 10 June 2005.

20. Lawrence and Elliehausen, "Payday Loan Customers," 313. CRG, *Customer Satisfaction Survey*.

21. Heather Vogell, "Payday Loan Center Patrons Denounce Regulations," *Chicago Tribune*, 14 September 2000; Sean Noble, "Gov. Ryan Draws Ire of Payday Loan Supporters," *State Journal-Register*, 14 September 2000.

22. "Payday Lending Fills a Need," *Chicago Tribune*, 13 August 1999.

23. Michelle Stevens, "No Pity for Deadbeats," *Chicago Sun-Times*, 22 April 2001.

24. John Chase and Gary Washburn, "Costly 'Payday' Loans Disturb State Officials," *Chicago Tribune*, 11 November 1998.

25. Mary Wisniewski, "Payday Lenders Start Credit-Building Program," *Chicago Sun-Times*, 6 June 2005.

26. Creola Johnson, "Payday Loans: Shrewd Business or Predatory Lending?" *Minnesota Law Review* 87 (2002): 70.

27. Becky Yerak, "Bill Would Widen Payday Loan Curbs," *Chicago Tribune*, 26 February 2008.

28. Adriana Colindres, "Legislators Seek more Regulation of Payday Loans," *State Journal-Register*, 1 November 2004.

29. Mike Ramsey, "Governor Bites Hand that Fed," *State Journal-Register*, 14 June 2005.

30. CRG, *Customer Satisfaction Survey*, 24–25.

31. Ibid., 30.

32. Lawrence and Elliehausen, "Payday Loan Customers," 313.

33. Hellwig, "Loansharks in Sheep's Clothing."

34. Gene Tharpe, "State Probes Lenders in Alleged Payday Loans," *Atlanta Journal*,

9 January 1999.

35. Walter Jones, "Groups Bolster New Bill," *Augusta Chronicle*, 10 April 2000.

36. Donald Morgan and Michael Strain, "Payday Holiday: How Households Fare after Payday Credit Bans" (staff report, Federal Reserve Bank of New York, February 2008).

37. Jabo Covert, "Tight Rules Make Case for Short-Term Cash Advances," *Atlanta Journal-Constitution*, 1 March 2007.

38. Ben Jackson, "Payday Firms' Defense now Aimed at CU's," *American Banker* 169 (30 March 2004), 1–2.

39. John McCarron, "Just an Illusion: Borrowing from Payday Lenders Turns into 'A Sentence of Perpetual Poverty'," *Chicago Tribune*, 13 December 1999.

40. Tony Davis, "County Seeks Curbs on Payday Loan Sites," *Arizona Daily Star*, 6 July 2005.

41. Neil Steinberg, "Lawsuit Challenges State on Payday Loan Centers," *Chicago Sun-Times*, 28 September 1999.

42. Raymond Coffey, "More than just a Pound of Flesh," *Chicago Sun-Times*, 2 March 1999.

43. Robert Manor, "City Sues Payday Loan Firm: Deception Charged," *Chicago Sun-Times*, 19 February 1999.

44. Johnson, "Payday Loans," 88.

45. Noyes, "Get Cash until Payday," 1639.

46. Bradley Keoun, "State Faces Lawsuit over Payday Loan Check Policy: Alderman Claims Agency Skirted Law," *Chicago Tribune*, 28 September 1999.

47. Curtis Lawrence, "Aldermen Want Payday Stores to Check Out," *Chicago Sun-Times*, 28 July 1999.

48. Stegman, "Payday Lending," 175.

49. Raymond Coffey, "Payday Loan Places Proliferate," *Chicago Sun-Times*, 5 March 1999.

50. James Janega and Margaret O'Brien, "State Pressed to Put Checks on Payday Lenders," *Chicago Tribune*, 11 August 1999.

51. Melissa Wahl, "Surge Puts Payday Loans under Scrutiny," *Chicago Tribune*, 7 May 2000.

52. Bob Wolfberg, "Payday Loans," *Chicago Tribune*, 20 June 2000.

53. CFA, *Show Me the Money!* 16–18.

54. Allison Kaplan, "Consumer Groups Push Rules on Payday Lending," *Daily Herald*, 2 February 2000.

55. Douglas Holt, "State Plans Crackdown on Payday Lending," *Chicago Tribune*, 5 August 2000.

56. Randy Blaser, "Payday Loan Rules back to Legislature," *Elk Grove Times*, 21 December 2000.

57. Dean Olsen, "News," *Lincoln Courier*, 15 November 2000.

58. In his 2008 presidential campaign, Obama expressed support for extending to all Americans the 36% cap imposed in 2006 on payday lending to members of the armed forces. The effect of a cap set at this level would be prohibition.

59. Blaser, "Payday Loan Rules."

60. Ibid.

61. Douglas Holt, "Payday Loan Rules Succeed," *Chicago Tribune*, 30 May 2001.

62. "'Payday' Loan Limits Begin to Take Effect," *Chicago Tribune,* 21 August 2005.

63. Tom Feltner and Marva Williams, "New Terms for Payday Loans: High Cost Lenders Change Loan Terms to Evade Illinois Consumer Protections," *Reinvestment Alert* no. 25 (2004): 1–8.

64. Cheryl Reed, "The 'Wild, Wild West' in Loans," *Chicago Sun-Times,* 15 August 2004.

65. Tammy Williamson, "New Limit Proposed for Payday Lending," *Chicago Sun-Times,* 26 February 2002; Tammy Chase, "Lawmaker Tries to Limit Loan Rates, Amounts," *Chicago Sun-Times,* 10 March 2004.

66. Brian Mackey, "Legislature to Consider Payday Loan Reform Bill," *State Journal-Register,* 7 February 2005.

67. Sabrina Walters, "3 Dems Jostle for Black Vote," *Chicago Sun-Times,* 10 February 2002.

68. Mary Wisniewsky, "Payday Loan Reform Would Limit Debts," *Chicago Sun-Times,* 4 February 2005.

69. Mike Fitzgerald, "Lawmaker Wants to Cap Payday Loans," *Belleview News-Democrat,* 12 February 2005.

70. Mary Wisniewski, "Payday Lenders Say They're Ignored," *Chicago Sun-Times,* 7 March 2005.

71. Chris Fusco, "Guv Signs Law Capping Payday Loan Rate," *Chicago Sun-Times,* 10 June 2005.

72. Woodstock Institute, *Hunting down the Payday Loan Customer*; and Woodstock Institute, *The Illinois Payday Loan Loophole* (Chicago: Woodstock Institute, 2008) .

73. Mary Wisniewski, "No Uncertain Terms," *Naperville Sun,* 7 December 2005.

74. Christine des Garennes, "Regulators on Lookout for Shiftiness," *News Gazette,* 5 February 2006.

75. Mike Ramsey, "Payday Loan Crackdown Blocked," *State Journal-Register,* 12 July 2006.

76. Stephen Franklin, "Interest still High in Payday Battle," *Chicago Tribune,* 29 June 2008.

77. "Payday Moles," *The Register-Guard,* 19 February 2007.

78. Tara Copp, "Easy Credit, Tough Costs," *Corpus Christi Caller-Times,* 28 May 2000.

79. Mary Spector, "Taming the Beast: Payday Loans, Regulatory Efforts, and Unintended Consequences," *DePaul Law Review* 57 (2008): 961–96; Mann and Hawkins, "Just until Payday," 877–79.

80. James White, "The Usury Trompe l'oeil," *South Carolina Law Review* 51 (2000): 445.

81. CFA, *Rent-a-Bank Payday Lending.*

82. Stephen Franklin, "Trapped by Web Loan with the 842% Interest Rate," *Chicago Tribune,* 11 May 2008.

83. Elizabeth Schiltz, "The Amazing, Elastic, Ever-expanding Exportation Doctrine and Its Effect on Predatory Lending Regulation," *Minnesota Law Review* 88 (2004): 575.

84. CFA, *Rent-a-Bank Payday Lending,* 19.

85. Pearl Chin, "Payday Loans: The Case for Federal Legislation," *University of Illinois Law Review* (2004): 734–37.

86. Robert Snarr, "No Cash 'til Payday: The Payday Loan Industry," *Compliance*

Corner (first quarter, 2002), 6.

87. Melissa Allison, "FHA Lenders to Face Closer Monitoring," *Chicago Tribune*, 18 August 2002; Tammy Wilson, "Bank Will Stop Funding 'Payday Loans'," *Chicago Sun-Times*, 18 September 2002; Tasha Winebarger, "Payday Lending: The Beginning of the End," *North Carolina Banking Institute* 7 (2003): 335–36.

88. Scott v. Lloyd 34 U.S. 418 (1835).

89. Oren Bar-Gill and Elizabeth Warren, "Making Credit Safer," *University of Pennsylvania Law Review* 157 (2008): 85.

Six—Culling the Shiver of Sharks

1. Paula Erickson, "'Payday' Loans Become Financial Trap for Some," *Daily Oklahoman*, 20 February 2005. According to the story, Pennington's "most recent advance was $500, on which he owed $565 plus additional late fees for rolling over outstanding balances. For the past 15 months, he's carried at least one loan and usually two—the maximum allowed under state law. 'I pretty much had to go down the street and borrow from one lender to pay another,' he said."

2. U.S. Department of Defense, *Report on Predatory Lending Practices Directed at Members of the Armed Forces and Their Dependents* (Washington, D.C.: DOD, 2006).

3. Graves and Peterson, "Predatory Lending."

4. Patrick Aul, "Federal Usury Law for Service Members: The Talent-Nelson Amendment," *North Carolina Banking Institute* 12 (2008): 163–84.

5. Obama for America, "Barack Obama's Plan to Strengthen the Economy for Working Families (press release, 2008).

6. Office of Senator Dick Durbin, "Durbin Introduces Bill to Crack Down on Excessive Interest Rates" (press release, 18 July 2008).

7. Fl. Stat. Ann. § 560.401 et seq.

8. Veritec Solutions, *Florida Trends in Deferred Presentment* (2009). Note that the Veritec reports count the number of loans every customer gets during the same twelve-month block of time. But because some debtors get their first loan near the end of the reporting period, it isn't possible for them to get more than one loan before the counts are tallied. As a result, the reports understate the average number of loans customers get in a twelve-month period. A recent national survey reports that only a fifth of payday-loan customers say they had less than five loans in the previous year. See Gregory Elliehausen, *An Analysis of Consumers' Use of Payday Loans*, Financial Services Research Program Monograph No. 41 (School of Business, George Washington University, Washington, 2009), 43.

9. Florida Office of Financial Regulation, "Response to Public Information Request for Deferred Presentment Loan Data" (press release, 26 September 2008).

10. Veritec Solutions, *Oklahoma Trends in Deferred Deposit Lending* (2009).

11. Washington State DFI, *Payday Lending Report, 2007* (Olympia: DFI, 2008); Veritec Solutions, *Michigan Trends in Deferred Presentment* (Jacksonville: Veritec Solutions, 2007).

12. One former payday loan employee confirmed that his shop "openly instructed customers to go to another borrower for money if they were unable to pay their loan." See "Payday Lenders Need a Lot more Regulation," *Springfield News-Sun*, 3 February 2008.

13. "Credit Union's Effort Avoids Loan Trap," *Patriot-News*, 21 December 2008.

14. Susan Block-Lieb and Edward Janger, "The Myth of the Rational Borrower:

Rationality, Behaviorism, and the Misguided 'Reform' of Bankruptcy Law," *Texas Law Review* 84 (2006): 1481–1565. See also Christine Jolls et al., "A Behavioral Approach to Law and Economics," *Stanford Law Review* 50 (1998): 1471–1550; Dan Ariely, *Predictably Irrational: The Hidden Forces that Shape Our Decisions* (New York: HarperCollins, 2008).

15. Stefano Della Vigna and Ulrike Malmendier, "Contract Design and Self-Control: Theory and Evidence," *Quarterly Journal of Economics* 119 (2004): 353–402; Patricia McCoy, "Predatory Lending Practices: Definition and Behavioral Implications," in *Why the Poor Pay More: How to Stop Predatory Lending*, ed. Gregory Squires (Westport: Praeger, 2004): 81–101; Paige Skiba and Jeremy Tobacman, "Payday Loans, Uncertainty, and Discounting: Explaining Patterns of Borrowing, Repayment, and Default" (working paper, Vanderbilt Law and Economics Research Paper Series, August 2008).

16. Oren Bar-Gill, "Seduction by Plastic," *Northwestern University Law Review* 98 (2004): 1411.

17. David Laibson, "Golden Eggs and Hyperbolic Discounting," *Quarterly Journal of Economics* 112 (1997): 446.

18. Uriah King and Leslie Parrish, *Springing the Debt Trap: Rate Caps Are the Only Proven Payday Lending Reform* (Durham: Center for Responsible Lending, 2007), 12.

19. On the determinants of profit in the payday-loan business, see Stegman and Faris, "Payday Lending: A Business Model"; Flannery and Samolyk, "Payday Lending."

20. Uriah King, Leslie Parrish, and Ozlem Tanik, *Financial Quicksand: Payday Lending Sinks Borrowers in Debt with $4.2 Billion in Predatory Fees Every Year* (Durham: Center for Responsible Lending, 2006).

21. Kartikay Mehrotra, "Law Makes It Tougher to Get Short-Term Loans," *Kane County Chronicle*, 6 August 2006.

22. King, *Springing the Debt Trap*, 1.

23. Coalition for Responsible Lending, "Payday Lending Industry Insiders."

24. Ginnie Graham, "Payday Applicants Lose Help," *Tulsa World*, 7 May 2004.

25. Veritec Solutions, *Florida Trends in Deferred Presentment* (2009), 16.

26. Veritec Solutions, *Michigan Trends in Deferred Presentment* (2007), 17.

27. Coalition for Responsible Lending, "Payday Lending Industry Insiders."

28. Colorado Department of Law, "Attorney General's Office Releases Annual Lending Data" (press release, 3 November 2008).

29. Dena Potter, "New State Payday-Lending Law Takes Effect Jan. 1," *Free Lance-Star*, 1 January 2009.

30. Ryan Keith, "State May Muzzle Payday Lenders," *State Journal-Register*, 28 August 2000.

31. John Allen Krout, *The Origins of Prohibition* (New York: Russell and Russell, 1967).

32. Richard Arneson, "Paternalism, Utility, and Fairness," *Revue Internationale de Philosophie* 43 (1989): 409–37.

33. John Stuart Mill, *On Liberty* (Indianapolis: Hackett, 1978), 95.

34. Benston, "Maine's '36 Month Limitation'," 41.

35. CCC, *Consumers after Payday Lending*, 11–18.

36. AMPG, *Department of Corporations Payday Loan Study*, 68–76 (69).

37. Jonathan Zinman, "Restricting Consumer Credit Access: Household Survey Evidence on Effects around the Oregon Rate Cap," *Journal of Banking and Finance* 34 (2010): 546–56. In the survey 35% said they used the debt to pay regular bills, and 15% said

the cash advance paid for groceries.

38. Bart Wilson et al., "An Experimental Analysis of the Demand for Payday Loans" (working paper, Economic Science Institute, Chapman University, Orange, California, April 2008). In the real world, of course, the typical customer borrows more than ten times in thirty months.

39. Adair Morse, "Payday Lenders: Heroes or Villains?" (working paper, Booth School of Business, University of Chicago, January 2007).

40. Donald Morgan, "Defining and Detecting Predatory Lending" (staff report, Federal Reserve Bank of New York, January 2007).

41. Donald Morgan and Michael Strain, "Payday Holiday: How Households Fare after Payday Credit Bans" (staff report, Federal Reserve Bank of New York, January 2008).

42. Scott Carrell and Jonathan Zinman, "In Harm's Way? Payday Loan Access and Military Personnel Performance" (working paper, Federal Reserve Bank of Philadelphia, August 2008).

43. Paige Skiba and Jeremy Tobacman, "Measuring the Individual-Level Effects of Access to Credit: Evidence from Payday Loans," *Federal Reserve Bank of Chicago Proceedings* (2007): 280–301. See also Paige Skiba and Jeremy Tobacman, "Do Payday Loans Cause Bankruptcy?" (working paper, Vanderbilt Law and Economics Research Paper Series, Nashville, Tennessee, February 2008). Contrast this paper with Petru Stoianovici and Michael Maloney, "Restrictions on Credit: A Public Policy Analysis of Payday Lending" (working paper, Department of Economics, Clemson University, Clemson, South Carolina, October 2008), which found no increase in bankruptcy rates where payday lending is permitted.

44. Dennis Campbell et al., "Bouncing out of the Banking System: An Empirical Analysis of Involuntary Bank Account Closures," *Federal Reserve Bank of Chicago Proceedings* (2008): 462–93.

45. Brian Melzer, "The Real Costs of Credit Access: Evidence from the Payday Lending Market" (working paper, Kellogg School of Management, Northwestern University, Evanston, Illinois, November 2007).

46. Brian Melzer and Donald Morgan, "Competition and Adverse Selection in Consumer Credit Markets: Payday Loans vs. Overdraft Credit" (working paper, Kellogg School of Management, Northwestern University, Evanston, Illinois, December 2008).

47. Jonathan Zinman, "Restricting Consumer Credit Access: Household Survey Evidence on Effects around the Oregon Rate Cap," *Journal of Banking and Finance* 34 (2010): 546–56.

48. For a similar argument before the rise of payday lending, see George Wallace, "The Uses of Usury: Low Rate Ceilings Examined," *Boston University Law Review* 56 (1976): 451–97.

49. Stegman and Faris, "Payday Lending: A Business Model," 29. For a recent example of a vest-pocket lender in a prohibition state, see "State Employee Involved in Illegal Lending with Co-workers," *Capital News*, 23 January 2009.

50. Venkatesh, *Off the Books*, 140–141, 399–400.

51. Dexter Filkins, "In Some Immigrant Enclaves, Loan Shark Is the Local Bank," *New York Times*, 23 April 2001.

52. Policis, *Economic and Social Risks of Consumer Credit Market Regulation* (London: Policis, 2004).

53. Andrew Leyshon et al., "Walking with Money Lenders: The Ecology of the U.K.

Home-Collected Credit Industry," *Urban Studies* 43 (2006): 161–86.

54. Policis, *Illegal Lending in the UK* (London: Policis, 2006).

55. Policis, *Economic and Social Risks*, 37–38.

56. CFA, *Internet Payday Lending* (Washington, D.C.: CFA, 2004).

57. Stephen Franklin, "Trapped by Web Loan with the 842% Interest Rate," *Chicago Tribune*, 11 May 2008.

58. Telzrow, "Payday Advance Industry," 10.

59. Oren Bar-Gill and Elizabeth Warren, "Making Credit Safer," *University of Pennsylvania Law Review* 157 (2008): 45.

60. A recent study found that large numbers of payday-loan customers have not yet maxed out their credit cards and also have credit scores that should qualify them for cheaper loans. See Sumit Agarwal, Paige Skiba, and Jeremy Tobacman, "Payday Loans and Credit Cards: New Liquidity and Credit Scoring Puzzles?" *American Economic Review* 99 (2009): 412–17.

61. Bair, *Low-Cost Payday Loans*, 21–22.

62. Ibid., 22–23; Mary Wisniewski, "How to Break Payday Loan Cycle," *Chicago Sun-Times*, 13 April 2005; Matt Carr, "Banks, CUs to Fill Payday Gap? Maybe," *American Banker* 172 (7 November 2007), 1–6.

63. John Leland, "Nonprofit Payday Loans? Yes, to Mixed Reviews," *New York Times*, 28 August 2007.

64. Susan Burhouse et al., "An Introduction to the FDIC's Small-Dollar Loan Pilot Program," *FDIC Quarterly* 2/3 (2008): 23–30.

65. Federal Deposit Insurance Corporation, *Study of Bank Overdraft Programs* (Washington, D..C.: FDIC, 2008).

66. Bair, *Low-Cost Payday Loans*, 4.

67. Michael Bertics, "Fixing Payday Lending: The Potential of Greater Bank Involvement," *North Carolina Banking Institute* 9 (2005): 133–58; Michael Kenneth, "Payday Lending: Can 'Reputable' Banks End Cycles of Debt?" *University of South Florida Law Review* 42 (2008): 659–713.

68. Richard Thaler and Cass Sunstein, *Nudge: Improving Decisions about Health, Wealth, and Happiness* (New Haven: Yale University Press, 2008).

69. On the pros and cons of overdraft lines of credit, see Steve Cocheo, "Follow the Bouncing Check," *ABA Banking Journal* (April 2003): 32–36.

Epilogue—The View from the Shark Cage

1. Agarwal, Skiba, and Tobacman, "Payday Loans and Credit Cards."

2. Kathleen Engel and Patricia McCoy, "A Tale of Three Markets: The Law and Economics of Predatory Lending," *Texas Law Review* 80 (2002): 1317–34.

3. Robert Mayer, "What's Wrong with Exploitation?" *Journal of Applied Philosophy* 24 (2007): 137–50; "Sweatshops, Exploitation, and Moral Responsibility," *Journal of Social Philosophy* 38 (2007): 605–19; "Payday Loans and Exploitation," *Public Affairs Quarterly* 17 (2003): 197–217.

Bibliography

Newspapers

Advocate. 1992. Baton Rouge, LA
Arizona Daily Star. 1879. Tucson, AZ
Atchison Globe. 1879. Atchison, KS
Atlanta Constitution. 1881. Atlanta, GA
Atlanta Journal-Constitution. 2001. Atlanta, GA
Augusta Chronicle. 1885. Augusta, GA
Aurora Daily Beacon News. 1912. Aurora, IL
Austin American Statesman. 1987. Austin, TX
Belleville News-Democrat. 1983. Belleville, IL
Chicago Defender. 1973. Chicago, IL
Chicago Sun-Times. 1948. Chicago, IL
Chicago Tribune. 1872. Chicago, IL
Corpus Christi Caller-Times. 1987. Corpus Christi, TX
Courier. 1992. Lincoln, IL
Daily Herald. 1977. Arlington Heights, IL
Daily Oklahoman. 1894. Oklahoma City, OK
Daily Press. 1896. Newport News, VA
Decatur Herald. 1899. Decatur, IL
Denver Post. 1901. Denver, CO
Edwardsville Intelligencer. 1868. Edwardsville, IL
Elk Grove Times. 1995. Glenview, IL
Fayetteville Observer. 1833. Fayetteville, NC
Free Lance-Star. 1926. Fredericksburg, VA
Kane County Chronicle. 1990. St. Charles, IL
Kansas City Star. 1885. Kansas City, MO
Mobile Register. 1903. Mobile, AL
Naperville Sun. 1935. Naperville, IL
News-Gazette. 1986. Champaign, IL
New York Evangelist. 1830. New York, NC
New York Herald. 1840. New York, NY
New York Times. 1857. New York, NY
Patriot-News. 1997. Harrisburg, PA
Register-Guard. 1983. Eugene, OR
Seattle Post-Intelligencer. 1921. Seattle, WA
Seattle Times. 1966. Seattle, WA
Springfield News-Sun. 1982. Springfield, OH
St. Louis Post-Dispatch. 1879. St. Louis, MO
Star Tribune. 1987. Minneapolis, MN
State-Journal-Register. 1974. Springfield, IL
Tucson Daily Citizen. 1929. Tucson, AZ
Tulsa World. 1977. Tulsa, OK
Wellsboro Agitator. 1872. Wellsboro, PA

Books and Articles

Advance America, Cash Advance Centers, Inc. "U.S. Securities and Exchange Commission Form 10-K." 2007.

Agarwal, Sumit, Paige Skiba, and Jeremy Tobacman. "Payday Loans and Credit Cards: New Liquidity and Credit Scoring Puzzles?" *American Economic Review* 99 (2009): 412–17.

AMPG. *See* Applied Management and Planning Group (AMPG).

Anderson, Annelise. *The Business of Organized Crime.* Stanford: Hoover Institution Press, 1979.

Anderson, Elizabeth. "Experts, Ideas, and Policy Change: The Russell Sage Foundation and Small Loan Reform, 1909–1941." *Theory and Society* 37 (2008): 271–310.

Applied Management and Planning Group (AMPG). *Department of Corporations Payday Loan Study.* Los Angeles: AMPG, 2007.

Aquinas, Thomas. *The Political Ideas of St. Thomas Aquinas.* Edited by Dino Bigongiari. New York: Free Press, 1997.

Ariely, Dan. *Predictably Irrational: The Hidden Forces that Shape Our Decisions.* New York: HarperCollins, 2008.

Arneson, Richard. "Paternalism, Utility, and Fairness." *Revue Internationale de Philosophie* 43 (1989): 409–37.

Asplundh, Owen. "Bounce Protection: Payday Lending in Sheep's Clothing?" *North Carolina Banking Institute* 8 (2004): 349–76.

Aul, Patrick. "Federal Usury Law for Service Members: The Talent-Nelson Amendment." *North Carolina Banking Institute* 12 (2008): 163–84.

Austin, Regina. "Of Predatory Lending and the Democratization of Credit: Preserving the Social Safety Net of Informality in Small Loan Transactions." *American University Law Review* 53 (2004): 1217–57.

Avery, Robert, Gregory Elliehausen, and Glenn Canner. "Survey of Consumer Finances, 1983." *Federal Reserve Bulletin* (1984): 679–92.

Avio, Kenneth. "An Economic Rationale for Statutory Interest Rate Ceilings." *Quarterly Review of Economics and Business* 13 (1973): 61–72.

Bachelder, Richard. "The Small Loan Business Unregulated." *Annals of the American Academy of Political and Social Science* 205 (1939): 35–42.

Bacon, Francis. *The Essayes or Counsels, Civill and Morall.* Edited by Michael Kiernan. Oxford: Clarendon Press, 2000.

Bair, Sheila. *Low-Cost Payday Loans: Opportunities and Obstacles.* Baltimore: Annie E. Casey Foundation, 2005.

Bar-Gill, Oren. "Seduction by Plastic." *Northwestern University Law Review* 98 (2004): 1373–434.

Bar-Gill, Oren, and Elizabeth Warren. "Making Credit Safer." *University of Pennsylvania Law Review* 157 (2008): 1–100.

Barr, Michael. "Banking the Poor." *Yale Journal on Regulation* 21 (2004): 121–237.

Beckner, Earl. *A History of Labor Legislation in Illinois.* Chicago: University of Chicago Press, 1929.

Benmelech, Efraim, and Tobias Moskowitz. "The Political Economy of Financial Regulation: Evidence from U.S. State Usury Laws in the 19th Century." Working paper, National Bureau of Economic Research, January 2007.

Benston, George. "An Analysis of Maine's '36 Month Limitation' on Finance Company

Small Loans." In National Commission on Consumer Finance, *Technical Studies* 2 (1975): 1–63. Washington, D.C.: U.S. Government Printing Office.

Bentham, Jeremy. "Defense of Usury." In *Jeremy Bentham's Economic Writings*, ed. W. Stark. London: George Allen and Unwin, 1952.

Bertics, Michael. "Fixing Payday Lending: The Potential of Greater Bank Involvement." *North Carolina Banking Institute* 9 (2005): 133–58.

Bertrand, Marianne, and Adair Morse. "Information Disclosure, Cognitive Biases and Payday Borrowing." Working paper, Milton Friedman Institute, University of Chicago, October 2009.

Birkhead, Joe. "Collection Tactics of Illegal Lenders." *Law and Contemporary Problems* 8 (1941): 78–87.

Blake, Guy. "The Validity of Laws Regulating Wage Assignments." *Illinois Law Review* 5 (1911): 343–49.

Block-Lieb, Susan, and Edward Janger. "The Myth of the Rational Borrower: Rationality, Behaviorism, and the Misguided 'Reform' of Bankruptcy Law." *Texas Law Review* 84 (2006): 1481–1565.

Bogert, George. "The Future of Small Loan Legislation." *University of Chicago Law Review* 12 (1944): 1–25.

Bonacich, Edna, and Richard Applebaum. *Behind the Label: Inequality in the Los Angeles Apparel Industry.* Berkeley and Los Angeles: University of California Press, 2000.

Bond, Philip, and Robert Townsend. "Formal and Informal Financing in a Chicago Ethnic Neighborhood." In Federal Reserve Bank of Chicago, *Economic Perspectives: A Review* 20 (July 1996): 3–26.

Boushey, Heather, and Christian Weller. "Has Growing Inequality Contributed to Rising Household Economic Distress?" *Review of Political Economy* 20 (2008): 1–22.

Brooks, Richard. "Credit Past Due." *Columbia Law Review* 106 (2006): 994–1028.

Bureau of Justice of Chicago. *Annual Report of the Bureau of Justice of Chicago.* 1st-17th, 1888–1904. Chicago: Hornstein Brothers.

Burhouse, Susan, et al. "An Introduction to the FDIC's Small-Dollar Loan Pilot Program." *FDIC Quarterly* 2 (2008): 23–30.

Burkey, Mark. and Scott Simkins. "Factors Affecting the Location of Payday Lending and Traditional Banking Services in North Carolina." *Review of Regional Studies* 34 (2004): 191–205.

Cahan, Richard. *A Court That Shaped America: Chicago's Federal District Court from Abe Lincoln to Abbie Hoffman.* Evanston: Northwestern University Press, 2002.

Calder, Lendol. *Financing the American Dream: A Cultural History of Consumer Credit.* Princeton: Princeton University Press, 1999.

California Department of Corporations (CDC). *California Deferred Deposit Transaction Law.* Los Angeles: CDC, 2007.

Campbell, Dennis, et al. "Bouncing Out of the Banking System: An Empirical Analysis of Involuntary Bank Account Closures." *Federal Reserve Bank of Chicago: Proceedings* (2008): 462–93.

Caplovitz, David. "Consumer Credit in the Affluent Society." In *Consumer Credit Reform*, ed. Clark Havighurst, 3–17. Dobbs Ferry: Oceana, 1970.

———. *The Poor Pay More: Consumer Practices of Low-Income Families.* New York: Free Press, 1963.

Carr, Matt. "Banks, CUs to Fill Payday Gap? Maybe." *American Banker* 172 (7 November 2007): 1–6.

Carrell, Scott, and Jonathan Zinman. "In Harm's Way? Payday Loan Access and Military Personnel Performance." Working paper, Federal Reserve Bank of Philadelphia, August 2008.

Carruthers, Bruce, Timothy Guinnane, and Yoonseok Lee. "The Passage of the Uniform Small Loan Law." Paper presented at the annual meeting of the American Sociological Association, New York, 11 August 2007.

Caskey, John. *Fringe Banking: Check-Cashing Outlets, Pawnshops, and the Poor.* New York: Russell Sage Foundation, 1994.

———. "Fringe Banking and the Rise of Payday Lending." In *Credit Markets for the Poor,* ed. Patrick Bolton and Howard Rosenthal, 17–45. New York: Russell Sage Foundation, 2005.

———. "Payday Lending." *Financial Counseling and Planning* 12 (2001): 1–13.

Center for Community Capital. *North Carolina Consumers after Payday Lending: Attitudes and Experiences with Credit Options.* Chapel Hill: Center for Community Capital, 2007.

CFA. *See* Consumer Federation of America (CFA).

Chapman, John, and Robert Shay. *Licensed Lending in New York.* New York: Columbia Graduate School of Business, 1970.

Check Into Cash. "About Check Into Cash Chairman and Founder W. Allan Jones." http://www.checkintocash.com/allan.htm.

Chessin, Paul. "Borrowing from Peter to Pay Paul: A Statistical Analysis of Colorado's Deferred Deposit Loan Act." *Denver University Law Review* 83 (2005): 387–423.

Chin, Pearl. "Payday Loans: The Case for Federal Legislation." *University of Illinois Law Review* (2004): 723–53.

Christen, Markus, and Ruskin Morgan. "Keeping Up With the Joneses: Analyzing the Effect of Income Inequality on Consumer Borrowing." *Quantitative Marketing and Economics* 3 (2005): 145–73.

Citizens Waterfront Committee. *The New York Waterfront: A Report to the Public of New York City.* New York: Citizens Waterfront Committee, 1946.

Clark, Evans. *Financing the Consumer.* New York: Harper and Brothers, 1930.

Coalition for Responsible Lending. "Payday Lending Industry Insiders Tell All: Unsavory Details Emerge about the Debt Trap and Much More." Press release, 11 September 2007.

Cobleigh, Ira. *How and Where to Borrow Money.* New York: Avon Books, 1964.

Cocheo, Steve. "Follow the Bouncing Check." *ABA Banking Journal* (April 2003): 32–36.

Collins, Jackson. "Evasion and Avoidance of Usury Laws." *Law and Contemporary Problems* 8 (1941): 54–72.

Colorado Department of Law. "Attorney General's Office Releases Annual Lending Data." Press release, 3 November 2008.

"Confessions of a 6-for-5 'Juice Man'." *Burroughs Clearing House* 49 (April 1965): 40–41.

Consumer Federation of America (CFA). *The Growth of Legal Loan Sharking: A Report on the Payday Lending Industry.* Washington, D.C.: CFA, 1998.

———. *Internet Payday Lending.* Washington, D.C.: CFA, 2004.

———. *Rent-a-Bank Payday Lending: How Banks Help Payday Lenders Evade State Consumer Protections.* Washington, D.C.: CFA, 2001.

———. *Safe Harbor for Usury: Recent Developments in Payday Lending.* Washington, D.C.: CFA, 1999.

———. *Show Me the Money! A Survey of Payday Lenders and Review of Payday Lender Lobbying in State Legislatures.* Washington, D.C.: CFA, 2000.

Corzelle, Charles. *The Small Loan Racket.* South Bend: Mirror Press, 1934.

Cypress Research Group (CRG). *Payday Advance Customer Satisfaction Survey.* Cleveland: CRG, 2004.

Daily News Almanac and Book of Facts. 18th ed. Chicago: Chicago Daily News, 1902.

Damar, H. Evren. "Why Do Payday Lenders Enter Local Markets? Evidence from Oregon." *Review of Industrial Organization* 34 (2009): 173–91.

Danieri, Cheryl. *Credit Where Credit Is Due: The Mont-de-Piété of Paris, 1777–1851.* New York: Garland, 1991.

Davis, Colin. "'All I Got's a Hook': New York Longshoremen and the 1948 Dock Strike." In *Waterfront Workers: New Perspectives on Race and Class*, ed. Calvin Winslow, 131–54. Urbana: University of Illinois Press, 1998.

Della Vigna, Stefano, and Ulrike Malmendier. "Contract Design and Self-Control: Theory and Evidence." *Quarterly Journal of Economics* 119 (2004): 353–402.

Dewey, Thomas. *Twenty against the Underworld.* Garden City: Doubleday, 1974.

DeYoung, Robert, and Ronnie Phillips. "Strategic Pricing of Payday Loans: Evidence from Colorado, 2000–2005." Working paper, Networks Financial Institute, Indiana State University, August 2006.

Drysdale, Lynn, and Kathleen Keest. "The Two-Tiered Consumer Financial Services Marketplace: The Fringe Banking System and Its Challenge to Current Thinking about the Role of Usury Laws in Today's Society." *South Carolina Law Review* 51 (2000): 589–669.

DuBois, James, and Gertrude Mathews. *Galusha A. Grow: Father of the Homestead Law.* Boston: Houghton Mifflin, 1917.

Durkin, Thomas. "Credit Cards: Use and Consumer Attitudes, 1970–2000." *Federal Reserve Bulletin* (September 2000): 623–34.

———. "An Economic Perspective on Interest Rate Limitations." *Georgia State University Law Review* 9 (1993): 821–38.

———. "A High Rate Market for Consumer Loans: The Small Small Loan Industry in Texas." In National Commission on Consumer Finance, *Technical Studies*, 2:1–99. Washington, D.C.: U.S. Government Printing Office, 1975.

Edelman, Daniel. "Payday Loans: Big Interest Rates and Little Regulation." *Loyola Consumer Law Review* 11 (1999): 174–87.

Elliehausen, Gregory. *An Analysis of Consumers' Use of Payday Loans.* Financial Services Research Program Monograph No. 41. School of Business, George Washington University, Washington, January 2009.

Elliehausen, Gregory, and Edward Lawrence. *Payday Advance Credit in America: An Analysis of Customer Demand.* Washington, D.C.: Credit Research Center, 2001.

Engel, Kathleen, and Patricia McCoy. "A Tale of Three Markets: The Law and Economics of Predatory Lending." *Texas Law Review* 80 (2002): 1255–366.

Eubank, Earle. *The Loan Shark in Chicago.* Chicago: Department of Public Welfare, 1916.

———. *Loan Sharks and Loan Shark Legislation in Illinois*. New York: Russell Sage Foundation, 1917.

Farrow, Thomas. *In the Money-Lender's Clutches*. Westminster: Yeoman, 1895.

Feingold, Kenneth. *Experts and Politicians: Reform Challenges to Machine Politics in New York, Cleveland, and Chicago*. Princeton: Princeton University Press, 1995.

Feltner, Tom, and Marva Williams. "New Terms for Payday Loans: High Cost Lenders Change Loan Terms to Evade Illinois Consumer Protections." *Reinvestment Alert* no. 25 (2004): 1–8.

Flannery, Mark, and Katherine Samolyk. "Payday Lending: Do the Costs Justify the Price?" Working paper, FDIC Center for Financial Research, June 2005.

Florida Office of Financial Regulation. "Response to Public Information Request for Deferred Presentment Loan Data." Press release, 26 September 2008.

Fortas, A. "Wage Assignments in Chicago: State Street Furniture Co. v. Armour & Co." *Yale Law Journal* 42 (1933): 526–60.

Foster, William Trufant. *Loan Sharks and Their Victims*. Dallas: Public Affairs Committee, 1940.

———. "The Personal Finance Business under Regulation." *Law and Contemporary Problems* 8 (1941): 154–72.

Fox, Stephen. *Blood and Power: Organized Crime in Twentieth-Century America*. New York: William Morrow, 1989.

Gallert, David, Walter Hilborn, and Geoffrey May. *Small Loan Legislation: A History of the Regulation of Lending Small Sums*. New York: Russell Sage Foundation, 1932.

Gallmeyer, Alice, and Wade Roberts. "Payday Lenders and Economically Distressed Communities: A Spatial Analysis of Financial Predation." *Social Science Journal* 46 (2009): 521–38.

Garcia, Jose, et al. *Up to Our Eyeballs: How Shady Lenders and Failed Economic Policies Are Drowning Americans in Debt*. New York: New Press, 2008.

Gates, Charles. "The Social Worker in the Service of the Small Loan Business." *Annals of the American Academy of Political and Social Science* 196 (1938): 221–24.

Gentzkow, Matthew, Edward Glaeser, and Claudia Goldin. "The Rise of the Fourth Estate: How Newspapers Became Informative and Why It Mattered." In *Corruption and Reform: Lessons from America's Economic History*, ed. Edward Glaeser and Claudia Goldin, 187–221. Chicago: University of Chicago Press, 2006).

Gisler, George. "Organization of Public Opinion for Effective Measures against Loan Sharks." *Law and Contemporary Problems* 8 (1941): 183–204.

Glaeser, Edward, and Jose Scheinkman. "Neither a Borrower nor a Lender Be: An Economic Analysis of Interest Restrictions and Usury Laws." *Journal of Law and Economics* 41 (1998): 1–36.

Glaeser, Edward, and Andrei Schleifer, "The Rise of the Regulatory State." *Journal of Economic Literature* 41 (2003): 401–25.

Glenn, John, Lilian Brandt, and F. Andrews. *The Russell Sage Foundation, 1907–1946*. 2 vols. New York: Russell Sage Foundation, 1947.

Goldstock, Ronald, and Dan Coenen. "Controlling the Contemporary Loanshark: The Law of Illicit Lending and the Problem of Witness Fear." *Cornell Law Review* 65 (1980): 127–289.

Graves, Steven. "Landscapes of Predation, Landscapes of Neglect: A Location Analysis of

Payday Lenders and Banks." *Professional Geographer* 55 (2003): 303–17.

Graves, Steven, and Christopher Peterson. "Predatory Lending and the Military: The Law and Geography of 'Payday' Loans in Military Towns." *Ohio State Law Journal* 66 (2005): 653–832.

Guidolin, Massimo, and Elizabeth La Jeunesse. "The Decline in the U.S. Personal Saving Rate: Is It Real and Is It a Puzzle?" *St. Louis Federal Reserve Bank Review* (2007): 491–514.

Hacker, Jacob. *The Great Risk Shift.* Oxford: Oxford University Press, 2006.

Hadley, Arthur. *Economics: An Account of the Relations between Private Property and Public Welfare.* New York: G. P. Putnam's Sons, 1904.

Haller, Mark, and John Alviti. "Loansharking in American Cities: Historical Analysis of a Marginal Enterprise." *American Journal of Legal History* 21 (1977): 125–56.

Halsey, Forrest. *The Bawlerout.* New York: D. Fitzgerald, 1912.

Ham, Arthur. *The Campaign against the Loan Shark.* New York: Russell Sage Foundation, 1912.

———. *The Chattel Loan Business.* New York: Charities Publication Committee, 1909.

———. *Remedial Loans: A Constructive Program.* New York: Russell Sage Foundation, 1912.

Hardy, Charles. *Consumer Credit and Its Uses.* New York: Prentice-Hall, 1938.

Harrison, W. M. "Foreign Usury Laws." *Journal of the Society of Comparative Legislation* 1 (1899): 215–36.

Hellwig, Diane. "Exposing the Loansharks in Sheep's Clothing: Why Re-Regulating the Consumer Credit Market Makes Economic Sense." *Notre Dame Law Review* 80 (2005): 1567–611.

Hodson, Clarence. *Money-Lenders, License Laws, and the Business of Making Small Loans.* New York: Legal Reform Bureau to Eliminate the Loan Shark Evil, 1919.

Horack, Benjamin. "A Survey of the General Usury Laws." *Law and Contemporary Problems* 8 (1941): 36–53.

House of Commons. *Report from the Select Committee on Money Lending.* London: Her Majesty's Stationery Office, 1898.

Hubachek, F. B. "The Development of Regulatory Small Loan Laws." *Law and Contemporary Problems* 8 (1941): 108–45.

———. "Progress and Problems in the Regulation of Consumer Credit." *Law and Contemporary Problems* 19 (1954): 4–28.

Huckstep, Aaron. "Payday Lending: Do Outrageous Prices Necessarily Mean Outrageous Profits?" *Fordham Journal of Corporate and Financial Law* 12 (2007): 203–32.

Hynes, Richard, and Eric Posner. "The Law and Economics of Consumer Finance." *American Law and Economics Review* 4 (2002): 168–207.

Iacoviello, Matteo. "Household Debt and Income Inequality, 1963–2003," *Journal of Money, Credit, and Banking* 40 (2008): 929–65.

Ianni, Francis. *A Family Business: Kinship and Social Control in Organized Crime.* New York: Russell Sage Foundation, 1972.

Illinois Crime Investigating Commission (ICIC). *Juice Racketeers.* Chicago: ICIC, 1970.

Illinois Department of Financial Institutions (DFI). Consumer Credit Division. *Short Term Lending: Final Report.* Springfield: DFI, 2000.

———. Division of Consumer Finance. *Analysis of Reports: Annual Report.* Springfield: DFI, 1934, 1964.

Illinois Department of Insurance. *Analysis of Reports: Annual Report.* Springfield: Division of Small Loans, 1934.

Illinois General Assembly. *Laws of the State of Illinois.* Vendalia: State Printers.

Io Data Corporation (IDC). *Illinois Payday Advance Customer Study.* Salt Lake City: IDC, 2002.

Jackson, Ben. "Payday Firms' Defense Now Aimed at CU's." *American Banker* 169 (30 March 2004), 1–2.

Johnson, Creola. "Payday Loans: Shrewd Business or Predatory Lending?" *Minnesota Law Review* 87 (2002): 1–152.

Johnson, Harold. "Nebraska Has No Loan Shark Problem Today." *Law and Contemporary Problems* 19 (1954): 42–53.

Johnson, Robert. "Conclusions for Regulation." In *The Consumer Finance Industry: Its Costs and Regulation,* ed. John Chapman and Robert Shay, 137–62. New York: Columbia University Press, 1967.

Jolls, Christine, et al. "A Behavioral Approach to Law and Economics." *Stanford Law Review* 50 (1998): 1471–550.

Juster, F. Thomas, and Robert Shay. *Consumer Sensitivity to Finance Rates: An Empirical and Analytical Investigation.* New York: National Bureau of Economic Research, 1964.

Kaplan, Lawrence, and Salvatore Matteis. "The Economics of Loansharking." *American Journal of Economics and Sociology* 27 (1968): 239–52.

Kelly, Charles. "Legal Techniques for Combating the Loan Sharks." *Law and Contemporary Problems* 8 (1941): 88–99.

Kelso, Robert. "Social and Economic Background of the Small Loan Problem." *Law and Contemporary Problems* 8 (1941): 14–22.

Kenneth, Michael. "Payday Lending: Can 'Reputable' Banks End Cycles of Debt?" *University of South Florida Law Review* 42 (2008): 659–713.

Kennickell, Arthur, and Janice Shack-Marquez. "Changes in Family Finances from 1983 to 1989: Evidence from the Survey of Consumer Finances." *Federal Reserve Bulletin* (January 1992): 1–18.

Kennickell, Arthur, Martha Starr-McCluer, and Brian Surette. "Recent Changes in U.S. Family Finances: Results from the 1998 Survey of Consumer Finances." *Federal Reserve Bulletin* (January 2000): 1–29.

Khoury, Sarkis. *U.S. Banking and Its Regulation in the Political Context.* Lanham: University Press of America, 1997.

Kilgore, John. "Legislative Tactics of Unregulated Lenders." *Law and Contemporary Problems* 8 (1941): 173–82.

King, Uriah, et al. *Race Matters: The Concentration of Payday Lenders in African American Neighborhoods in North Carolina.* Durham: Center for Responsible Lending, 2005.

King, Uriah, and Leslie Parrish. *Springing the Debt Trap: Rate Caps Are the Only Proven Payday Lending Reform.* Durham: Center for Responsible Lending, 2007.

King, Uriah, Leslie Parrish, and Ozlem Tanik. *Financial Quicksand: Payday Lending Sinks Borrowers in Debt with $4.2 Billion in Predatory Fees Every Year.* Durham: Center for Responsible Lending, 2006.

King, Willford. *The Small Loan Situation in New Jersey in 1929.* Trenton: New Jersey Industrial Lenders Association, 1929.

Kogan, Herman. *Lending Is Our Business: The Story of Household Finance Corporation.* Chicago: Household Finance Corporation, 1965.

Kolaian, Alicia. "Appendix B: A Survey of the Regulatory Structure Governing the Check-Cashing Industry." In *Economic Profile of the Check Cashers' Industry*, B1–27. Albany: New York State Banking Department, 1991.

Krout, John Allen. *The Origins of Prohibition*. New York: Russell and Russell, 1967.

Laibson, David. "Golden Eggs and Hyperbolic Discounting." *Quarterly Journal of Economics* 112 (1997): 443–77.

Landesco, John. *Organized Crime in Chicago*. Chicago: University of Chicago, 1968.

Lawrence, Edward, and Gregory Elliehausen. "A Comparative Analysis of Payday Loan Customers." *Contemporary Economic Policy* 26 (2008): 299–316.

Leinen, Oscar. "A Wolf at the Stock Yards." In *Told Out of Court*, 172–77. Chicago: P. G. Smyth, 1909.

Lenihan, B.J. "Progress in Consumer Credit in Kentucky." *Law and Contemporary Problems* 19 (1954): 54–67.

Leyshon, Andrew, et al. "Walking with Money Lenders: The Ecology of the UK Home-Collected Credit Industry." *Urban Studies* 43 (2006): 161–86.

"Loan-Sharking: The Untouched Domain of Organized Crime." *Columbia Journal of Law and Social Problems* 5 (1969): 93–110.

Lyle, John. *The Dry and Lawless Years*. Englewood Cliffs: Prentice-Hall, 1960.

Maas, Peter. *The Valachi Papers*. New York: G. P. Putnam's Sons, 1968.

MacCoun, Robert, and Peter Reuter. *Drug War Heresies: Learning from Other Vices, Times, and Places*. Cambridge: Cambridge University Press, 2001.

Mann, Ronald, and Jim Hawkins. "Just until Payday." *UCLA Law Review* 54 (2007): 855–911.

Maryland Administrator of Loan Laws. *Annual Report*. Baltimore: The Administrator, 1939.

Mayer, Robert. "One Payday, Many Payday Loans: Short-Term Lending Abuse in Milwaukee County." Working paper, Department of Political Science, Loyola University Chicago, April 2005.

———. "Payday Loans and Exploitation." *Public Affairs Quarterly* 17 (2003): 197–217.

———. "Sweatshops, Exploitation, and Moral Responsibility." *Journal of Social Philosophy* 38 (2007): 605–19.

———. "What's Wrong with Exploitation?" *Journal of Applied Philosophy* 24 (2007): 137–50.

McCoy, Patricia. "Predatory Lending Practices: Definition and Behavioral Implications." In *Why the Poor Pay More: How to Stop Predatory Lending*, ed. Gregory Squires, 81–101. Westport: Praeger, 2004.

Meador, Victor. *Loan Sharks in Georgia*. Washington, D.C.: American Bar Association, 1949.

Melzer, Brian. "The Real Costs of Credit Access: Evidence from the Payday Lending Market." Working paper, Kellogg School of Management, Northwestern University, Evanston, Illinois, November 2007.

Melzer, Brian, and Donald Morgan. "Competition and Adverse Selection in Consumer Credit Markets: Payday Loans vs. Overdraft Credit." Working paper, Kellogg School of Management, Northwestern University, Evanston, Illinois, December 2008.

Michelman, Irving. *Consumer Finance: A Case History in American Business*. New York: Frederick Fell, 1966.

Mill, John Stuart. *On Liberty.* Indianapolis: Hackett, 1978.

Morgan, Donald. "Defining and Detecting Predatory Lending." Staff report, Federal Reserve Bank of New York, January 2007.

Morgan, Donald, and Michael Strain. "Payday Holiday: How Households Fare after Payday Credit Bans." Staff report, Federal Reserve Bank of New York, February 2008.

Morse, Adair. "Payday Lenders: Heroes or Villains?" Working paper, Booth School of Business, University of Chicago, January 2007.

Morton, Richard. *Justice and Humanity: Edward F. Dunne, Illinois Progressive.* Carbondale: Southern Illinois University Press, 1997.

National Commission on Consumer Finance. *Consumer Credit in the United States.* Washington, D.C.: U.S. Government Printing Office, 1972.

———. *Technical Studies.* Washington, D.C.: U.S. Government Printing Office, 1975.

National Consumer Finance Association. *The Consumer Finance Industry.* Englewood Cliffs: Prentice-Hall, 1962.

National Film Preservation Foundation. *Treasures III: Social Issues in American Film, 1900–1934.* Chatsworth: Image Entertainment, 2007.

Neifeld, M. R. "Institutional Organization of Consumer Credit." *Law and Contemporary Problems* 8 (1941): 23–35.

———. *Neifeld's Manual on Consumer Credit.* Easton: Mack, 1961.

———. *Personal Finance Comes of Age.* New York: Harper and Brothers, 1939.

Neifeld, M. R., and A. E. Robichaud. "Lenders Exchanges in the Personal Finance Business." *Journal of Marketing* 4 (1940): 268–73.

Nelson, Paula. *Where to Get Money for Everything.* New York: William Morrow, 1982.

New York Office of the State Inspector General. "Loan Shark Taps Co-Workers in Illegal Lending at State's Student Loan Agency." Press release, 22 January 2009.

New York Temporary Commission of Investigation. *An Investigation of the Loan-Shark Racket: A Report.* 1965

Nord, David. *Newspapers and New Politics: Midwestern Municipal Reform, 1890–1900.* Ann Arbor: UMI Research Press, 1981.

Noyes, Kelly. "Get Cash until Payday! The Payday-Loan Problem in Wisconsin." *Wisconsin Law Review* (2006): 1627–81.

Nugent, Rolf. *Consumer Credit and Economic Stability.* New York: Russell Sage Foundation, 1939.

———. "The Loan-Shark Problem." *Law and Contemporary Problems* 8 (1941): 3–13.

———. "Small Loan Debt in the United States." *Journal of Business of the University of Chicago* 7 (1934): 1–21.

———. "Tendencies in Consumer Credit." *Journal of the American Statistical Association* 33 (1938): 42–50.

———. "Three Experiments in Small-Loan Interest Rates." *Harvard Business Review* 11 (1933): 35–46.

Obama for America. "Barack Obama's Plan to Strengthen the Economy for Working Families." Press release, 2008.

Office of Senator Dick Durbin. "Durbin Introduces Bill to Crack Down on Excessive Interest Rates." Press release, 18 July 2008.

Orchard, Dorothy, and Geoffrey May. *Moneylending in Great Britain.* New York: Russell Sage Foundation, 1933.

Oron, Assaf. "Easy Prey: Evidence for Race and Military Related Targeting in the Distribution of Payday Loan Branches in Washington State." Working paper, Department of Statistics, University of Washington, 2006.

Pegram, Thomas. *Partisans and Progressives: Private Interest and Public Policy in Illinois, 1870–1922.* Chicago: University of Illinois Press, 1992.

Peltzman, Sam. "Toward a More General Theory of Regulation." *Journal of Law and Economics* 19 (1976): 211–40.

Pennisi, Carolyn. "A Bird's-eye View of the Loan Shark Problem from the Offices of the Legal Aid Society in Atlanta, Georgia." *Law and Contemporary Problems* 19 (1954): 81–95.

Pennsylvania Department of Banking. *Report on Small Loan Companies.* Harrisburg: Department of Banking, 1935.

Penny, J. M. *The Dallas Loan Shark Fight.* Dallas: Better Business Bureau, 1939.

Peterson, Christopher. *Taming the Sharks: Towards a Cure for the High-Cost Credit Market.* Akron: University of Akron Press, 2004.

———. "Usury Law, Payday Loans, and Statutory Sleight of Hand: An Empirical Analysis of American Credit Pricing Limits." *Minnesota Law Review* 92 (2008): 1110–64.

Peterson, Virgil. *Barbarians in Our Midst: A History of Chicago Crime and Politics.* Boston: Little Brown, 1952.

———. "Chicago: Shades of Capone." *Annals of the American Academy of Political and Social Science* 347 (1963): 30–39.

Phelps, Clyde. "Monopolistic and Imperfect Competition in Consumer Loans." *Journal of Marketing* 8 (1944): 382–93.

Piketty, Thomas, and Emmanuel Saez. "Income Inequality in the United States, 1913–1998." *Quarterly Journal of Economics* 118 (2003): 1–39.

Policis. *Economic and Social Risks of Consumer Credit Market Regulation.* London: Policis, 2004.

———. *Illegal Lending in the UK.* London: Policis, 2006.

Posner, Eric. "Contract Law in the Welfare State: A Defense of the Unconscionability Doctrine, Usury Laws, and Related Limitations on the Freedom to Contract." *Journal of Legal Studies* 24 (1995): 283–319.

Pride, Robert Edwin. *Loan Sharks of America.* Philadelphia: Harper Stokes, 1940.

Projector, Dorothy, and Gertrude Weiss. *Survey of Financial Characteristics of Consumers.* Washington, D.C.: Board of the Federal Reserve System, 1966.

Raab, Selwyn. *Five Families: The Rise, Decline, and Resurgence of America's Most Powerful Mafia Empires.* New York: St. Martin's Press, 2005.

Rabino, Adele. "The Small Loan Law and Its Application in Illinois." Master's thesis, Northwestern University, 1942.

Raymond, Allan. *Waterfront Priest.* New York: Henry Holt, 1955.

Reuter, Peter. *The Organization of Illegal Markets: An Economic Analysis.* Washington, D.C.: U.S. Department of Justice, 1985.

Reuter, Peter, and Jonathan Rubinstein. *Illegal Gambling in New York: A Case Study in the Operation, Structure, and Regulation of an Illegal Market.* Washington, D.C.: U.S. Department of Justice, 1982.

Rhine, Sherrie, and Maude Toussaint-Comeau. "The Use of Formal and Informal Financial Markets among Black Households." *Consumer Interests Annual* 45 (1999): 146–51.

Robinson, Louis, and Rolf Nugent. *Regulation of the Small Loan Business.* New York: Russell Sage Foundation, 1935.

Robinson, Louis, and Maude Stearns. *Ten Thousand Small Loans.* New York: Russell Sage Foundation, 1930.

Rosen, Ellen. *Making Sweatshops: The Globalization of the U.S. Apparel Industry.* Berkeley and Los Angeles: University of California Press, 2002.

Ryan, Franklin. *Usury and Usury Laws.* Boston: Houghton Mifflin, 1924.

Schelling, Thomas. "Economic Analysis and Organized Crime." In *Task Force Report: Organized Crime,* 114–26. Washington, D.C.: U.S. Government Printing Office, 1967.

Schiltz, Elizabeth. "The Amazing, Elastic, Ever-Expanding Exportation Doctrine and Its Effect on Predatory Lending Regulation." *Minnesota Law Review* 88 (2004): 518–626.

Schneider, B. "Usury as Related to Illinois Law." *John Marshall Law Quarterly* 4 (1938): 489–503.

Scurlock, James. *Maxed Out: Hard Times, Easy Credit, and the Era of Predatory Lenders.* New York: Scribner, 2007.

Seidl, John. "'Upon the Hip': A Study of the Criminal Loan-Shark Industry." Ph.D. diss., Harvard University, 1968.

Shergold, Peter. "The Loan Shark: The Small Loan Business in Early Twentieth-Century Pittsburgh." *Pennsylvania History* 45 (1978): 195–223.

Simon, Carl, and Anne Witte. *Beating the System: The Underground Economy.* Boston: Auburn House, 1982.

Simpson, William. *America's Small Loan Problem with Special Reference to the South.* Columbia: University of South Carolina, 1963.

———. *The Small Loan Problem of the Carolinas.* Clinton: Presbyterian College Press, 1941.

Skiba, Paige, and Jeremy Tobacman. "Do Payday Loans Cause Bankruptcy?" Working paper, Vanderbilt Law and Economics Research Paper Series, February 2008.

———. "Measuring the Individual-Level Effects of Access to Credit: Evidence from Payday Loans." *Federal Reserve Bank of Chicago: Proceedings* (2007): 280–301.

———. "Payday Loans, Uncertainty, and Discounting: Explaining Patterns of Borrowing, Repayment, and Default." Working paper, Vanderbilt Law and Economics Research Paper Series, August 2008.

Smith, Adam. *An Inquiry into the Nature and Causes of the Wealth of Nations.* Chicago: University of Chicago Press, 1976.

Smith, Alson. *Syndicate City: The Chicago Crime Cartel and What to Do about It.* Chicago: Henry Regnery, 1954.

Snarr, Robert. "No Cash 'til Payday: The Payday Loan Industry." *Compliance Corner* First Quarter (2002): 1–8.

Spector, Mary. "Taming the Beast: Payday Loans, Regulatory Efforts, and Unintended Consequences." *DePaul Law Review* 57 (2008): 961–96.

Spink, J. *Judge Landis and Twenty-Five Years of Baseball.* New York: Thomas Cromwell, 1947.

Steffens, Lincoln. *The Shame of the Cities.* New York: Hill and Wang, 1957.

Stegman, Michael. "Payday Lending." *Journal of Economic Perspectives* 21 (2007): 169–90.

Stegman, Michael, and Robert Faris. "Payday Lending: A Business Model that Encourages Chronic Borrowing." *Economic Development Quarterly* 17 (2003): 8–32.

Stiglitz, Joseph, and Andrew Weiss. "Credit Rationing in Markets with Imperfect Information." *American Economic Review* 71 (1981): 393–410.

Stoianovici, Petru, and Michael Maloney. "Restrictions on Credit: A Public Policy Analysis of Payday Lending." Working paper, Department of Economics, Clemson University, October 2008.

Stolberg, Mary. *Fighting Organized Crime: Politics, Justice, and the Legacy of Thomas E. Dewey.* Boston: Northeastern University Press, 1995.

Stone, Robert, and Jack Thomas. "California's Legislature Faces the Small Loan Problem." *California Law Review* 27 (1939): 286–312.

Sullivan, James. "Administration of a Regulatory Small Loan Law." *Law and Contemporary Problems* 8 (1941): 146–53.

Sullivan, Teresa, Elizabeth Warren, and Jay Westbrook. *The Fragile Middle Class: Americans in Debt.* New Haven: Yale University Press, 2000.

"Syndicate Loan-Shark Activities and New York's Usury Statute." *Columbia Law Review* 66 (1966): 167–77.

Teletrack. "$howmethemoney." http://www.teletrack.com/successes/show.html.

Telzrow, Dennis. "Present and Future of the Payday Advance Industry." Presentation at the annual conference of the Community Financial Services Association of America, Las Vegas, 6 March 2008.

Temin, Peter, and Hans-Joachim Voth. "Interest Rate Restrictions in a Natural Experiment: Loan Allocation and the Change in the Usury Laws in 1714." *Economic Journal* 118 (2008): 743–58.

Texas Legislative Council. *The Small Loan Business in Texas through 1961.* Austin: Texas Legislative Council, 1961.

Thaler, Richard, and Cass Sunstein. *Nudge: Improving Decisions about Health, Wealth, and Happiness.* New Haven: Yale University Press, 2008.

Thrasher, Frederic. *The Gang: A Study of 1313 Gangs in Chicago.* Chicago: University of Chicago Press, 1936.

"To Control Loan Sharks in Illinois." *Charities and the Commons* 21 (1908): 407–8.

Toussaint-Comeau, Maude, and Sherrie Rhine. "Access to Credit and Financial Services among Black Households." Working paper, Consumer and Community Affairs Division, Federal Reserve Bank of Chicago, June 2000.

Trebilcock, Michael. *The Limits of Freedom of Contract.* Cambridge: Harvard University Press, 1993.

Turkus, Burton, and Sid Feder. *Murder, Inc. The Story of "The Syndicate."* New York: Farrar, Straus, and Young, 1951.

Tyree, Donald. *The Small-Loan Industry in Texas.* Austin: University of Texas Press, 1960.

U.S. Department of Defense. *Report on Predatory Lending Practices Directed at Members of the Armed Forces and Their Dependents.* Washington, D.C.: 2006.

U.S. Federal Deposit Insurance Corporation. *Study of Bank Overdraft Programs.* Washington, D.C.: 2008.

"The Uniform Small Loan Law." *Harvard Law Review* 42 (1929): 689–93.

Uptown, Miller. "An Economic Appraisal of Convenience and Advantage Licensing by Small-Loan Statutes." *Journal of Business* 25 (1952): 249–63.

Venkatesh, Sudhir. *Off the Books: The Underground Economy of the Urban Poor.* Cambridge: Harvard University Press, 2006.

Veritec Solutions. *Florida Trends in Deferred Presentment.* Annual report. Jacksonville: Veritec Solutions.

———. *Michigan Trends in Deferred Presentment.* Annual report. Jacksonville: Veritec Solutions.

———. *Oklahoma Trends in Deferred Deposit Lending.* Annual report. Jacksonville: Veritec Solutions.

Wallace, George. "The Uses of Usury: Low Rate Ceilings Examined." *Boston University Law Review* 56 (1976): 451–97.

Washington Department of Financial Institutions. *Payday Lending Report.* Annual Report. Olympia.

Wassam, Clarence. *The Salary Lending Business in New York City.* New York: Charities Publication Committee, 1908.

Weaver, Findley. *Oklahoma's Small Loan Problem.* Oklahoma City: Bond Printing, 1938.

Webb, James. *A Treatise on the Law of Usury.* St. Louis: F. H. Thomas Law Book, 1899.

White, James. "The Usury *Trompe l'Oeil.*" *South Carolina Law Review* 51 (2000): 445–65.

Wiebe, Robert. *Businessmen and Reform: A Study of the Progressive Movement.* Cambridge: Harvard University Press, 1962.

———. *The Search for Order, 1877–1920.* New York: Hill and Wang, 1967.

Wiles, Marti, and Daniel Immergluck. "Unregulated Payday Lending Pulls Vulnerable Consumers into Spiraling Debt." *Reinvestment Alert* no. 14 (2000): 1–9.

Williams, Brett. *Debt for Sale: A Social History of the Credit Trap.* Philadelphia: University of Pennsylvania Press, 2004.

Williams, Jeffrey, and Peter Lindert. *American Inequality: A Macroeconomic History.* New York: Academic Press, 1980.

Williams, Marva, and Kathryn Smolik. "Affordable Alternatives to Payday Loans." *Reinvestment Alert* no. 16 (2001): 1–6.

Willrich, Michael. *City of Courts: Socializing Justice in Progressive Era Chicago.* Cambridge: Cambridge University Press, 2003.

Wilson, Bart, et al. "An Experimental Analysis of the Demand for Payday Loans." Working paper, Economic Science Institute, Chapman University, April 2008.

Winebarger, Tasha. "Payday Lending: The Beginning of the End." *North Carolina Banking Institute* 7 (2003): 317–37.

Wisconsin Department of Financial Institutions. *Review of Payday Lending in Wisconsin.* Madison: 2001.

Wolf, Irving. "The Licensed Check Cashing Industry in New York City." M.B.A. thesis, Pace University, 1975.

Woodstock Institute. *Beyond Payday Loans: Consumer Installment Lending in Illinois.* Chicago: 2009.

———. *Hunting Down the Payday Loan Customer: The Debt Collection Practices of Two Payday Loan Companies.* Chicago: 2006.

———. *The Illinois Payday Loan Loophole.* Chicago: 2008.

Yntema, Theodore. "The Market for Consumer Credit: A Case in 'Imperfect Competition'." *Annals of the American Academy of Political and Social Science* 196 (1938): 79–85.

Young, Ralph. *Personal Finance Companies and Their Credit Practices.* New York: National Bureau of Economic Research, 1940.

Zinman, Jonathan. "Restricting Consumer Credit Access: Household Survey Evidence on Effects Around the Oregon Rate Cap." *Journal of Banking and Finance* 34 (2010): 546–56.

Index